Queer Frontiers

Queer Frontiers

Millennial Geographies, Genders, and Generations

Edited by

Joseph A. Boone
Martin Dupuis
Martin Meeker
Karin Quimby
Cindy Sarver
Debra Silverman
Rosemary Weatherston

THE UNIVERSITY OF WISCONSIN PRESS

The University of Wisconsin Press
2537 Daniels Street
Madison, Wisconsin 53718

3 Henrietta Street
London WC2E 8LU, England

Library of Congress Cataloging-in-Publication Data
Queer frontiers : millennial geographies, genders, and generations / edited by the Queer
    Frontiers Editorial Collective, Joseph A. Boone . . . [et al.].
      394 pp.   cm.
      ISBN 0-299-16090-4 (cloth: alk. paper)
      ISBN 0-299-16094-7 (pbk.: alk. paper)
         1. Homosexuality—Philosophy.   2. Homosexuality—Political aspects.   3. Gays in
    popular culture.   4. Homosexuality in literature.   I. Boone, Joseph Allen.   II. Queer
    Frontiers Editorial Collective.
    HQ76.25.Q37   2000
    306.76'6'01—DC21   98-48151

Contents

Preface

As much as this book is shaped by the social and theoretical concerns of its chapters, it is also a reflection of a specific time and place. *Queer Frontiers* grew out a conference by the same name—"Queer Frontiers: the Fifth Annual National Gay, Lesbian, and Bisexual Graduate Student Conference"—hosted by the University of Southern California (USC) on March 23–25, 1995. The inception of the conference series in 1991 at the University of Wisconsin–Milwaukee came during a period of radical change within lesbian and gay studies and politics, a time marked by the publication of the first wave of what are today considered some of the hallmark texts of queer studies—Eve Kosofsky Sedgwick's *Epistemology of the Closet* (1990), Diana Fuss's *Inside/Out* (1991), Bad Object-Choices' *How Do I Look? Queer Film and Video* (1991), and the special "Queer Theory" issue of *differences,* edited by Teresa de Lauretis (1991). A new generation of scholars committed to exploring possibilities of a more inclusive, celebratory, yet contentious sexual politics vigorously responded—some positively, some negatively—to the then emergent queer studies. The 1991 National Gay, Lesbian, and Bisexual Graduate Student Conference created a national forum for showcasing just how this cutting-edge queer scholarship was being received, refined, and put to work by student scholars coming of age in the academy in the early 1990s. Subsequent conferences were held at Ohio (1992), the University of Minnesota, Twin Cities (1993), and the University of Texas at Austin (1994). (Following "Queer Frontiers," the conference was held at Miami University, Oxford Campus [1996] and the Graduate Center of the City University of New York [1997].)

By 1995, a *new* generation of queer scholars had emerged—scholars that one of our editorial collective members, Rosemary Weatherston, suggested we might well call "second-generation queers." These ranks are comprised of graduate students and nonacademic writers, artists, and community builders who, as Joseph A. Boone notes in his introductory chapter, "have grown up with the concept of 'queer' as a theoretical and political tool already in play," and their unique critical perspectives have brought a dynamic challenge to, while simultaneously incorporating, more established lesbian/gay studies. It is at this theoretical and political crossroads that *Queer Frontiers* is set.

At the "Queer Frontiers" conference over 250 participants gathered from all over the world to share scholarship, activism, and art. In addition to four days of panels, keynote addresses by Sue-Ellen Case, George Chauncey, Cherríe Moraga, and John Rechy, and a welcoming address by Walter Williams, the event included workshops on oral history methodologies, queer resources on the World Wide Web, sessions with avant-garde filmmakers, performances by queer artists, film screenings, and a banquet honoring the pre- and post-Stonewall activists who pioneered the lesbian and gay movements in Los Angeles and San Francisco. The conference's objective, hence, was not simply to provide a forum for up-and-coming queer scholars and cutting-edge artists, but to situate their work within a self-reflexive social, political, and historical context that acknowledged the legacy of feminism, lesbian and gay studies, and activism as well as current trends in postmodern queer inquiry. We hoped, in other words, to inspire a serious interdisciplinary and cross-generational dialogue about the possibilities *and* problems presented by a newly emerging queer theory and activism.

This book grew out of a desire to continue the conference's commitment to sustaining this important dialogue. In the months following the conference, an editorial collective formed to further pursue the themes that made the conference so exciting and, for many of its participants, groundbreaking in the form of an anthology. Early on, however, our editorial group decided that this anthology should not simply be a "proceedings" volume, but rather that it should attempt to establish a dialogue between the conference and the present moment by tracking the continuing debates triggered by some of the most significant issues raised during the conference. To this end, we first requested submissions from about two dozen of the most promising conference papers, narrowed this group to the eight essays that were most innovative and that lent themselves to the themes that structure this project. We also brought back together three of the keynote speakers—Case, Chauncey, and Rechy—for a dynamic discussion of each others' contributions as well as for self-reflexive commentary on the transformations their own thinking has undergone; likewise, in place of Moraga's performance piece at the conference—a collage of her already published works—we solicited from her a lengthy interview, to which she graciously consented and which was conducted in January 1997.

Were it not for the support of the Los Angeles and University of Southern California queer and queer-friendly communities, this project would have never come to fruition. A debt of gratitude is due to David Román, who first suggested to several of the graduate students involved in this conference that they form a group (which eventually became our editorial collective) to consider transforming the conference's papers into a collection; our gratitude extends, as well, to Tania Modleski for agreeing to moderate the roundtable discussion concluding this volume, and to Walter Williams for assuming the responsibility of faculty adviser to the graduate student committee organizing the conference. We would also like to acknowledge the expert assistance and goodwill of Rebecca Chavez and Nellie Ayala-Reyes for their hands-on help with the various unforeseen administrative duties entailed in assembling this book. In addition, thanks to Hugh Farrington, the USC Department of English, and the USC Center for Feminist Research for the generous financial support that has helped make *Queer Frontiers* a reality. We also applaud our editor at the University of Wisconsin Press, Raphael Kadushin, for his patience and persistence in seeing this manuscript through to its end. And finally, our deepest gratitude to all the original conference participants for the vision, enthusiasm and scholarship that initially inspired this project and without which this volume would have not been possible.

Queer Frontiers

Go West
An Introduction

Joseph A. Boone

Together   we will go our way
together   we will leave some day
together   we will start life anew
together   this is what we will do:
    Go west . . .
This is where the air is free
we'll be what we want to be
now if we make a stand
we'll find our promised land
—Pet Shop Boys, "Go West" (Village People cover)

Moving: feeling in motion
Grooving on a notion
Feelings getting higher
Dealing with desire
Just keep me moving:
    Freedom. . . .
—k. d. lang, "Just Keep Me Moving"

What feminism was for the 1970s and 1980s—the galvanizing political and intellectual force reorganizing mainstream culture's understanding of gender and sexuality—queer theory is well on its way to becoming for the present moment. This is not to say that the latter has merely replaced or subsumed the former, or that the future of queer sexualities is stable or certain—indeed, the destabilization of any givens inherent in the very concept of queerness, as well as the volatile political climate of the *fin de millennium*, militates against such predictions. What this collection of interdisciplinary essays—composed by scholars, artists, and writers—attempts to do is to test out the proposition offered in the first sentence above by catching a movement in the process of its unfolding without freezing or fixing it. To this end, these essays

3

canvass the myriad ways in which the explosion of theory taking place under the term *queer* is continuing to shape our present historical moment, and they go about this exploration by situating contemporary debates about the politics (and future) of sexuality in the specific geopolitical and historical spaces or locations in which they have developed. As a corollary of this focus on how our current lives are being shaped in and by this historical moment, *Queer Frontiers* also examines the degree to which the practice of queer theory in literature, popular culture, politics, and academia portends "the millennium" and its attendant anxieties in the popular imagination: literally, the turn of the century; figuratively, the utopian horizons of desire and possibility that beckon beyond the limits of the rigid binaries that have shaped twentieth-century understandings of sexuality; and, symbolically, the threshold into the unknown that faces global culture as constructions of East and West continue to loosen their grip on local and national formations of sex and gender.

Like all acts of naming—which in the case of queer theory has not been without its very vocal critics—the title bestowed upon an essay collection necessarily overdetermines, in sometimes unexpected ways, the reading and reception of the material that follows. Part of my goal in this introduction, then, will be to unfold the implications—euphoric to some of our contributors, disturbing to others, and already anachronistic to at least one—of the moniker *Queer Frontiers*, with which this volume's editorial collective has decided to promote this collection's vision. But before I turn to the various, sometimes contradictory meanings that issue from the yoking of the words *queer* and *frontier*, I first want to address the title of this introduction, "Go West," which carries its own sets of assumptions and provocations.[1] Indeed, to some readers the injunction to "Go West," given the imperialist underpinnings of the doctrine of Manifest Destiny that spurred the relentless westward migration of the United States during the previous century, may seem a less-than-promising trope with which to espouse a queer politics. But my initial inspiration to use this phrase originated in neither U.S. politics nor the mythos of the Old West as the "final frontier," but rather in a gay video bar—the same video bar, in fact, whose spatial dimensions Richard C. Cante analyzes in a chapter in this book—where I first viewed the Pet Shop Boys' 1993 music video version of the 1978 Village People disco hit, "Go West."[2] The meanings that attach to words or phrases—as the contemporary use of the word *queer* illustrates—are not only subject to change but sometimes to radical revision, as the saying "Go West" has proved in its various transformations: from patriotic rallying cry for westward expansion evoking covered wagons and Indian war parties in Americana lore; to a paean to ecstatic gay "liberation" when parlayed into the insistent disco beat of the Village People song; to the Pet Shop Boys' synthesized pop anthem, in which the original song's appeal to various clichés of the old/new American West (the macho cowboy, San Francisco as gay mecca) is rescripted as a transglobal ode to queer possibility. But what fascinated me most about the Pet Shop Boys' version was not just the way in which it provides an intriguing example of a contemporary "out" duo (Neil Tennant and Chris Lowe) reinterpreting for a new era—and hence, in a sense, paying homage to—the work of the first gay-identified group to achieve crossover success, but the way in which the 1993 cover evokes, in a rather sophisticated fashion, several of the associations that have led to the choice of *Queer Frontiers* as the title to head this collection. These associations, however, as my second epigraph is meant to intimate, are not without their lacunae and hence might usefully be expanded by adding to the Pet Shop Boys' vision of them the equally but differently utopian resonances that "going west" takes on in k. d. lang's song, "Just Keep Me Moving," composed for the soundtrack of gay filmmaker Gus Van Sant's 1993 adaptation of Tom Robbins's 1976 *Even Cowgirls Get the Blues*.[3] For in the conjunction of lang's lesbian profile, Van Sant's status as a queer auteur in film, and Robbins's paean (however ambivalent) to lesbian feminist separatism, the mythic freedom associated with the "Wild West" becomes synonymous with the iconic queerness of the cowgirls of the novel's title and of the large-thumbed Sissy Hankshaw, an erstwhile "cowgalpal" and hitchhiker extraordinaire whose response to the conventional world in which she can never fit is to "just keep . . . moving."

I want to begin, though, with the queer resonances in the Pet Shop Boys' version of the song that first inspired me to think of titling this introduction "Go West." What I find most fascinating in this postmodern vision of a manifestly queer destiny is the way that the boundaries differentiating East and West as geopolitical metaphors literally dissolve, such that the summons "Go West" ceases to signify *either* in its local, historical sense (that is, the American Wild West), in its hemispheric connotation (Western culture as the one true haven of freedom, democracy, and progress), or in its eschatological meaning (the West as the realm of death, of the dying sun[4]). Accompanying the lyrics sung by a chorus of marching men (the Gay Men's Chorus of New York) united in a communally shared, transcendent vision whose realization depends upon an act of exodus or emigration in the name of a "love" that is at once individualistic and collective ("Together, we will leave some day . . . start life anew . . . this is what we will do"), the video screens a series of images that insistently blur the boundaries between the United States and the Soviet Union, two of this century's most potent symbols of (one version of) East versus West.[5] In the process, "Go West" envisions the future as a literally unknown frontier of possibility. We might well surmise that lying behind and inspiring this vision is the 1989 toppling of the Berlin Wall, which, as Peter Coviello suggests in his chapter in this book, has changed the way we think about apocalypse and about human relations as we enter the new millennium. Metaphors of "borderlands" and "liminal spaces" have now become commonplace in contemporary criticism, but the no-man's-land demarcated by the Berlin Wall presented a particularly visceral representation of the power of constructed (and hence, one hopes, deconstructable) borders to divide the world into restrictive binaries, ones thereby legislating what national—like sexual—identities are allowed to include and exclude. The Pet Shop Boys' video borrows from such Cold War imagery by featuring troops of soldier-athletes marching in perfect rhythm (too perfect, one first thinks, to be anything but Soviet formations!) and dressed in campily futuristic, yet homoerotically alluring, costumes. These marching hordes provide a rousing choral backup to Tennant's lead vocals that underline the communal endeavor of the lyrics which, if only heard and not seen, might be mistaken as a conventionally romantic ode ("Together, your hand in my hand . . . baby you and me / this is our destiny"). The eroticizing camera, however, quickly makes it clear that these comrades are not traditional soldiers (likewise, they are not identifiably "Western" or "Soviet"). Their goal is not one of militaristic conquest; rather, they constitute, to use Walt Whitman's phrase in "Calamus," an "army of lovers" or, even more evocatively, a queer activist movement, such as ACT UP (the AIDS Coalition to Unleash Power), joyously and defiantly leading the way to a new world order, a fully queer one in which, "if we make a stand / we'll find our promised land," along with the freedom to "be what we want to be."

Significantly, however, this "promised land," in contrast to the mythic San Francisco conjured up in the Village People's rendition, does not lie off to the west in any traditionally geographical sense: what is being represented on the screen is most definitely *not* an army of once-abject-now-liberated Soviet gay boys joyously rushing into the embrace of the capitalist "land of the free" or abjuring the collective for the individual pursuit of happiness. Rather, opening with a computerized image of a spinning globe whose continual rotation already anticipates the transformation of the injunction to "Go West" from a linear, end-directed project into a transglobal movement that has no end—if you go far enough west you'll run into east again—the video locates its marching chorus in a variety of settings and amid a host of iconic visual references. Including the Statue of Liberty, red flags, hammer and sickle, and Red Square, these references suggest a blurring of *both* the Soviet and U.S. domains, creating the pathway to a futuristic utopia where the communal ideal of the former, and the ideal of individual freedoms of the latter, might coexist. This transcendent movement is signaled by the soldiers' march up a stairway suspended in the sky, flanked by a singing Statue of Liberty—a black woman—on one side and a statue of Joseph Stalin on the other, as Tennant and Lowe lead the way through a door frame that opens onto the empty stratosphere, the final frontier or "nowhere" of utopia. These political reverberations are firmly placed within contexts that are both postmodern and queer—contexts that include the Pet Shop Boys' longstanding appeal to a gay following, the degree to which the entirety of their compact disk *Very* can easily be read as meditation on the coming-out process; the Herb Ritts–inspired use of the camera to eroticize the athlete-soldiers' bodies; and the campily sublime transformation of the Statue of Liberty into a singing black diva dressed in red. The queer ambience of these political and sexual contexts is amplified, moreover, by visual choices that inculcate a subtle but clear message celebrating the embrace of difference—sexual, political, and racial— as the way of the future. Not only is Liberty herself an African American woman and, as the video progresses, the troops increasingly racially integrated, but the colors of the uniforms worn by the marchers— yellow, red, and blue—are the primary pigments from which the entire spectrum of colors can be created: they embody, that is, a veritable "rainbow" of possibility, and the rainbow, of course, has become contemporary shorthand for racial and sexual coalition-in-diversity, which in turn has been a foundational principle of the queer agenda in its attempt to establish alliances across categories of difference.

The visual omission in this panoply of queer difference, of course, is *women*, in the plural. What the video offers us, instead, is a single woman, the iconic representation of the Statue of Liberty (albeit as an exoticized diva who, in contrast to the moving men, remains frozen in place), as well as Tennant's high-pitched voice, which insinuates a gender ambiguity into the masculine baritones of the chorus; but the fact remains that all the marching emigrants to this promised land are men. One might argue, of course, that the subversive edge of this video lies precisely in the *totality* of its presentation of men, and men alone, singing these lyrics: this defiantly all-male ubiquity—the most taboo because the most threatening visual representation of sexual difference for patriarchy—is what makes the song inescapably homoerotic and, in line with its overall politics, "queers" it for any viewing audience, making it impossible to be read or seen outside of its gay aesthetic. But even if such an argument holds some legitimacy, the fact remains that women themselves have no place in this video's vision of "going west" (repeating, in a sense, one of the lacunae in traditional histories of the westward movement in U.S. history), and we might thus see in this instance—however "justifiable" in terms of the specific message of the video—an allegory of one of the pitfalls often attributed to the concept of queer: for this omission repeats the same elision of much queer theory and praxis, from which many women, including lesbians, feminist activists, and gay-sympathetic women, have at times felt excluded or, in spite of their participation, rendered more or less invisible by a movement that is most often associated, especially in the media, with white, urban gay men.

It is in this vein that I present as the second of my epigraphs an excerpt of the lyrics from "Just Keep Me Moving," the opening cut from the soundtrack of the 1993 film *Even Cowgirls Get the Blues*, since this song, given its context, serves as an unabashedly feminocentric vision of "going west" and forms an interesting companion text to the Pet Shop Boys' anthem. As sung by k. d. lang—this decade's premier icon of lesbian crossover success in the world of popular music, not unlike the Village People were for an earlier generation—these lyrics mark the lesbian feminist separatist themes of the 1976 novel from which Gus Van Sant adapted the film with the signature of an ineluctably 1990s queer female icon. The plot of both novel and film centers on Sissy Hankshaw's insider-outsider relation to the takeover of the Rubber Rose Ranch, a tony women's health spa in Oregon, by its brazenly lesbian, separatist, and racially diverse cowgirl ranch hands.[6] Within this context, k. d. lang's lyrical injunction for the nonnormative female "misfits" of the dominant culture (like the "abnormally" large-thumbed Sissy) to "just keep ... moving" to realize "desire[s]" and "freedom[s]" that the narrative explicitly associates with queer love (embodied in Sissy's love affair with the head cowgirl Bonanza Jelly-bean and with her impregnation by a cave-dweller mystic called the Chink) works to transform the metaphor of Wild West frontier into a more universal call-to-arms that sets the frontier of the unknown, the moving road of desire, against all stultifying forms of normativity and queer oppression.[7] In this sense, the continuity that lang's vocals suggest between 1990s queerness and 1970s lesbian feminism serves as a useful reminder of the often overlooked legacy that the contemporary queer movement owes to the feminist movement of the 1970s and

1980s: without the precedent of feminist activism, scholarship, and theory, there would be no queer frontier for us to explore today. Michael Warner, for instance, has already written eloquently of the degree to which early radical lesbian documents such as the manifestos collected in the 1972 anthology, *Out of the Closets,* serve as prototypes of significant aspects of postmodern queer ideology. Thus, even while both the novel and the film versions of *Even Cowgirls Get the Blues* form a kind of allegorical warning of one of the pitfalls of queerness—the appropriation of feminist- or lesbian feminist–originated ideas for a male-centered vision—nonetheless the very topos of radical lesbianism that *Cowgirls* conjures forth serves to remind us, especially as mediated through the vocals of lang's 1990s soundtrack, of the rich if complicated history of antipatriarchal and often antinormative resistance that links the goals of feminism, in its most radical expressions, and those of contemporary queer theory.[8]

When so reenvisioned by lang and the Pet Shop Boys, the conceit of going west does not simply repeat the scenario of conquest associated with U.S. imperialism or Western cultural hegemony. In fact, as conceptualized in these contemporary versions, and particularly as visualized in the "Go West" video, the new resonances given to the metaphor of going west explicitly overwrite the scenario of conquest with a global vision of frontiers and of imaginative possibility. In this vision, the West becomes a liminal space rather than a final goal or resting place, a borderland traversed on the way to a new dispensation that lies beyond the horizons of the seen or known. Queer theory and queer studies, too, may be conceived as a borderland and a frontier, a space of transition and a still largely unexplored geography that both portends a real break from limiting modes of conceiving human sexuality and that, at this historical moment, serves as one of the conceptual sites or spaces within which the various futures of sexuality are currently being created, as we speak, and, more problematically, commodified and marketed, as several of our contributors warn.

Such an understanding of the title I have chosen for this introduction, then, turns out to be intrinsically related to the title we editors have given this book. For *Queer Frontiers* is meant, first of all, to signify those horizons of possibility, as yet incompletely demarcated and thus subject to revision and experimentation, that lie ahead, in a social and political environment whose power to oppress gay men, lesbians, and other sexual dissidents nonetheless still remains enormous and maddeningly depressing. In the chapters that follow, this frontier is figured as a geographic, cultural, psychic, and political entity. It can be seen— as in the familiar trope of the Wild West—as a liminal, lawless space in which traditional roles and rules are suspended or freely transgressed, while new ones, still in the process of formation, are up for grabs: everything, as lang sings, is indeed "in motion," a state of productive flux. Not only conceived as that which lies ahead, on, or over the horizon, the metaphor of frontiers—as in the phrase, "the frontiers of knowledge"—also evokes for many of our contributors the groundbreaking intellectual foment and emergence of a radical avant-garde *already* in full force among queer activists, thinkers, artists, and scholars. So defined, the frontier functions as a dividing line or schism between different states of being, thus driving home the crucial importance of an epoch-defining break, a seismic shift in world orders, as a fact that may have *already* occurred yet remains to be fully discovered. As Richard C. Cante suggests in his chapter in this volume, such a break in the realm of sexuality is phantasmically present in the subject formation of all individuals who have "come out." And, as another of our contributors, Peter Coviello, reminds us, this differentiation of the time "before" from the time "after" has already happened, historically speaking, as a consequence of the simultaneous and not coincidental demonization of AIDS and the downplaying of the threat of nuclear holocaust in the post–Cold War dispensation: "In or about November, 1989," Coviello writes, echoing Virginia Woolf's famous pronouncement at the beginning of this century, "Apocalypse changed and, by virtue of that change, all human relations have shifted." In cultural understandings of sexuality and its practice(s), both writers imply, a new frontier has been broached because a decisive break—however unconscious of the shift the majority of human being the world may yet be—has *already* transpired, and the consequences are of paramount importance not only for gay-identified men and women but for everybody, our friends and foes alike.

Even if this desire to imagine queerness as the harbinger of an absolute paradigmatic shift is perhaps as unfounded at the present as it is grandiose, the *power* of such imaginings in helping to shape the future that lies beyond that other marker of change and futurity—the frontier marked by the new millennium, with all its symbolic power to suggest an irreversible shift from one order to another—cannot be underestimated. In the chapters that follow, the trope *queer frontiers* also takes on other shades of meaning: as several contributors remind us, envisioning future frontiers depends as well on recognizing the pioneering efforts of lesbian feminist and gay pioneers working on the front lines and at the outposts of early gay activism, since the future frontiers envisioned by current queer theory and practice depend on knowing the history of how we got to where we are to today, or, as Cante pithily phrases it in a related context, "How did *that* (the before) turn into *this* (the after)?" For other writers in this anthology, the body itself—particularly the intersexed or transsexual body—becomes the frontier, the site of contested meanings of sexuality and gender that go directly to the heart of queer theory's goal of displacing the primacy of the heterosexual/homosexual binary (and that binary's critical dependence on an absolute gender divide) that has dictated modern sexual epistemologies. Other contributors make the similar point that the frontier not only lies "out there," in some imagined "other" land (which can too easily tip into unconsciously colonizing rhetoric), but that it also exists "in between," in the interstices, on the boundaries that bridge categories of being and meaning.

Even though the chapters included in *Queer Frontiers* take seriously these possibilities, our contributors do not naively assume that "queerness" as a lifestyle or "queer theory" as an intellectual approach to understanding sexuality is a stable entity whose future is guaranteed. As George Chauncey, in particular, notes in his comments in the roundtable discussion that concludes the volume, queerness assumes very different valences depending on context, user, and audience. One goal of this book, then, is to push the meanings of the term in order to explore its limitations as well as possibilities—in effect, to create a self-conscious space in which the political as well as polemical efficacy of queerness as distinctively postmodern praxis and theory can be debated and questioned as well as celebrated. Many of our contributors do not shy away from addressing the contestatory issues and competing agendas, often taking the form of generational debates, that have been brought into play by the rise of queer theory and by the expanding field of those who claim membership within a queer community. Although some of the questions being asked of and about queer theory are by now familiar, they nonetheless bear repeating in an introduction such as this. For example:

- Should queer theory and praxis be seen as paradigmatic shifts in ways of conceptualizing sexuality, or do they simply represent one phase in the always evolving history of sexuality? Can and should queerness be institutionalized within the academy and within the political realm? What happens to a specifically lesbian/gay politics in the process?
- Likewise, how can advocates of queerness work to maintain the visibility of both lesbian- and feminist-oriented agendas within its penumbra, given (to some observers) the overwhelming maleness of its advocates and given the historical tendency of most move-

ments for social change—excepting the feminist and lesbian movements—to erase the presence and contributions of its female participants? The same question applies to the interrelation of, or
impasse between, (socially imposed) racial identities and (volunta-
rily assumed) queer identifications, as Cherríe Moraga and David
Román note in their contributions to this volume.

- Given the postmodern commodity culture in which "the age of
  the queer" has come about—and which, arguably, is one of its
  "causes"—is the incorporation of queerness into more mainstream
  ways of thinking inevitable? Can there be an upside to such mainstreaming, or is the "selling of queer" the sign that queerness has
  failed in its challenge to the status quo?
- Similarly, does the influx of gay, lesbian, and queer representations
  in popular cultural forms such as television, music, film, stage, and
  journalism contradict queerness's claim to represent a position of
  intellectual avant-gardism and radical oppositionality in contemporary society? Can one, that is, claim allegiance to *Ellen*'s mainstreaming of sitcom lesbianism and Sex Panic!'s militant advocacy
  of nonnormative sexuality at once?
- Who is excluded from access to the term *queer*, and who chooses
  not to join its ranks? To what degree do these answers expose—in
  addition to the race and gender issues noted above—the generational, national, and class biases of queer theory's practitioners?
- Is queer theory a product of American consciousness that is largely
  irrelevant outside the United States, or worse, a concept that, like
  modern "homosexuality" in its exportation abroad, stands to erase
  or subsume the sexual particularities of other cultures?
- Is the queer claim to alliances across categories of difference an
  indiscriminate invitation to all takers, one that ignores the hard
  work of materialist coalition-building—such as that characterizing
  Marxist and feminist coalitions in previous decades—in which
  consensus or identification is not assumed, but earned through
  labor?

In self-consciously addressing these and similar issues, the chapters in
this volume, when viewed as a whole, suggest that the controversies
arising *from within* the field of current queer theory and practice are
among the most productive factors at work in redefining both the frontiers being opened by queer theory and the meanings that queerness
might come to embrace for the future—whether or not *queerness* remains the privileged term for such a future. Furthermore, by including
chapters that represent both utopian visions of a queer future and the

hard questioning of such vanguardist claims, our editorial collective seeks to capitalize on and draw attention to a *deliberate* tension within these pages. We strongly believe that calling into question some of the more cutting-edge claims of queer theory is *not* to abandon the hope or desire for the sexual-political advances that we have here inscribed under the trope of the millennial, the apocalyptic, or the revolutionary. Rather, such a questioning ensures that the concept of queerness—or the term or terms that may succeed it—is all the more fully equipped to carry forth that mission successfully, that its principles and practices are in fact made resilient enough through ongoing self-critique to participate in the creation of those conceptual frontiers that portend real transformations in the realm of sexuality, rather than merely rhetorically gesture toward such changes through what Sue-Ellen Case in her chapter calls "the slippery sex appeal of postmodern discourse." In effect, we suggest that this tension, rather than forming a contradiction, is a local/spatial context through which queer theory must necessarily pass in order to realize its potential.

There is one more sense in which this book imagines itself as the expression of a "queer frontier," one that returns us as well to the title of this introduction. This level of meaning has to with the fact that most of the material in *Queer Frontiers* was first presented in a conference of the same name held in Los Angeles on the campus of the University of Southern California in 1995. In the popular imagination, California has long loomed as the endpoint of the continental United States and the "final frontier" of the mythic Old West; and Los Angeles has become the nation's premier psychic embodiment, unlike any other city in the United States, of racial diversity and ethnic hybridity, of mass culture and celluloid dreams, of futurism and apocalypse (just recall Nathaniel West's *The Day of the Locust*), of unrest and mindlessness, of sexual promiscuity and perversity, of the Pacific Rim's meeting point of Asia and America, and, as recent immigration controversies have highlighted, the meeting point of North and Central America. As one of the press readers of this book noted in her report, paraphrasing Claude Lévi-Strauss, "We [Angelenos] are the place where something has occurred."[9] *Queer Frontiers* deliberately attempts to make the most of its inception in this location and, without engaging in undue East Coast bashing, to remind its readers that New York City is not the only metropolis in the United States that has given rise to a powerful queer voice in politics, the arts, popular culture, and intellectual spheres—that, in point of fact, the relative newness of Los Angeles enables a perhaps more catalytic, experimental relationship among such variables as sexuality, race, ethnicities, and nationalities than other cities inured in centuries of tradition. To highlight this volume's geopolitical siting, two of the chapters address the degree to which Los Angeles has served as the frontier of important groundbreaking lesbian and gay activist work in both pre- and post-Stonewall eras. Relating the legacies of the queer past to the present moment remains, as the chapters by John Rechy, Sue-Ellen Case, and George Chauncey all variously demonstrate, one of the most important critical tools at hand for shaping a queer future. Walter Benjamin, in "Theses on the Philosophy of History," warns that we have to look back unremittingly at the rubble of history in order to conceive any real break in its tragic continuum. "The most dangerous thing," Tony Kushner writes, apropos of Benjamin, "is to become set upon some notion of the future that isn't rooted in the bleakest, most terrifying idea of what's piled up behind you."[10]

The relation of past to present, and of present to future, raises another of the grounding assumptions that has guided our editorial group in conceiving *Queer Frontiers*. This assumption is that queer theory has *already* generated a second wave of queer scholars and activists who are expanding the scope of gay, lesbian, and queer studies in exciting new directions, including disciplines that have often been neglected in studies of sexuality. In fact, one might hypothesize three major stages of relatively recent intellectual foment: the evolution throughout the 1970s and 1980s of gay and lesbian studies; the burst of scholarship in the early to mid-1990s inaugurating queer studies proper; and, now, the great number of undergraduate and graduate students in multiple fields of inquiry for whom gay, lesbian, and queer perspectives have been an integral part of their curriculum and training. It should come as no surprise, given this evolution, that some of the most productive, cutting-edge work in the field is being done by current and recent graduate students who have grown up with the concept of "queer" as a theoretical and political tool already in play, who have inherited a now substantial history of lesbian and gay scholarship, and who have been privy to training in the academy unavailable to the first wave of queer-identified scholars. To represent the powerful perspectives emerging from these second-generation queers, this volume incorporates the work of eight writers who were graduate students at the time of the "Queer Frontiers" conference. Their chapters bring into relief the fascinating reorganization of mainstream understandings of gender and sexuality that follows as queer theory and practice is taken up by new groups of queer scholars, including "straight queers," persons of color, intersexuals, and transgendered individuals.[11] If the claim that "We are in the place where something has occurred" holds for the geotheoretical conflation that this book posits between Los Angeles and queer theory as parallel liminal zones, it also pertains for queer students across the nation, for whom the possibilities of gay scholarship and faculty mentoring have radically altered what it means to be gay *and* to be a student of higher education today. Something significant *has* happened; and, whether or not that change is figured as a violent rupture or gradual evolution, this shift, as Virginia Woolf said of the beginning of the century, augurs the possibility that, here at the end of the twentieth century and the beginning of a new millennium, human relations have indeed shifted.

The contents of this anthology have been organized into three thematic sections. The first, "Troubling Frontiers: Genders and Generations," plunges directly into some of the more fraught controversies troubling the frontiers *of* queer studies as well as queerness *as* a frontier. In the case of the forceful chapters written by Sue-Ellen Case and John Rechy, and in Rosemary Weatherston's revealing interview with Cherríe Moraga, these controversies often assume the form of generational critique, looking at the degree to which concepts of queerness either divide or link those who have "come of age" as lesbian, gay, or bisexual in different periods and/or under different political dispensations, as well as those with different perceptions of the relation of historically rooted divisions of class and race, or of feminist or lesbian feminist politics, to a contemporary queer agenda. The uncanny coordination of the rhetorics of nuclear and sexual apocalypse that Peter Coviello sees in the evolution from the Cold War era to the AIDS era also traces a generational movement that carries inevitable and not always comforting implications for the rise of queer studies as an academic discipline. A second "troubling" frontier explored in this section involves issues of the nonnormatively gendered body as a site of sexuality and futurity: if *queer* has emerged as an umbrella term to include all sexual outlaws and dissidents, exactly what, Morgan Holmes and Jill St. Jacques ask in their respective chapters, are the stakes and liabilities that such an affiliation offers for intersexed and transgendered individuals?

The chapters in the second section of this book, "Urban Frontiers: Queer Space and Place," reflect one of the most interesting developments in recent cultural criticism and gay-influenced study: the impact of twentieth-century urban spatial arrangements on the production of individual subjects and minority sectors. It goes without saying that the modern metropolis has played a vital role in the rise of gay and lesbian culture, providing the sites where identities, cultures, and communities based on same-sex desire have taken root, evolved, and flourished, often providing the blueprint for the revitalization of urban culture at large. Two of the chapters in this section take Los Angeles as a test case for such analysis. Through the reproduction of key documents and archival photographs, Karin Quimby and Walter Williams examine the city as the site of early gay activism, as the home of pioneering homophile publications, and as a repository of queer history in the making. In turn, Yolanda Retter focuses on the complex processes of institution-building among lesbian feminists in the city during the 1970s. Two other chapters, by Ira Tattelman and Richard C. Cante, theorize the relationship between queer spaces and queer subjectivities by turning their eyes to two fixtures of urban gay male life—the bathhouse and the video bar, respectively—in the one instance projecting, through an architectural design project, a futuristic queer (bath)house that builds on the literal and figurative remains of a now (arguably) obsolete model of gay male sexuality; and in the other instance demonstrating how the recycling of nostalgia within the space of the video bar—as a stay against the specter of AIDS—has established itself in opposition to the tenets of postmodern queer identity.

We have titled the third section "Crossing Frontiers: Activism and Academia," since many of us view our work and our lives as ideally bridging both these fields of endeavor at the same time that most of us deeply suspect that this crossing is where we most often fail to satisfy both ourselves and others. The chapters and roundtable discussion included in this section ponder, among other topics, the discursive and material relationship between queer trends in the academy and the aims of queer politics, between theory and activism, and between theory and popular culture: Liana Scalettar asks whether representations of violence in lesbian "zine" culture may serve as a mode of political resistance to dominant systems of queer oppression; Michael Bacchus shows how popular culture's fascination with fashion, gossip, and celebrities has infiltrated the academy—and particularly queer theory—in ways that have inalterably changed both academic and queer claims to longevity; George Chauncey provides a thumbnail sketch of the evolution of present-day queer theory out of what was previously known as gay and lesbian studies so that he can address the political and professional risks still involved for the present generation of graduate students who seek to stake out a queer space in the academy. These meditations are followed by a roundtable discussion, moderated by Tania Modleski, among Sue-Ellen Case, John Rechy, George Chauncey, and several members of our editorial group, in which the three writers speak about how their perspectives have shifted in the years since presenting their keynote addresses at the "Queer Frontiers" conference. The result is a frank discussion by some of the leading voices in the field as to what they view to be the most volatile issues facing the future of gay, lesbian, and queer studies at this paradoxical historical moment, one in which the increase of queer and gay presence in public life is counterbalanced by ever more vicious attacks from the political and religious opponents of gay rights. Among the topics canvassed in this discussion are the impact of conservative agendas on sexual progressivism; the troubling commodification and even globalization of queerness as a Western phenomenon; the sometimes hopeful and sometimes paradoxical dissemination of gay images in the media and popular culture; the role of the continuing culture wars in circumscribing gay and queer agendas; the highly public and divisive debate now occurring within the gay community about the deployment of sexuality, ranging from the ad-hoc creation of Sex Panic! in New York to combat what it perceives as sexual gay conservatism to the battles for legitimization of same-sex marriages and domestic partnership benefits occurring on legislative and corporate levels. This section, and the book as a whole, concludes with epilogues written by two professors, David Román and Richard Meyer, two widely published scholars in queer theory who joined the faculty at the University of Southern California after the "Queer Frontiers" conference was held, but during the production of this anthology. Anticipating that they would therefore have a unique perspective to bring to the concepts of "queer frontiers" and "going west," both in terms of their own scholarship and the future of queer theory, we invited them to write a conclusion for this volume. In response to our invitation, Meyer and Román have opted to write a pair of separate but linked meditations—joined under the rubric "Afterwards/Afterwords"—on the relation of queerness to history, to the archives, and to the future. Drawing on their respective fields of expertise—art history and performance studies—both writers turn to community-based projects recently mounted in California. From different perspectives, their chapters—Román's "Visa Denied," on the representation of emigration from a queer Asian American perspective in theater, and Meyer's "Back to the Future," on artistic renderings of queerness that predate "official" queer theory—form a dialogue on the multiple horizons that the trope *queer frontiers* holds open to our imagining, here at the beginning of the millennium.

It seems appropriate to close an introduction to a volume entitled *Queer Frontiers* with some lines from the opening of *Millennium Approaches*, the first part of Tony Kushner's *Angels in America*, in which the rabbi presiding at the funeral of the character Louis's grandmother proclaims that no more crossings from east to west, such as she has made in coming to America, are possible: "Great Voyages in this world do not any more exist." Yet he immediately qualifies this proposition by adding, "every day of your lives the miles that voyage between that place and this one you cross. Every day. You understand me? In you that journey is."[12] Going west, staking out the queer frontier in what Kushner subtitles a "gay fantasia on national themes," is now refigured as an unending movement, a weave of psychic, political, spiritual, geo-graphical, and cultural crossings and recrossings whose global reper-cussions override the constructed, antediluvian boundaries of nation, race, or sexuality. If, as the rabbi also intones, "You do not live in America. No such place exists," it is because his addressees, like the audience members who hear these words, are *already* exilic inhabitants, within Kushner's imaginative project, of a millennial dispensation that they are only now discovering is already in the process of announcing itself. So the ghost of Ethel Rosenberg will taunt Roy Cohn at the cli-max of part 1, when she prophetically declares, "History is about to crack open. Millennium approaches."[13] We can only hope that this an-thology will approximate something of this utopian hope—the "no place" of fantasy that is, by definition, "utopia"—in its attempt to ges-ture toward the queer frontiers whose arrival is dependent on a history that we are still making:

> So go then   there are many ways
> to live in   in the sun or shade
> together   we will find a place
> to settle   there is so much space . . .

[*The song fades out, with echoes of the "Go West" refrain intercut with a lone voice singing "When are you leaving?"*]

Notes

1. In addition to the song references noted below, I would also like to ac-knowledge the dissertation of the same title, a study of immigration patterns to San Francisco, that one of the coeditors of this volume, Martin Meeker, is completing in the history department at USC. Thanks also to Karin Quimby, Cindy Sarver, and David Román for their helpful comments on this chapter.

2. The Village People recording, which appears on their *Can't Stop the Music* album (Scorpio, 1978), was written by J. Morali, H. Belolo, and V. Willis. The Pet Shop Boys' version appears on *Very* (EMI-Virgin, 1993), and includes addi-tional music and instrumentation written by Neil Tennant and Chris Lowe. I am grateful to Keith Smallhair, the owner of the video bar Revolver in West Hollywood, Los Angeles, for making the Pet Shop Boys' video available for my review.

3. Cowritten by k. d. lang and Ben Mink, from the *Even Cowgirls Get the Blues Soundtrack* (Sire, 1993).

4. Here I have in mind the archetypal associations that have accrued to the West as the site of the death of the day since prehistoric times, an attitude graphically embodied in the city planning of Thebes in ancient Egypt, which sited its great temples to the life-giving sun-god Ra on the eastern banks of the Nile and its Valley of the Dead on the western shore. In England, as Matthew Stone reminded me, the term *going west* is still often used as a euphemism for dying. In light of such connotations, the Pet Shop Boys' video, like many of the other songs on the *Very* compilation, could indeed be interpreted as a kind of transglobal AIDS eulogy. The magic of the video's reinterpretation of the song and phrase, to me, however, seems to be the way in which what might on the surface level be read as the march toward death is overwritten by a utopian, visionary impulse, transforming this end-directed Thanatos into a lyric celebration of an Eros that, under the sign of a new, queer world order, is open-ended and ongoing, having outlasted the nightmare of AIDS and having transformed the genre of elegy into an euphoric anthem of possibility.

5. Other permutations of this opposition might focus on China (independently or as part of the former Soviet bloc); or the Vietnam/Korea/U.S. conflicts; or the Near and Middle East of the Desert Storm operation; or the "Orient" of occidental scholarship.

6. Some readers of Robbins's novel have found his use of women-centered themes problematic, especially given the character Sissy's on-again, off-again relation to the cowgirls at the Rubber Rose Ranch, whose revolt against patriarchy at times verges on unflattering parody. Interestingly, despite the near-universal critical dismissal of Van Sant's film as a "misfire," I'm not aware of any critique of his representation of lesbianism in the film for being inappropriate. I cannot help but wonder, however, whether some of the negative reaction to the film has to do with his attempt to find a visual medium and create a mode of narrative desire to depict women loving women, which creates an uneasy blending of "queer" aesthetics and seventies lesbian "ideology" that might be as intentional as it is unsettling.

7. This is an appropriate place to note the complex history of the "cowgirl"—and of the place of women more generally—in the mythos of the American West and its representations in fiction and film. Whereas the image of the cowboy has most often connoted masculine strength and heroism, the very idea of the cowgirl has most often been used to signal oddity and to incite mild amusement if not outright derision: thus Annie Oakley, who can "do anything you [men] can do better" in the musical *Annie Get Your Gun*, becomes a symbol of potentially excessive female self-reliance in need of the constraints of romance, and Calamity Jane, particularly as played on screen by Doris Day, becomes a kind of laughable parody to general audiences at the same time that her butch persona becomes, for the lesbian audience, a coded lesbian representation. The same might be said of Joan Crawford's high-camp performance as a pistol-toting, overly ambitious independent woman in *Johnny Gui-*

tar. For an interesting perspective on the relation of women to the genre of the western and to western "drag," see Tania Modleski, "A Woman's Gotta Do . . . What a Man's Gotta Do? Cross-Dressing in the Western," *Signs* 22, no. 3 (spring 1997): 519–44.

8. Michael Warner, "From Queer to Eternity: An Army of Theorists Cannot Fail," *Village Voice Literary Supplement,* June 1992, 18. For various perceptions of the sometimes troubled relation between feminist and queer ideology and goals, see, for instance, the special issue of *differences* entitled "More Gender Trouble: Feminism Meets Queer Theory" (*differences* 6, nos. 2–3 [summer-fall 1994]).

9. Thanks to Susana Chávez-Silverman for this insight.

10. David Savran interview with Tony Kushner, "Tony Kushner Considers the Long-standing Problems of Virtue and Happiness," *American Theatre* 2, no. 8 (October 1994): 25.

11. On the phenomenon of the "straight queer," see Ann Powers, "Queer in the Streets, Straight in the Sheets: Notes on Passing," *Village Voice,* 29 June 1993, reprinted in *Utne Reader* (November-December 1993): 75.

12. Tony Kushner, *Angels in America, a Gay Fantasia on National Themes. Part One: Millennium Approaches* (New York: Theatre Communications Group, 1992), act 1, sc. 1, lines 10–11.

13. Ibid., act 3, sc. 6, line 112.

Part One

TROUBLING FRONTIERS
GENDERS AND GENERATIONS

1

Toward a Butch-Feminist Retro-Future

Sue-Ellen Case

After throwing a major temper tantrum about the feminist tradition in my article "Toward a Butch-Femme Aesthetic," I now want to emphasize the fact that the tantrum was intended as a dramatic event that would, I hoped, by the force of its critique, initiate a dialogue to correct what seemed to me to be persistent omissions and oppressions in the history of feminist discourse around lesbian issues.[1] The scenario I sought to write was a butch seduction/bar fight with feminism, with no exit from the feminist arena on my mind. For, dysfunctional as the feminist family of critical notions proved to be, it was still "home" to my lesbian identity. And I mean specifically a "lesbian" identity. If the bar culture had given me "butch," feminism had given me "lesbian." Now maybe the reason I was entangled with feminism had to do with my premovement, oppressed habit of bringing out straight women— particularly straight middle-class women, who seemed to best grace my working-class arm. I kept trying to seduce feminism, then, as it toyed with representations of me. Classic behavior for a butch bottom.

Yet, while "butch" provided a way back into the bars, subcultural history, and signs, "feminism" had provided a way out of the bars, onto the streets, in coalitions with other women, and into theories of representation. Theoretical prowess—is that another name for academic upward mobility? Possibly. Barbara Christian and others have revealed the operations of class in such theory building. But, as those very authors have illustrated, it isn't in the theory that the class markers are embedded. After all, they theorize against theory, or theorize through autobiography and poetry. The class-specific signs, then, reside in the language of the theory. Part of an early feminist concern— that. The general proscription was not to duplicate the impersonal, unmarked language of the patriarchal tradition. Refined by some women of color and white-trash lesbians, the creative impulse within the movement was to abandon elitist, class-privileged language for experiments in the personal voice of the author. As in what was once called the arts, an embodiment of the abstracted position of the author was the practice. Author, as floating signifier, presumed access to the realm of timeless, genderless, subjective-less knowledge. In the case of the early feminist critique, the abstract, situated author, apart from "personal" or explicit historical and material attributes, practiced gender, class, and ethnic privilege. Slippage, then, signaled upward mobility. Dorothy Allison, author of *Trash*, quotes, in *Skin*, from a speech delivered by Bertha Harris that contrasts what she calls "lower class" writing with such signs of privilege: "[D]irect, unequivocating, grabby, impolite, always ready for a fight, and with a nose that can smell bullshit a mile away. The ecumenical, appeasing, side-stepping, middle-class mind never ever produces a great work of art, nor a great work of politics."[2] Now, Allison reports that Harris delivered this homily in a manner that "scared" her. Harris "put her hands on her hips, glared out at us." Scared, seduced, and supported in one, Bertha's attitude and her admonition produced a therapeutic effect for Allison. She took them as a challenge to believe in herself—to overcome her class-based insecurities and lack of self-esteem. She then quotes how Harris threw down the gauntlet to stop shuddering and get busy: *"Remember, the central female organ that makes us different and strong and artists is not the womb but the brain."*[3] Allison is citing a speech Harris delivered at the Sagaris feminist institute in 1975. Here is an essentialism of 1970s lesbian feminism—an appeal to the biological, delivered through that "unequivocating, grabby" style, aimed at the material practice of writing, and received within the class practices of she who would write. Harris's call to the body (the brain) is a rhetorical strategy, insisting upon a hands-on relation to the meat of mentality. To write, for Allison and Harris, is to work—appeals to the body reference manual labor— a far cry from the elitist notions of "ontology" or "presence" later ascribed to lesbian feminists. But those later charges presume the referents of writing to be philosophical systems. Their distance from the assumption of manual labor and class shame mark more the authors who deploy such charges than those they were set against.

In order to reframe the debates over critiques of lesbian and queer, I want to erect Harris, standing, feet apart, like a feminist butch colossus, overseeing the divide between the tradition of feminism and its *All about Eve* successor—the queer dyke. Allison's Harris, big, bad, gender- and class-specific, seductive and butch in her positioning of writing and the body, challenges the later charge of essentialism that has been funneled through the term queer in order to undo that pose of the feminist butch. The charge of essentialism, from those queer quarters, would bury that butch feminist and her likes beneath an image of lesbian feminists that look like button-wearing naive politicas. Queer dykes, flipping through fashion magazines while boarding at Northeastern private universities, proffer, instead, the semiotic copy of such material practices as a correction to the "essentialist" fallacy. If Allison sees in Harris a kind of *Night of the Living Dead*, starring brain-eating butch writers teaching at a 1970s feminist institute, the queer dyke sees herself seeing k. d. lang on the cover of *Vanity Fair.* How is it that Condé Nast(y) has become more poststructurally correct than Allison's *Skin?* The answer resides in the deployment of the term queer.

Queer, Not!

Early on, before its assimilation by postsomething or other's positioning of the discourses constructing sexuality, "queer" theorizing still emulated the sense of taking back the insult—inhabiting the "bad girl"—playing the monster—as 1970s lesbian feminism had taught some of us to do. Antiassimilationist in its intent, "queer" moved away from good-girl civil-rights petitioning. Some people thought "queer" originated that pose, but Allison reports, from that 1975 feminist writing institute, that big Bertha admonished them: *"Dare to be monstrous,* she told us in that tone of irony that warned of puns and witticisms to follow."[4] The tradition of antiassimilation, then, could be perceived as emanating from a 1970s working-class butch feminism, rather than a late 1980s New York queer coalition. Embedded in camp irony and wit (a discourse some writers of lesbian history deny to lesbians), these shared moments of Dorothy Allison and Bertha Harris at the feminist writer's institute could promote the kind of move that would embrace the insult of queer, in order to retrieve a contestatory site for political intervention.

Moreover, "queer" might reposition lesbian—moving the term out of its subcategorical position within feminism to one of (one hopes) equal status within discourses and practices of homosexuality. In order to safeguard the status of lesbian within feminist practices, and in association with gay men, Teresa de Lauretis organized a conference in Santa Cruz in 1990, proposing "queer" as a tactic that would so move the lesbian into a queer coalition that would, however, continue to trouble the conjunction between "lesbian AND gay." As de Lauretis explained it, in her introduction to the special issue of *differences* that was culled from the conference, "queer" was set at the site of difference, to call for an articulation of historical/material specificity in regard to sexual and gender practices where "and" had simply conjoined them.[5] In other words (some of them penned by Mary McIntosh), there is a separate development of lesbian and gay male history inscribed in their shared strategies.[6] Terms such as constructionism and queer, rather than inhabiting a gender-free or beyond-gender theoretical position, would be examined to reveal the uneven development of lesbian/ gay politics along the social, historical axis of gender difference, while also forging a common front.

Persuaded by de Lauretis's call through queer to critically explore the homosexual divide, I wrote "Tracking the Vampire" for her conference and to be published in the ensuing collection of articles. For me, queer mobilized a vampiric (in)visibility within systems of representation that would feed along an axis of both gay and lesbian texts which had nourished me prior to feminism. Again, ever in dialogue with feminist constructions, I tried to retrieve "lesbian" from an ill-got *jouissance* that cast her in *Whatever Happened to Baby Jane?* Smarting (hopefully) at the feminist "recreational use of the lesbian" that assigned her to the wings in order to stage mother/daughter conjunctions, I hoped to provide an entrance for lesbian from upstage center by aligning her with homosexuality—the queer. Within that critical context, situating lesbian representational strategies in proximity to those of the gay, or homosexual, man, was intended as a correction to the way in which feminist discourses had subsumed or "topped" the lesbian. The social movement ever in mind, it also seemed high time to end the historical labor relations between the lesbian and the feminist activist movement which had domesticated lesbian labor. After all, the lesbian feminist had provided activist labor in many causes, not necessarily her own, such as abortion rights, and for which the straight feminist did not return the favor by, say, marching in PFLAG units in Pride marches. Where were those legions of feminists marching in support?

When I delivered the paper "Tracking the Vampire," I was critiqued by the local community in Santa Cruz for performing "whiteness" and privileging complex, abstract theorizing, unavailable to working-class people. I revised my paper by founding the theorizing in my historically-geographically specific experiential situation that had produced the theory and by working anti-Semitic codes of blood along with vampiric images. This process of self-criticism and answerability to the local community seemed a familiar practice within lesbian feminist cultural production. However, the editors at the Pembroke Center for Teaching and Research on Women, who would publish the article in *differences,* had (to me) a surprising reaction to what I considered to be a standard materialist feminist correction. They sought to edit out the initial experiential foundation of the piece as an example of 1970s feminist essentialism. First they suggested that I italicize the personal base of the argument, so that it would read like a biographical sketch of the author, separated out from the theorizing. Then they sought to cut it entirely. I'm relating this publishing gossip, not to elevate the stature of my work, nor to seek some balm for wounds to my ego, nor to *j'accuse* those editors, but to compose a parable, bound in the business of publishing, that illustrates the shift in the reception of the construction of "lesbian" in representation, and situates that shift specifically within the rise of the term queer. The deconstructive break with the personal as political sought to reaffirm the author as floating signifier. Slippage, once perceived as privileged mobility, became the preferred mode of intellectual travel. The queer call was to return to that unmarked patriarchal, Eurocentric language of, well, the French and German philosophical traditions. "Philosophy to the fore!" cheered queer. Queer thus functioned as the sign of sexual politics cut loose from earlier, grass-roots lesbian feminism.

Burial Rites of the Feminist Butch

From the developing perspective of queer, lesbian became conflated with what was once more specifically identified as radical feminist politics. The preponderance of socialist/materialist feminist practices in the 1970s was buried in such revisionism, along with the critique devised by working-class, manual-laboring butch feminists. Soon, in queer quarters, it seemed that all lesbian feminists had been wearing Birkenstocks and ripping off their shirts at the Michigan Womyn's Music Festival. Some of us chortled at the revisionist image of bar/butch/feminist dykes listening to acoustic guitars. We remembered, for example, the girl group called the Contractions, who whacked their electric instruments at top volume and flirted impossibly with the audience of dykes (sigh). The culture, always variegated by its wildly divergent feminisms was, through the charge of essentialism and the newly organized perspective of queer, being represented by one small subset. Slapping each other on the back, we joked, "was lesbian S/M invented by Gayle Rubin and Pat Califia in an argument with antiporn advocates?" Leafing through our old phone books and photos of friends flamed out in one affair after another, we snorted at the queer dykes' belief that they were originating the practice of multiple sexual partners, S/M scenarios, the use of sex toys, and the habit of hanging around bars. Beebo Brinker, Ann Bannon's 1950s seducer and abandoner, who found someone else's flannel pajamas in the faithful Laura's apartment, took it as a familiar sign of lesbian social practices, and her progeny peopled at least two succeeding decades. What a surprise, then, to learn that queer dykes associated such sexual promiscuity as more narrowly particular to a gay male culture that they would then need to assimilate and imitate. Butch feminists, it seemed, had been having monogamous, vanilla, Saturday-morning slight sex since the 1970s. We snickered. Then it wasn't funny anymore.

Such revisionist history thus promoted a queer ascension, through a valorization of gay male practices, arising from lesbian feminist ashes. The new queer dyke is out to glue on that gay male mustache and leave those dowdy, gynocentric habits behind. The *lesbian* body, perforated by discursive intrusions as early as Monique Wittig's, disciplined by materialist production as early as the manifestos of Ti-Grace Atkinson and the Combahee River Collective, and radiated out through the hard work of coalition-building, was spanked by the queers for its so-called ontological status and antisexual proclivities. Although, by now, we are surely bored with the spectacle of the debate over the essentialist charge, the charge continues to brand "queer" onto the disciplined, upended bottoms of what were once fleshly figures of lesbian desire. Further, queer's consort, "performativity," links "lesbian" to the tarnished sweating, laboring, performing body that must be semiotically scrubbed until the "live" lesbian gives way to the slippery, polished surface of the market manipulation of its sign. Better to circulate the queer dyke body through zines and fashion rags than to travel its orifices and tissues in Wittig's speculum-script. Body-less transcendence is produced through the process of semiosis. Isn't that the same desire for transcendence that was identified earlier by lesbian feminists as a masculine, Eurocentric trope? That gay male mustache, garnishing the lip of the queer dyke, then, also garnishes her critical strategies. Even if, as Peggy Shaw contends, testosterone is better in the hands of women, appropriating the masculine is not, obviously, beyond gender.

Right after those queer dykes slammed the door on the way out of lesbian feminism, the dowdy old women-centered places began to close down: most feminist and lesbian theaters, bookstores, and bars have disappeared. One of the underground movies making the circuit the past few years is called *Last Call at Maud's*—about the last night at the oldest lesbian bar in San Francisco and the end of many such lesbian bars. I walk the streets of West Hollywood and the Village in New York to jealously observe packed bar after bar of gay men. I stand in the book chain A Different Light on a Saturday night in West Hollywood—one of four or five lesbians among, say, fifty gay men. I'm flipping through the zines. I'm checking out the special photo shots of daddy-boy-dykes in *Quim.*[7] Back on the streets. Everyone is looking good. I stand outside the gym on Santa Monica, in front of the huge picture windows, reminiscent of shop windows, where I can watch everybody working out. The women are looking strong. Slim. Young. I look down at my aging, overweight, academic body. They've cleared us out, I think. It's true—the Birkenstocks are gone, but so are what we used to call "women of size" and well, uh, older women. Two of my gay male friends call me up—they're freaking out because they're now in their 30s—how will they retain their sexual currency—do they have to become tops—do they have to go over to the leather scene, where older men still find them desirable? So now we all have *their* problems, I think.

Never mind, I'll go to the theater. I like *Angels in America*—it has a big cast and a big theme—a critique of nationalism and, well, I'm pretty sure the angel is a lesbian. That's what we used to say about the Holy Ghost—you know, the Father, the Son and. . . . Anyway, there are some great one-person dyke shows making the circuit and lots of new lesbian stand-up comics. Forget Broadway—we have "intimate" sites such as P.S. 122, or I can always go to the movies with my other professor friends and "read," as we say, something like *Single White Female* as signifying, as we also say, lesbian. The privileging of gay male culture by queer dykes, along with the disdain and mis-remembering of lesbian feminism, has produced the dwindling away of lesbian cultural resources—socially and economically and theoretically. Oh well, I comfort myself with the option of those lesbian luxury cruises sponsored by Olivia—if only I could afford one. Then I'm caught up short with this thought—those old dowdy lesbian feminist hangouts—almost all of them were organized as collectives: theater collectives, bookstore collectives, food collectives, collective living quarters. Lesbian dowdy politics had been intrinsically tied to collective ownership and collective labor. They locked the mode of material production to cultural production and to the production of sexual, personal relationships . . . and then there was interactive commodity dildoism. Does it matter that A Different Light is not a collective and is, in fact, a chain? Is someone getting rich? Is someone not? Does it matter?

Up (Your) Market

What was once a lesbian or gay community is now becoming a market sector. The *Journal of Consumer Marketing* ran an article that summarized the finding of several studies to discover just how lesbians and gays consume market goods.[8] Several studies (some produced by gay public relations agencies) concur that gays and lesbians make more money per household than the U.S. average, buy more airline tickets, own more cars, are better educated, and spend more money on consumer goods. Clearly this market sector has disposable income. They are becoming a target market, but how are they accessible to the market? This study suggests that it is primarily through their publications. The article lists the *Advocate, Deneuve, Genre, On Our Backs, Out,* and *10 Percent* as likely venues for effective ads. The new, glossy formats with upscale-looking models and ads encourage corporations to consider buying their pages.

Sarah Schulman has taken such studies to evidence a rising "management class," warning that there is a "class war emerging within the gay and lesbian world."[9] She details how some gay organizations are even organizing to profit from HIV-positive buyers. Particularly poignant, notes Schulman, is the growth of viatical companies that purchase the life insurance policies of persons with terminal illnesses. After all, people with AIDS, who have no children or other heirs, may be eager to spend and thus sell their insurance money, at any percentage, to a viatical company. Schulman details how this new management class creates the image of a gay/lesbian market sector that conceals the class differences within it. She quotes from the literature published by the gay-owned Mulryan/Nash advertising firm—the one that marketed *Angels in America* to gay tourists and worked for the government of Holland to develop advertising that would attract gay tourists. Mulryan/Nash contends that 61 percent of gay people have college degrees, household incomes of $62,000, and CD players, work out in gyms, and drink sparkling water. Schulman contrasts these figures with some published in the *New York Times* asserting that homosexual men earn 12 percent less than heterosexual ones and lesbians 5 percent less than heterosexual women, who earn 45 percent less than heterosexual men. Schulman's conclusion, then, is that a privileged gay class is entering the market economy and creating a fiction that erases the "others" in what was once called a community. The aim is to produce sexual identities as powerful consumers with discretionary incomes and good taste.

The once-activist Queer Nation has formed the Queer Shopping Network of New York. "Queer" may be found on coffee mugs, T-shirts, and postcards sold at Gay Pride parades and in new marketing chains across the country. One can buy queer and wear it. In some circles, "queer" seems to be primarily constituted by body piercings, leather, and spike haircuts. One might applaud such signs of commodification as signs of success. Good. We are not necessarily poor, nor downwardly mobile. Lipstick lesbians are cute. Sex can be fun. We are visible, strong, making more money, dressing better, eating out, and enjoying sex.

Many "queer" academics write this affluent, commodity fetishism. Some are concerned with Rock Hudson's body, some with k. d. lang's and Cindy Crawford's photo display in *Vanity Fair*, others with the radical purchasing of dildoes—"subversive shopping," as Danae Clark refers to it in her article "Commodity Lesbianism." They invent queer discourse out of an addiction to the allure of the mass market. Fandom queered. *Melrose Place* reruns as Castro Street. Class privilege and the celebration of capitalism are compounded with the queer sex industry. Likewise, certain theoretical strategies have been embodied in new, surprising ways. The much-touted practice and theory of masquerade, once written as subversive cross-dressing, has literally turned into a uniform. Recent Gay Pride parades sport a uniformed color guard of Marines and the like, accompanying the flag. The people on the sidewalk cheer as the presumably "queer" or "gay" U.S. flag and military march by. If only we could make the military-industrial complex gay-friendly. From queer planet to queer Pentagon. Antiassimilationist in its move away from pleading civil rights, the queer movement insinuates sexual citizenship through affluence in the market and the willing participation in national agendas. Wouldn't it be victory for the movement if Colonel Margarethe Cammermeyer, mother of four sons, Vietnam vet, could be reinstated into the army?

Mommie Dearest

The Reagan 1980s, ushered in by Joan Crawford's attack on any of those hideous wire hangers still found in the closet, produced a routing out of any associations with the iron curtain that continued to inform the political movements concerning alternative sexualities. Contesting capitalism, along with providing alternative economic practices such as collective ownership and labor, in discourses of so-called sexual dissidence was out. Following its successful purge, the privileged compound "queer performativity" ushered in the 1990s, having detonated the ground of lesbian feminism—shattering its socialist roots through the charge of essentialism. The trick was, as post–Berlin Wall discourse also performed, to invert the traditional meanings of political terminology, thereby confusing the actual development of power relationships. After the wall's fall, Euromediaspeak repositioned communism as signifying the Right and the reactionary and global capitalism as the leftist, outsider position. Such sleights of terminology masked material conditions: former property owners in the West appropriated the properties of the former East, while portraying themselves as the oppressed, shaking off the shackles of collective ownership. Similarly, the lesbian feminist position, imbricated with socialist/communist strategies, such as collective practices of ownership and labor, were represented as essentialist, reversing the nature of the critique in order to overcome its materialist practices with formal discursive ones. The rise of "queer performativity," then, accompanied the victory of global capitalism in the new Europe as well as the complete commodification of the sexual movement. The charge of essentialism rousted the iron curtain out of the closet.

The notion of the Bad Binary also functioned to resituate the queer movement within market strategies. Second terms were out. Hetero/homo made homo suspect. Likewise for capitalism/communism. After all, Baudrillard had already depicted the two as the twin trade towers in New York in his *Simulations*.[10] Global capitalism could contain everything, all differences within its shifting economic zones, just as the new Individual could contain multiple subject positions. Down with the binary went oppositional economic and cultural alternatives. Queer emulated global capitalism in order to gain status within it. Certain revisions of history would have to be performed, of course, in order to cleanse any sense of oppositional affiliations from the sexual rights movement. Enter the case of Colonel Cammermeyer. Antiwar demonstrators? Not! Instead, the bid to reinstate the lesbian Vietnam hero into high ranks in the army revised the image and the agenda of the movement. Soldiers and marketeers of global expansion, avid and capable consumers, loyal fans, even (one hopes) good wives and husbands could gather under the banner of queer. Oppositional struggles fade before simple iterations that queer includes everyone who is antinormal and hypernormal all at once. Who could but envy us? At last we're competitive, as they say.

Nevertheless, those of us who were in a relationship, so to speak, with the old dowdy "I" of i-dentity politics, the "I" of dialogue or the dialectic, continue to interpret "presence" as politically showing up. As a base of operations, that "I" signals the old theatrical, the old dare I say communist, the old feminist collective dialogues of contradiction—"I know, let's do a show—I'll play," as Lois Weaver once said onstage to Peggy Shaw, "Katharine Hepburn to your Spencer Tracy." Or, in the old communist sense, "I know, let's redistribute the land—let's collectivize the labor—what? It's not fair, given your college education, your student loan, your expertise? How can we work this out?" Or, in the old feminist sense, I can still hear the voice of the African

American activist Bernice Johnson Reagon, speaking to a group of feminists struggling over issues of ethnicity and sexual practice. She described the experience of building coalitions: "The first thing that happens is that the room don't feel like the room anymore. (The audience laughed) And it ain't home no more. It is not a womb no more. And you can't feel comfortable no more. . . . [Yet] the 'our' must include everybody you have to include in order for you to survive. . . . That's why we have to live in coalitions. 'Cause I ain't gonna let you live unless you let me live. Now there's danger in that, but there's also the possibility that we both can live—if you can stand it."[11]

The sound of dialogue, the collective, resounds in these threats and hurts of the clash of conflicting positions, or the joy of temporary agreement which, like Rome, is not made in a day, or by the fiat of a term like queer that sweeps down from the discourse to gather up oppositional positions by force of its own definition AS embracing AS multimulti, acting like the movies, or the old well-made plays that conclude all problems with a kiss, a marriage, or, in this case, a dildo.

And "presence"—showing up—at activist disruptions, at live performances, in collective venues, reclaims the "live"—the body—the visible—looking for lesbians in the political sense. It is "live" performance as politics, as theater, the play of positional masks, sweating flesh and clapping hands that finally animates what cyberpunks call the "meat." For presence as body, as visibility, in the collective, once abandoned, i-dentity once gone, promotes the new sense of performativity in which the body is a trope and performance part of the allure of reading and writing.

Work Not, Want Not

The year 1982 might be regarded as the Great Divide. Along with *Mommie Dearest*, the Barnard conference staged the outbreak of open conflict between the lesbian S/M community and the feminist antiporn adherents—a conflict that was never resolved. The debates were hot and the rifts were deep. What later became the "sex radicals" tired of feminism's het "missionary position," while the feminist critique stalled out in its persistent blindness to heterosexism. Moreover, the socialist critique remained obsessed with labor, ignoring issues around sexual practice and pleasure.

Meanwhile, the beginning of what would become the AIDS crisis was forging new alliances between lesbians and gay men. Patriarchal privilege aside, gay men were in life-or-death struggles around sexual practices. Sex was a given, open focus in their community, while the feminist community, where heterosexism forced a silencing of the debate they were afraid to continue, seemed to be formulating neopuritanical prescriptions against erotic materials and the exploration of sexual pleasure. So lesbian feminists became queer dykes among gay men. The rise of the fundamentalist Right demanded a new, more aggressive political activism. The failure of government institutions to respond to the need for AIDS treatment became more and more reactionary. ACT UP, formed in the late 1980s in New York, produced "live" agitprop street performances within a coalition. For awhile. While some ACT UP organizations survived, others, such as the ones in San Francisco and Seattle, split into ACTS UPS, or whatever. Lesbians split from gay men over the focus of concern: is AIDS a gay male disease, or how do we also address the problems of the category "women," straight or lesbian, of color who bear a high incidence of AIDS? Latent feminist coalitions with other women, particularly women of color, still haunted the new dyke. It seems girls don't just wanta have fun, but they also don't wanta have none. In queer coalitions, proceeding out from New York's urban center, how could those queer dykes still remain in old feminist coalitions with women of color and third-world women?

If queer, as sex-positive and antiassimilationist, claims to cut across differences—including bisexuals, transgendered people, S/M practitioners—and all the "antinormal" could be included in its embrace, and if it also claims multicultural representation at its base, then why do we read things like the following? Cherríe Moraga, the lesbian Chicana poet and dramatist writes, "We discussed the limitations of 'Queer Nation,' whose leather-jacketed, shaved-headed white radicals and accompanying anglo-centricity were an alien-nation to most lesbians and gay men of color."[12] Even the queer enthusiast Michael Warner offers a chilling description of the "queer community" in his introduction to *Fear of a Queer Planet:* "In the lesbian and gay movement, to a much greater degree than in any comparable movement, the institutions of culture-building have been market-mediated.... Nonmarket forms of association . . . churches, kinship, traditional residence—have been less available for queers. This structural environment has meant that the institutions of queer culture have been dominated by those with capital: typically, middle-class white men."[13] Terry Castle, in *The Apparitional Lesbian,* adds this dimension: "As soon as the lesbian is lumped in—for better or for worse—with her male homosexual counterpart, the singularity of her experience (sexual and otherwise) tends to become obscured . . . to the extent that 'queer theory' still seems . . .

to denote primarily the study of male homosexuality, I find myself at odds with both its language and its universalizing aspirations."[14] Charles Fernández, in "Undocumented Aliens in the Queer Nation," identifies queer as a "melting pot" term of "bankrupt universalism."[15]

I think an important clue to the element in the notion and practice of queer that led to its embrace of commodification and its emulation of dominant class and gender practices may be found in Alexander Chee's historical account of the origins of Queer Nation: "The name stuck simply for the sake of marketing. The original idea was this: choose a name around each action, keep responsibility with each individual and not with an institution. . . . People are tired of groups with egos, processes, personality cults, and politicking. So far Queer Nation is individuals confronting individuals."[16] Chee underscores that any practice of continuity was a marketing choice. The queer retention of individualism, changing tactics, venue, and organizations, was designed to invigorate those who are "tired" of group processes. The interest, then, is not in collective agency—in fact, collectives are perceived as infected with "politicking"—but in the individual's action of intervention into the marketing process. In fact, if Chee is correct, Queer Nation arose as a direct contradiction to collective, group-process-oriented politics. At the same time, it does seem to unfurl that same old banner of the individual that liberal democracy keeps hanging out to dry. Sarah Schulman, writing from a slightly different perspective in *My American History*, indicates that the AIDS crisis catalyzed the correction of traditional forms of coalition-building. She offers "processing" as the problem, through which coalition-building became therapizing, continually postponing activism—a delay the new, fatal progress of AIDS could ill afford.[17] Yet, when the process is aborted and the coalition simply iterated, the skills that had been learned in antiracist, antisexist training groups become lost and those dominant structures remain intact within the coalition.

Queer coalitions, then, in a hurry to get onto the streets, began to interrogate the "normal," as if outside of the normalizing operations of patriarchy, capital, and nation. For, without arduous attention to dominant contexts, single-issue politics operate within them. The term queer, then, circulating out from Queer Nation, asserts itself as an umbrella term without the hard rain of coalition-building. Thus it reinstates the dominant social structures, lending its power to those who are already vested in the system, with the exception of their sexual identification. Not surprisingly, then, white middle-class men will form the constituency. Their culture, sub or not, will continue to be representative.

You Have Nothing to Wear but Your Chains

Now thoroughly depressed, I wonder if this writing is only nostalgic. The good old days of butch feminism. Not only. I mean, the child whines because she wants something she can't have—in the present. It isn't all fort/da, as the Freudians would have us believe—I mean, it isn't all because mommie left the room. If this writing did begin by wriggling through those spread thighs of the colossal Bertha Harris I erected to guard the portals between butch feminist and queer, it isn't satisfied to remain there, curled up in the fetal position, stammering fort/da to some Freudian who likes to watch. Toward a butch-feminist retro-future seeks an agenda that might animate both a modernist project of doing something historical about the future and the ironic, postmodern sense of retro that, by the conjunction, still performs a critique of the categories of historical past and future.

Employing retro in this way is in contradiction to the way the term and the practice are typically theorized. Critics such as Celeste Olalquiaga in *Megalopolis* contend that any retro future is always already "attracted by an image of progress only possible to an apocalyptical fin de siècle as a melancholic appropriation—one that refuses to accept death, fetishistically clinging to memories, corpses, and ruins."[18] Farting the old fetishistic gas, as usual. Crucial to my argument, however, is the way in which Olalquiaga discovers retro as a specifically gay male practice. She contends that the "two most conspicuous subcultures involved in retro fashion are children of the baby-boomer era: yuppies and young gay men." Never to be left out, I want to imply queer dyke subculture in such practices. Here's how Olalquiaga sees it:

While yuppies use money as a means of neutralizing difference, many young gay men use their bodies as a celebratory means of camouflage and the absorption of difference. Rather than the explicit transvestism of drag . . . these men are prone to . . . the body as the territory on which infinite characters and personas can be explored on a daily basis. . . . Money and body alike, then, serve as conduits for the circulation of signs, enabling a swift exchange void of the weight of referentiality. It is not history or a peculiar culture that is being referred to in this way of quoting, it is rather an iconographic richness that is being happily cannibalized.[19]

Something in the style of retro quoting, then, makes it unspecific—the general play of signs that, finally, celebrates a significatory emptiness. The past is dead. This sense of retro depends upon a rather wide bandwidth of signs—that is, unlike drag, not signs of a specific historical or collective past. Retro butch feminism is more specific in its referent, butch feminism, than queer has been in its operations that would dismantle the generalized, revisionist lesbian feminism. So first the retro I have in mind requires a knowledge of the specific historical and discursive strategies of butch feminism to cite. Retro, in this sense, is a kind of discipline. On the one hand, retro confounds the melancholic nostalgia of a dead retro with an agenda for the future; on the other, it corrects the tendentious quality of utopian agendas with a camp citation of history. What does this mean? Partially, it mandates a reconsideration, back through queer, of a class specific, self-consciously gendered political program that situates the practitioner within coalitional politics while playing out traditionally lesbian seduction scenarios within the political practice. Economic structures once again codetermine sexual politics, and the inscription of the different histories of gay men and lesbians reconfigure what now seem to be common, agendered forms, which encourage the belief that there is another, nongendered discursive space within which such politics may emerge. The composition seeks a certain playful sobriety, oxymoronic compounds that actually do suggest, once again, agency and responsibility in a time which puts on a good show in order to distract the audience from the irreparable damage it inflicts on those who continue to play by its rules.

Notes

I am indebted to the organizers of the conference entitled "Queering the Pitch" in Manchester and to Karin Quimby and the other organizers of the "Queer Frontiers" conference at the University of Southern California for inviting me to deliver the keynote address that led to this chapter.

This chapter originally appeared in Dana Heller, ed., *Cross-Purposes: Lesbians, Feminists, and the Limits of Alliance* (Bloomington: Indiana University Press, 1997), 205–20, and is reproduced with the permission of Indiana University Press.

1. Both this chapter and its title overwrite the femme with feminist. Partially, this new conjunction means to place the butch and feminism in a similar desiring coupling, as the earlier butch/femme had suggested. Polemically, the conjunction also means to reforge a lost, troubled connection. However, "dropping" the femme is definitely part of the theoretical process here—an unhappy one. I can only hope that she will make me regret every minute of it—will force herself back into the theorizing. Thanks to Laura Harris for pointing out this problem in my article. I eagerly await her forthcoming femme flirtation with the discourse.

2. Dorothy Allison, *Skin* (Ithaca, N.Y.: Firebrand, 1994), 206.

3. Ibid., 207; emphasis in the original.

4. Ibid.

5. Teresa de Lauretis, "Queer Theory: Lesbian and Gay Sexualities: An Introduction," *differences* 3, no. 2 (summer 1991): iii–xviii.

6. See McIntosh's notion of the triad of "queer," "feminist," and "lesbian" strategies at the conclusion of her article "Queer Theory and the War of the Sexes," in *Activating Theory: Lesbian, Gay, Bisexual Politics,* ed. Joseph Bristow and Angelia R. Wilson (London: Lawrence and Wishart, 1993), 30–52.

7. "Daddy Boy Dykes," *Quim* (winter 1991): 32–35.

8. Douglas Fugate, "Evaluating the U.S. Male Homosexual and Lesbian Population as a Viable Target Market Segment," *Journal of Consumer Marketing* 10, no. 4 (1993): 46–57.

9. Sarah Schulman, "Now a Word from Our Sponsor," paper delivered at the University of California, San Diego, January 1995.

10. Jean Baudrillard, *Simulations,* trans. Paul Foss, Paul Patton, and Philip Beitchman (New York: Semiotext(e), 1983), 135–36.

11. Bernice Johnson Reagon, "Coalition Politics: Turning the Century," in *Home Girls: A Black Feminist Anthology,* ed. Barbara Smith (Brooklyn, N.Y.: Kitchen Table Women of Color Press, 1983), 359, 363.

12. Cherríe Moraga, *The Last Generation* (Boston: South End Press, 1993), 147.

13. Michael Warner, introduction to *Fear of a Queer Planet,* ed. Michael Warner (Minneapolis: University of Minnesota Press, 1993), xvii.

14. Terry Castle, *The Apparitional Lesbian* (New York: Columbia University Press, 1993), 12–13.

15. Charles Fernández, "Undocumented Aliens in the Queer Nation," *Out/Look: The National Lesbian and Gay Quarterly* 11 (spring 1991): 20.

16. Alexander Chee, "A Queer Nationalism," *Out/Look: The National Lesbian and Gay Quarterly* 12 (summer 1991): 13.

17. Sarah Schulman, *My American History: Lesbian and Gay Life during the Reagan/Bush Years* (New York: Routledge, 1994), 6.

18. Celeste Olalquiaga, *Megalopolis: Contemporary Cultural Sensibilities* (Minneapolis: University of Minnesota Press, 1992), 23.

19. Ibid., 32.

2

Apocalypse from Now On

Peter Coviello

The once-and-for-all eradication of gay populations, however
potent and sustained as a project or fantasy of modern
Western culture, is not possible short of the eradication of the
whole human species.
—Eve Kosofsky Sedgwick, *Epistemology of the Closet*

If it's not love, then it's the bomb, the bomb, the bomb that
will bring us together.
—The Smiths, "Ask"

Speaking on May 18, 1924, to a group called the Heretics, Virginia
Woolf proposed "that in or about December, 1910, human character
changed." With that disarming mix of bravado and imperturbable tact,
she strode to her first conclusion: *"All human relations have shifted . . .*
those between masters and servants, husbands and wives, parents and
children. And when human relations change there is at the same time
a change in religion, conduct, politics, and literature."[1] Given the authority of Woolf's modernist precedent, I want to begin with an assertion just as abrupt and just as tendentious—but, for that, no less crucial
to an understanding of the conditions of *our* knowledge, here in
America, at the *fin de millennium*. My hypothesis is this: in or about
November 1989, apocalypse changed and, by virtue of that change, all
human relations have shifted. One may want to situate this shift as
early as January 1986 when, in the words of Mikhail Gorbachev, "the
Soviet Union put forward a historic program, that of stage-by-stage
elimination of nuclear weapons,"[2] or as late as the ratifications of disarmament treaties under the Clinton administration. In any event, in
or about November, 1989, the Berlin Wall fell; the Cold War, as it had
been practiced for roughly forty years, ended, and nuclear weapons—
"the most momentous development in the history of the species," according to novelist and writer Martin Amis[3]—all but vanished from

representations of the world's geopolitical climate, or, at the very least, ceased to be *the* omnipresent and determining contingency, under the rubric of which all life on the planet quietly carried on.

One forgets, in these late days, how comprehensively the threat of nuclear destruction marked the day-to-day cultural life of an America now only a decade or so behind us. Indeed, the remarkably comfortable fit of what I would call our nuclear amnesia may well be one of the most puzzling legacies of the Reagan era. Where, one wants almost nostalgically to ask, did the nuclear go? Certainly, nuclear "threats" continue to be trotted out before the national public, and come typically in the guise of one or several "rogue states," whose presumed political (not to say national and psychic) instability makes requisite an intensified American defense.[4] But these familiar stories, however obligatory they may be to the maintenance of American imperial relations, do seem notably mundane when set against the sweeping geopolitical melodramas of the early 1980s: they have none of the heart-stopping urgency, and certainly none of the seductive narrative grandeur, of that great nuclear saga which, by the mid-eighties, had so fully enmeshed itself in the fabric of American culture as to be the subject of—what else?—a made-for-TV movie. (Few, I think, are the members of my generation who will not remember, with perhaps a tiny quickening of the pulse, either watching or, in my case, being forbidden to watch that melodramatic nuclear horror show *The Day After.*) If nuclear arsenals stand ready even at this moment to unleash themselves at the punch of a proper series of keys, their once incontestable *cultural* potency would seem, by contrast, far less susceptible to revivification. The culture of the nuclear warhead is simply, strangely, gone. And so emphatically are nuclear weapons "of the past" that now, in all but the most rarefied of circles, the very phrase "nuclear anxiety" fairly trembles with all the beguiling opacity of any other manifestly *eighties* fascination—as though the nuclear were as outdated, and as faddishly retro, as junk bonds, white denim Calvins, and feathered hair. Where *did* the nuclear go? Given the fairly untroubled completeness of its disappearance, shouldn't we revise the governing critical aphorism of the day, and say that rather than a postmodern age ours is, more exactly, a *postnuclear age*?[5]

Perhaps. But to claim that American culture is at present decisively postnuclear is not to say that the world we inhabit is in any way postapocalyptic. Apocalypse, as I began by saying, *changed*—it did not go away. And here I want to hazard my second assertion: if, in the nuclear age of yesteryear, apocalypse signified an event threatening everyone and everything with (in Jacques Derrida's suitably menacing phrase) "remainderless and a-symbolic destruction,"[6] then in the postnuclear world apocalypse is an affair whose parameters are definitively *local*. In shape and in substance, apocalypse is defined now by the affliction it brings *somewhere else,* always to an "other" people whose very presence might then be written as a kind of dangerous contagion, threatening the safety and prosperity of a cherished "general population." This fact seems to me to stand behind Susan Sontag's incisive observation, from 1989, that, "Apocalypse is now a long-running serial: not 'Apocalypse Now' but 'Apocalypse from Now On.'"[7] The decisive point here in the perpetuation of the threat of apocalypse (the point Sontag goes on, at length, to miss) is that apocalypse is ever present because, as an element in a vast economy of power, it is ever useful. That is, through the perpetual threat of destruction—through the constant reproduction of the *figure* of apocalypse—agencies of power ensure their authority to act on and through the bodies of a particular population. No one turns this point more persuasively than Michel Foucault, who in the final chapter of his first volume of *The History of Sexuality* addresses himself to the problem of a power that is less repressive than productive, less life-threatening than, in his words, "life-administering." Power, he contends, "exerts a positive influence on life ... [and] endeavors to administer, optimize, and multiply it, subjecting it to precise controls and comprehensive regulations." In his brief comments on what he calls "the atomic situation," however, Foucault insists as well that the productiveness of modern power must not be mistaken for a uniform repudiation of violent or even lethal means. For as "managers of life and survival, of bodies and the race," agencies of modern power presume to act *"on the behalf of the existence of everyone."* Whatsoever might be construed as a threat to life and survival in this way serves to authorize *any* expression of force, no matter how invasive or, indeed, potentially annihilating. "If genocide is indeed the dream of modern power," Foucault writes, "this is not because of a recent return to the ancient right to kill; it is because power is situated and exercised at the level of life, the species, the race, and the large-scale phenomena of population."[8] For a state that would arm itself not with the power to kill its population, but with a more comprehensive power over the patterns and functioning of its collective life, the threat of an apocalyptic demise, nuclear or otherwise, seems a civic initiative that can scarcely be done without.

A number of questions present themselves: how, in a postnuclear world, is power dispersed and seized and operated? Can we discover, in this age of disarmament, presences not so much new as newly articulated that form equivalent threats to, say, "bodies and the race," to

"the existence of everyone," threats through which a postnuclear regime might reconstitute itself with all the more efficiency? If the nuclear has vanished so entirely from the cultural stage, might some
other apocalyptic spectacle have more or less seamlessly replaced it,
and have taken over some of the civic *utility* once extracted from the
threat of nuclear destruction? To anyone possessed of an at least passing familiarity with the last decade of American public life, my referent
should now be clear: nothing exemplifies the postnuclear localization
of the figure of apocalypse more visibly, or more harrowingly, than
AIDS. Sometime around 1989, and with a thoroughness and a rapidity
that I think we are only now beginning to grasp, the menace of AIDS
unseated nuclear warfare as the defining apocalyptic threat to American health and security. What I want to take up in this chapter, then,
are the uncanny transactions between these two genres of apocalypse,
the nuclear and the sexual, and the quietly sweeping rearrangements
of American civic life their interchange effects. It would of course
startle no one to say that queer communities are a great deal more
visible now than they were fifteen years ago, and that such visibility
comes, at least in part, as a rather direct result of AIDS, which has in
that brief time turned upon gay men in particular the full glare of any
number of differently calibrated public gazes. Still, it's remarkable—
and, I think, necessary—to consider how deeply scored this multifac-
eted national investment in homosexuality has been by the shifting
political imperatives of a nuclear state on the verge of détente. I mean
to suggest, broadly, that in the wake of a rapidly deflating nuclear
threat, violently homophobic responses to AIDS came to operate in
America with all the decisiveness and utility of a defensive, fully *national* initiative. I look in the first half of the pages that follow at the
often arrestingly lurid figures of nuclear discourse, to show how intimately bonded the nuclear and the sexual actually were, *before* the
advent of AIDS gave to such bonding a ghastly quality of inevitability.
In the second half, I take up the matter of "the new queer visibility"
by considering the extractions from, and inflictions upon, gay life and
gay possibility that the various narrative mechanisms of popular gay
enfranchisement seem to demand. Part of my concern is thus to trace
a few of the salient transformations in national polity, whereby queer
peoples became at once the targets of a uniquely virulent condemna-
tory campaign, *and* the objects of sustained, and not always spiteful,
public fascination. Figuring out exactly how this double movement
works seems to me a matter of some analytic importance, especially
since this unprecedented national interest in homosexuality manifests
itself not least consequentially in the emergence of the very discipline

under whose auspices this collection of essays has been gathered together: queer studies. One might say that the undertaking of this chapter is thus a kind of genealogy: not so much a genealogy of queer studies per se as of the conditions of American public life in which it became possible for such a critical discourse to emerge, in institutions (like the university) otherwise not wholly amenable to gay life. The overarching point I want to make here, though, is simply that in the shift from a nuclear to a postnuclear political dispensation what unfolds is not a diminishment, but rather a series of calculated adjustments in the state's capacity to administer to its citizens carefully regulated quantities of *life*. As a result of this readjustment, a pivotal figure in the legitimation of a power over life is now, more than ever before, the gay man.[9]

These uncanny rumblings go back a long way, and certainly predate the Reagan presidency. It might be said, in fact, that the sexualization of nuclear warfare was evident from the moment of its conceptual inception, and took a form as blaringly unsubtle as simple *naming:* from an atoll called Bikini, soon to be visited by an explosive named Little Boy, to the sexual hygienics of an almost comically allegorized American "nuclear" family is, after all, a very short step.[10] But things get curious indeed when a specifically *homo*sexuality begins to locate itself with respect to this nuclear familialism. James Merrill's five-hundred-page nuclear epic, *The Changing Light at Sandover,* is uniquely instructive in this regard. In its weird intergalactic ecologies, its self-consciously daffy spiritualism, and not the least in its persistent cross-wirings of militaristic and sexual apocalypses, Merrill's poem might be said to crystallize a number of the profound affective pressures of what we now call, almost derisively, "nuclear anxiety." Indeed, part of what I think makes the poem so uniquely indicative (especially when compared with the more securely ironic latter-day appraisals of sex and apocalypse in the Cold War, such as Tony Kushner's *Angels in America*) is the amazing thoroughness with which its every gesture or thematic turn is scored by elements of plain, unguarded nuclear panic. Composed during the seventies and early eighties, *The Changing Light* consists of three discrete books of verse, each longer than the one before it, and a short "Coda." The poem is, to quote the end of its first canto, "The Book of a Thousand and One Evenings Spent / With David Jackson at the Ouija Board / In Touch with Ephraim Our Familiar Spirit."[11] That is, the book unfolds as a loving reconstruction of decades' worth of conversations between Merrill (JM, as he is called for short), his lover and partner David Jackson (DJ), and the spirit world they access via a Ouija board. Through this novel device, JM and DJ manage to converse with their dearly departed, as over a kind of interworld telephone, and through its ghostly speakers they are gradually told the history of the universe (that history consists of God Biology, of the three Edens he created, and of creatures who long ago fell from grace into the rigid hierarchy of an atomically threatened earth and now labor in the manufacture of souls—the cosmology, like the verse, is nothing if not baroque). If the poem can be said to have something approximating a plot, it goes like this: in the first book, "The Book of Ephraim," which spans over twenty years of life with DJ and details the domestic minutiae of their partnership, Merrill offers a meditation on long-term attachment and its many emotional perturbations. Here, Merrill presents the beneficent Ephraim as a kind of mentor, who teaches "the boys" (as he affectionately calls them) how to love one another without "FEAR OF LOSING TOO MUCH" (15). In particular, "The Book of Ephraim" teaches the reticent JM to renounce his conception of gay love as an affair of "pure mind," encourages him to reinhabit the earthly, and, "Through superhuman counterpoint to work / The body's resurrection sense by sense" (76). Such are the otherworldly, homespun lessons of a book that, as a document concerned essentially with the literarily unpromising topic of monogamy and its travails, has few works in this century to rival it, either in formal grace or emotional acuity.

Then, very strangely, with the opening of the very next book, more sinister voices take over and dominate the poem for the next four hundred or so pages. These are the voices of the fallen angels, warning of the threats to the earth's very existence, and their message is this: the world is overpopulated with "lesser soul-densities," who respond too quickly to nature's implanted urge to "MATE PROPAGATE / & DIE" (229), and who do not know the scope of the dangerous, world-threatening power they wield. Rather inexplicably, the domestic meditations of "The Book of Ephraim" modulate into this novel-length exposition on the necessity to Earth's survival of the annihilation, or "thinning," of all but two million "elite souls" (the poem calculates the death toll at roughly 3.5 billion). Gay men, it turns out, occupy a unique position of privilege in the aristocratic celestial hierarchy precisely because they facilitate, by virtue of being nonreproductive, that necessary "thinning," that somewhat limited apocalypse. In the latter half of the poem, the biological nongenerativity of male homosexuality reads as the proof that same-sex desire is in fact an abstract love of "pure mind," beyond the instinctual drives of brute nature, forestalling population growth and so participating in the heroic rescue of the Earth from its dullwitted inhabitants. But all is not so well, despite the quasi-divine status thus conferred by the snobbish spirits on gay men everywhere, and on JM and DJ in particular. For as a result of its proximity to and its alignment with the very violent means through which the angels propose to enact their "minor" apocalypse—war, famine, mass suicide—male homosexuality itself becomes invested with an intrinsic, and often inward aimed violence. Despite Merrill's insistence that homosexuality is "beyond" the brute instinctual drives so rampant in the commoner, the poem insinuates what we might call, in today's parlance, a gay death drive.[12]

What is so disturbing about the latter half of the poem is not so much the manner in which it unravels the most wrought conclusions from "The Book of Ephraim" about love, loss, and homosexuality, only so that homosexuality itself might be secured as a signifier of status and celestial privilege. More disquieting still, in a poem completed at the advent of the AIDS epidemic, is the turn to a narrative of innate gay morbidity. Merrill's remapping of same-sex biological nongeneration (the "childlessness" of same-sex couples) onto a field of cultural and historical legitimation anticipates uncannily the mobilization of religious, pseudoscientific, psychoanalytic, and biological narratives in and around the figure of the gay man in response to AIDS. As Paul Morrison writes, "The AIDS epidemic has resolved, rather than occasioned, a crisis in signification"; that resolve "has been to stabilize, through a specifically narrative or novelistic logic, the truth of gay identity as death or death wish."[13] If the occult hermeneutics of the second half of Merrill's poem tell us nothing else, they do make stunningly clear how easily, and with what little tropological difficulty, the transitions from one figuration of apocalypse (the nuclear) to another (relating to AIDS) might be made, and how useful the figure of the gay man might be in the execution of such transitions.[14]

There is of course nothing particularly new about the writing of same-sex desire as intrinsically moribund, or as symptomatic of a world-threatening moral malady. Indeed, so familiar are these narratives that we might generously say that the novelty of Merrill's poem lies in its rewriting of homosexual moribundity *not* as an agent of the decivilizing force that threatens to eradicate humanity in some Gomorrah-esque malaise, but as the *antidote* to that force. The history against which we could imagine Merrill writing would be a history of the conceptual circuitry that links sexual acts to degrees of moral and physical health, and finally to the well-being of society and the state.[15] This system of linkages makes up what Eve Kosofsky Sedgwick has elegantly described as "the inveterate topos of associating gay acts or persons with fatalities vastly broader than their own extent."[16] Though such a circuitry may, as Sedgwick suggests, be as old as the hills, I would insist that something quite remarkable happens to it in the 1980s, something at which Merrill's poem very hauntingly glimpses: suddenly, the time-worn narrative of gay morbidity is called upon not merely to dismiss a medical epidemic as an inevitable moral punishment, *but to ratify a culturally potent figure of dangerously excessive state power.* As in Merrill's inexhaustibly strange poem, the gay man and the nuclear warhead begin to be made weirdly coordinate.

But before we allow this thumbnail historical sketch completely to evaporate the specificity of those apocalyptic anxieties at work in *The Changing Light,* we need to ask: what *is* the context in which Merrill's poem is written? In what, precisely, does the nuclear context consist? We might begin by noting the veritable avalanche of pertinent sources—the great proliferation of nuclear discourse—that the election of Reagan itself precipitates. Aside from Jonathan Schell's enduring and much publicized *The Fate of the Earth,* there occur during Reagan's tenure literally countless government speeches, sociological profiles, military analyses, and macabre medical ruminations (with wonderfully improbable titles like "Long-Term Consequences of Prospects for Recovery from Nuclear War" and "Atmospheric Perturbations of Large-Scale Nuclear War"[17]). What this great explosion of nuclear *discourse* may attest to—in an era of both intensified militarist speculation *and* nuclear freeze—is what we might call, following Frances Ferguson, the "becoming sublime" of nuclear weapons.[18] That is, by the mid-eighties the nuclear seems to be more a matter of the proliferation of discussion, of rhetoric and exegesis, than of arms or bomb shelters. And this makes a certain sense: for part of what seems to drive even the most humane of these discussions (Schell's among them) is a certain ghastly *thrill* in imagining scenes of mass death. Even in the most sober disquisitions—like Jack C. Greene's frighteningly earnest "Recovery from Nuclear Attack"[19]—one recognizes the not intangible pleasure taken in enumerating in unhesitatingly grisly detail the various horrors of nuclear winter, which simply by describing and quantifying one seems, thrillingly, to have survived. An eerie sort of triumphalism winds through these many documents, the pleasure of which increases proportionally as the horizon of nuclear possibility recedes, inch by inch. The matter is not, as pronuclear advocates insisted, that in repeated visions of mass death the cowed population solaces itself with the thought that something so absolutely horrible is surely beyond the capabilities of any rational state; on the contrary, at least part of the appeal of these fantasies resides in their capacity to enact exactly that destruction, again and again, which one then has the peculiar pleasure of calculating, mapping, surviving. Nuclear weapons are indeed made sublime by nuclear discourse, where that sublimity is understood to include an ability to thrill and to please deeply with the prospect of a potentially self-eradicating devastation.

One of the most fascinating examples of, and commentaries upon, this discursive sublimity of the nuclear is an issue of *Diacritics* entitled "Nuclear Criticism," in which selected essays from a conference of the same title, held at Cornell University in 1984, are gathered and prefaced with the colloquium's call for papers. What the various authors more or less uniformly propose is an institutional response to a power they all conceive to be ever present, though never fully visible, whose force has already determined the parameters of what might be said. "Nuclear criticism," the conference proposal tells us, is "a new topic and an explication of what is already everywhere being done." Such criticism must respond to "(t)he power of horror, which the nuclear horizon proposes," a power that "has its own abject influence on the quality of our lives and on the cultural climate we engender, and may determine in ways we do not yet understand our capacity to act, even to will."[20] For critical thinkers in the American academy in 1984, then, nuclear weapons—those streamlined, siloed, inert tubes of machinery—realized materially a kind of power not at all unlike that which a writer such as Foucault had theorized: a power that is everywhere, immanent in all relations yet bound up in an intricate network of (super)power negotiations; a power that impresses itself into the will and the inclinations of its subjects, that is incorporated and so actively produced by and through the bodies it regulates. But if the embodiment of such a form of power in the nuclear warhead is clearly a figure of some critical convenience, it is also, just as clearly, an incoherent one. For one of the essential points Foucault makes about power is that it is fundamentally *relational*; for Foucault, "power" denotes the relations of force that are immanent between two or more entities, and as such cannot be properly embodied or materially "realized" (though his discussion of "the atomic situation" makes these claims suggestively problematic).[21] We might say, then, that among the most important characteristics of a specifically nuclear regime of power is this structure of critical misrecognition. The spectacle of nuclear weaponry appears to sponsor a notable misrecognition of the plurality of immanent forces that constitute a field of power. Remarkably, though, it is a misrecognition that pins the blame for the dangerous excess of power *securely on the state*. The agencies of a nuclear state are visibly possessed, in other words, of the authority to subject to horrifying death entire populations, and to do so as if on their own behalf. Only the state possesses such a power, and so only the state can be assailed for the risk to which its citizens are constantly subject. More remarkable still, this political and epistemological climate, abstracted perhaps in its theoretical articulations, is virtually transparent to anyone who, in 1984, cares to look around; thus Derrida can write, *"As no doubt we all know, no single instant, no atom of our life (of our relation to the world and to being) is not marked today, directly or indirectly, by that speed race."* [22] Nuclear weapons, in these formulations, both define and, in a jargon-free language, make readily apparent for all the world to read—both signify and stand in for—the capacity of modern agencies of power to monitor, sustain, and fully articulate our being-in-the-world.

We should not be surprised, then, that the nuclear—and the nuclear sublime—occasions a wonderfully vivid parade of fantasies, the tenor of which never strays too far afield of the manifestly sexual. Martin Amis, the British novelist who wrote quite fixedly about the threat of nuclear holocaust throughout the eighties, seems to recognize with all the paranoid subtlety of Foucault's *Discipline and Punish* the nearly boundless powers of surveillance activated by a standing nuclear arsenal. "The nuclear arsenal," he writes in 1987, "is not nowhere—it is everywhere. Every minute, in thousands of locations, in the oceans, in the heavens, there are reports, readings, dispatches, exercises, posturings, provocations. The Defense Mapping Agency has 'digitised' one third of the earth's 39 million square miles." [23] With Amis, however, this state of celestial surveillance gets a specifically psychological or, more accurately, psychosexual turn. Describing the effects of nuclear weapons on "everybody," Amis contends that "the process, the seepage, is perhaps preconceptual, physiological, glandular. *The man with the cocked gun in his mouth may boast that he never thinks about the cocked gun. But he tastes it, all the time."* [24] Now, one need not be a Freud or Lacan to unpack the sexual dynamics of this lurid and arresting figure. The effect Amis strives for here is clearly one of fascinated revulsion, and it is a revulsion at an intimate and sexualized abasement before power: at forced incorporation, at violating penetration. In Amis's nuclear age, the cocked gun of power—the penile warheads, slumbering ever erect in their silos: power's cock—demands that the virtuous citizen take it in the mouth, and forever anticipate, by taste, the obliterating ejaculate to come. (And not just any citizen: we have before us in this case an ostentatiously heterosexual male citizen, who can go scarcely a page without hauling out once more his imperiled wife and children.) For Amis, power in the nuclear age is thus already a thoroughly sexualized phenomenon, and sexualized in such a way as to unseat perpetually any solacing straight-male fantasy of boundedness and impermeability.[25] In a smoother, if less vivid version, Amis might have written: *power in the nuclear age is horrifying and unlivable because it makes me—or wants to make me—thoroughly, irremediably queer.*[26]

Such power—state power as sedimented in and represented by nuclear weapons—seems, then, none too efficient. The menacing presence of nuclear arsenals may well foster some tactical misrecognitions: concerns about "the fate of the earth," for instance, make it notably easier for one either to dismiss out of hand, or simply to ignore, more local calamities, and for the Reagan administration these calamities most assuredly included AIDS.[27] But power in its terminal form as nuclear weaponry both disrupts certain crucial phantasmatic operations, and, worse still, makes too great a spectacle of itself. "Power," Foucault reminds us, "is tolerable only on the condition that it mask a substantial part of itself."[28] Though hidden by American imperatives in remote silos and invisible submarines, nuclear weapons were, by the mid-eighties, simply too much in evidence, and had attracted to themselves, as by gravitational pull, too much discursive commentary—so much so, in fact, that in 1984, Cornell could think to hold a colloquium entitled "Nuclear Criticism," during the course of which none other than Jacques Derrida would forecast "that soon, after this colloquium, programs and departments in universities may be created under this title (nuclear criticism), as programs or departments of 'women's studies' and 'black studies' and more recently 'peace studies' have been created."[29]

Here, a dozen years later, one snickers perhaps a bit too easily at such grand prophecy. And it is, perhaps, with too little critical attention to the crossings and transferences of meaning, fantasy, and power that one concludes, in a word, *no:* nuclear criticism never leapt, fully born, from the womb of a Cornell colloquium and out into greater academia. What came in its place, and what now bends the very shelves where volumes of nuclear criticism were to have rested, is an altogether different critical genre, called gay, lesbian, and bisexual studies. From nuclear criticism to queer theory—a more unlikely substitution seems difficult to imagine. I would suggest, though, that a powerful sort of continuity inheres in the two critical paradigms. What provides the form for that continuity is a pervasive apocalypticism, in whose changing contours we might best begin to read the decisive shifts that occur between "the nuclear age" and "the age of AIDS." In some respects, the transformations are painfully obvious: where once had been the apocalyptic proclamations of an armed and unflinchingly anticommunist nuclear state, we observe the discursive formulations of the AIDS epidemic. We observed in 1987, calls for mandatory testing, as well as some for quarantines and branding of the infected.[30] ("AIDS," Thomas Yingling writes, "has provided a site for surveillance of the most private bodily practices."[31]) We observe a regime of public health education intent on teaching the population (particularly the youth population) how to make use not of their cellars or their school desks "in the event of a nuclear emergency," but of their sex, in a manner publicly ordained as "safe"—this under the rubric of the oddly stammering Helms Amendment (1987), which forbids federal funding to any organizations "that promote or encourage, directly or indirectly, homosexual sexual acts."[32] We observe the full-scale and unilateral vilification of homosexuality in the phantasmatics of life, death, and power, such that it is no longer the nuclear phallus in the mouth of the innocent American subject, threatening to destroy family, home, and happiness, but the diseased and death-delivering, endlessly copulating cock of the gay man, the "[p]romiscuous" and "suicidal" gay man, "practicing [his] vehement sexual customs."[33] Finally, if we understand "apocalypse" in its classical sense, meaning an unveiling or revelation of final truth, we observe in the remapping of same-sex couples' biological childlessness onto ontological categories (like "generative" and its counterpart "moribund") the constant revelation of a final "truth" whose use value, in the postnuclear age of AIDS, cannot be underestimated: the truth of the preordained doom of homosexuality and homosexuals. To quote Paul Morrison again, "The AIDS epidemic has resolved, rather than occasioned a crisis in signification," and that resolve "has been to stabilize . . . the truth of gay identity as death or death wish."

I think we can begin to see here how a violently fantasized homosexuality has served not only to suture an already sexualized discourse of nuclear apocalypse to a discourse of AIDS-related apocalypse, and to make the transition between them all but seamless; it has also provided one site for the consolidation of a power all the more efficient at the level of the individual because it is all the more intimate. We can without much difficulty see how public discourses about AIDS authorize a more comprehensive grasp on individual life than the threat of a wholesale annihilation from the heavens: installed by an invidiously self-assured "popular belief" as a menace whose lethal origins are to be found in no enzyme or antibody, but can be traced most reliably to an improperly functioning desire, AIDS demands of every citizen a body fully available, down into its most subterranean stirrings, to the searching scrutiny of civic hygiene. No one subject to an institutionalized sexual "education" in the 1980s could fail to have noticed the confidence and authority with which intimate matters still quite hazy and vague to oneself (if fully arresting to the attention) were taken, as it were, in hand, and duly organized around that enduring narrative polarity, "Safe/Unsafe."

What's more, in the translation of discourses of apocalypse from the nuclear to the sexual, there has ensued a fairly massive reorientation of the elements that define and delimit state power. By thus fashioning as the locus of apocalyptic threat a desiring gay body to whom its only relation is one of unhesitating disregard, the postnuclear state manages, in the first place, to disarticulate entirely its agency within, much less culpability for, scenes of mass death. The oft envisioned human carnage of nuclear winter had about it, as we have seen, a certain thrill of survival, even if that thrill was made everywhere uneasy by the state's unforesworn capacity to produce such a world, surely without one's consent, but nevertheless on one's own behalf. The AIDS epidemic quite palpably returns to the fabled "general population" a duplicate thrill of survival; one need only think of the weekly expositions on the evening news about "the ravages of AIDS," which often seem to me fueled by no more humanitarian motive than the desire to make widely available, under the guise of a sickeningly morbid sentimentality, this frightening pleasure in surviving the deaths of a great many others. But the disseminated pleasure of surviving AIDS may lie less in simply surviving than in the flattering proposition that one is, *definitionally*, one of those who survives. For by its presumed adherence to those much renowned high-risk *groups*, the human destructiveness of AIDS can and has been made deliberately, absolutely separate from the state, its policies, or indeed from any structure of causality located exterior to the downright ontological pull ascribed to certain stigmatized identities.[34] ("Risk" continues to be popularly understood in terms of individual and group identity, not acts: that there is nothing at all unsafe about unprotected anal sex between two HIV-negative men remains, for many, a lot less elementary than you might think.) The epidemic thus presents to the American public a threatened civic apocalypse whose undeniable menace tacitly sanctions the mobilization of any number of state forces. But unlike any previous apocalyptic menace, this one can be understood, with only a very little cognitive leverage, as an attack decisively *from without*. The lever here, of course, is homosexuality, or, more exactly, homophobia: to the degree that the postnuclear state can, without widespread disapprobation, effect the deliberate expulsion of gay sex from a general economy of American health and prosperity, it can secure by its response to AIDS an aspect no longer thuggish and potentially homicidal, but blamelessly hy-

gienic, preventative, protective, even (as some have had it) *beneficent*.
Perhaps the least grisly of the ironies at work here is that such power,
however transformed and beneficent from the purview of global nuclear aggressivity, continues to take as its proper point of application simple human survival: anyone even remotely familiar with the
sprawling networks of force and adjudication that surround the AIDS
epidemic can testify that the power of the state, and of its many appa-
ratuses, to seize as manipulable objects human life and survival has
diminished not in the slightest.

There is, however, what we might sardonically call a flip side to this
coin. For as Gilles Deleuze reminds us, "power does not take life as its
objective without revealing or giving rise to a life that resists power."[35]
And so, in the transformations enumerated above, we might discover
not simply the increased efficiency of a disciplining hold on individual
bodies that the translation from figures of nuclear to sexual apocalypse
so seamlessly effects, but also a more ironic side effect. If the deployment of some fantasized version of homosexuality as a term utterly
indispensable to a new apocalyptic dispensation is apparent there as
well, it may begin to bring into focus the corollary fact that, as the
apocalyptic threats to civic life have shifted centers, so too the "use
value" of homosexuals has increased exponentially.

We have, as a result, an intensified cultural investment in homosexuality—in its behaviors, its predilections, its psychoses—such that
homosexuality itself has acquired in public discourse an altogether
new currency. The veritable efflorescence of things queer and "queer-
positive" in the marketplace of American culture in recent years is only
one manifestation of this new and, in its way, unprecedented investment. Perhaps Eve Kosofsky Sedgwick framed it all best while re-
flecting, in her foreword to 1993's *Tendencies*, on the New York City Gay
Pride parade of 1991: "I suppose," she writes with a fully warrantable
diffidence, "this must be called the moment of Queer."[36] The magazines *Time, Newsweek,* and the *Nation,* the Hollywood film and TV industry, and a host of other more and less improbable sources seemed,
by their attentions, to concur. (I cannot help but wonder: is the film
Philadelphia a later generation's *The Day After*? Surely some more meaningful continuity inheres between them than the shared quality of
treacly techno-horror. I'll leave it for tomorrow's video theorists to decide.) Such various manifestations of public "interest" in homosexuality is of course not without some very important rewards: it has promised, in the first place, to bring into the realm of legitimate public
visibility a variety of urgent, and not at all inconsequential, claims to
queer entitlement. That these words appear between the covers of a

university press book is itself no small measure of the extent of this new credibility.

I want to consider for a moment, though, exactly how the mechanisms of popular enfranchisement actually function in postnuclear America, and what they exact in their functioning from the realm of gay life and gay possibility. It is, after all, a matter of some consequence that claims to queer entitlement tend to be heard *as legitimate* to precisely the extent that they concur with, or fail to disrupt, a manner of enforced amnesia at least as potent in its erasures as our latter-day misrecollections of the nuclear era. For instance, none would deny that the spectacle of AIDS extends to gay men, and to queer communities generally, the prospect of a safer, more easily countenanced social narrative in which to fit themselves. As Walt Odets has written: "Having any disease, AIDS included, is much more respectable than being homosexual; and many who do not 'condone' homosexuality but are not profoundly homophobic have been able to separate AIDS from homosexuality."[37] In a culture that seems often to adjudicate claims for popular political legitimacy on no other basis than their suitability for various kinds of sentimental narration, this is perhaps unsurprising. Whatever the stigma it carries, AIDS remains a more than serviceable vehicle for narratives whose principal elements are morbid sentimentality, the extraction of atonement, and, most crucially, the regretful but always inevitable exercise of *punishment*. There are, it appears, few personages more embraceable in American popular culture than the gay man who renounces utterly his sexual "misconduct" and, his hour upon him, unprotestingly accepts his death as the form of punishment proper to his sins.[38] *Philadelphia*, though certainly vivid and uniquely celebrated, is hardly singular in bestowing upon gay men a modicum of social legitimacy whose underside is this desexing, blithely punitive quality of affection.

Distressingly, the injunction to gay men to *forget their sex* is certainly not the only, and probably not even the worst, bit of enforced ignorance these familiar social narratives of AIDS have to offer. For in the renunciations they so casually demand, in the tepid "moral" victories they offer in the face of vaster and vaster human catastrophe, such narratives call upon us day after day to forget, deny, or simply pretend away the gruesome fact that, in some not strictly figurative sense, *the apocalypse has happened*. The fantasized wreckage of the nuclear age—the destruction beyond one's capacity fully to conceive—has in point of fact been realized in the disappearance of what often seems like an impossibly monumental number of men and women. We are talking, after all, about an enormity of loss in whose stark light once meaningful words like *devastation* and *grief* stare inertly back at us, as though uncomprehending, broken. And there is a cruelty particularly keen in the assertion, bandied about quite freely in certain circles, that from the purview of mass culture, AIDS has really been something of a boon to the gay community. The telling elision here, of course, is of a gay community irredeemably gutted by untimely death. That gay life will never be the same, that AIDS has with terrible efficiency effected a crippling reduction in the realm of gay possibility, that this lost promise might itself demand a process of mourning, of grieving, just as intense as our grieving over the too great number of men and women taken from us already—all of this is unequivocally denied by the mechanisms of popular enfranchisement, and denied with a wantonness only more brutal for its banalizing platitudes. The simultaneously hygienic and sentimental strictures of the new gay enfranchisement demand, in other words, not only a tacit renunciation of gay sex (if you *must* do it, they seem to say, at least have the decency not to tell); it seems we must admit as well that the truncated possibilities of gay life are simply not worth grieving, and that, in essence, *nothing has been lost*. The sentimental narrative in which the gay man finds himself today would, like all sentimental narratives, educate him. But what is to be educated away are any remaining shards of affection for or identification with expressions of gay life. In the perhaps (though perhaps not) unconscious utopia of these narratives, the gay man and all his "kind" will be educated soundly and conclusively out of existence.

Leo Bersani thus seems to me exactly right when he observes, "The heightened visibility conferred on gay men by AIDS is the visibility of imminent death, of a promised invisibility."[39] Surely, the quality of imminent invisibility extracted from gay men in response to AIDS continues to pressure gay lives in ways we are only now beginning to recognize and adumbrate.[40] It remains worth noting, however, that the promise of invisibility, which may indeed stand behind *any* substantial public investment in homosexuality, carries with it a number of not so easily managed effects. For all the killing efficiency of its hygienic narratives, the intensified public investment in homosexuality is not, in other words, without its volatility. It has, as I have already suggested, given rise to an entire order of discourse—a fully functioning cultural analytics—whose intents, though hugely varying, might be said to converge in the attempt to think through the panics and paradoxes of homophobia, as they are traced across vectors of gender, race, region, serostatus, or general affiliation. Outside of such an upsurge of national interest in gay life, is it even conceivable that an entity called queer studies could emerge and flourish, and do so within a variety of institutions that only recently would have seemed unlikely sanctuaries at best?

Queer studies, to put it more plainly, is perhaps most profitably understood as one of the more unruly stepchildren of this peculiar, and at moments savage, postnuclear investment in homosexuality. Saying this, I do not for the life of me mean to dispute any of the numerous genealogies of queer studies offered in recent years, nor would I diminish in any respect the positively Herculean efforts by many scholars and activists to forge a new and vital field in environments often belittling, disapproving, and downright hostile.[41] But I do think that by understanding the national derivation of some our discipline's newly won institutional force we might better equip ourselves, analytically, to guard against a potentially dangerous kind of complacency in our work. My concern is that in the context of the revised apocalypticism we have been observing, the practice of queer theory is itself perhaps a bit more vexed than we commonly admit. I worry, to be more precise, about the odd *appropriability* of an emergent critical discourse on homosexuality, insofar as the civic economy into which it emerges has displayed as one of the essential elements in its functioning an ability to fit any form of knowledge about homosexuality into a pattern of narratives designed especially to chasten, if not altogether eradicate, homosexuals. Undoubtedly, queer work provides an indispensable kind of leverage against such narratives, and provides as well a desperately needed site for queer identifications, and for the validation of aspirations that might otherwise seem patently unwelcome in the world; resistance is quite clearly far from futile, and one would be cynical indeed to deny that thoughtful and discriminating intellectual work is an always potent tool in political endeavors. But it seems to me equally evident that the utility of our words, and of the institutions we build, within causes decidedly not our own must everywhere be recognized.[42] If, in other words, we suddenly find ourselves invited to discuss, to debate, to testify, and to think intently about queer existence and queer possibility, it is surely worth recalling the new centrality of homosexuality in an apocalyptic dispensation in which queer desires, pursuits, and persons are located, precisely, *as targets.*

We need little reminder, after all, that the targeting of gay persons for purposes explicitly national and, indeed, *defensive* remains a quite visible civic imperative. If one cares to see the bizarrely militarist origins of our present-day sexual apocalypticism on full and unguarded display, one need look no further than the much ballyhooed Defense of Marriage Act. Signed late in the evening by our unimpressively diffident president, this document must stand among the most weirdly

self-negating initiatives ever passed into law. One scarcely knows
which word to lean upon incredulously: *Defense?* Defense of *Marriage?*
Apparently, the champions of normative heterosexuality have become
so confident in its presumably natural inevitability that they would
enshrine it in law, even though the necessity of legislating the normativity of heterosexuality speaks as plainly as any queer "kiss-in" of its
anxious susceptibility to contention, displacement, aggression, or (perhaps most frightful) unconcern. The imperious propositions of the act
are in this way unraveled even as they proceed, which is again perhaps
not surprising: no one ever credited homophobia, at the national level,
with an elegance of thought. But whatever its internal incoherence, the
act *was* signed, and now actively circumscribes the lives and aspirations of gay people in America, spelling out in its passage the continued political efficacy of homophobia and, perhaps more crucially, the
utterly provisional status, in these late days, of any achievement in gay
rights. And there had been achievement: we could look, for example,
to the adoption debates, where (in the unironic words of the *ABA
Journal*) cases "go both ways."[43] The publicity given throughout 1993
to the Sharon Bottoms case (in which a lesbian lost custody of her
child because of her sexual orientation) might be read as an emblem
of the vexingly unmoored status of homosexuality—and in this case
specifically lesbianism—within the framework of a popular American
"moral code," since as recently as 1989 the cases publicized were those
in which lesbians *were* granted child custody. What seems to be at
stake, though, in the micromanaged call and response of queer initiative and state legislation, is not merely the status of lesbians within an
American moral framework, but the framework itself. "I think something important is happening in this country," a family law expert is
quoted as saying back in 1993. "Little by little the definition of family
is undergoing a change."[44] Four years down the road, one can't but
wonder if the transformations he had in mind were those of pluraliza-
tion, or a repelling exclusivity.

   "All human relations have shifted," wrote Virginia Woolf, "and
when human relations change there is at the same time a change in
religion, conduct, politics, and literature." I propose to you then that
we are in the midst of just such a historical change—here in America,
with the new millennium beginning—and that a few of the key terms
in this change have been, and are, and may or may not continue to be,
apocalypse, AIDS, and *homosexuality.* It is clear at least that our responses to the popular narratives of AIDS must in every imaginable
fashion contest their casual disregard for gay life, and must continue
to give testament to the too often ignored fact that something utterly

cherishable—indeed, a great deal—has been lost. But I would suggest by way of conclusion that what is required of us additionally by this frenetic and terminally unstable epoch, this postnuclear age, are critical languages attuned to the discontinuities of meaning over time, and to the local and radically contingent quality of every act and its interpretation. What we need, then, especially out there on those queer frontiers, is a critical sensibility intent on scrutinizing the conditions of its own production, rather than on recognizing—in every discursive song, in every historical dance—the confirmation of its own assumptions.

Notes

This chapter has benefited from more conversations, squabbles, and unpremeditated rants than I would dare enumerate here. Thanks go to the most faithful interlocutors: Bonnie Blackwell, Dana Luciano, Scott MacKenzie, and my heaven-sent editors, Rosemary Weatherston and Martin Meeker. My gratitude extends as well to the remarkably generous and forthcoming audiences at Cornell, at USC, and at Tufts, where different versions of this chapter were nervously debuted.

1. Virginia Woolf, "Mr. Bennett and Mrs. Brown," in *Collected Essays*, ed. Leonard Woolf (London: the Hogarth Press, 1966), 1: 320–21; emphasis added.

2. Mikhail Gorbachev, public address, Moscow, 28 February 1987; reprinted in *Vital Speeches of the Day* 53, no. 13 (15 April 1987): 386.

3. Martin Amis, *Einstein's Monsters* (New York: Vintage Books, 1987), 7.

4. Nations luckless enough to be neither European nor North American must, as a matter of American diplomatic course, be presumed "unstable"— and the deployment of unhesitatingly racist characterological presumptions as easefully connotative (if never tastelessly denotative) of political pathologies has not been difficult to observe. What may be most unnervingly displayed, then, in those uniformly blustering and nationalistic responses to nuclear "threats" from nations as diverse as North Korea, Iran, and Libya, is the alarmingly protean quality—the international portability—of American racism.

5. Might it be time, in other words, to insinuate a difference where, for a great many earlier critics, none had seemed to exist? It's well worth remembering, I think, that nuclear weapons have functioned—in the work of such critics as Derrida, Foucault, José Ortega y Gasset, and Jean-François Lyotard—as both signs for and material embodiments of what has been called the postmodern. One concern that underwrites this chapter, then, is the following: how might the postmodern be reinterpreted, here in the postnuclear? Public narratives concerning AIDS and homosexuality, it seems to me, are essential in this translation of discourses pertaining to power and knowledge, sex and the individual, disease and the state.

6. Jacques Derrida, "No Apocalypse, Not Now (Full Speed Ahead, Seven

Missiles, Seven Missives)," *Diacritics* 14, no. 2 (summer 1984): 28. The fully inclusive quality of nuclear apocalypse suggested here might well make us think of the concluding sentence to Thomas Pynchon's exuberantly apocalyptic novel *Gravity's Rainbow* (New York: Bantam Books, 1973): "Now everybody!"

7. Susan Sontag, *AIDS and Its Metaphors* (New York: Farrar, Straus and Giroux, 1989), 88.

8. Michel Foucault, *The History of Sexuality,* vol. 1, *An Introduction,* trans. Robert Hurley (New York: Vintage Books, 1980), 137.

9. This essay focuses mainly, if not exclusively, on gay men, despite the clear fact that AIDS is absolutely not, epidemiologically, a distinctively gay and/or male disease. The terrible rise in the incidents of AIDS among differently situated constituencies—especially among women of color—has made the fact of—dare we say—the *plurality* of AIDS more than evident. But in many instances this latter fact has been cynically joined with the already established energies of homophobia surrounding the epidemic, for the purpose of turning the screw once more upon gay men: in nauseating screeds like Michael Fumiento's *The Myth of Heterosexual AIDS* (New York: Basic Books, 1990), and also increasingly in the parlance of "common sense" that seems so elusively to govern the climate of American public discourse generally, the downright assaultive force of homophobic scapegoating inspired by AIDS is attributed not to a homophobic culture, but, amazingly, to AIDS activists themselves, who are then straight-facedly accused of insisting *(insisting!)* upon a somehow distinctive relation of homosexuality to AIDS—to the deliberate exclusion of the minority communities that are also truly suffering the ravages of the disease at present. The elisions in such formulations as Fumiento's are too numerous even to begin to describe (the most damaging, perhaps, being the conceptual elision of any person who is both nonwhite *and* not straight), but they do make clear that a certain analytic vigilance is required of us. Insofar as the deliberate confusion of violently homophobic targeting with something like gay self-promotion continues to govern "common sense" accounts of AIDS and its links to homosexuality, a cultural critic would do well to attend as closely as possible to the particular uses made of gay men in response to AIDS, even as the gay-specificity of the disease is gradually (and never definitively) diffused.

10. For more on sex, gender, and the nuclear, see Elaine Tyler May's *Homeward Bound: American Families in the Cold War Era* (New York: Basic Books, 1988), especially chapter 4, "Explosive Issues: Sex, Women, and the Bomb."

11. James Merrill, *The Changing Light at Sandover* (New York: Knopf, 1993), 4; hereafter, page numbers for this work will be cited parenthetically.

12. See, for a most vivid example, pages 303–4, in which Merrill and W. H. Auden, who appears as a character in the poem, adumbrate the desire to "die of complications / invited by the way we live," in which Auden, who claims he died of lead poisoning after he "SUCKED ON A PENCIL THINKING," wonders "ARE PENCIL & KNIFE / & COCK ALL ONE," thereby suggesting (with, of course, the greatest of tact) that sucking pencils, having one's guts penetrated by a knife, or either sucking or being penetrated by a cock all come to the same inevitable end: death. For more on Merrill and the trope of gay death drive,

see Jeff Nunokawa, "'All the Sad Young Men': AIDS and the Work of Mourning," in *Inside/Out*, ed. Diana Fuss (New York: Routledge, 1991), 311–12.

13. Paul Morrison, "End Pleasure," *GLQ* 1 (1993): 54.

14. Here is Lee Edelman on the gendering of homosexuality, and on the privileging of male homosexuality in the national imaginary: "The erotic economy of homosexual relations continues to be traced for our culture in the enduring equation of homosexuality with *male* homosexuality, of male homosexuality with sodomy, and of sodomy with anal intercourse, and, in particular, with the so-called 'passive' or receptive position in anal intercourse—an equation that the eighties reinforced through the telling cliché of anal penetration as the 'most efficient' mode of HIV transmission and the attendant identification of HIV infection with the condition of gay men as such." See his *Homographesis* (New York: Routledge, 1994), 133–34; emphasis in the original.

15. One way to specify this history would involve a history of medicine. Foucault, for example, notes in *The Birth of the Clinic* that at the turn of the nineteenth century medical knowledge began to constitute itself in a distinct but completely homologous relation to social space. That is, as medical knowledge began to orient itself less toward the curing of particular ills and more toward the comprehension of an ideal, "non-sick," essentially normative healthy being, it assumed for itself a domain perfectly reciprocal to the domain of statecraft: "In the ordering of human existence," Foucault writes of late-eighteenth-century medical knowledge, "it assumes a normative posture, which authorizes it not only to distribute advice as to healthy life, but also to dictate the standards for physical and moral relations of the individual and of the society in which he lives." Medicine exists "in that borderline, but for modern man paramount, area where a certain organic, unruffled, sensory happiness communicates by right with the order of a nation, the vigor of its armies, the fertility of its people, and the patient advance of its labors." Disease can thus articulate the state; and the fact that their domains are so homologous—the fact that both take as their field of application the normative, healthy citizen—sponsors a completely promiscuous crossing, in which each is allowed to indicate the other. The abnormally behaving body in this way becomes an effective analogue for the poorly functioning state, for the state whose citizenry would be, en masse, at risk. By the mid-nineteenth century, a new medical discourse intent as well on fashioning the normal healthy citizen is being born, and sometime between 1860 and 1890 it specifies one very particular form of abnormality by locating an abnormal *type* of person. Psychology invents the homosexual person, and ascribes to this person a series of pathologies which, in turn, stand in for the ills of the state, and of civilization generally. See Michel Foucault, *The Birth of the Clinic: An Archaeology of Medical Perception*, trans. A. M. Sheridan-Smith (New York: Vintage, 1973), 35.

16. Eve Kosofsky Sedgwick, *The Epistemology of the Closet* (Los Angeles: University of California Press, 1990), 128.

17. These titles are from Frederic Solomon and Robert Q. Marston, eds., *The Medical Implications of Nuclear War* (Washington, D.C.: National Academy Press, 1986). This book contains very sober and studied chapters on these and

other equally alarming or improbable topics. See also Jonathan Schell, *The Fate of the Earth* (New York: Avon Books, 1982).

18. See Frances Ferguson, "The Nuclear Sublime," *Diacritics* 14, no. 2 (summer 1984): 4–10.

19. See Jack C. Greene, "Recovery from Nuclear Attack," in *The Apocalyptic Premise: Nuclear Arms Debated*, ed. Ernest W. Lefever and E. Stephen Hunt (Washington, D.C.: Ethics and Public Policy Center, 1982), 255–70.

20. Preface to *Diacritics* 14, no. 2 (summer 1984): 2.

21. One of the concerns of this chapter is to articulate an internal tension in Foucault's work that has not garnered much thoughtful attention. That tension is located precisely in the much debated concept of power, and its irreducibility to, say, the state. Foucault is very clear on this point in the "Method" chapter of his *The History of Sexuality*, in which he insists that law, or simple, politically sedimented power not be mistaken for the complex relations of force that he means to denote with the term *power*. And yet his notion of a power that "administers life" strikes me as a formulation to which the context of its articulation quite remarkably adheres; that is, it seems in no small part a product of what he calls "the atomic situation," in which "at stake is the biological existence of a population." The power to take life—to take survival, its extension or its termination—as a manipulable object can after all be traced securely back to agencies of the state with perhaps the least threat of reductiveness or imprecision. I have for this reason persisted in referring nuclear and AIDS-related discourses back to an entity I have called, for shorthand, "the state," whose policies, medical and military, seem to me the most salient forces of circumscription in these fields. But I want also to say that this fact does not make Foucault flatly wrong about power and its irreducible modality (as a fair number of his detractors have claimed) nor does it justify the even more distressing tendency of work that takes Foucault as a model to insist upon the comprehensive instrumentalization of persons by some abstracted force like "culture"—to insist, that is, on their top-to-bottom "construction." What a close look at the economies of power instituted around nuclear weapons and around AIDS *does* make clear, I think, is the fact that there are in Foucault's work certain basic, and potentially useful internal tensions. Historicist followers of Foucault have seemed to me a bit too monolithic in their advocacy, and have as a result been incapable of exploring Foucault's texts with the discrimination, subtlety, and attention to detail that have characterized some of the best rereadings of the psychoanalytic canon. That a "power over life" refers back more directly to a state power that Foucault tells us, almost in the same breath, we must not imagine to be power's proper locus, may show us simply that Foucault's texts, by their very incoherences, are as available to insightful and productive *interpretation* as any of Freud's case studies or Lacan's disquisitions. For more on Foucault and his uses in the realm of queer studies generally, see David M. Halperin, *Saint Foucault: Towards a Gay Hagiography* (New York: Oxford University Press, 1995).

22. Derrida, "No Apocalypse," 20; emphasis added.

23. Martin Amis, *Visiting Mrs. Nabokov and Other Excursions* (New York: Harmony Books, 1994), 17.

24. Amis, *Einstein's Monsters*, 7; emphasis added. Amis likes this formulation so much that it appears again in the later collection of essays *Visiting Mrs. Nabokov and Other Excursions:* "The fact that the planet has a cocked gun in its mouth will inevitably be absorbed in some way—psychologically, physiologically" (199).

25. For thorough treatment of masculine fantasies of self-enclosure, and of the use of the gay man in those fantasies, see Leo Bersani, "Is the Rectum a Grave?" in *AIDS: Cultural Analysis, Cultural Activism*, ed. Douglas Crimp (Cambridge, Mass.: MIT Press, 1988), and D. A. Miller, "Anal *Rope*," in *Inside/Out*, ed. Fuss, 197–222.

26. Nothing indicates nuclear destructiveness for Amis as convincingly as sodomitical acts. Nicola Six, the doomed heroine of his novel *London Fields*, who by her rapacious self-destructiveness is called upon to represent the excesses and excitations of her century, is distinguished for us not only by her astounding facility with all varieties of the kiss, but also, and fundamentally, by her "surrender" to sodomy. "Sodomy pained Nicola," we are told, "but not literally": it is the act that figures for Amis a manifestly destructive creativity. A vicious parody of reproductive sex, sodomy "was just [Nicola's] strategy for sending love back the other way." See Martin Amis, *London Fields* (New York: Vintage Books, 1989), 67–69.

27. "The final indifference to AIDS during the Reagan years cannot be separated from what were national priorities of the political right—increased militarism, a renewal of Cold War hostility with the Soviet Union, a flat denial of funding for domestic issues." Thomas Yingling, "AIDS in America: Postmodern Governance, Identity, and Experience," in *Inside/Out*, ed. Fuss, 310. Similarly, Amis, writing in 1987 about London boiling in nuclear fires, fails to notice that a number of districts in London are, in point of fact, burning, as a result of IRA bombings, of protests against the Thatcher regime, and, as it would happen, of demonstrations concerning homosexual rights and AIDS. More generally we might observe that one of the primary discursive effects of something like "nuclear criticism" (that of both *Diacritics* and Amis) is the radical leveling of all markers of difference—most notably class, race, and nationality—in response to a threat constantly invoked as "universal." That is, because nuclear weapons threatened to annihilate all persons, regardless of cultural situation, talking about nuclear weapons became a way to *avoid* talking about other, rather pressing inequalities.

28. Foucault, *The History of Sexuality*, 1: 86.

29. Derrida, "No Apocalypse," 30.

30. See Douglas Crimp, "AIDS: Cultural Analysis/Cultural Activism," in *AIDS: Cultural Analysis, Cultural Activism*, ed. Crimp, 8–12.

31. Yingling, "AIDS in America," 294.

32. Quoted in Douglas Crimp, "How to Have Promiscuity in an Epidemic," in *AIDS: Cultural Analysis, Cultural Activism*, ed. Crimp, 264.

33. These quotations come from none other than Susan Sontag, *AIDS and Its Metaphors*, 26. See also Sander L. Gilman, "AIDS and Syphilis: The Iconography of Disease" and Leo Bersani, "Is the Rectum a Grave?" in *AIDS: Cultural Analysis, Cultural Activism*, ed. Crimp. The most comprehensive account of the invention of AIDS in public discourse, and of the violences enacted therein, remains Cindy Patton's *Inventing AIDS* (New York: Routledge, 1990).

34. Sedgwick writes compellingly that "It's been one of the great ideological triumphs of AIDS activism that, for a whole series of overlapping communities, any person living with AIDS is now visible, not only as someone dealing with a particular, difficult cluster of pathogens, but equally as someone who is by that very fact defined as a victim of state violence" (Eve Kosofsky Sedgwick, *Tendencies* [Durham, N.C.: Duke University Press, 1993], 261). Given the vehemence of phobic responses to the epidemic, that persons living with AIDS might be seen by anyone beyond the perimeter of their relations as victims of state violence is most certainly a commendable and consequential triumph. But the number of people to whom persons living with AIDS are visible precisely as enemies to, or at best pitiable fiscal drags upon, the healthy functioning state, seems to me still disconcertingly high—which perhaps explains the inspecificity of those "overlapping communities" Sedgwick mentions. When at last these vital communities overlap with, say, the communities capable of reorganizing the dispensation of health care on a national or even local level, or those that make, alter, or proscribe public policy, we will have a real triumph on our hands.

35. Gilles Deleuze, *Foucault*, trans. Sean Hand (Minneapolis: University of Minnesota Press, 1988), 94.

36. Sedgwick, *Tendencies*, xii.

37. Walt Odets, *In the Shadow of the Epidemic: Being HIV-Negative in the Age of AIDS* (Durham, N.C.: Duke University Press, 1995), 106.

38. Other targets of normalizing social hygiene have available to them modes of narrative recuperation that are, in the end, less manifestly lethal: the junkie can kick the habit (perhaps with the help of God and a life mate of a different gender); the single mother, short of landing that upwardly mobile corporate internship, can marry and at least no longer be single. Insofar as domestic heterosexuality is a switch point in all these narratives of legitimation, unapologizing gay men and lesbians will be foreclosed from their recuperations.

39. Leo Bersani, *Homos* (Cambridge, Mass.: Harvard University Press, 1995), 21.

40. Walt Odets's staggering book, *In the Shadow of the Epidemic*, brings frighteningly into view a desire—shared, he argues, by many gay men—not to survive. The matter is not simply that the wish for a gay eradication, made so tangible in public responses to AIDS, has itself begun to infect gay men's self-perception (though this is surely part of the problem); Odets writes also of an identification in queer communities with the ill and the dying that is so powerful, so self-consolidating, so affirming, that the very desire to remain HIV-

negative is experienced as nothing short of betrayal. How, Odets asks, does one explain to oneself *not* wanting to be like so very many men who together form the community in which one is most approved of, most desired, most cherished? If the straight world has proven in its responses to the epidemic that it little cherishes—and indeed has small difficulty in imagining as extinct—gay life, how can queer people then be expected to harbor anything other than these vehement and perhaps self-endangering identifications? What Odets's book reveals, finally, is a profound disinvestment among some gay men in the prospect of survival. That such a radical emptying out of cathectic force from the very concept of futurity recalls, quite strikingly, descriptions of a kind of fully normative despair among the American urban poor, and so suggests that a fairly startling political coalition might be at least conceivable, is only the most challenging among the many possibilities Odets's book brings to the table.

41. For one such genealogy, see the introduction to *Hidden from History: Reclaiming the Gay and Lesbian Past*, ed. Martin Duberman, Martha Vicinus, and George Chauncey, Jr. (New York: Meridian Press, 1989).

42. This is perhaps simply to replay, with respect to somewhat different coercive social mechanisms, the cautionary note struck by Sedgwick in her introduction to *The Epistemology of the Closet*, where she writes of the vexing concept "homosexual panic": "Yet I feel, as well, with increasing dismay, in the increasingly homophobic atmosphere of public discourse since 1985, that work done to accentuate and clarify the explanatory power of this difficult nexus may not be able to be reliably insulated from uses that ought to be diametrically opposed to it" (21).

43. Henry J. Reske, "Lesbian Loses Custody," *ABA Journal* 79 (December 1993): 24–25.

44. Ibid.

3

An Interview with Cherríe Moraga
Queer Reservations; or, Art, Identity, and Politics in the 1990s

Cherríe Moraga with Rosemary Weatherston

San Francisco
10 January 1997

ROSEMARY WEATHERSTON: Let's start with your ideas about the term *queer*. You've described yourself as knowing since you were eight or nine that you were queer, and you've used the term in every work of yours I've read—how has your understanding of queer changed over the years?

CHERRÍE MORAGA: Well, it's funny, when you said I'd used it in every work of mine you've read, I was thinking, "Damn—did I?" Because to me it is such a contemporary word. But in fact, that's true. In *Loving in the War Years* there's a piece, "It Is You, My Sister, Who Must Be Protected," in which I repeat the line, "It's this queer that I run from."[1] That was published in 1983, certainly before there was a so-called queer movement. In the piece I was talking about my father. My dad is a heterosexual man and he loves women, but I was talking about that place in him, as a man, that was queer in the sense of being too "soft" for a man, you know? Traditionally there are ways men are supposed to be, and my dad has never fit that image. He's a very soft, kind man, the opposite of macho. So, it's kind of his vulnerable place. There is also a negative side to that place, a kind of passivity that is not good. In that particular piece I was talking about how *that's* that queer I run from—that person in me who is passive, or who's beaten down, or who can't express herself fully. It's a sore spot. I was relating to a place in a man that is vulnerable to attack. But, in terms of naming myself, I've always called myself a lesbian, and I still do. My own use of language evolves and changes with the time, but also remains the same on a certain level.

RW: Becoming layered . . .

CM: Yes. When I was growing up, *dyke* was, of course, a derogatory term. In the early days of the lesbian and gay movement, the word was reclaimed as a statement of self-affirmation, a kind of in-your-face label of resistance. It's not my generation, but the generation after me who began to call their movement a "queer movement." Personally, I had used *queer* not just to describe how I was a lesbian, but to describe that I was different, odd. Later, when I began working with queer youth, I began to understand the term *queer* somewhat differently.

RW: In what capacity were you working with queer youth?

CM: It was a lesbian/gay/bisexual theater group for kids under twenty-one. They called themselves the DramaDIVAS.[2]

RW: For people who aren't familiar with your theater work, could you describe what you were doing with this particular group and how you got into youth theater?

CM: Well, for many years I have been a playwright-in-residence at Brava! Theater Center, a women's multicultural theater company here in San Francisco. In addition to writing essays and poetry, I've been writing theater for I guess now twelve or thirteen years. I also teach at Stanford University in the drama department. So, more and more, theater has involved a good deal of my creative energies, and is where I am directing my energies as a teacher. DramaDIVAS was born in the early 1990s through a California Arts Council Artist-in-Communities Grant. The two communities that I chose to work with were Native and Chicana women, and queer youth, because the two, in a way, represent the span of my interests.[3] I was especially committed to working with queer youth, because I really believe in the power of art to change peoples' lives. Most of these kids had gone through every kind of social service agency, halfway house, and support group available to them. Some of them were very hip, so my hunches that they needed more than counseling, they needed art, were absolutely right. The group wrote and performed their own material. That's how I usually try to teach writing and acting, hand in hand; the DIVAS performed all over the state. It really was a wonderful program. Some of these kids were living on the street and doing heavy drugs, but they'd come in and clean up because they had to do a show. For all the rhetoric about self-esteem that all these youth support groups try to promote, there is nothing like getting a kid's self-esteem together by saying, "Write your experience, we'll turn it into some art. We'll put it on stage and you get to do it." Suddenly, their lives become the stuff of art and that totally changes them.

RW: And it was through working with these kids that your understanding of *queer* changed?

CM: At the time I started with these kids, they wanted to name *themselves*, so when we first started doing brochures and publicity to get kids to come, we did the typical long-ass list: "a group for gay/lesbian/bisexual/transgendered/or questioning youth." We did this out of respect for whatever contemporary terms were being used by the kids, so kids could find a place to identify themselves and find a space to question themselves about their sexual identity. When you are talking about young people, you have to be very careful with language in order not to eliminate or to intimidate anyone. But, when I started teaching the DIVAS, they were tripped because I came in an *out* lesbian, and very few of them used that word; very few of the boys used *gay* and very few of the girls used *lesbian*. Some of them did, when they were talking really specifically about themselves as individuals, but when they were talking about themselves as a group they used *queer*. So their use of language did affect me. At the same time, though, I was always really adamant with them that I would never give up calling myself "lesbian," that I had worked long and hard to be able to claim that term and the specificity of it, and I wasn't interested in losing the specificity of being *female* and gay, and of loving women exclusively and *not* being bisexual. Lesbian to me is *that* specific.

RW: And how did they respond to your adamancy?

CM: We'd get into these big debates about it. I said, well, when you look at the history of their sex lives, at least half the lesbians I know are really bisexual. But if they are from my generation, and they are in a lesbian relationship, they are still calling themselves lesbians, so on a certain level it's a generational thing. But, on another level, I think it has more to do with the act of naming. If their commitments were really to women, feminists of my generation, regardless of whether or not they had had a history of sexual relations with men, still thought of themselves as "lesbians," as "dykes." So, I will always keep that term and always use it. But I think what happened for me is that when I began to try and articulate a sexual politics within a Latino context that included men, I had to address my understanding of sexuality which acknowledges the whole spectrum. However we actually *enact* our sexuality—lesbian, straight, heterosexual, bisexual—human beings do not conveniently fit within those strict categories of homosexual or heterosexual. How, for instance, does transgenderism fit into either of those categories? So, *queer* was a good term to incorporate all those identities and they taught me that, nineteen-year-olds taught me that. There was something persuasive about some of them saying, "I'm not a lesbian in my sex life but I know I'm queer and my allies are people who are queer." The "queer" category included not only a range of sexualities but also a position of opposition to heterosexual dominance. I thought, "Well, that's cool." And so my prejudice—which was that *queer* was a softening or neutralizing of the specificity, the power, the radicalism of calling oneself a lesbian—was challenged by their perspective. Rather than seeking integration into society, their understanding of *queer* was to draw alliances with those who considered themselves sexual outsiders on multiple levels of experience and self-conception. I thought that was good. But I still only use the word for those purposes. For alliance or coalition-building. When I speak of my own identity I am always a lesbian or "queer" in the prefeminist sense of the term: which is just not a "normal" heterosexual, a sexual outlaw. If the root of one's outsidership is sexuality, then you just know you're queer kid, you spot other queer kids—it's all before politicization. So, ironically, for me the term conjures both a kind of prequeer movement sentiment, which was depoliticized, and a politicized kind of 1990s definition. My greatest passion, however, remains with the word *lesbian*.

RW: Given the importance you place on that type of specificity, what's been your take on the rise of the queer movement(s) of the nineties? How do you view their relationship with lesbian and gay political movements?

CM: Well, queer is problematic, too. I have to frame my response within the context of people of color. Truth is, I'm not even thinking about white people in most of this discussion. I think that is another set of questions that we should talk about.

RW: Definitely.

CM: On a certain level, a young, gay man who is very effeminate (who is really a queen), or a young woman, a lesbian, who is really butch (just a little dyke), will relate to and identify with the terms *faggot* and *dyke*. They will see themselves reflected in those terms. That way of being queer is very, very different from somebody who is essentially bisexual and who can pass within a heterosexual context. Some people experience much more prejudice and oppression based on their sexuality than do others. People suffer around sexuality. So, the part to me that can be the most problematic is when terms like *queer* are used to neutralize politics, or when they don't respond to the specific needs of an oppressed people.

RW: What about those "queer, leather-jacketed, shaved-headed, white, anglocentric, radicals" you describe in your final essay in *The Last Generation*, "Queer Aztlán?"[4] In that piece you were contrasting Queer Aztlán and Queer Nation.

CM: Right. But, you see, the idea of a Queer Nation doesn't have any bearing for me. I am not in dialogue with that movement. Just because the same word is used doesn't mean there is a relationship. It's like the way I've felt about the use of the term *feminism*. People assume by using the term *feminist*, one is in direct dialogue with white feminism. In fact, I feel like my conversations have primarily been within a context of women of color for so long, even more specifically within a Latino or Chicano context, that I just claim the term *feminism* as part of my own Chicana territory. It's not a dialogue in that sense. On one level that's naive, because, of course, I'm a writer and anything one puts down is in conversation or dialogue; white people are reading my work and vice versa. But I try to self-define those terms while claiming them. The fact that the first person who uses a given term might be a white person is not really that significant to me. One of the things about *queer* that I think is dangerous is that the term includes men. There is great promise and there are great problems in that. The greatest problem is that feminism can disappear.

RW: How do you see that happening?

CM: Well, it's kind of like the lesbian and gay movement; I never really felt a part of the lesbian and gay movement, I felt a part of the lesbian *feminist* movement, but I really had no conversation with white gay men, I still don't. There is *nothing* to talk to them about. It doesn't mean that I don't have something to talk about with individual white gay men, who may be my friends. But, as a woman of color, and lesbian of color, one's idea of oppression is so informed by class and race and gender. For the most part, when you are connecting with white gay men politically, you are relating through only one shared identity (sexuality) that is on some level disenfranchised. And even that disenfranchisement may not even be experienced equally on a daily basis—for example if you live in the Castro in San Francisco and you're moneyed. If you're not moneyed, homophobia is experienced very differently. Money protects. So really, I don't automatically consider them brothers. I am not in alliance with gay white men in a movement. I am much more in alliance with straight Chicanos than I am with gay white men. Culture, class, and racial oppression can be a powerful source of connections. Still, it is not without its problems. Within the queer movement, just like any movement that is both male and female, feminism can so easily disappear. Unless a movement and the language of that movement specifically articulates all the sources of disenfranchisement within its ranks, it's guaranteed that the power base will not reside amongst its most oppressed members. It will be among the named ones. The thing about the queer movement is that those who are named are white, privileged males. It ensures that they are named because they're the ones who have only that singular identity. It doesn't ensure that women are named, it doesn't ensure that people of color are named, it doesn't ensure that working-class people are named, or poor people are named—it doesn't ensure any of those things. I have spent my time trying to define a feminism and a Chicanoism that is inclusive and that keeps me in conversation with women and Latino men, which is problematic enough as it is. *Queer* does not blind those whom I consider "us" together.

RW: Do you think queer studies or queer politics are even capable of addressing these other aspects of identity? Are there some approaches to queerness that are better equipped to address multiple identities than others?

CM: Are there ways in which to ensure, for example, that queer studies really grapples with issues of race and class and all of it? There is no way. The only queer studies conference I ever went to was one where I gave a keynote address at Rutgers University and I remember having this most shocking experience. I was standing looking at this audience and they all looked like every other Ivy League faculty group across the nation, they didn't even look *queer*—

RW: [*laughter*]

CM: They were like queer people in drag! When you are talking about university faculty you are talking about an elite group of people, so they were, by and large, still tweed-jacketed, white males who were queer. They were gay, so what? When you looked at the things that they were writing about, and the papers they were presenting, for the most part their concerns had very little to do with the rest of us. They reflected very rarified concerns. There's a way in which gay male culture is part and parcel of Western culture at large. This is no news. I'm not saying anything that's original. We all know that there is a verifiable history of homosexual male culture that is in agreement with the values of western culture at large. So to me, that is not where the pressing questions are.

RW: Where are the pressing questions, then?

CM: Well, again, for me it's always been "The more specific you are the better." So, what is pressing sometimes changes depending on the circumstances. One uses different languages in different contexts. The reason I wrote "Queer Aztlán" and used the word *queer* in that context was because it was the more radical thing to do, the more radical language to use. I wanted to look at Chicano nationalism in a way that would be inclusive. My critique of Chicano nationalism has always been the homophobia and sexism of "El Movimiento." As a lesbian and a feminist, Aztlán (the Chicano homeland, presently the U.S.

Southwest) doesn't belong to me, because Chicano nationalism, is, by definition, a masculinist concept, and as we speak, it remains homophobic. Again, it's a question of my reclaiming these terms: I'm going to take *queer* and *Aztlán* and I'm going to color *queer* brown and reconfigure *Aztlán* as queer (which includes the female queer). There is potential within the context of specific race-based movements to do the kind of intracultural feminist critiques that we need in order to become a stronger people. This requires men and women of the same culture and class background to work together. My challenge in "Queer Aztlán" had very little to do with white people. My challenge was really to my brothers, straight and queer. I've said this many times, the men of my generation (including the queer ones) have done virtually nothing, *nothing* to make space for younger gay men of color. They were too invested in propping up their manhood. It was lesbians who made that space, and you can ask any young gay man of color about that. Every place that I have ever taught, young gay men of color have come to me and said, "If it hadn't been for black lesbians, if it hadn't been for Chicana lesbians, I wouldn't know how to understand being queer." So what is it? Lesbians of color are making space for these young men—man-haters that we are supposed to be—ironically, we're making space for these young men. That's where I began to have some faith because I saw this new generation of queer, colored men growing up. On a certain level, they are really the crème de la crème because they are privileged young men to the degree that I meet them through universities. So even if they are coming from working-class or poor homes, they are getting their college education and they hold the promise of leadership for the next generation. But, unlike the Chicano counterparts of my generation, they are using feminism.

RW: Are they using feminism automatically? Is it something they have been formally taught? Or is feminism just in the air of this generation and queers have taken parts of feminism as their own?

CM: Well, like I said, I'm not talking about the white movement at all, I am talking within the context of men of color.

RW: I see.

CM: But yes, it's all across the board. I know this has been the case with young Asian men I've talked to, and young black men, Native men, and Chicano/Latinos. Because as they were coming up and coming out, the people that they were reading were us, women. They were reading lesbian feminist texts, to try to get an understanding of their own oppression and their own issues. The problem is what we are writing isn't sufficient because it doesn't really break down maleness. The people who have to break down masculinity are *them*. My generation never did it and so the challenge was, and the challenge remains: are these young men going to do it? What gives me hope is the fact that these young men's comprehension of their masculinity has been influenced by feminism, which is very different from the men of my generation. Historically, in the white gay movement, in the Chicano movement, in any of the movements where men have been involved, feminism was not an integrated part of the analysis. The New Left movement had nothing to do with feminism. Feminism had to happen in the 1970s without men. So, the fact that a new generation of men can use feminism, to me, is a very optimistic sign.

RW: That is another thing I want to talk about: this notion of who should be able to use, or to have access to, different identities and resources. You mentioned young, colored gay men reaching for feminism as part of forming their identities and their ways of living—in the 1990s there seems to have been, at least in academia, a huge proliferation of the use of terms like *queer* and *border* and *colonization*, words that originated in very specific experiences but that are now being used almost metaphorically to describe a wide range of experiences. Do you have any thoughts on this trend? Do you think there are such things as "identity metaphors" that should be limited in use, or is it that we couldn't stop such appropriations if we tried?

CM: Well, you can't stop it if you tried. No matter what you or I think. That's a function of language: language gets appropriated and movements get appropriated. I find it very distressing but I've given up being distressed about it. I think probably the first thing that comes to mind is the proliferation of "discourse" around "borders." I'm thinking about Gloria Anzaldúa's book *Borderlands: La Frontera = the New Mestiza*.[5] I think, very sincerely, she was really talking about queers when she was talking about all these "others," all these people including white gay men, all these different sectors of people who were living in this kind of border region of identity. But she is from the literal border between the U.S. and Mexico and that metaphor is for her as a Chicana, a lived experience. The Mexican/Chicano performance artist, Guíllermo Gomez-Peña, is another case in point. He's talking about the U.S./Mexican "border" relationship and how he functions as a "Mexican-born Chicano" artist. Just recently I was reading his new book, *The New World Border*,[6] in which he moves from the use of the term *border* to the term *hybrid*. He warns that this term will also become depoliticized and appropriated and we will have to find another term, and we will continue to have to find another term to counter the appropriation and to describe the complexity of our identities. On one level, he is indicting the appropriators, pointing his finger to the fact that in creat-

ing metaphors of identity, particularly if they are emerging out of
people of color or whatever disenfranchised group, those metaphors
will quickly be appropriated by the mainstream. So now white queers
or white academics or even straight, white academics can suddenly
see themselves as residing in this metaphoric border land—

RW: —and everyone has been colonized in some way or another, and
everyone is a little queer.

CM: Yeah. Language is a very elusive thing, it is a very tricky thing.
As Guillermo says, you just keep inventing new terms, and more new
terms. He is reminding us that we must keep language from being
bought off, so to speak, by capitalism, even the capitalism/cannibalism
of art and art criticism. But, with all due respect to Gomez-Peña, I feel
that this is a little bit of a cop-out. I feel like that there are certain words
that are very difficult to appropriate.

RW: Such as . . . ?

CM: Such as *nationalism*. That's why I like *Queer Aztlán*. I feel part of
the deal is to use words that get everybody upset, that are, as my
students say, "in your face." You can't say the word *nationalism* without
thinking KKK, and Bosnia, and "ethnic cleansing." It's dangerous.

RW: It's a "bad" word.

CM: Right, it's a dirty word. The thing of it is, in the 1960s it wasn't
a bad word, there were nationalist movements of color altering the
consciousness of an entire nation. As a person who witnessed those
movements, I am looking into the twenty-first century and thinking,
"Wait a minute. Chicanos are suddenly being told we are now 'Hispan-
ics.'" Our identities have all been totally neutralized politically. Everybody is everything. We're just another immigrant population. The national message is: "No, in fact we Chicanos don't have Indian blood,
no, in fact we don't have indigenous roots in this country, no, we don't
have a right to this land, and we didn't have the land before all y'all
came." This is racial amnesia and a historical lie. When you use words
that are more encompassing, what tends to happen is that they become
more easily appropriated. When you use language that is more confrontational, people say you are angry and they don't like it, or they
say you are playing into the hands of fascists or Nazis. But, if you are
specific in your meaning, you do not have to compromise the radicalism of your position. I don't want to give up nationalism yet, because
I want Chicanos to remember that we are a nation of people by blood
and history, and that all of these geopolitical borders are a lie. That's
important for my kid to know, it's important for my students to know
and to remember that we are a nation of people regardless of the fact

that we live in this monolithic nation-state of the United States. But everything in the United States, including our metaphors for identity, is telling us to forget that.

RW: Right.

CM: I feel that sometimes you have to use very dangerous language and risk people calling you bad names or saying to you that you're reactionary or saying that you are playing into the hands of the right wing in order to counter liberalism which, to me, is the most dangerous of all. I don't worry about the Christian Right, I think that it's fine. I mean I don't think *they* are fine, but I think we have something to learn from the Christian Right. For one thing, people are wanting some God. On one level you can call it escapism, but on another level you can document the success of political movements that were driven by a spiritual mandate. The civil rights movement, the black power movement, even Chicano nationalism were being driven by a sense of spirituality that emerged from a people.

RW: Do you think that queer movements have that sense of spirituality behind them?

CM: No. I don't think so. The problem with it—and this is what makes things very, very difficult—the problem is that queer is not cultural. It's not cultural in the sense that it is not an identity emerging from a culturally ethnic group. It's an identity that can encompass many, many cultural groups. But, as a people, we still emerge out of a particular class, a particular race, a particular geography, a particular language, particular foods that we eat, et cetera—all of these things form who we are culturally. When we even consider our own liberation, what moves us about our liberation, and the way we use language and metaphor to define our own liberation, it all emerges out of our own cultural base.

RW: So you would say then that there isn't such a thing as a particular "queer experience" from which queers emerge into a political realm? That it's strictly a coalitional, rather than cultural, term?

CM: I think it is a coalitional term because I think that even our understanding of *queer* is culturally based. Your understanding of queer is different than mine. We may use queer and shape it from within our own experience and background, but the word itself, like *feminism*, isn't a culturally based term. And being queer, that is, being homosexual, being transgendered, being any of those things, you create a way of expressing yourself with certain codes and with certain languages that you use to communicate and to send the right signals to others like you. But, even all of that still is nuanced by issues of class, race, sex, et cetera. I agree with you that *queer identity* does suggest some point of connection and therefore holds strong potential for coalition, but it can't be a cultural movement in the historical sense.

RW: But then what is that point of connection? I keep coming back to the question of who has access to that potential. In her article about gay and New Right identity discourses called "Tremble, Hetero Swine!," Cindy Patton describes political identities as something you take up and that suture you to particular moral duties.[7] She argues that identities like queer or New Right are more a matter of specific responsibility than, say, of "being" or ontology. First of all, is that a definition of identity that you would even consider?

CM: That it's a responsibility?

RW: That identity can be defined as a matter of responsibility and action, rather than as states of being—the ontological sense of identity.

CM: I agree with that idea when you are talking about identities that may imply choice. Like when you have a choice to claim yourself as queer politically or you have the choice to call yourself a feminist, or even when as a light-skinned person you have a choice whether or not to "come out" about your racial identity. When you don't have a choice about it, Patton's position makes less sense, for in those instances it's not about you being responsible to your identity, you just *are*. Everyone experiences you that way, you don't have the choice about being a woman, you don't have any choice about being visibly colored, you don't have a choice about your class or being a stone bull dagger. You are living it, and so it's not a question of being responsible to your identity. You live it whether you are politicized about it or conscious of it or not. It really doesn't matter because you are it, it's your identity. If you are a black woman, you're a black woman, *punto final.* That's it. The notion of responsibility to one's political identity does make sense, though, when you are talking about identities which one could on the negative side appropriate or on the positive side choose. Patton's position weeds out people who just want to claim certain identities simply because they are advantageous to them at a particular period in their lives.

RW: Do you think there is a place in queer political movements for academics who identify themselves as queer scholars, or straight people who feel aligned with queer agendas, if there's an understanding that it is a choice on our part?

CM: I think the irony of it is that one would know if they are being responsible to a political identity, particularly if the identity is somehow related to oppression, because they're going to lose something in the deal. By assuming a disenfranchised identity, that identity may open some doors for some people because it may be politically or professionally advantageous in a certain context. But those same folks will go to another place with the same identity and the doors will be shut. That's where the responsibility comes in; the responsibility means that one doesn't change their tune when they go to the other door. You assume that identity in every situation, and if you do that in every situation, *regardless* of who you are sleeping with (if we are just talking about queer here), and you passionately identify with that term—

RW: —then you're willing to lose something for it.

CM: Yes, you will lose. That person loses stuff. Because queer ain't good in society, it ain't good. [*laughter*] I mean, at least as far as last time I checked. It is outsiderhood, so it's about giving up privilege. I can say this as a light-skinned person, that I can go into situations and nobody necessarily knows I'm Latina. I know nothing can change the fact that if I'm walking down the street and not opening my mouth and if someone was really a racist, they probably ain't going to be giving me no flak, because I don't look colored enough for that. So I can't do anything about that, being light-skinned is an inherent privilege that I have. But I can do something about where I stand politically, and about the risks that I take. And taking those risks, I lose the privilege that my light skin—when left unchallenged—affords me. So even if, as you were saying, even as a straight woman, as somebody who doesn't look particularly queer—

RW: —In terms of fitting gender expectations?

CM: Yeah. No one can take that away from you—thank god—I would hate to lose femmes in the world! But by assuming a queer position, some of that privilege is lost. I think of my own partner, who I always see as a high femme. She can get into situations of opportunity with men that I never could because she is physically and commercially attractive by their standards. But, she opens her damn mouth, and she alienates every damn man in the room! Her feminism is uncompromising, so I'm saying that, by her lesbian feminism, she loses privilege.

RW: Not compromising is the responsibility she has in her identity as a feminist?

CM: Yes, that's the responsibility. There are doors that are shut to her because of her politics. She carries weight, she carries the burden of having those convictions, and that's what it is about, ultimately. That's also, ultimately, what coalition is all about. You end up making alliances with people based on their practice, not on their identities. The people whom I end up calling allies in my world are not necessarily other Chicana lesbians; they are every shape, size, form, color, class, gender. They are allies based on their practice, and based on where they assume responsibility.

RW: Let's take off on another tangent and talk about where that practice comes from. In an article, I think it was written in 1983, you and Amber Hollibaugh had a conversation in which you both asserted that specific individual experience is the place sexual theory should come from. One of you suggested the best way to approach a theory of sexuality was through something like the consciousness-raising of feminism in the seventies.

CM: Yes, that was Amber's suggestion.

RW: Do you see the idea of sexual theory based on personal experience as feeding into, or as contradicting, the notion of queer as a coalitional term?

CM: That conversation was very much generated in reaction to an understanding of lesbianism at the time that was very classist. Back in the 1970s, lesbianism was being redefined through a feminist movement consisting mostly of middle- and upper-middle-class women. If you didn't fulfill their prescriptions about what a lesbian should be, then you weren't a lesbian. You were something else, but you weren't a lesbian.

RW: You were queer.

CM: Yeah, you were back to being queer, you were back to being a dyke. It absolutely echoes what I just said, which is that, for any coalition to work, one has to remain very specific about their experience and be responsible to the identity they are assuming. The only way you can build coalitions with people is to bring all your specificities together then find where the point of commonality, the point of juncture is, and then pick the project that reflects your shared concerns. It doesn't mean that you have to be pals or that you have to make a life together. Bernice Reagon said as much many years ago in her article on coalitional politics in *Home Girls*.[8] It's great—she says, "Who said you have to like the people you do coalition work with?" If people were to come together under the rubric of being queer, and if it were truly representative of the queers in the U.S. alone, it would be the most diverse coalition known to humankind, because it represents every aspect of society. Queers happen in every level of society. This brings me back to the point that *queer* is not cultural, I mean, of course it's not.

RW: And that's what, in particular, makes finding points of political or theoretical connection difficult?

CM: That's part of the problem. Since being queer is so informed culturally, and so determined by our cultural experience, what is the basis of commonality beyond experiences of oppression that are still very much informed by class, race, gender, et cetera? It becomes a little awesome to me. Is there *a* queer experience? It's sort of like when feminist artists and art critics begin to ask, "Is there a female aesthetic?"

RW: Would you say there is a queer aesthetic?

CM: I don't know. You can't find someone more different from me than Walt Whitman, but I remember reading him as an English major in college and there was a passion in the poetry that I related to. Was that all about being queer? I don't know. So is there a queer aesthetic? Is there a female aesthetic? I know that *that* makes more sense to me.

RW: Why?

CM: Because to me being female and being male is a much more profound marker of identity than desire is. That's why transgendered people are so frightening to people, because they challenge what we thought was so fundamental about those identities. Being female and male so much determines how you are treated in this society. In a way, even being the *wrong* kind of male or female, like if you are a faggoty male or you're a butchy female, the reason you are getting the shit is because you are male or female, right?

RW: Or "should be."

CM: Exactly. As an artist, I am interested in how gender may influence how we write. One can make generalities based on gender, such as, men use more action-based kinds of plot structures than women. Not that women can't do that, or that *all* men do, but why is it that women tend not to be interested in doing that? What is it about being in the domestic realm as girls, being indoors more so than boys, around the hearth, so to speak, that informs the kind of art we produce, and the images we produce? *That* makes more sense to me, because gender is so enforced in this society.

RW: More so than sexuality?

CM: Yes, because when I think of my own experience, my desire came second. For me, my first conflicts with society were all about being a girl, not a lesbian. You see, that was the problem—I was the wrong kind of girl, the problem was the girl thing. The problem was—

RW: —How can there be a wrong kind of girl?

CM: Yeah! How come you can't be just a girl? You have a little body and this is the little body you have. My definition of being female influenced everything, including my terror about the fact that I didn't fit the definition. That's why feminism meant so much to me and why feminism became the way for me to understand my lesbianism. I always knew I was queer. I knew I was queer before I was ever a feminist, right? But, my queerness had to do with the fact that I didn't fit the "correct" role of being a girl. So gender seems so much more profound than my desire. That I liked girls was secondary. The fact I liked girls, and I knew that early on, too, really problematized things, but that was partly because I was the wrong gender.

RW: You refer to having the wrong gender several times in your work. You wrote of dreaming that you were a hermaphrodite, of having hybrid experiences of yourself, and not quite feeling like the right kind of woman because you felt like a butch. Two of the essays in this collection, Morgan Holmes's and Jill St. Jacques's, are about this kind of transgendered experience and question whether transgenderism should locate itself under or within the rubric of queer. Do you feel you would have identified with a transgendered movement if it had been around when you were growing up?

CM: Well, I did identify with transgender people in the sense that I knew more about that than I did about gay and lesbian. I mean, in my ignorance I thought it was almost the same thing. As a child you see images, you see faggots and you see bull daggers and you know that these people have some relationship to you. I remember once as a child seeing this magazine article, I think it was in *Life* magazine, and there was this woman standing on a low stool having her dress hemmed. The caption read that she was a man, and I remember looking at this photo and looking at it and looking at it, and my heart was going boom, boom, boom—pounding a hundred miles an hour. I was so struck with the fact she was a man and that she felt she was really a woman trapped in this man's body. She was what we called then a "transsexual," and I knew that was me. Those people weren't other, they were me, even this white man in this dress was me. My secret was that I was a boy trapped in a girl's body. I wanted to be a boy and that came before—

RW: —Did you want to be a boy, or did you want what you saw boys having?

CM: It wasn't like I wanted a dick, I never got that specific. I didn't even think about dicks, I never saw dicks, I barely saw myself. We came from a very Catholic background, so it wasn't that you thought in terms of genitalia. Later I'd say I wanted men's freedom. Of course I wanted to be a boy, they had a better life, but I wanted to be a boy before I wanted girls.

RW: Oh, okay.

CM: When I got older, and I reached puberty, that's when I knew that I wanted girls. Eleven maybe. I'd always known that I loved girls—women—but it became sexualized at eleven when I felt physically attracted to females. But what I thought was that I was a transsexual. I didn't think I was a lesbian, it didn't work that way. I mean, there were men and there were women and men wanted women and women wanted men and if you wanted the wrong one, you weren't gay, you were, you were . . .

RW: Queer?

CM: Yeah, you were queer. But you were transsexual, you weren't gay. There was a way that gender was more profound than one's desire, desire just complicated it. That's why it got very confusing to me, particularly the more acquainted I became with transgenderism. For example, it fascinates me that there are men who are born men who become women in order to become lesbians. They want nothing to do with dick—they don't want one on 'em or in 'em. I think it's very interesting, and it totally contradicts my earliest convictions that transsexuals were all homosexuals who had a sex change because they sexually wanted the "wrong" gender. Then, because of feminism, I began to get an analysis that the problem wasn't that I was the wrong gender, but that what was defined as appropriate for my gender was wrong.

RW: Instant paradigm shift.

CM: Exactly. "The society is wrong, not you." The birth of political consciousness. It's the same thing with issues of race. Political consciousness requires our knowing, "I'm not inherently wrong for being Mexican, society is wrong for having a prejudice against me as a Mexican." It's a very simple and significant thing—the sudden politicization of one's identity. Feminism to me became the way for me to politicize and understand my lesbianism, and that isn't necessarily the case for everybody. A lot of people don't have that analysis and, in fact, really do believe in those gendered roles, really do believe that those roles are there for a reason and that the roles are just, and if you don't have the right one, you want to change it. What's hard for me to understand about the transgendered movement and transgenderism is the conviction that you have to fuck up your body to fit a fucked up world. I understand people making those choices because they ain't going to change that world (at least not in their lifetime), but the idea of societally enforced mutilation still makes me really outraged. I don't really think one can change one's perspective on one's own genitalia. There's very little in society that challenges our fixed perceptions of ourselves as gendered beings. But where I want to put my work is in changing that society, not in changing my organism. I think another part of the problem is that even a post-op transgendered person is never totally the opposite gender. They're just queer, and they will stay queer their whole lives. It doesn't matter if their genitalia changes, if they were a queer boy and become a woman later, they are still not a woman. They're just queer, because they grew up a boy. They grew up a queer boy, they grew up an unacceptable boy, they grew up an outsider boy, they were an inappropriate boy, they were all these queer notions of boyness, but they were still a boy.

RW: They still have all that experience and history.

CM: You can't undo it. You can't undo it and so they're queer; they really remain a third category in terms of gender, that "third sex" kind of thing I use to identify with so much as a child. It doesn't matter. You change your body so that you can function in society better and you feel more at peace with yourself, but that doesn't make a person-born-as-a-man into a woman. I guess I agree with the "standard" feminist position on that. I mean, I am raising a son, and regardless of my influence, the degree of enforced superiority that males feel, even if you are an inappropriate kind of male, is amazing. I think of the phrase in Spanish of being given "el don," the gift. You've been endowed with a superior existence.

RW: [*laughter*] That is the rumor.

CM: I don't think you can undo that. So a man becoming a woman doesn't necessarily make him suddenly my female ally. It's very complicated.

RW: Let's talk, if we could, about your experience of raising a son. When *The Last Generation* came out you identified yourself as "a woman who is forty without children, a lesbian without a partner." How then, has having a child changed your sense of your self? Admittedly, a huge question.

CM: I always feel that books have their own lives. A book, even an autobiography, is not the biography of its author. The book has its own biography. So, whoever I was as the author at that time of writing *The Last Generation*, I felt everything as passionately as I wrote it. The book will just go on with that message. So anybody who opens that book will experience the writer—the author or the voice—with all of those preoccupations that that person had at the time of the writing regardless of what I, as an individual, go on to do. So, for example, when I wrote the lines in the 1980's, "There will be nobody calling me mamá, mami, abuelita, grandma," I meant that to my core. I didn't see motherhood in my future. I didn't see it in my own life. And yet, ironically, my obsession with family has preoccupied every single thing I've ever written in my life.

RW: Especially around mothers and your own mother.

CM: Right, starting with her. I am finishing a book right now called *Waiting in the Wings*,[9] which is kind of a memoir about my getting pregnant and the birth of my child. He was born very premature, so he had a very threatened beginning. He is fine now, but he was in the hospital for a long time. In *Wings* I describe how I tried to make family with every lover I ever had. Being a lesbian was always about, "I'll make family with her, I'm going to make my own queer family." My attachments to my blood family remain very strong. I have a big ol' extended blood family, but I always knew that since I couldn't really be a lesbian there, it also was essential that I build my own kind of queer family. Because I was a lesbian, I always just assumed that that meant I'd never have kids. *Punto final.* You raise other women's kids. And I think that was coming from a really butch place, sort of like, "I'm not the one that has kids, *they*—the femmes—have kids." After being a non-biological mother, and raising a kid and losing him very suddenly, it just came to me that I *could* have children if I wanted. It was a choice, I had a choice. This seemed like a very kind of novel notion, that I actually had a choice, that being a dyke didn't mean I was destined to be childless.

RW: That it was no longer a matter of "butches don't"?

CM: Yeah! Being in a relationship that I felt was sane and supportive helped me see that. And for me—well, this is so much a part of my own sort of spiritual beliefs—my *destino* was, in fact, to have this child. I just hadn't been listening to those subterranean messages telling me so. I know this is true because I became pregnant on my very first try. I had never been pregnant in my life!

RW: O——kay.

CM: I mean, that was it. My feeling about getting pregnant was that if it wasn't meant to be, I wasn't going to trip on it. I'd try it a few times, and if it wasn't happening, I was going to adopt. It wasn't like I had any big agenda. It was really just a question of, "Is this in your path or not? Have you not been listening?" And so, I started to listen and my son came into my life right away. Very quickly.

RW: *Very* quickly.

CM: People asked me what I did over the summer, and if I hadn't seen them and I'd say "I had a kid." I mean, that's how fast everything went. It really was for me a sense of this is just destiny. Whatever the entity that is my son was out there waiting to hook up with whatever entity I am. Once that happened—and it happened so quickly—I really understood that it was that this had been in my path all along and that, thank God, I started to listen. I was forty years old. Of course, it changed many, many things, but on a certain level, having my son has just reinforced the sense of family I'd already cultivated for so many years. Not only with my blood family, which is very supportive, but also with a circle of, as we say "comadres," of women—and some men—who are making family with this child.

RW: Godparents?

CM: Yes, I feel very blessed in that sense. On a certain level, my preoccupation with notions of family are being given a chance to be realized. There is something about intergenerational connection (and I don't mean just children, but also old people) that is what I understand to be family. It's not just two dykes together, not that that's not totally legitimate, nobody has got to have kids, nobody has to raise kids. But for me, the intergenerational stuff is what I understand as family. And as a queer, as a lesbian, I can have that in this very protective world of San Francisco. I can say that because the reality of being a lesbian mom in less tolerant environments is, as you know, that they take away your kids. I have a family that supports me. There are so many things that could fall in harm's way about trying to have and raise a child as an open lesbian, but so far I'm very lucky. To me, it just was the logical next step, or illogical next step . . . on the path.

RW: So, in addition to the book *Waiting in the Wings*, what other projects have you got going?

CM: I'm trying to finish a play, *The Hungry Woman: A Mexican Medea,* that I started many years ago but that got interrupted by another play, *Watsonville*, which premiered in 1996.[10] *The Hungry Woman* is based on both the Greek Medea and also the Mexican myth La Llorona (The Weeping Woman). In both stories, a mother kills her children. I started the play before I was ever pregnant and now my son is three-and-a-half years old and I am finishing it. It has been a very difficult play for me to write, because it's a lesbian play and it's probably the most dangerous thing that I could think to write. It's like, "Oh yeah, let's write about lesbian child killers." That's really the image we want to project into this homophobic world. But, for me, my preoccupations as a writer remain the same, which have to do with really trying to understand what I call "female wounding," both within the context of my own Mexican culture and within the broader dominant culture. I know that, as women, we have been deformed, by not being allowed full humanness. With this play, I have picked one of the most taboo, antisocial acts a woman can commit as the essence of the plot. The only role women are given sanction for in society is motherhood, right? I mean, a good woman is a good mom. And so, what's the worst thing you can do against society, i.e., against patriarchy? Kill motherhood. The child killer is a greater aberration to society than is a dyke. I want to understand the mind of a woman who would be so desperate as to commit this "unspeakable" act. A midwife once told me that when a woman kills her child, it is not a homicide but a suicide. Having a child, I now understand what she means. I'm just dying to know what would cause a woman to commit this most unthinkable/unspeakable act. It just began to preoccupy me so much, and the play is trying to answer that question. Within a Mexican and Chicano context, the child killer la Llorona has been looked at over and over again through a very patriarchal lens. The standard explanation is (as with the Greek Medea): "She killed her children because some man dumped her." It's a very sexist understanding of why a woman would kill the very thing she most values, the very life she has created. I want to understand that. It's been a hard play to write, but necessary for me on some level. Ironically, both writing projects, *Wings* and the play, are about lesbian motherhood.

RW: At the same time very old and very new themes, right?

CM: The concern for me remains the intersection of culture and womanhood and desire, how all those things come together, and I'll probably keep writing those themes until I am gone.

RW: Thank you; thank you very much.

Notes

1. Cherríe Moraga, *Loving in the War Years: Lo Que Nunca Pasó por Sus Labios* (Boston: South End Press, 1983).

2. Moraga founded the theater troupe DramaDIVAS, and was its director for over five years. At present the group is on temporary hiatus.

3. The Native/Chicana creative writing group was called Indígena as Scribe.

4. Cherríe Moraga, *The Last Generation* (Boston: South End Press, 1993), 145–74.

5. Gloria Anzaldúa, *Borderlands: La Frontera = the New Mestiza* (San Francisco: Spinsters/Aunt Lute, 1987).

6. Guillermo Gomez-Peña, *The New World Border: Prophecies, Poems, and Loqueras for the End of the Century* (San Francisco: City Lights, 1996).

7. Cindy Patton, "Tremble, Hetero Swine!" in *Fear of a Queer Planet: Queer Politics and Social Theory,* ed. Michael Warner (Minneapolis: University of Minnesota Press, 1993), 143–77.

8. Bernice Johnson Reagon, "Coalition Politics: Turning the Century," in *Home Girls: A Black Feminist Anthology,* ed. Barbara Smith (New York: Kitchen Table Women of Color Press, 1983), 356–68.

9. Cherríe Moraga, *Waiting in the Wings: Portrait of a Queer Motherhood* (Ithaca, N.Y.: Firebrand Books, 1997).

10. At Brava! Theater Center, San Francisco.

4

Queer Cut Bodies

Morgan Holmes

> I don't think there is any questions [*sic*] that [the patient] has
> an isolated clitoral hypertrophy and that surgical revision
> would give her *the best cosmetic effect*.
> —author's medical file, 1974

Intersexuality and *genital ambiguity* are terms often interchangeably
used to refer to a bodily condition traditionally known as "hermaphroditism." In general, *intersexuality* refers to a physical and/or chromosomal set of possibilities in which the features typically understood as
belonging distinctly to either the male or the female sex are combined
in a single body. The term *genital ambiguity*, while popularly used in
much medical and the social science literature as a substitute for intersexuality, is in fact a misnomer on two counts: first, because there are
incidences of intersexuality in which the genitals appear quite clearly
and unambiguously as one or the other of the two recognized sexes;
and second, because the word *ambiguous* implies that intersexed genitals do not really look like *anything*. This perception and its enunciation
speak volumes about the cultural anxieties attending issues of sexuality and categories of sexual identity. In an attempt to unfold these anxieties, this chapter seeks to refute the idea that intersexed genitalia are
examples of "gender ambiguity," arguing instead that the very fact that
such bodies are neither male nor female makes them clearly intersexed
rather than confused or incomprehensible. My title is thus meant, on
the one hand, to suggest that intersexed bodies are *clear cut* bodies, as
neatly fashioned as any human form, and, on the other, to draw attention to the medicocultural forces that have nonetheless persisted in
their attempts to "cut" these bodies, quite literally, in order to make
them fit patterns that align with and do not threaten heterosexist
hegemony.

To put the latter proposition another way: intersexed bodies—when
understood as those that do not fit into the symbolic realm of Western

culture—have been physically and literally cut, bound, and sutured in order to appear, in a most violent paradox, "normal" even if not "natural." Previously regulated through juridical intervention, around the turn of the century hermaphrodites came increasingly under the control of the medical gaze, whose power to enforce its pronouncements of "disease" and to impose disciplinary "cures" on such diseased bodies, worked in tandem with the late-nineteenth-century desire to reduce the threat of similarities within and between the categories male and female.[1] This interventionist medical response to the hermaphrodite's body also emerged concurrently with new definitions distinguishing between heterosexuality and homosexuality and hinged upon the development of hormonal research. Indeed, at one time, the definitions of the intersexual and homosexual overlapped to so great a degree that same-sex desire was interpreted as a mental form of hermaphroditism, while hermaphrodites were viewed as deeply disturbing physical entities who presented the threatening possibility of living as *natural* or *auto-sodomites*.[2]

This interpellation of the intersexual body in medical and social discourse raises both material and discursive questions of what, if anything, constitutes "normalcy," and it invites a (re)consideration of the wider spectrums of possibility that inhere both in sexual desire and sex/gender identifications grouped under the rubric "queer." While shock treatment of homosexuals has ceased, and homosexuality has been removed from the *Diagnostic and Statistical Manual* (the primary sourcebook for mental health professionals), intersexed bodies continue to be carved, cut, and sutured in an attempt to place them within a symbolic realm of the comprehensible. This medical and surgical management is performed at all the major children's hospitals in Canada, as well as in various hospitals across the United States. This chapter examines some of the long-term implications for children subjected to such forms of treatment and interrogates the cultural reasons for the standard mode of treatment—namely, early surgical intervention to reshape the genitals.

I first wrote a version of this chapter for an adviser who required that topics be framed in terms of interpersonal violence, which he defined as the type of abuse *one* person suffered at the hands of *one other* person. I had to stretch the definition and challenge its narrowness in order to make the point that both sex, as a biological/anatomical description, and gender, as a set of cultural requirements, could be interpreted as violent impositions written onto the bodies of many separate individuals, impositions executed by authorities that we individuals might never even see. My concern in that paper was to examine the sexing and gendering of children diagnosed as intersexed, a focus that this chapter has retained. However, rather than continue to try to adhere to the original mandate to see everything in terms of interpersonal violence, herein I define this sexing and gendering process in terms of a set of *controls*. As physically and psychically violent as some of the text that follows is, *control* now strikes me as a much more suitable organizing principle because it enables a more accurate analysis of the social and cultural systems of thought, the linguistic constructions of subjects and identities, and the actual physical interventions attending the medical establishment's treatment, in all senses of the word, of intersexuality. Violence of a physical sort is merely one of the many means employed in this process of control and intervention, functioning as part and parcel of *medical* discourse rather than as a series of isolated surgical *acts*. Indeed, the acts of medicine discussed in the following pages, ranging from diagnostic procedures to surgical cuts, may all be interpreted as inscriptions of particular forms of meaning onto bodies and, as such, part of a larger field of cultural discourse and cultural demands.

Perhaps most famously, but by no means solely, Michel Foucault has argued that medical discourse has shaped and controlled the way in which people think of, approach, and experience "the body." According to temporal location and political requirements, the limits placed upon bodies through medicine have differed radically. Thomas Laqueur's cross-temporal study of Western medicine, *Making Sex*, for example, shows that at one time there was only one sex: male, and it was divided into a hierarchy in which there were males who could conceive (those we now call males) and males whose reproductive organs were internal and who could not conceive, but only carry the fetus as a jug carries wine (those we now call females).[3] In addition to Laqueur, Nelly Oudshoorn, Donna Haraway, and Judith Butler have all provided commentary on the ways in which cultural and medical discourses have intersected to set parameters on bodily intelligibility and significance. In the sense that bodies are thus constituted as cultural products, and hence contrary to liberal individualist understandings of subjectivity, "one" is never alone in one's body; there are always already other people, histories of meaning, and changing terms used to describe identities and practices, all of which continue to shape and act upon bodies as fields of meaning. This is true of any person's body for, as Foucault has shown, there is no nature outside culture.

My task here, however, begins neither with Foucault nor the other theorists whom I have already mentioned. For although they have compellingly argued for the construction and active production of "the body," it remains unclear just exactly what this term *the body* is or could be. Therefore, my study turns first to the early-twentieth-century anthropological work of Marcel Mauss, who analyzed bodies as instruments of technology. Mauss's work is interesting because, first, he looks not only at the ways in which people "talk" about bodies, but also at the very physically different ways in which whole cultures learn to use and live in their bodies. Through understanding bodies as technological productions, I then turn to my actual field of interest: the management and control of intersexed bodies, I suggest, should be considered not only as an example of a technical creation of gender and sexuality, but also as a general *habitus* in which the possibility for resistance as well as domination exists.[4] The question that readers ought constantly to keep in mind as an organizing principle is, "Who gets to decide?" This question applies not only to the juridicomedical history of intersex management, but also to current social and semiotic analyses of bodies and their meanings. In particular, the question applies to the meanings that intersexed bodies can, should, and do convey.

Meaningful Bodies

In 1950, anthropologist Marcel Mauss theorized that human beings learn to use their bodies in accordance with culturally specific mannerisms that he referred to as "body techniques." Mauss's study proved useful for interpreting the culturally specific significations of bodily habits and activities, and it remains an interesting theory when applied to the ways in which we learn to use our bodies to transmit those meanings that make gender performances intelligible. Mauss's observations of how individual subjects come to bear meaning also illuminate how a culture demands and privileges some meanings— including sexual meaning—over others, and how it achieves this fiat *through* the bodies of its citizens. Mauss observes that "'habits' do not vary just with individuals and their limitations; they vary especially between societies, educations, proprieties and fashions. In these habits we should see the techniques and work of collective and individual practical reason."[5] Most important, it is incorrect to assume that there are any natural bodily techniques, even when we consider an activity as simple as walking for, as Mauss cautions, "there is perhaps no 'natural way' [of walking] for the adult. *A fortiriori* when other technical facts intervene: to take ourselves, the fact that we wear shoes to walk transforms the positions of our feet: we feel it sure enough when we walk without them."[6] Unfortunately, Mauss does not push his observations of bodily techniques further, noting that gender and sexuality are differently enacted, performed and coded across cultures as well. Of course, Judith Butler has firmly established gender as a performance that must be deliberately reconstituted on a daily basis if it is to continue to convey the illusory seamlessness of gender. The paradox of this constant need to re-create what is supposed to be a natural consequence of one's sex is an extremely compelling and provocative argument; however, the point that is lacking in both Mauss's and Butler's analyses is that one's biological sex is also a performative and technical transmitter for the cultural demands centered on sexuality. The clothes we wear, the spaces we inhabit, and the activities we are trained to fulfill are just a few of the most apparent examples of the technical impositions through which we come to signify gender and sexuality. At least since the publication of *Gender Trouble* in 1988,[7] these spatial and behavioral organizations have been understood in queer theory as "obvious" examples of gender performance. What may be less obvious is that gender does not rest upon a scientifically neutral backdrop with biology as its incontrovertible basis. The highly specific conceptualization of sex as determined by chromosomes and hormones is, in fact, a quite historically specific, mid- to late-twentieth-century, Western medical/technical concept that circumscribes the way we approach the terms *male* and *female*. That all of us are subject to assumptions about chromosomes, genitals, and hormones is not the same as saying that all persons arrive at technical interventions from equal positions on a level playing field; bodies are not neutral pages waiting to be inscribed with the same message by the same means. Thus, for some, the imposition of meaning may seem quite seamless, while for others the technical interventions that culture imposes upon our bodies are both more obvious and more crude. Although one might assert that they are simply that—obvious impositions of the same technical genres that *make* our bodies signify and significant—I will argue that they are also more physically violent and invasive than the standard modes of cultural inscription.

The focus of this chapter centers on a group of bodies subjected to these more obvious and violent cultural impositions of sex and gender: the bodies of intersexed infants and minors. I am only marginally interested in what the process teaches us about more "typical" gendering processes. Much has been written on how the management of intersexuality elucidates the production of the feminine/female.[8] For approximately thirty years, since the beginning of John Money's work on hermaphroditism and gender, intersexed bodies have been used as examples of how mutable gender identity can be before a certain age.[9]

Since then, theorists who have opposed Money's treatment paradigm have argued that the standard treatment of intersexuality stands as an example of the effects of misogynist practice in medicine. While I agree that such practice is largely misogynist, premised upon seeing female bodies as bodies that *lack* and are, therefore, the easiest ones into which to convert an intersexed child, I believe that the time has come to examine intersexed bodies not as examples of what is wrong with how we treat women, but as examples of what is wrong with how we treat intersexuality. While I agree that gender is a mutable social category, that fact should not be used to justify the alteration of the bodies of children who cannot consent to the kinds of management that will be discussed in this chapter. I am not interested in intersexed bodies as vehicles that transport meanings for others; I am interested in intersexed bodies as bodies that *do not fit*.

How does culture enforce not only the technique(s) of bodily use, but also make assignments regarding what bodies should signify? By "assignments" I mean those acts that organize humans into the categorical envelopes of "male" and "female." How does one acquire the ability to signify, both *to be* and *to bear* meaning through the body?[10] For this acquiring is not a simple process in which a subject is free to choose the ways in which s/he will embody a subject position. How are bodies that "do not fit" brought into the symbolic realm in Western culture, and what are the limits of this confinement? How does medical observation, diagnosis, and management bring some bodies into being while refusing others? Anne Fausto-Sterling, in her discussion of this process, states that "the treatment of intersexuality in this century demands scrutiny. . . . Society mandates the control of intersexual bodies because they blur and bridge the great divide; they challenge traditional beliefs about sexual difference. Hermaphrodites have unruly bodies. They do not fall into a binary classification: only a surgical shoehorn can put them there."[11] While it is true that it is a *surgical* shoehorn that engenders the intersexual, this process occurs in tandem with a larger *ideological* shoehorn of a sex/gender binary. What the treatment of intersexed children underscores is that we are all forced to conform to specific, binarized, heteronormative gender roles. The surgical violence to which intersexed infants and children are submitted may be likened to the torture device described in Franz Kafka's *In the Penal Colony*. The body itself does not learn that the price ex(tr)acted for nonconformity is extreme; it is those who witness the punishment that take this lesson home. In the case of Kafka's story, punishment results in the death of the body; in the case of intersexuality, punishment results in a death or paralysis of the soul. One intersexed woman that I know, Kira Triea, writes: "I was 'treated' (experimented upon) at the PRU [Psychohormonal Research Unit]. . . . Up on the roof of that hospital they keep primates . . . many of which had been made intersexed while in utero. We kids downstairs were treated a little better . . . we didn't have to live on the roof. But we were just experimental animals, smarter ones. The doctors were very impressed with how smart I was . . . I was a very interesting little lab rat and unusual too! Yes . . . an interesting little creature to do experiments about sex, hormones, surgery and gender upon!"[12] The experimentation upon the bodies of the children in the PRU, was, according to this informant, highly punitive. But what is astonishing is that the professionals in the unit were so convinced that they were correct they did not even realize that what they were doing was impeding the personal and physical freedoms of the children who were their patients. The above informant related that she bumped into her endocrinologist a few years later and the doctor, believing herself to be totally in the right, approached Kira as though everything had been made normal and happy at last; there was not even a hint during their conversation that the doctor thought that things might not be as she had envisaged them.

We tend to overlook the technical constructions of bodies and posit them as "natural"; therefore, when doctors make a gender assignment, they somewhat paradoxically believe that they are simply aligning intersexed bodies with natural categories and not with social constructions. The ability to diagnose intersexed conditions as deviations depends upon a conflation of the idea of the "natural" with statistical norms—that is, that a majority of babies are born with typical genitals, therefore, binary sex categories are "natural." In fact, though less common, intersexuality is as "natural" an occurrence as any other sex/genital/chromosomal presentation. Furthermore, what is decidedly cultural and not natural at all, regardless of anatomical or biological presentation, is the imposition of gender upon bodies.

A more current anthropologist than Mauss, Pierre Bourdieu has a theory of embodiment that takes into account labor and spatial—as well as temporal—organizations of bodies according to gender.[13] Taking up where Mauss leaves off, Bourdieu shows how the imposition of behaviors effectively organizes bodies into intelligible roles. His theory of the habitus describes how cultures actively produce the contexts in which bodies come to be meaningful such that, for example, one may expect to find men and women doing specific and different tasks at specific and definitive times and not at others; this organizational structure may indeed be one of the ways in which cultures recognize the difference between "masculine" and "feminine." Thus, to be a man in Western culture means that one is not to stay home with children, take another man as a lover, be sexually attracted to men, and so on; opposite tenets are used to bound the conceptual and temporal space of what it means to be a woman. However, cultural meanings and locations of intelligibility are not necessarily static, and though they are totalizing, they do not go absolutely unquestioned by all citizens in Western culture.

As Susan Gal indicates, Bourdieu's conceptualization of the habitus as one of "symbolic domination" leaves us without a firm sense that "such cultural power rarely goes uncontested. Resistance to a dominant cultural order occurs when devalued linguistic strategies . . . are practised and celebrated despite widespread denigration."[14] Gal continues her critique of Bourdieu by indicating that he misses the everyday challenges to the symbolic domination he posits. Indeed, although Kira Triea's above testimony indicates an abusive enforcement of gender, her statement is also imbued with a sense of angry resistance that defies any *total* medical containment of her body, one that stands as an everyday challenge to the medical measures taken against her.

When theorizing resistance, it is necessary first to identify what is being resisted and how it operates—in this case, as the following pages enumerate, the medical discourse of discovery surrounding the treatment and management of intersexed bodies. The second step is to consider how the emerging discourse of an intersexed community resists the dominant view of intersexed bodies as diseased or deformed bodies whose sexualities are therefore doomed to pathology.

Discovery

In the opening pages of her book *Beyond the Natural Body*, Nelly Oudshoorn points out that prior to the "discovery" of hormones in the early years of the twentieth century, women discussed neither sexuality/desire nor behavior/mood in terms of hormones: "We will never know precisely which words women used in those days to express themselves, but we know one thing for sure: women did not refer to hormones to explain their lives. Simply because the very word hormones did not exist in the nineteenth century."[15] Oudshoorn is not contesting the idea that women and men already thought of themselves as distinct and opposing genders/sexes. Indeed, the logic of her argument presumes a dialogue between research directions taken (and avoided) in science and what she calls "prescientific" ideas that are already present in culture.[16] Oudshoorn cites Aristotle's *History of Ani-*

mals and the ancient notion of "male gonads [as] the seat of masculinity" as evidence that from very early on in Western medical discourse, links between behavior and anatomy have been posited.[17] It is this long development of a theory of consistency between anatomy and gender that, Oudshoorn argues, set the direction for the study of hormones and their biological role in the development of gender.

How does the discovery of hormones, which Oudshoorn links primarily to the constitution of a biological binary between the sexes, relate to the treatment of intersexuality? The first and most obvious relationship is the idea that hormones produce phenotype. Many diagnoses of intersexuality are diagnoses of inappropriate phenotypes, that is, of bodily appearances that seem "ambiguous." Until the discovery of hormones, diagnoses of intersexuality were relatively unheard of. This is not to say that hermaphroditism or atypical genital features were altogether unheard of or that they went without notice; it is simply to state that however unusual these things may have seemed, they were not necessarily diagnosed as illnesses. More troubling than how to diagnose their health—and the precursor to the standard present practice of sex assignment for intersexed infants—was how to understand the desires of the hermaphrodite.[18] In the dossier contained in Foucault's publication of the Herculine Barbin story we see, in the discussion of Barbin's phallus, an inclusion of the properties of the clitoris. This discussion centers on the problem of aligning desire and use with biology: "As we shall see later when it is described, this organ was a large clitoris rather than a penis; in fact, among women we sometimes see the clitoris attain the size of the index finger."[19] Yet in Barbin's case, it was not the *size* of the clitoris that was the problem, rather it was her *use* of that organ in a relationship with the headmistress's niece that was the cause for alarm and impetus for the revision of her sex to male. In Barbin's account and in the accompanying dossier, the fact that most seems to disturb the physicians who presided over her case was that Barbin failed to desire the phallic power of the male, and, instead, used her own female body as a powerful possessor of the phallus. Because Barbin insisted on behaving as the possessor of the phallus, those who managed her case could only make her desire acceptable by reassigning her as the appropriate possessor of such power: a man.

The revision of hermaphrodites under such juridical controls accomplished the same goal as the present revision of the intersexual under current medical controls: placing desire firmly along an axis of heterosexuality. But if the juridical was so efficiently able to determine what kinds of desires a person had and what that said about his/her true sex, one might logically ask why Western culture shifted to surgical controls? The most obvious "drawback" of the juridical paradigm was that it entailed waiting until the hermaphrodite had matured to make a final determination or pronouncement on "his" or "her" sex. The appeal of surgical intervention, in contrast, is that in a matter of a few hours doctors can produce a sexed subject who will either function within the sanctioned bounds of heterosexuality or not—either way, the medical establishment will *know* what it is faced with: "male" or "female."

In the present, we no longer wait to find out how girls with large clitorises and boys with small penises will use their organs. Instead, we diagnose and "cure" them using a discourse of hormones and chromosomes and a practice of "routine" surgery. Girls with large clitorises and boys with small penises are "worked up" for endocrine "disorders." Etiologies are sought as to whether or not a definitive cause can be found; medical wisdom on the subject advocates clitorectomy and, sometimes, "trimming" of the labia minora to produce a "normal appearance."[20] In intersex management, even the removal of a small penis from a genetic male is referred to postoperatively and in counseling of parents as a "clitoral reduction," as this tactic helps to assure parents that they really do have a baby girl; it is commonly believed—and repeatedly written in medical texts on the subject—that the use of terms that suggest that the organ is a "phallus" will only confuse the parents. Because "reduction" and its alternative, "recession," sound like fairly benign procedures—much less gory sounding than "female circumcision," "infibulation," or "mutilation," for example—it is necessary to point out what the surgery actually entails. Lest it be thought that these surgical interventions are either minor or necessary to the health of the child, I draw attention to the following comments:

I don't think there is any questions [*sic*] that [the patient] has an isolated clitoral hypertrophy and that surgical revision would give her *the best cosmetic effect*.[21]

With pen and ink a U-shaped dorsal incision was marked out on the clitoris with the apex at the base of the pubis. With the glans under tension, the U-shaped incision was carried out around the dorsal aspect of the clitoris to the glans. The dorsal hood of skin was then removed and heavy dexon sutures were placed through the base of the crura of the enlarged clitoris. The *redundant* corpora was then excised dorsally. . . . The glans was then recessed into the infrapubic area with several fine dexon sutures and then the skin approximated as a new clitoral hood with interrupted fine dexon sutures.[22]

The above quotations are taken from my own medical files, which permits me to view this record not only as an external reader of a text, but also as one who has clear memories of the surgical event—I was seven—and the procedures that led up to it. It is worthwhile pointing out that "the best cosmetic effect" mentioned here is one that would please the five male doctors in charge of my surgery and that the decision regarding what constitutes "redundant" tissue was made while I was unconscious on the operating table. Effectively, everything except the glans was considered redundant. According to all the measurements taken, what they left was one-half centimeter of glans, which was then pushed backward into the surrounding flesh and sutured down. In terms of a body coming to bear meaning, this is a body that was quite literally bound and sutured down to a particular representation of absence. Most people are not built this way, because most people are not *built*.

The procedure outlined in this postoperative report is typical of the kind of surgery that intersexed children have been subjected to since the 1970s; I have several files in my possession that detail exactly the same procedure. Prior to the 1970s, intersexed children who were to be assigned female would not keep even the glans of the clitoris. That my generation and those who followed it have been allowed to retain the glans is a point that we are continually reminded to be thankful for by doctors who proclaim that we are the beneficiaries of a more modern and technically perfected procedure, not at all like those horrible days of total extirpation. That surgeons have always proclaimed their great advances is continually obfuscated in any commentary on the issue.

All such surgeries, whether they are feminizing or, more rarely, masculinizing, are implicitly heterosexualizing. This is true even when a child who is genetically male is assigned a female sex, for in spite of all the scientific questioning about whether or not homosexuality is biologically determined, it is only the *social role* of the intersexed child that matters. Ironically, it is the combination of the strict conviction that sex is natural and that gender is social that allows medical experts to assure parents that their XY-chromosome children assigned female will grow up to be completely heterosexual. This involves the finest hairsplitting dissemblance on the part of medical professionals who explain procedures and biology to the parents of intersexed children.

The discourse of hormones, and even of the chromosomal determination of sex, is at once amazingly rigid and ironically flexible. Although medical science follows the basic principle that the male sex is determined by a chromosome profile of 46 XY, its practitioners will nonetheless assure parents that their 46-XY children with small penises, severe hypospadias, or androgen insensitivity are really girls with confused biological information:

> With parents who know that the karyogram is 46 "XY" . . . we emphasize that the sex of a child is not only directed by the sex chromosomes. . . . When we talk about the sex organ of the child, we use only the female terms, for example: "The clitoris is too large and will be reduced leaving the top . . . intact; the labia are joined together and will be separated; the vagina is missing and will have to be constructed. . . ." We speak only about gonads, not testicles. . . . *Parents will feel reassured when they know that their daughter can develop heterosexually just like other children* and that male characteristics are impossible.[23]

The case posited above is the clinical profile of a person with partial to complete androgen insensitivity (AIS). As the name implies, androgen insensitivity—which used to be called "testicular feminization syndrome"—cannot be separated from the concept of hormones and what they are *supposed* to do. In this case, the idea is that male hormones, and the androgens such as progesterone and testosterone, create the phenotype that we recognize as that of male—that is, the presence of a penis, scrotum, and testicles.[24] Because testes produce estrogen as well as testosterone, these children, who respond quite typically to estrogen, tend to look typically female. In cases of partial androgen insensitivity, it may be possible for the clitoris to be deemed "enlarged," although in complete AIS this would not be the case as the body does not respond at all to the androgens that are presumed to affect the size of the phallus.

Prior to the advent of a discourse on hormones, intersexed children were designated and reared as girls without ever being diagnosed as intersexuals. In fact, prior to the establishment of endocrinology as a discipline, the absence of menstruation and the short or absent vagina of persons with AIS may have only made them remarkable women, but *not* malformed men or intersexuals. As women, should they be partnered with men, they would have been considered heterosexual, while if they had been partnered with other women they would have been considered homosexual. This set of designations would have been dependent upon a conceptualization of sexual orientation as a purely social phenomenon. However, since the "discovery" of chromosomes, sexual orientation has become much more essentialized as a scientific phenomenon. It is then an irony that according to its own standards, the socially heterosexual androgen insensitive person is a biologically homosexual person. The contradiction is not one that I have created; it is merely one that I am pointing out. Indeed, the issues around sexuality and genetics, hormones, "gay genes," and "gay brains" is so troubled by this scenario that some have begun to posit that AIS males, lacking androgen receptors, would not have masculinized brains and would, therefore, have typically feminine desires. That science has not yet been able to determine what a typically feminine or masculine desire is and that it cannot account for social lesbianism in genetic XY individuals is not highlighted in the literature on the subject of desire and the hermaphrodite.

The rise of science typified in the Enlightenment and post-Enlightenment discourse of "rational knowledge" has come to mean, in the case of individuals and their health, that medicine *informs* us of the reality of our bodies.[25] In the case of intersexuality, the ability of medicine to tell us what our bodies are for and about is exacted through violent means. Through an assertion that its fictions of hormones and chromosomes are facts that are not contingent upon historical and cultural contexts and exist independently of their applications, medicine is able forcibly to confine and contain intersexed bodies within disciplinary boundaries that did not exist before the late nineteenth and early twentieth centuries. Oudshoorn's text reminds us that the process of "discovery" was not a naive and neutral process; rather, this discovery was a deliberate course of study informed by what she calls "prescientific" ideas. Hence the great dividing line of so-called male and female hormones is predicated upon an already controlling idea of the binaristic and oppositional differences between men and women. The ossification of this polar difference certainly imbued medicine with more power to enforce the idea that intersexuals, as intermediary bodies, run against what John Money has referred to as "the phylogenetic scheme of things." As Foucault suggests in *The Birth of the Clinic*, "There is . . . a spontaneous and deeply rooted convergence between the requirements of *political ideology* and those of *medical technology*. In a concerted effort, doctors and statesmen demand, in a different vocabulary . . . the suppression of every obstacle to the constitution of this new space: the hospitals, which alter the specific laws governing disease."[26] Although I disagree with his use of the term *spontaneous* to describe this process of convergence, I agree with his analysis: namely, that the hospital, as a community of people who could know and ascertain "the truth," required full freedom to explore and enforce its ideas and discoveries. This freedom was, in fact, neither undirected nor neutral. Rather, the process of discovery had to conform to the already present mandates of domination and control within the political sphere.

In the context of sexuality and the sexes, discovery could have led down a path that would inform us that there was a broad range of human sexual diversity and potential; instead, it upheld the course toward an ever more narrow definition of "male," "female," and "normal." What had previously been controlled by juridical intervention—the birth of a hermaphrodite—became controled by a medical gaze that could enforce a pronouncement of disease and enforce a disciplinary "cure" capable of reducing the threat of a diminished set of differences between male and female, and one result was that of abetting the concurrent evolution of separate sexual identities: heterosexual and homosexual.

Working from Foucault's now famous argument that prior to the nineteenth century there were heterosexual and homosexual *practices* but not heterosexual and homosexual *people*,[27] it is possible to see that the movement of the management of hermaphrodites from the courts to the clinics coincides with the construction of stricter identity categories, pathologies, and norms. The intersexual, like the homosexual, came to be identified under a disease category for which a cure might be found and imposed, thus maintaining and privileging the industrial age's organization of the family, and of the roles of men and women within it.

Resistance

Because we now live in an age in which hormones and chromosomes are largely accepted as the biological marshals of sex, gender and sexuality,[28] it is easy to look upon the intersexed child's body as a "sick" one—one which is diseased and in need of "repair" or "corrective" measures. However, what I am positing in this chapter is that the treatments to which intersexed children are subjected constitute a violent imposition of cultural norms and restrictions on their bodies and behaviors. As such, this arguably punitive set of "corrections" cannot be justified by labeling intersexed bodies as "diseased." Rather, it is the culture around the child which is *dis-eased*, as it were, made uneasy by the child's intersex characteristics. Because the intersexed child's bodily configuration flies in the face of what are taken to be essential truths about males and females, about masculinity and femininity, and about heterosexuality and homosexuality, the intersexed child threatens all the borders that separate the normal from the abnormal, the powerful from the weak.

To try to separate what is really true about gender, sex, and sexuality from what is only provisionally true is larger than the parameters of my project here. I recognize, as Diana Fuss indicates in *Essentially*

Speaking, that to conceive of bodies, behaviors, and sexualities as culturally determined products that either conform to, or diverge from, "normal" and "essential" truths, is as dependent upon the linguistic intelligibility of the terms *man* and *woman, male* and *female, heterosexual* and *homosexual*, as are all essentialist arguments.[29] However, to be dependent upon the intelligibility of the terms is not necessarily to employ them for the purposes of re-creating the same. When I use the terms *heterosexual, homosexual,* or *lesbian,* to name a few examples, I do so because I recognize them as politically cogent categories and because the idea of "intersexuality," when set amid these terms, undoes much of their stability. When I describe someone as an intersexed woman or intersexed man, it is because that is how these people have described themselves to me. Each of us who has been diagnosed as an "intersexual" understands the term as a referent for a certain experience of pathologization, and although each of us may have a *roughly* equivalent, as in an equi*valent,* sense of the terms *man* and *woman,* the deployment of the term *intersex* transgresses the division of those terms and creates different, indeed "queer," territories and frontiers of meaning. These meanings are not bounded by and through strict categorization; what one intersexed person means by that individual's chosen self-description—pseudo-hermaphrodite, female pseudo-hermaphrodite, intersexed, intersexed male or female, man or woman—may be quite different from the next. Furthermore, there are different ways in which each individual may describe hirself (note my conflation here of the personal pronouns him and her) according to different contexts.

When, for example, I describe myself as a "dyke," there is implied in my understanding of the term a sense of political experiences of sexuality and desire, predicated upon an understanding of mixtures of masculinity and femininity in desire, that derives from Monique Wittig's assertion that lesbians are not women. I refuse the term *lesbian* because of its more popularly understood meaning of being a *woman-identified woman who loves other women.* As an intersexed person, I do not find that the concept "woman-identified" is a useful or accurate definition of myself. I also define myself as a dyke out of a certain political commitment, for I find that the label *bisexual* lacks the power to disconcert in the way that the label *dyke* does. To me, being a dyke is as much an attitudinal stance as one of desire or sexual practice, although the latter shapes my sense of myself as well. But the crux of my identification as a dyke comes out of being perceived as very "femme," a perception that has made me an easy target for the heteronormative medical discourse that has looked upon me since I was a child and said, "She is so feminine looking; we can't allow her to have those masculinized genitals." By taking on the identity "dyke" I can at least refuse to acquiesce quietly to the script that the medical establishment would place upon me.

When I call myself an "intersexed woman," in contrast, I refer to the dual experience of living in the world through an embodied position that has been pathologized and regimented in medical discourse and management, as well as perceived by the general public as "typically female." When I describe myself as "intersexed," I am positioning myself within a group that has, as yet, not acquired an intelligible field of signification. This latter point is both positive and negative, affecting how people understand and represent what an intersexed person is, and it often veers out of my control, particularly when the terms *intersex*, *dyke*, and *queer* converge in the media interviews in which I have participated. Unfortunately, even reports derived from interviews in which I am careful to construct my personal sexuality as an unintelligible frontier between different sexualities, ranging from "dyke" to "straight" and from "woman" to "intersexual," get reinscribed along a binary that elides the subtleties I have tried to signify. An interview in *XTRA*, a major Canadian gay and lesbian journal, that appeared with the subtitle "Queer Seven-Year-Old Was Turned into a Woman," remarks twice upon my marriage and status as a mother.[30] The article also reports that I "was born with the genitalia of both men and women." I was not born with the genitalia of both *men* and *women*; I was born with *child-sized* intersexed genitals. However, the reporter's comments show that without some point of articulation hinged on already accepted categories, the term "intersex" has no meaning to a lay readership. The subtitle, combined with the statements that imply that I am a woman who is married to a man, shows that the writer accepts the idea that the surgery made me a woman, and not, as I would hold, an intersexed person minus a few parts. The title and article seem to indicate that no matter what I may say about myself, people are free to interpret my surgery as having "made me a woman."

The acceptance of terms and what they signify in culture returns me to Judith Butler's argument in *Bodies That Matter*, which explains that people come to expect certain performances to follow from certain initial statements: "[T]he initiatory performative, 'It's a girl!' anticipates the arrival of the sanction, 'I pronounce you man and wife.' Hence . . . the peculiar pleasure of the cartoon strip in which the infant is first interpellated into discourse with, 'It's a lesbian!' . . . the queer appropriation of the performative mimes and exposes both the binding power of the heterosexualizing law *and its expropriability*."[31] Butler's statement leads me to wonder what the potential might be for the proc-lamation "It's an intersexual!" However, the expropriation of citational laws is much more difficult than simply overturning linguistic utter-ance. I recognize that Butler is partly engaged in wishful thinking and is not prescribing an easy subversion of norms, but a reminder that some bodies are controlled not just through language and meaning is in order here. Although the example of the *XTRA* reporter's miscon-struction of my sexuality and sexual identity is a powerful indication of the ability of people to subsume terms under an umbrella of mean-ing that makes sense to them, it says nothing of the violence expressed by the clinical enforcement of meaning upon intersexed bodies. How these complexities will play out in future articles and a popular notion of intersexuality are yet to be seen. What it means within the vocal group of intersexuals who comprise the Intersex Society of North America (ISNA) and the Intersex Society of Canada (ISCa) is that we exist in a constantly shifting discourse that can both evade and chal-lenge the medical control of our subjectivities, but that also risks an easy assimilation into anyone else's categories.

Domination

All intersexed infants and children with an XX karyotype and all those considered to have an "inadequate" phallus are assigned female.[32] Ac-cording to a 1992 article in the *Annals of Surgery,* 90 percent of in-tersexed infants are assigned a female sex.[33] Only those who are be-lieved to possess a phallus that matches an XY karyotype and a minimum size standard for heterosexual penetration are assigned male. The "heterosexual imperative [that] is inextricably linked to the treatment of intersexuality" is an imperative that operates as much to heterosexualize males as females.[34] This is evident in the fact that the goal of surgery on intersexed infants is to produce adults who will function as either female receptacles *for* the penis, or male possessors *of* the penis. Thus, it is only those males with hypospadias (a shortened urethra) on an otherwise adequate penis (one that measures greater than two-and-one-half centimeters at birth) who are assigned a male sex, and the hope is that they will grow up to have heterosexual, pene-trative sex. This hope is apparent in various follow-up studies, all of which focus attention on the ability of a greater percentage of patients to penetrate female partners while diverting attention from patients who identify their activities as homosexual or as nonexistent. Such studies often suggest outright that these latter "abnormal" cases are simply the result of extreme hormonal anomalies: "The development of the gender identity of the patients that had incomplete virilization at birth [six patients of eight] had a greater chance of disorders than that of the children with the [complete] androgen insensitivity syndrome ... these children have had a greater chance of prenatal brain androgynization, which may cause abnormal gender identity and gender role development."[35] This scenario hypothesizes the long-term outcome for a genetic male assigned a female sex and discusses the different possibilities for gender identification in those whose tissue has partial response to androgens versus those whose tissue has none. The principle being put forth is that sexual desire is determined, at least in significant part, by the effect of so-called male and female hormones upon the brain. The concern is that those genetic males with partial response might also have brains with a partial tendency to desire females as sexual partners; this is what would constitute the "abnormal gender identity" of such great concern and anxiety to the doctors. Thus, the question of why they would assign children to a female sex must remain a source of consternation for the medical pundits. Why then do they assign an overwhelming portion to the female sex?

The justification for the overwhelming assignment of intersexed children to a female sex—in addition to the preservation of fertility in genetic females—is that it is considered technically easier to make females than it is to make males. In a word, it is easier for the medical establishment to realize its view of heterosexual function by making a receptacle for the phallus; hence Dr. John Gearheart's thoughtless quip that it "is easier to make holes than build poles." Gearheart argues the uselessness of a micropenis: "A child who has a micropenis ... that's not going to be of use to him for sexual satisfaction, urination, ejaculation."[36] His concern is that the genetic male with a small penis is not going to be able to have appropriately penetrative heterosexual sex. What Gearheart fails to make explicit in his comments is that the amputated phallus and constructed vagina that replace the male genitalia are not going to provide sexual satisfaction for the child who is supposed to grow up to be a woman; they will only provide sexual satisfaction for her *presupposed* male lover. The surgery—like the declaration/command "It's a girl!"—presumes and commands a heterosexual future; it serves a masculinist set of demands. Paradoxically, however, this overdetermined fantasy of the child's future erases something essential from the definitions of maleness, femaleness and homosexuality. For if such a child matures to take a female lover, she will be "straight" at the chromosomal level and lesbian at the social level. If she takes a male lover, the opposite will be the case. How we define sexual identity categories in such scenarios thus becomes quite complicated, particularly for those who rely upon biological definitions of sexuality and sexual desire as the final arbiters.

The intersexed body, whether medically revised or left intact, flies in the face of taken-for-granted definitions of sexuality because an intersexed body cannot be contained under strict anatomical, functional or chromosomal categories. Hence, the behaviors that we normally ascribe to one or the other of only two possible sets of biological characteristics, male or female, cannot be strictly delineated as either heterosexual or homosexual. Intersexed bodies thus operate as an incommensurable frontier between and across sexualities and genders. As such, intersexuality as a threatening territory can only be conquered through the invasive surgeries that are used to make the bodies align with one or the other of the two recognized sexes. As Julia Epstein argues, "Suppression [of intersexuality] achieves its perfect form in 'excision,' and the Other's potential for subversive social arrangements is eradicated altogether. The varying approaches to gender ambiguity . . . suggest that the assignment of a place in or the expulsion from legitimate social enmeshment represents an ideological project, a particular and paradigmatic instance of the cultural construction of gender and one that reveals the powerful operations of homophobia in social practice."[37] Epstein pinpoints the homophobia evident in the surgical interventions that align intersexed bodies into neat sex and gender categories. For even when the revised intersexed person refuses to play by the rules and the wishes so vehemently imposed through families and medical professionals and thus turns out to assume what is at least socially a same-sex sexual orientation, medical, psychiatric, and "common sense" discourses can resort to labeling that sexuality as deviant. This definition, in turn, opens the way to explaining (away) the intersexed person's sexuality as either (a) a biological glitch stemming from the intersexed condition, or (b) a pathological response to their sexuosocial environment. Left unrevised, the intersexed body and its practices would defy categorization from external points of view.[38]

However, Epstein's notion that *all* of the intersexed body's ability to subvert social categories is erased by medical interventions has been contraindicated by the creation and establishment of an intersex community that has come together through the Intersex Society of North American and the Intersex Society of Canada. Likewise, I find it somewhat troublesome that Epstein bemoans the inability of "Others" to effect changes in homophobic cultural practices. Since when are intersexuals necessarily interested in subverting anything? There are some members of both ISNA and ISCa who are not interested in being welcomed under a queer rubric; indeed, some are quite vehemently opposed to the close associations that the founding members have made to the queer and transgendered communities. An additional question that Epstein does not consider is whether being born "different" necessarily means that one is "Other"? "Other" to whom? To be able to label someone as an "Other" is a privilege that goes unrecognized in Epstein's work. And however valuable Epstein's work may be, there is still an element in it that views intersexed bodies as "frontiers" in the very worst sense: as mascots for projects that intersexed persons, by Epstein's own definition as voiceless "Others," have had no say in defining. The same etiologies that may produce atypical genitals are also the most common causes of infertility, hence a large number of the general population share the same genetic, chromosomal, or hormonal makeups as those of us who are "intersexed." Are we all then "Others," or is being "Other," as opposed to "self-same," a label that is placed on us from those who think that they are not like us? What would happen if we imagined a world in which we might all be in some way intersexed? Epstein herself recognizes that "sexual ambiguity [sic] threatens the possibility of gender contrariety as the basis for social order and thereby threatens the hegemony of heterosexuality."[39] This is quite a promising kind of troublemaking. However, Epstein's argument is weakened by the assumption that the surgical artillery used to bring intersexed bodies under control is actually able to effect a permanent silencing of the community. The increased difficulty in subverting norms and the refusal by some intersexuals deliberately to embrace subversion is not equivalent to an absence of possibilities. Although it is absolutely true that social heternormativity assigns a legitimate space for persons as only one sex or the other, and although this is exacted upon the intersexed child's body with a scalpel, the control of the intersexed person's body can never be *total*, for the intricacies of both biology and identity are more complex, and a set of surgical practices can never entirely control them.

For example, my own surgery, which was explained to my father as an intervention that would ensure "normal sexual function as an adult,"[40] was not—however silencing it was for many years—an intervention that could control either my desires or my identity. In spite of the promise that the doctors made to my father, I did not turn out to be your average straight woman. I am always going to be an intersexed woman, and that is always going to complicate who I am and what I do; it makes it logically impossible to taxonomize me or my practices as deviant or pathological. This is where there is an "upside" for intersexuals seeking community, voice and identity: we are able to insist that however hard they may have tried, the surgeons could not *enforce* their measures over time because who and what we are (becoming) is more complex than what we look like. The "downside" for many intersexuals is that sexual function, in terms of normal physical response, has been impaired by the surgery and so, in that sense also, sexual normalcy becomes a cultural fantasy. In fact, in the latter sense, the surgery *creates* a sexual abnormality; it, however, is one that the dominant culture can live with, particularly in the case of the subjects that it overwhelmingly casts as female.

Decisions to alter an intersexed child's genitals are made in early infancy and childhood. Standard medical texts are promoting ever sooner interventions to the point that there is now some discussion of *in utero* gene therapy to obliterate some kinds of intersexuality. This type of gene therapy was proposed as a possible solution by Dr. Len Pensky at the November 1996 Canadian Bioethics Society meetings and has also been put forth by Dr. Maria New on ABC's *20/20* television special on congenital adrenal hyperplasia (CAH). The justification for making decisions so early in the child's development is based upon the declared interest in protecting children from the trauma of later medical and surgical interventions, which John Money and Margaret Lamacz have written may be perceived by the child as abuse.[41] I would strongly suggest, however, that the declared interest of protecting the child obfuscates the actual premises that inform current practices. Until quite recently in Canadian law, children were officially the chattel, or property, of their parents, and more specifically, of the father. Although those laws changed in the 1970s, social attitudes toward familial structures, evident in recent debates over corporal punishment, indicate that society still views children as the property of their parents. Hence, parents assume that they have the right to try to ensure that their children grow up "sexually normal." Because the objective in these cases is to make "normal," which is to say *heterosexual*, children, doctors advise early surgeries in the hopes that the child will have no memory of the surgery and may not ever have to be told about it. Children who have their testicles removed, as in the case of XY children assigned female, will be lied to, told that they have to take hormones because their ovaries did not function properly, or that their gonads were not properly developed. These children will not be told that they are genetic males who were born with functioning testes.[42] And at a 1996 ISNA educational seminar at a Manhattan hospital where these kinds of surgeries are performed, one surgeon responded to the charge that even very early surgeries could be traumatic by suggesting that in the future they might perform clitoral surgeries on children in the first twenty-four hours of life so that patients would have no memory of it and would not have to be told about it later.[43] Ethical issues about properly communicating with patients aside, this set of practices and recommendations indicates just how badly the medical world wants to erase intersexuality from the human spectrum, and how badly it wants to silence intersexed persons.

Is there a different world that we could imagine? A world in which intersexed children would not be forced into one sex or the other? Can we imagine a world in which we are not taxonomized and pathologized along axes of gender, sexuality, and desire? In my refusal to lay to rest the designation "intersexual" as a description of myself, I see myself as taking up a project inspired by Donna Haraway: "The refusal to become or to remain a 'gendered' man or woman, then, is an eminently political insistence on emerging from the nightmare of the all-too-real imaginary of sex and race."[44] Of course, the trouble with this kind of refusal is that people who have little knowledge or understanding of how "hermaphrodites" are managed in current medical and cultural practice are inclined to say "Cool!" when they find out that I make this kind of refusal. I have lost count of how many times people who should know better have fetishized my body and the bodies of other hermaphrodites as "cool." There is a cultural fascination with intersexuality which is derived from, and continues to promote, the intersexual as a mythological figure liberated from the bounds of gender and sex. For example, when I first came out as a hermaphrodite about six years ago, a local playwright was putting together a play called *The Whore's Revenge,* in which the main protagonist was a female prostitute with a big clitoris who, thus, could fulfill the homosexual fantasies of one of her clients. This representation of the whore as the vehicle of gay male desire was doubly troubling to me when an acquaintance who was also in attendance at the play's reading declared that my own intersexuality (which I then referred to as hermaphroditism) was "neat!"

In a larger social context, the fascination with "chicks with dicks" and the idea that intersexed persons have two complete sets of opposing genitals are not productive for those of us who live not as fantastic imaginary specters, but as "real" people. Kira Triea, of whom I spoke earlier, keeps as her "sign-off" on e-mail: "Don't quote Ovid to me!" This frustration—and it is one that I obviously share—comes from the sense that people are free to make intersexuals into anything that they want us to be. As we have not yet established any recognized or respected definition of ourselves, it seems ironic that even communities that rail against their own expropriation into "queer chic" have no problem writing us into their own fantasies.

This tension between the representation, eroticization, and appropriation of intersexuality for nonintersexed persons is similar to the heterosexual appropriation of lesbian sexuality in male heterosexual pornography. Likewise, the fact that people are creating and commodifying erotic images of intersexuality is no guarantee that they will support us in our battle against medical pathologization and interference. Furthermore, just as there is no guarantee that a heterosexual male who gets a kick out of lesbian images made palatable for his gaze will support "real" lesbians, there is no guarantee that the either producers or viewers of fetishized images of intersexuals will be supportive or understanding of a "real hermaphrodite." I would not mind being another person's fantasy so much if I were able to have some access to that fantasy as a reality. But because the appeal of the intersexed body is in fact predicated upon its taboo position, for straights, gay men and lesbians, or even queers to continue to fetishize the intersexed body as the ultimate "Other" is, I believe, irresponsible.

Is there a responsible way in which we could conceptualize the intersexed body? First, we need to locate our initial efforts at effecting change at the very first site of intervention, childhood. Intersexed adults are first intersexed minors who have been subjected to the wills of their families and doctors. Avoidance of surgeries serving no purpose except to make the intersexed child more appealing to parents and to their culture is a fine place to start reconceptualizing the intersexed body. However, more than simple avoidance of cosmetic surgery needs to occur if the lot of intersexed children/persons is substantially to change. We need to transform the way we think about our children's sexualities and welcome all possible sexual futures, not just heterosexual orientations, into our habitus. We need to wrest intersexuality from its taboo designation and make it into something that people can talk about, can experience as valid and be proud of being. This latter process is not something that others can do for us, although they can help to make it easier by being responsible and supportive listeners, parents, and medical professionals. Ultimately, however, it is up to those of us who are intersexed to refuse to be silent, to seize the name "intersexual" as our own and take away its pathologizing power. This is *our* frontier.

Notes

1. The larger debates around education and voting rights for women depended upon interpreting the sexes as radically different, with one suited solely for reproduction and the other suited for public life. Hermaphrodites, if allowed to continue to *choose* their sex, would have threatened the dawning discourse with regard to the stability of the distinct separation of male and female.

2. *Sodomite* and *sodomy*, as shown in Vern Bullough's collection *Sex, Society and History* (New York: Science History, 1976), were not specific terms at all, but rather terms that could apply to anyone at any time as long as what was being practiced was not reproductive sex. Thus, my use here should not be taken solely to signify a particular set of penetrative or receptive practices, although *sodomy might* actually refer to such practices in some cases; rather, I am simply indicating that the juridical model had no way of interpreting hermaphrodite eroticism as primarily reproductive, assuming as they did that hermaphrodites would not be able to reproduce.

3. The term *conceive* meaning, literally, to think of the idea of the child. It was believed by Aristotle and Plato that the blood passed through the brain of the male, acquiring intellect, before passing through the *vas* and becoming semen.

This is a gross reduction not only of Laqueur's detailed study, but also of the Platonic, Hippocratic and Aristotelian discourses on reproduction. However, as this chapter is not about classical medical approaches to sex, I am providing this gloss merely to indicate the *kind* of differences in sex and gender that one might expect to see discussed in these works.

4. The term *habitus* is taken from anthropologist Pierre Bourdieu's theorization of how a culture creates and signifies its own cultural meanings and conditions. There is a more detailed discussion of this term later in this chapter.

5. Marcel Mauss, *Sociology and Psychology: Essays*, trans. Ben Brewster (London: Routledge & Kegan Paul, 1950), 101.

6. Ibid., 102.

7. Judith Butler, *Gender Trouble: Feminism and the Subversion of Identity* (New York: Routledge, 1990).

8. See: Julia Epstein, "Either/Or, Neither/Both," *Genders* 7 (spring 1990): 99–142; Deborah Findlay, "Discovering Sex: Medical Science, Feminism and Intersexuality," *Canadian Review of Sociology and Anthropology* 32, no. 1 (February 1995): 25–52; Suzanne Kessler, "The Medical Construction of Gender," *Signs* 16, no. 1 (autumn 1990): 3–26; Marjorie Garber, "Spare Parts: The Surgical Construction of Gender," in *The Lesbian and Gay Studies Reader*, ed. Henry Abelove et al. (London: Routledge, 1993), 321–36.

9. A recent flurry of media reports following the publication of Dr. Milton Diamond's and Dr. Keith Sigmundsen's contact with the patient, John/Joan—whom Money used as his proof of gender mutibility—has shown that the ability to influence gender outcome is more complicated than a simple surgical intervention. The fact that the patient's parents had been raising two identical twin boys (until John lost his penis in an accident) and accepted/perceived their son as a boy, combined with the fact that John grew up with an identical, male twin have been completely overlooked in media reports such as Natalie Angier's *New York Times* article, which broke the story to a mainstream readership. The popular media have used the story to swing the pendulum to the "chromosomes determine sex" side of the argument and are all too pleased to report on the proof that biology is destiny in the John/Joan case. In both Money's approach and that of the popular media, a crucial error is made in that

they take a single case as the model that can set the standard for everyone else. Money evaluated the success of the gender revision according to whether or not the parents were convinced that John's genitalia had been reshaped to make an appropriate looking set of female genitalia; the news evaluates the failure of all gender revisions according to John's self-reports of dissatisfication. That John is one person with a special set of circumstances is entirely over-looked; this too, is the problem with the clinical management of intersexed children.

10. This statement echoes the Lacanian argument that the female/mother cannot *have* phallic power because her desire for the father subordinates her power to the imagined power of his phallus. However, my argument is not so much about a presumed end result of *being*, but rather, of how that process is effected. The Lacanian argument is relevant, of course; as I discuss later in the chapter, so many intersexed children are assigned a female sex and, as such, do not *have* meaning, do not have the phallus as the object of desire, but bear the cultural imposition of a desire for the phallus. By removing the phallus from the intersexed child assigned female, the desire for the phallus is reinscri-bed onto the body of the intersexual. The privilege of *having* the phallus is thus reasserted as the domain only of the certifiably male child/man with a "real" penis of an "adequate" size.

11. Anne Fausto-Sterling, "How Many Sexes Are There?" *New York Times,* 12 March 1993, op-ed section.

12. Kira Triea, Personal ISNA e-mail correspondence, 16 November 1996.

13. The argument explained here is taken from Pierre Bourdieu, *Outline of a Theory of Practice* (Cambridge: Cambridge University Press, 1995).

14. Susan Gal, "Between Speech and Silence: The Problematics of Research on Language and Gender," in *Gender at the Crossroads of Knowledge,* ed. Micaela di Leonardo (Berkeley: University of California Press, 1991), 177.

15. Nelly Oudshoorn, *Beyond the Natural Body: An Archeology of Sex Hor-mones* (London: Routledge, 1994), 15.

16. Ibid., 17–19.

17. Ibid., 17.

18. For several case studies on desire and hermaphroditism in the eigh-teenth and nineteenth centuries see Alice Dreger, "Hermaphrodites in Love," in *Science and Homosexualities,* ed. Vernon Rosario (New York: Routledge, 1996), 46–66.

19. E. Goujon, "A Study of a Case of Incomplete Hermaphroditism in a Man," in *Herculine Barbin: Being the Recently Discovered Memoirs of a Nineteenth-Century French Hermaphrodite,* trans. Richard McDougall (New York: Random House, 1980), 130.

20. Personal medical file, hospital number 10144, 19 June 1969.

21. Personal medical file, 25 October 1974, emphasis added.

22. Personal medical file, 18 March 1975, emphasis added.

23. F. M. E. Slijper et al., "Neonates with Abnormal Genitalia Development Assigned the Female Sex: Parent Counselling," *Journal of Sex Education and Therapy* 20, no. 1 (spring 1994): 14–15; emphasis added.

24. Although progesterone is considered a "female" hormone, its effect on the human fetus can be virilizing or androgizing.

25. I use the term *inform* in its double sense of education and imperative enforcement. This double sense of the conjoined function of "informing" a person or population of what to do is meant to gesture at the investments of scientists in "pronouncing the true sex" of the child.

26. Michel Foucault, *The Birth of the Clinic: An Archaeology of Medical Perception*, trans. A. M. Sheridan-Smith (New York: Vintage, 1975), 38–39.

27. Michel Foucault, *The History of Sexuality*, vol. 1, *An Introduction*, trans. Robert Hurley (New York: Vintage, 1977), 43.

28. Although there is a great deal of argument about hormones and their effect upon sexual desire, people generally accept the idea that hormones influence much of our behavior and that our chromosomes determine our biological sex.

29. This line of reasoning is derived from her argument concerning the linguistic intelligibility of categories in her chapter, "The 'Risk' of Essence," in *Essentially Speaking*, ed. Diana Fuss (New York: Routledge, 1989), 3–5.

30. Karen Hill, "The Surgeon's Knife: Queer Seven-Year-Old Was Turned into a Woman," *XTRA* 315 (21 November 1996): 24.

31. Judith Butler, *Bodies That Matter* (New York: Routledge, 1993), 232; emphasis in the original.

32. Some very masculinized XX infants were raised as males before karyotyping was a common diagnostic tool. However, present practice mandates the preservation of fertility in XX children and karyotype analysis is a routine diagnostic procedure.

33. Kurt Newman et al., "The Surgical Management of Infants and Children with Ambiguous Genitalia," *Annals of Surgery* 215, no. 6 (June 1992): 644–53.

34. Ellen Hyun-Ju Lee, "Producing Sex" (bachelor's thesis, Brown University, 1992), 35.

35. F. M. E. Slijper et al., "Neonates," 15–16.

36. Melissa Hendricks, "Is It a Boy or a Girl?," *Johns Hopkins Magazine* (November 1993): 10.

37. Epstein, "Either/Or," 130.

38. I know several unrevised intersexuals who identify themselves in different ways depending on their political/community affiliations, but this is a definition from inside and the definitions may be changeable. I know one unrevised hermaphrodite who identifies as the ultimate heterosexual because s/he has never met anyone like hirself, I know one who identifies as bisexual because of the social gender of the lovers she has taken on, and I know one who identifies as straight heterosexual, partly in the interests of adopting a child and partly because that is how her life looks to all viewers.

39. Epstein, "Either/Or," 130.

40. This promise, both according to my father's reports and to a much later entry in my personal medical files, was the major factor in promoting surgical intervention in my case.

41. John Money and Margaret Lamacz, "Genital Examination and Exposure Experienced as Nosocomial Sexual Abuse in Childhood," *Journal of Nervous and Mental Disease* 175, no. 12 (December 1987), n.p.; emphasis added.

42. A 1994 article in the *Canadian Medical Association Journal* advocating this policy of nondisclosure to the patient won the medical student essay prize for that year. See Anita Natrajan, "Medical Ethics and Truth Telling in the Case of Androgen Insensitivity Syndrome," *Canadian Medical Association Journal* 154 (1996): 568–70. It is obvious that the medical authorities still value paternalistic approaches to patient care and favor that approach over greater honesty or respect for patient intelligence and autonomy.

43. Dr. S., *ISNA Symposium, Mt. Sinai Hospital,* 18 May 1996, available through Intersex Society of Canada video archives for limited, personal viewing. Write to P.O. Box 1076, Haliburton, Ont., K0M 1S0.

44. Donna Haraway, *Simians, Cyborgs, and Women: The Reinvention of Nature* (New York: Routledge, 1991), 148.

5

Embodying a Transsexual Alphabet

Jill St. Jacques

> Paintings, tattoos or marks on the skin embrace the multi-dimensionality of bodies. Even masks ensure the head's belonging to the body, rather than making it a face. Doubtless, there are profound movements of deterritorialization that shake up the coordinates of the body and outline particular assemblages of power; however, they connect the body not to faciality but to becomings-animal.
> —Gilles Deleuze and Félix Guattari, *A Thousand Plateaus*

This text began as a performance.

Performance relates to paintings, tattoos, and skin in much the same way that printed words relate to a book, brushstrokes relate to a painting, or frame-by-frame exposures relate to a film: performance is a process in which the medium is skin, as opposed to paint, clay, or celluloid.[1] As far as the artist is concerned, the most important thing is the process—not the product. The end result is merely a relic, a shell that identifies activity. In the case of certain types of conceptual art, such as the columns of moving air Michael Asher has set up within different museum spaces, it could be said that the process continues within the form of the piece—but it would be hard to deny that the creator of the piece has moved on to other climes, having left his production machine behind.

Consider:

What were the writings of the transsexual Jan Morris,[2] before Morris became a transsexual, back when she still considered herself a man? Were they the writings of a man? Or were they the writings of a man-becoming-transsexual (-and-then-becoming-female)? How does Morris perceive these writings when she looks back on them? Relics of the past? The writings of a former self? There is no doubt that the writings still retain a life of their own, and retain the "voice of a man"—even though Morris has since made alterations to her former gender and her politics. Yet, the question remains: now that the thing referred to as Morris has moved on to a differently gendered expression, do the writings retain their "original" gender? And is Morris still connected to some degree to the gender of her former writings? Or, has the document of the performance taken on a new gender, a new politic—a politic one step removed from the performer?

Initially, the performance from which this document derived was a monologue/strip show/laboratory experiment examining the "scientific" Freudian theory that transsexuality is nothing more than the transsexual's "hysterical reaction." According to Freud, the transsexual performance was designed by the transsexer to win the love of an uncaring father by taking on the physical appearance of the father's love object. In Freud's view, these hysterical reactions were the same for both female-to-male as well as male-to-female transsexuals.[3] As the text for my performance evolved, however, I became less interested in the hypothetical hysterical reaction, and more interested in "moments-of-becoming."[4] Beginning with the belief that moving a theoretical text throughout my body could make such a text become flesh (while at the same time decomposing and transforming it into something else), I became obsessed with the notion that by passing information through my body and into the body of others, a text could shift its original structure, yet maintain its particular flavor.

There were several theoretical influences inspiring my aims from the start—the first of whom was the French structuralist Roman Jakobson. I liked Jakobson because his early work concerned functions of "poeticity" in grammatical structures.[5] It was Jakobson's suggestion that language uses "shifters" to disengage the metonymic (contiguous) structures of linguistic arrangement. Jakobson also asserted that shifters enable individual speakers to engage the flow of language and to use it as if it were their own property, while at the same time packaging their message to "fit" into the code of the addressee. In addition, Jakobson asserted that language was only used to a fraction of its potential, and that for the sake of "order" language was normally limited to the most regulated of functions (to serve the metonymic order).[6] I was interested in seeing how Jakobson's theory of poeticity applied when used as a vehicle to understand the reorganization of both the transsexual body and transsexual text as an open-ended structure with metamorphosis (and the subsequent acquisition and dispersal of knowledge) as its goal, and I wanted to construct a critical/performance text that mirrored this transsexual reorganization—that is, a text that went through the same process as the process it was describing.

To make matters even more complicated, I soon added another ingredient to my ungainly intellectual stew—the concept of *rhizome*, as described by the French theorists Gilles Deleuze and Félix Guattari, who saw information as reproducing itself in much the same way as organic rhizome structures do, burrowing and boiling underground. What Jakobson did for linguistics, Deleuze and Guattari did for subjectivity. Instead of using poeticity as a shifter to restructure language, Deleuze and Guattari used poeticity and language to subvert the subject:

The linguistic relation between the signifier and the signified has, of course, been conceived in many different ways. It has been said that they are arbitrary; that they are as necessary to each other as the two sides of the same leaf; that they correspond term by term, or else globally; and that they are so ambivalent as to be indistinguishable. In any event, the signified is thought not to exist outside of its relationship with signifier, and the ultimate signified is the very existence of the signifier, extrapolated beyond the design. There is only one thing that can be said about the signifier; it is Redundancy, it is the Redundant. Hence its incredible despotism, and its success.[7]

Deleuze and Guattari view the most flexible forms of language as nonspecific life forms that constantly need to flee the bonds of definite categorization in order to thrive. According to them, clusters of information are constantly copulating and spreading out—much like rhizome structures of plant life exploding underground. A good example of rhizome would be the explosion of fungal activity that takes place beneath the fruit of a mushroom. This fungal activity has no identifiable shape or form, yet as the fungus decomposes other organisms beneath the earth the mushroom thrives, shooting up its reproductive fruit. The thing we see above the ground and identify as "mushroom" is merely the reproductive organ of the rhizome that is exploding underground. When the mushroom reaches the end of its reproductive phase, the rhizome disintegrates, as does the reproductive organ. This structure resembles information-in-the-raw, in that when information becomes closed off or shut out from other information the rhizome activity halts—at which point the information has a tendency to stagnate, to insulate itself—and become a fascist pocket, carefully policing its well-defined boundaries and guarding them from any attack or threat to its status quo. As Deleuze and Guattari explain it, "Rats are rhizomes. Burrows are too, in all of their functions of shelter, supply, movement, evasion, and breakout. The rhizome itself assumes very diverse forms, from ramified surface extension in all directions to concretion into bulbs and tubers. When rats swarm over each other. The rhizome includes the best and the worst: potato and couchgrass, or the weed."[8]

Rhizome structures smack of transsexuality, in their rawest moments of becoming. The "trans" elements of the linguistic rhizome are "shifters"; they allow the rhizome of identity to slide between male-to-female, female-to-male, and so on. Yet, what is the thing that slides around and between male and female, and, more important, what are the other points the shifter may well be shifting among and between? Are male and female the only possibilities? This would be a productive question, were it not for the awkward observation that transsexuality has no medium point, no "trans central station." Likewise, the identity rhizome has no fixed platform of operations, whether male or female. In addition, the gender polarity of male and female does not exist as anything more than a hypothesis, a diversion, a pastime—something the transsexual-becoming-transsexual falls back on only when other avenues of expression fail. If we agree that male and female are not preordained points on a binary pole, but, rather, two interesting possibilities of representation out of many possibilities, we reach the active schizo state of transsexual existence—both textually and performatively speaking.

Given such a schizo modus operandi, I hoped in my performance to run the tablets of linguistic plurality through my body and the schizophrenic "body" of the viewers as a whole,[9] engaging the rhizome of transsexuality that runs from subject to subject—while at the same time avoiding the endorsement of some kind of "transsexual bureaucracy" at all costs. The absolute identification of transsexuality and the subsequent "that's it" categorization of its components would stifle the rhizome, and qualify its moment-of-becoming, thereby limiting it to a Kafkaesque claustrophobia that, instead of expanding the borders of sexuality, would instead set up the parameters of a "trans central station," from which nobody would come or go without the stamp of approval.

Perhaps, by identifying "bureaucracy" in the Deleuzian sense, we can see the dangers involved:

It is not sufficient to define bureaucracy by a rigid segmentarity with compartmentalization of contiguous offices, an office manager in each segment, and the corresponding centralization at the end of the hall or on top of the tower.

For at the same time there is a whole bureaucratic segmentation, a suppleness of a communication between offices, a bureaucratic perversion, a permanent inventiveness or creativity practiced even against administrative regulations. If Kafka is the greatest theorist of bureaucracy, it is because he shows how, at a certain level (but which one? it is not localizable), the barriers between offices cease to be "a definite dividing line" and are immersed in a molecular medium (milieu) that dissolves them and simultaneously makes the office manager proliferate into microfigures impossible to recognize or identify.[10]

By cutting through the underpinnings of bureaucratic language, the transsexual body becomes not a system with set parameters, but rather a location of activity, a nexus of informatic copulation. Such transsexual vortices are similar to the rhizomes Deleuze and Guattari describe in *A Thousand Plateaus*. In considering such nexes, the term *intent* looms vital, as well as the question of precisely who or what is "intending"; for there is a possibility that the "intender" may, in fact, be a multiplicity or rhizome in and of itself.

If language is premised on the agreement that meaning may or may not exist, then sexuality is based on a similar agreement about gender: to what degree and how much, maleness and femaleness will be utilized—and with what nuances—are all variables. A combination of factors decides whether sexuality is seen as just a plain fuck or an experience of religious intensity. When a self-defined straight boy copulates with a self-defined straight girl, their encounter is governed by an implicit agreement as to role, representation, and intensity. The degree to which they perform within their gender roles will denote the "success" of the sexual adventure; how much dick, how quick the climax, whether or not he calls the next day, or whether he breaks down after intercourse and begins to cry (which can be seen as either "sensitive" [increase-of-femininity] or "wimpy" [decrease-of-masculinity]). Perceived rules of behavior are expected to be observed, or crisis arises. If the straight boy who picked up the straight girl at the Bruce Springsteen concert suddenly appears at the foot of the bed dressed as Madonna, there will probably be trouble—unless the straight girl has a certain amount of flexibility. In the same fashion, when the seasoned leather daddy lies down with the teenage speedfreak he purchased with a quarter-bag of methamphetamine, or when the vanilla dyke gets fistfucked by the raging butch, there is a scripted space for their sexual performance. It is at the point that signifiers and definitions get confused, or "bent," that new possibilities arise.

Thus, every step I took with both text and performance of my original text reminded me I was no transsexual Überfrau or Übermensch.

In fact, every step I took to unite my flesh with the pluralistic nature of language resulted in the acute awareness of my own "creatureness," and a dawning sexual/semiotic exhaustion. In the words of Ferdinand de Saussure, "I am more and more aware of the immense amount of work required to show the linguist *what he is doing* . . . the utter inadequacy of current terminology, the need to reform and, in order to do that, to demonstrate what sort of an object language is, continually spoil my pleasure in philology."[11]

I began to rethink my goals. Was it such a radical step to posit gender as a type of rhizomatic philology? Certainly, if other political groups around me defined my gender for me, there was some stake in making this my battle cry: to make sure inadequate definitions did not imprison me, and so on. I came to the conclusion that if identity was composed of a plurality of genders (rather than one of essential gender), this was a crucial question—especially if I defined myself as transsexual-becoming-transsexual.
    Not man.
    Not woman.
    Not man-becoming-woman.
    Not woman-becoming-man.
    Transsexual.
    In the way that bats navigate in caves, or that rivers flow around rocks, language becomes the rudder that steers a course—to warn other creatures of approach, to identify friends and comrades, or even just to enjoy the sound of your own voice singing in the dark:

A rhizome ceaselessly establishes connections between semiotic chains, organizations of power, and circumstances relative to the arts, sciences, and social struggles. A semiotic chain is like a tuber agglomerating very diverse acts, not only linguistic, but also perceptive, mimetic, gestural, and cognitive: there is no language in itself, nor are there any linguistic universals, only a throng of dialects, patois, slangs, and specialized languages. There is no ideal speaker-listener, any more than there is a homogenous linguistic community. Language is, in Weinrich's words, "an essentially heterogeneous reality."[12]

    I presume we all agree that the root of language is desire.
    From desire comes speech, singing, music, and the representation of desire, which signifies its components with an alphabet. Yet, at the point we agree that the nature of existence is not binary, but plural, a fundamental difficulty occurs. To construct a pluralistic text-self utilizing an "alphabet" as it is known under the present contexts is a contradiction in terms.

Webster's Ninth New Collegiate Dictionary gives us this definition:

alphabet ... **1a:** a set of letters or other characters with which one or more languages are written esp. if arranged in a customary order **b:** a system of signs and signals that serve as equivalents for letters **2:** RUDIMENTS, ELEMENTS.[13]

Which leaves us to wonder:

What are these elements rudiments of? Where did they come from, these elements, rudiments? Is it possible to trace them back, like bits of breadcrumbs strewn along Hansel's and Gretel's path, to a home where gingerbread cookies once danced in circles, the childhood dream, mice singing cheerfully/defiantly from the cupboards as you lay in your bed in pain, stinging from your father's/mother's belt? Is it possible to trace these rudiments back to god's own Disneyland, where good is good, evil is evil, male is male, female is female and somewhere Plato's Ideal Book really exists? Do we agree that these principal bits are all chips off the principal block; rudiments of the rudiment, elements of the element?

Or, is it possible that they are merely relics, in fact, of a previous decomposition? Like the penis of the scientist Brundle in David Cronenberg's 1986 remake of *The Fly*—I am thinking of the scene where Brundle is transforming from Brundle into Brundlefly, and his penis falls off. He looks at his fallen organ casually, and says: "What's this? Another relic." Brundle realizes he is becoming something more than Brundle, and that his sexuality is taking on unknown rhizomatic (and possibly dysfunctional) dimensions. Because Brundle is aware that his physiognomy is changing, he is nonplused—aware that his situation may get either better or worse. With Brundle, there is an eerie (perhaps "scientific") detachment from his own plight. This detachment could be seen as inhuman, except that Brundle is already part fly, part human, or fly-becoming-human, or human-becoming-fly.[14] He is also flying apart. At the grizzly end of the movie, Brundle enters the transformer again in hopes that the computer will straighten out his chromosomal confusion, but the ensuing techno-disaster leaves Brundle's misshapen head part fruit fly, part scientist, and part transformer canister. Ultimately, Brundle's head is splattered apart with a shotgun wielded by his girlfriend—who at least has her identity perfectly aligned with the norm.

In this fashion, a Brundlefly has left its original binary canister to spread itself out in many directions, leaving us to wonder if Brundle ever really did exist—or was he/it merely Brundlefly all along?

Perhaps *Webster's New Ninth Collegiate Dictionary* gives us a hint when it comes to interrogating the genealogy of an alphabet's "rudiments, elements." In the entry immediately preceding "alphabet," the dictionary defines the concept of the supreme binaristic coupling—the "alpha and omega"[15]:

alpha and omega . . . **1:** the beginning and ending **2:** the principal element.[16]

Perhaps the alpha-alphabet is comprised of only one alpha-and-omega bit.

Perhaps a third definition should be: **3:** mythical.

Perhaps the sound of gender-becoming-rhizome or alphabet-becoming-language is the sound of one hand clapping.

I would like to suggest that concepts such as alphabet and alpha-and-omega rely on the use of arbitrary signs and signifiers in order to function. It is only by a process of mutual resignation (and assignation) that we agree the letter *A* is not the letter *B*, or that "beginning" is not "ending." To create our language, we set aside an ever-present yearning toward poeticity, blocking out realms of possibility, like a warden sealing off all possible routes of escape from a prison. The problem is, when we use a male-female alphabet to express transsexuality, we lose our shifters among false conclusions, conventional nomenclature, and bureaucratic process. The dilemma occurs because the metonymic chain is faulty, beginning with the slippery assumption that alphabet and alpha-and-omega (*a*) exist to be employed, (*b*) at the point of employment reach completion, and (*c*) at the point of completion become "meaningful" (*a–b–c*?). On the contrary, in a transsexual alphabet, meaning at the end of the chain might not exist, except as a possible representation of pluralistic meaning, replete with connections. This is in much the same way the letter *A* in the traditional male-female alphabet represents an idea of a rudiment or an element of an alphabet—except that in the transsexual alphabet there is no first letter *A* because there is no original myth: "There is no mother tongue," say Deleuze and Guattari, "only a power takeover by a dominant language within a political multiplicity. Language stabilizes around a parish, a bishopric, a capital. It forms a bulb. It evolves by subterranean stems and flows, along river valleys or train tracks; it spreads like a patch of oil."[17]

This may seem a radically utopian approach, which of necessity involves a certain amount of risk—similar to the risk of becoming-transsexual. It seems an optimistic stance at best to deal with reality by deterritorializing what most people consider to be at the center of it: identity (and often, gendered identity).[18] The risk occurs when optimism collides with the bleak resignation of those who have already formed their own fascist empires, composed of rigid gender stereotypes. As Deleuze and Guattari often observed, active rhizomes are often seen as a threat by fascist arrangements of control.

Alphabet and alpha-and-omega smack of centrality, declaring themselves to exist at the heart of language and being. The alphabet, for example, would have us believe that without it, there is no language. The alpha-and-omega observes a similar rationale:

"Within me is completion. Without me there is nothing."

Both approaches are closed corridors, positivist refuges, metonymic regimes that react as if they are already under siege. Thus they have created walls around their citadels—walls to be policed and defended, admitting only those with proper identification codes, attempting to keep the challenge to their supremacy at bay—and, most important:

Both definitions are vulnerable to subversion.

Historically, the existing definitions of transsexuality have been devised by political factions whose goals in defining transsexuality were in the interest of their cause. In the case of 1970s lesbian separatists, the goal of defining transsexuality was to minimize the threat of "outside" definitions of, as well as access to, femininity. Gay men also showed a propensity to dismiss transsexuality as "drag" or "camp," thereby distancing themselves from the explosive transsexual rhizome that called the significance of the phallus into question. Yet, it has been pointed out to me, with great impact, that this "conspiracy theory" regarding transsexual definition is a paranoid reaction. It also highlights an interesting dispute within the so-called gay community, in which separatist lesbians and gay daddies are seen two binary sides of a homosexual pole, with transsexuals lurking dubiously in the middle. Nonetheless, by brutally attacking transsexuality with confused definitions, feminists such as Mary Daly and Catherine Millot, scores of clinical psychologists, and talk-show hosts at large have succeeded in muddying the pool of transsexual discourse with their own ridiculous arguments. These political wars between gay and straight bureaucracies have managed to categorize transsexuality in order to fit it within the perimeters of their own bureaucratic codes, using the binary languages they understood to define and straitjacket a nonbinary subject. Rather than dismiss these political naysayers out-of-hand, I have chosen instead to investigate their bureaucratic forms so that I might perhaps give utterance to an alphabet that defies bureaucratic definitions such as this one:

The male transsexual is someone who has always felt himself to be a woman. When dressed as one, he easily passes for one. He is feminine, but not effeminate. He takes no sexual pleasure from wearing women's clothes. While he is attracted to men, he does not consider himself to be a homosexual: men please him inasmuch as he feels himself to be a woman, and only if they are heterosexuals. In his love relations he can never tolerate any interest shown in his penis. If he masturbates it is in a feminine way, for example by pressing his thighs together, and without touching his organ.[19]

To which one might reply:

But how can one still identify and name things if they have lost the strata that qualified them, if they have gone into absolute deterritorialization?[20]

The same deterritorializing devices of rhizomic deconstruction employed to subvert a closed alphabet/language circuit can also antagonize polarized definitions of gender—in particular, the "gender" of transsexuality. As I have attempted to suggest, the state of gender, like the state of "meaning," is mythical. Relationships or states implying innate systems of gender such as male and female (or innate "subcultures" such as homosexual, heterosexual, and transsexual) are also mythical. When such scripted relationships or states are referred to as "transsexuality," yet contain caveats of innate male or female essence (such as "male-to-female transsexual," or, "female-to-male transsexual"), these circuits find themselves particularly open to subversion.

Why?

Because the initial state of male or female is mythical, and therefore it is impossible for the male to ever become female, or for the female ever to become male; and even if she or he did what's the point, if one myth simply exchanges its trappings for the wardrobe of another? In contrast, it is the state of becoming that never becomes fascist, never becomes an empire unto itself, alpha-and-omega, complete. The possibility of Brundlefly is the thing that exists in (e)migration between the two transformation canisters. Transsexuality as a state is never completely manifest. As soon as the shifter becomes fluid, it skips among records, patois, vocabulary.

Choosing to form an identity from the myth of absolute gender (as if the myth preexisted the *initial desire to live it out*) is to raise an identity from a foundation of grandiose denial. Phallus-or-lack-thereof, alpha-or-omega, and especially male-or-female are concepts that are centralized, regulatory, and designed not for communication, but to control identity through an ethic of binary fear.

We are not born into an initial state.

There are no initial states of anything. Before male, female, and transsexual ever existed on this particular planet (in what is generally considered by many to be this specific place and time), there existed a heady state of hermaphroditism. Yet, hermaphroditism is also not an essence, not a "principal bit." The fact is, we are all transsexuals, no matter what we say—even if only by proxy, because we are all sliding through self-defined sieves of male and female. Yet the sieves themselves are full of holes, connections and decomposition. The sieve today may not be the same sieve it was yesterday. Time and class move through the sieves, both connecting and disassociating.

Expansion.

Without room to breathe, the rhizome cannot expand, and the root structure develops tumors. Within the context of the male, female, and transsexual arrangement, the transsexual process is often viewed not as a "work in progress"—but as a performance with an end, a "completed work" by which one gender "becomes" the other. In contrast, a transsexual alphabet is a fight against completion, a fight against enclosure within a binary alphabet of alpha and omega, a gender always beginning with the one and ending with the other.

This is why a transsexual alphabet might be viewed as a quixotic venture. The moral of the story: Icarus never reaches the sun, Lancelot never finds the Grail, and Brundlefly gets his head blown apart with a shotgun.

So what?

Writing has nothing to do with signifying. It has to do with surveying, mapping, even realms that are yet to come.[21]

Letters or rudiments composing the transsexual alphabet are moments-of-becoming. Opening into possibility, connected by threads of desire, a desire-to-become, a transsexual alphabet has no first and last letter, no alpha and omega. Transsexual letters operate from several positions at once, spawning a plurality of gender and a multiplicity of possibility. If gender is indeed a performance enacted to fulfill the thirst of our own desire, it stands to reason that every once and a while the subject will stand naked between genders, viewing itself from different points of view, desire running through its every pore, boiling and burrowing through sieves of identity, down corridors of possibility. Like rhizome, a transsexual alphabet is becoming.

Notes

A special thank you to Kirsi, Karin, and Joe.

1. During my performance, the skin performing the action was transsexual skin at the time. It is my premise that transsexuality is an activity that is constantly deterritorializing, yet reterritorializing in duration and intensity of gender. An interesting case can similarly be made that duration is a fundamental connection between painting, tattooing, throwing a pot, filming a scene.

2. Morris is a famous British war correspondent turned transsexual travel writer.

3. Phallic approval.

4. For Deleuze and Guattari, moments-of-becoming are moments of possibility, when codes copulate and exchange information (which is sexed): "Even blacks, as the Black Panthers said, must become-black. Even women must become-woman. Even Jews must become-Jewish (it certainly takes more than a state). But if this is the case, then becoming-Jewish necessarily affects the non-Jew as much as the Jew. Becoming-woman necessarily affects men as much as women" (Gilles Deleuze and Félix Guattari, *A Thousand Plateaus*, trans. Brian Massumi [Minneapolis: University of Minnesota Press, 1987], 291). Yet, who does it affect when a man or woman becomes a transsexual (especially if transsexuality is a transit point as opposed to a permanent location)?

5. Roman Jakobson, "What Is Poetry?" in *Selected Writings*, trans. M. Heim (The Hague: Mouton, 1981), 3: 40–50.

6. Although he did not invent the term, Jakobson's work on shifters (I, you, we, etc.) questioned the idea of personal subjectivity in language. How do you become "you"? Because "he" said so. See "Shifters, Verbal Categories, and the Russian Verb," in *Selected Writings*, 2: 130–34, 136, 146.

7. Deleuze and Guattari, *A Thousand Plateaus*, 66.

8. Ibid., 7.

9. The audience is another form of rhizome.

10. Deleuze and Guattari, *A Thousand Plateaus*, 214.

11. Ferdinand de Saussure to Antoine Meillet, Letter of January 4, 1894, cited in Jonathan Culler, *Ferdinand de Saussure* (Ithaca, N.Y.: Cornell University Press, 1986), 24; emphasis in the original.

12. Deleuze and Guattari, *A Thousand Plateaus*, 7.

13. "Alphabet," *Webster's Ninth New Collegiate Dictionary* (Springfield, Mass.: Merriam-Webster, 1991), 75.

14. Brundle is able to become fly and fly is able to become Brundle with the aid of a powerful computer that unlocks the secret "language" of DNA strands, then reforms them in a transformer chamber elsewhere. Yet, when a fly enters the transformer chamber, the computer becomes "confused"—it melds the two DNA strands together to become Brundlefly, a creation that the movie implies is unsuccessful—similar to the way clinical medicine views transsexuals who cannot make the "transformation" from male-into-female or female-into-male, but become "stuck" in the gray area in between.

15. A coincidence? Freud said there were none.

16. "Alpha and omega," *Webster's Ninth New Collegiate Dictionary*, 75.

17. Deleuze and Guattari, *A Thousand Plateaus*, 7.

18. People usually assign themselves a relationship to reality based on a premise of gender: (*a*) he was a man caught in a mid-life crisis; (*b*) she died an unhappy woman; (*c*) he hoped one day to reconcile himself with his father. Confusion ensues when the statement becomes "she died an unhappy man," or "he hoped one day to reconcile herself with their father." Yet, this is a goal of transsexual alphabetizing, as well as of rhizome language.

19. Catherine Millot, *Horsexe* (Paris: Autonomedia, 1983), 2. Obviously, this "definition" of a transsexual is about as accurate as describing a tomato as "a red round thing," or defining a lesbian as "a woman who has a deadly fear of men, and therefore seeks to rid existence of all vestiges of anything 'male'; the separatist lesbian only has sex with other separatist lesbians, and when she does so she never uses a dildo or any other object that resembles a phallus or penis." Such definitions are, obviously, anthropological at best. At worst they are degrading, and grossly inadequate.

20. Deleuze and Guattari, *A Thousand Plateaus*, 70.

21. Ibid., 4.

6

The Outlaw Sensibility in the Arts
From Drag and Leather to Prose,
the Mythology of Stonewall, and a Defense of Stereotypes

John Rechy

Please do not understand me too quickly.
—André Gide, *Corydon*

The question persists: Is there indeed a gay sensibility? (I use the word *gay* deliberately here and elsewhere for reasons explained later.) Yes, there is such a sensibility, and at its best it confounds the entrenched norm, stirs the stagnant mainstream, proclaims our presence, and asserts the proud defiance of the outlaw who challenges unjust laws.

What creates this unique sensibility?

We are the only minority born into the opposing camp. Nongay blacks are born into supportive black families; so are other minorities into theirs. We are born into a heterosexual world, the opposing camp—call it "enemy territory." We become strangers in a strange land, sinners in the eyes of religionists, criminals in the eyes of some lawmakers—that is, outlaws.

That early separation forces the homosexual into roles and camouflage in order to survive a hostile environment. In later life that separation defines a prominent aspect of the gay sensibility. It includes a terrific sense of dramatic presentation that veers at times toward extremity. We might even call it gay theater. Let's locate three powerful manifestations of that aspect of the gay sensibility—in the drag queen, the "leatherman," and the gay "macho."

Emphatically not a parody of women, the drag queen is a creation unto herself. Her flamboyant drag is a costume, not mimicry. It is brazen, unavoidable, superb at its best. One might even call it an elaborate uniform worn by a most distinctive, if unconventional, army that constantly disorients the rigid concept of only two allowed "genders."

On a seemingly opposite extreme in this theater of visual confrontation is the leatherman—only "seemingly opposite" because he is profoundly linked to the queen. Both share an awesome knowledge of the decorative power of sequins. Although I have long questioned and continue to question what I see as the ritualized self-hatred in gay S/M, a charade of heterosexual oppression, I admire the bold glamour of its uniform, silver on black, an intricate crisscross of glittery designs. A mainstay on our horizon, the doggedly "macho" leatherman is as easily identifiable as "gay" as is the queen in highest beaded drag.

Some years back I stood posturing shirtless on a street corner. "Oh, hon," a queen said, with the profound wisdom that God grants only to queens, "loosen up. Your muscles are as gay as my drag." Indeed, iron-pumped muscles are as exaggerated a form of decoration as is high drag, high leather. It may be that both pay homage to cauterized wounds.

Take a walk down Los Angeles's Santa Monica Boulevard or San Francisco's Castro Street, or through New York's East Village, and you will see, resplendent, a third figure of this unique gay sensibility, a newer figure, born—oh, terrific irony—out of a strict aversion to looking "gay": the gay macho. The body is by Soloflex. The outfit? Levi Strauss worn as arrogantly if it were Versace. The walk is defined by a strict avoidance of swishing; the result is a grand gay strut, part Madonna, part Clint Eastwood.

These figures are our unique inventions, to be acknowledged because they proclaim that we are here, assertively visual, despite myriad denunciations, and because they assert on the frontlines of outlaw extremity that—goddammit!—in many respects we *are* richly different, and so what?

Early in our lives secret longing clashes with demanded "acceptable performance"—that is, with the established heterosexual modality. That accounts for yet another powerful manifestation of the gay sensibility: its reconciliation of seeming contradictions, not unlike those that exist among the queen, the leatherman, and the gay macho.

Our literature abounds with examples of this duality. William Burroughs's orgiastic anarchy is contained within a highly conceptualized form. Jean Genet's super-hung studs easily become drag queens. Carson McCullers uncovers a very special beauty in grotesquerie, and grotesquerie in beauty. Truman Capote writes about criminals, and he does so in his high-drag style, not unlike the effect of shimmery darkness in Djuna Barnes's prose. Allen Ginsberg celebrates angel-headed hipsters—and does so in powerful literary low drag.

Much of our prose, especially that by men, reflects elements of gay-bar cruising: seductive, full of subtle messages of constant courtship—

Edmund White and Andrew Holleran endlessly flirt with their readers. Dennis Cooper's protagonists long to love the objects they violate.
Gore Vidal's cool intellect contains a tone of trashy "dishing." (Vidal
strongly denies the existence of a "gay sensibility." Yet in a television
interview he provided a hilarious inadvertent example of it, he said
that when homosexuals start talking to him about a "gay sensibility"
he reaches for his "revolver.")

Tennessee Williams's tough Stanley Kowalski (can't you see him in
a leather bar?) is as gay as is frail Blanche DuBois (who is more than
just a bit of a fading queen)—and let's note that the swoony Blanche
and the bruised macho Stanley could have been created only by a gay
writer; both in their respective extremes are clearly inspired by a gay
sensibility.

The gay sensibility does not in any way restrict the artist from illuminating *all* aspects of human experience; indeed, it may be enriched
by a broadened perspective. Indeed, there is more astute revelation of
heterosexual relationships in Marcel Proust's *Remembrance of Things
Past* than in all of Philip Roth's aggressively heterosexual male explorations. Pedro Almodóvar, André Gide, Virginia Woolf, Rainer Werner
Fassbinder, and Genet—these artists have all broadened the exploration of sex roles by examining their interchangeability. Oscar Wilde's
Dorian Gray is as much a rake who seduces women as he is a gay
narcissist who entices elegant queens. Though he denies it, Edward
Albee is a master of such camouflage: his Martha and George in *Who's
Afraid of Virginia Woolf?* are as believable as a gay couple as they are as
a straight one, especially when played with such campy bitchiness by
Elizabeth Taylor and Richard Burton.

Oh, there was a time in our recent history—the fifties, the sixties,
even the seventies—when homosexual acts even in private might result in imprisonment for years, even life. (In some states the threat of
prison remains.) Entrapment was rampant. Homosexuals were often
followed home by the police, who then might break in and arrest, or—
so it was bruited—perhaps join in the outlawed festivities. Same-sex
dancing was against the law, permitted only to heterosexual women;
in gay bars, an alerting code of flashing lights would signal gay men
to shift to lesbian partners. Squad cars and vans routinely gathered
outside bars, bullhorns demanding that all customers file out for identification before glaring lights. The next day, headlines proclaimed yet
another "roundup of queers," in the words of the newspapers of the
times.

Within such an ambiance, taboo subjects were introduced into our
literature without overt identification. Christopher Isherwood master-

fully avoided pronouns in order to depict gay sex encounters. Everyone except Charlton Heston knew that Ben Hur, in that gorgeously gaudy movie, had a crush on his fellow charioteer. Federico García Lorca got away with sexual imagery by exploring repression. Proust turned some of his males into females, and Gertrude Stein informed us that "rose"—not *a* rose—is a rose is a rose." These admirable subversives educated an audience that did not know it was being educated, and they did so through the refined and noble art of infiltration—sabotage through camouflage.

Then came Stonewall.

On a hot June night, the eve of Judy Garland's funeral, when sad flags waved half-mast on Fire Island, drag queens of both sexes resisted arrest at a bar in New York's Greenwich Village. Overnight—or so the myth has come to indicate—gay liberation was born. The next morning, freed, everyone sprang out of closets dank with decades of oppression and proclaimed their proud identity under a showers of light auguring a new day. Gay writers sat down joyfully at their typewriters and wrote "liberated literature."

The truth is that the Stonewall riot was only one event on the long road to assert ourselves in the evolution of our freedom. Used as the point of separation—before it, repression and after it, liberation—the mythologizing of Stonewall creates serious complications and distortions on our landscape. Not only does it implicitly lessen the courage of warriors who fought bravely on the frontlines when it was much more dangerous to do so, but it reduces in importance other equal—yes, equal—acts of resistance and protest. In 1967, two hundred gay men and lesbians powerfully protested a violent raid by cops on the Black Cat Bar in Los Angeles. In 1968, in that city's Griffith Park, men kissing men and women kissing women during a startling "gay-in" dumbfounded cops who were forced by the vast number of gay participants to remain on the sidelines. Throughout the country—unrecorded because of the tenor of the times that censored even our rebellions—other acts of equal pride and defiance were occurring long before Stonewall.

Even more seriously, the myth of Stonewall allows extending problems to be relegated entirely to the past and therefore obviates the need to explore their manifestation in the present. That relegation includes the festering dilemma of self-hatred and self-oppression, a subject that cannot be minimized and that was loudly denied during the heady decade of the seventies, when many demanded that wish be celebrated as reality.

The mythology of Stonewall negatively affects a correct evaluation

of our literature. *The Violet Quill Reader,* a recent book given wide attention, puts current gay literature exclusively in the hands of seven white
male writers of widely varied talent.[1] It identifies them clearly as products of the post-Stonewall decades. (In fact, these men became a group
by sharing extravagant desserts during only eight literary-evening
chats in Manhattan.) Like increasing others, that book spuriously identifies, and implicitly judges, pre-Stonewall literature as the literature
of repression and the literature produced after Stonewall as that of
liberation.

Yet what do we find in the novels of those writers currently held up
as heralds of a liberated gay literature? Tortured gay men pining after
impossible figures of desire, most often "straight;" dishy, "doomed"
Fire Island queens; rampaging sadists ravishing the objects of their
lust. Fine—everything is permitted for exploration by the artist. But
the implications of the attitudes depicted in that literature have been
largely left unquestioned by too many post-Stonewall gay reviewers
and critics, attitudes romanticized, and canonized as liberated.

Now listen!

Vidal's *Myra Breckinridge,* Burroughs's *Naked Lunch,* Isherwood's de-
ceptively genteel *A Single Man,* and other novels published before
Stonewall—and let's not forget Radclyffe Hall's *The Well of Loneliness*
in 1928, and Gertrude Stein's fabulous "Melanctha" before that, in
1909—each in its own way reveals more insurrectionary power than
the half dozen or so vaunted novels that now form the misguided
canon of post-Stonewall recognition.

After Stonewall, a body of work labeled "gay lit" emerged, or was
renamed—and it was quickly thrust into a new closet. Separated but
not exactly equal, our books are now located in bookstore in shelves
reserved for various "alternative lifestyles." There are many more manifestations of the creation of a literary ghetto, in which we often acquiesce with a mistaken notion of what constitutes liberation.

Our varied literary voices are routinely corralled into a chorus
known as "the gay writers." This occurs in insulting articles that duti-
fully appear in the *New York Times Book Review,* with its deeply homophobic roots, *Time, Newsweek,* and—with pompous "correctness"—in
the *Nation.* Those earnest articles discuss our literature as if it were a
genre, separate, as exotic as gothic romances.

The insult of such herdings is clear when we try to imagine a similar
corralling of John Updike, John Irving, Joan Didion, and others to dis-
sect aspects in common in the literature of self-avowed heterosexuals.
How about an article on the work produced by self-confessed hetero-

sexual male Jewish authors, led by flamboyant Norman Mailer and screaming heterosexual Philip Roth? (As far as being, myself, a self-avowed homosexual, I do not remember ever having taken a vow of sexuality, although I believe at one time or another Philip Roth may have done so.)

I applaud the emergence of gay literature courses in our colleges—but not when they become the final goal for the locating of our literature. All too often the emphasis is such courses will be on historical importance and political attitudes rather than on literary quality. That may help to ensure that our literature will not graduate into the mainstream of art, where it belongs with the best.

To applaud meager tokens of recognition as "success" is to accept and contribute to a new segregation: This is *literature;* this is *minority literature.* There is a vast difference between proudly proclaiming our identity and having it used as a label to separate us into a relatively spacious closet, where we see and are seen, only by each other.

In *Corydon,* André Gide wrote: "What I have to say about such things does not bring them into existence. They exist."[2] In the post-Stonewall era, the writer is increasingly pressured to turn away from what exists. The artist, it is decreed, must be a "role model." The artist as role model! What a reckless exhortation of the quintessential questioner, the outsider, the outlaw!

I suggest that the demand for "role modeling" is an insidious call for conformity, with its accompanying exhortation that "stereotypes" be banished. Rita Mae Brown was recently criticized for using as a character in her latest novel a "flamboyant antique dealer." I would venture to say that there is not one of us here who does not know a flamboyant antique dealer, perhaps even two—very courageous veterans of the wars.

Banish stereotypes? The call for such an inquisition grows louder daily.

Banish stereotypes and you banish figures of daring—outlaws who fought on the frontlines even before the war was declared: questioning, redefining, challenging, courageous, these noble flaming queens, these unflappable antique dealers and others we dismiss simply as "flamboyant." Banish the roaring bull dykes—undaunted even by Betty Friedan? Banish all these figures and you reject some of the strongest sources of confrontational rebellion, quintessential courageous outlaws often shunned even by their own, shock troops who proclaim most loudly, "I am not what you want me to be."

We have entered the riskiest of current territories, the area—I shall

call it an *arena*—of political correctness, which too often edges dangerously close to establishing a new conformity, a chorus of obedient
voices.

Many of you have chosen to call yourselves "queers." I believe that
this trend, entrenched, will divide our own ranks disastrously. I and
others of my generation and later will never use the word *queer* to
identify ourselves or each other, because we will never be able to erase
its association with the twisted faces of gay bashers, including cops;
that word, for us, will always belong to the violent enemy. In our
world, the divisions between the young and the old have always been
sharp—a lingering problem. We do not need another chasm-like separation within our ranks.

I confess that I have never been entirely at ease with the term *gay,*
either. The noun *gays,* makes us sound like "bliss ninnies," I heard
Christopher Isherwood say once. I agree. I suggest that the use of that
word to identify ourselves has been at the core of our being often
viewed as flippant. I use it now, however, because there is no other. I
envy lesbians their thrilling designation. I wish we gay males would
consider calling ourselves "Trojans." That would confound the football
team here (the University of Southern California Trojans), of course;
perhaps force out of the closet even Tommy Trojan with his pre–
International Male toga; and also act as a steadfast reminder of safe sex.

I wince at the excess of misguided political correctness, on whatever
front it may occur. Every year when I watch the spectacularly awful
Academy Awards, I lament the passing of the grand word *actress* as
woman after woman refers to herself as an "actor." (I imagine Sarah
Bernhardt stiffening in resistance.) Doesn't using the formerly only
masculine designation suggest that it is to be preferred over the one
that identifies the female? If there is to be one collective word, why
not "actress" for all? Actress John Travolta—instead of actor Michelle
Pfeiffer. There may be something to be learned from the fact that the
Spanish, French, and Italian languages award gender even to sexless
objects. The sturdy rock is the feminine *la roca,* the flickering earring
is the masculine *el arete.* No sexism there. What about the male organ
in Spanish? It is honored with a grandiose feminine designation—*la
verga!* Shall political correctness lead us to deny the special beauty of
a woman, the special beauty of a man?

Some of you reading this may well go on to write your own books,
to teach, to shape the thinking of your generation and those to come.
I would exhort you not to be restrictive, to allow dissent, not to become
conforming nonconformists—yes, and to explore and explode the
myths that have long oppressed us.

I have a favorite myth that I like to explore, a myth that is also a favorite of the Christian Right. That is the story of the fall of Sodom, the passage used most powerfully to indict us.

In the Book of Genesis, Lot, an unpleasant braggart disliked even by his wife and two daughters, proclaims loudly that two angels have come to visit only him. A group gathers insisting they, too, would like to get to know the angels. (To *know* is tortured in the preferred translation in order to give the word a sexual connotation that still remains ambiguous.) Now who wouldn't want to see an angel, better still, two? Lot petulantly refuses the request and instead offers his virgin daughters to be violated by the inquisitive group! God warns that the city of Sodom is to be destroyed. Why? Clearly because Lot offered his terrified virgin daughters to be abused by strangers? Oh, no, because an insistent group wanted to see two angels. Lot flees, with his wife and daughters. The wife looks back at the terrible excess of the destroyed city, and for her "woman's curiosity," she's turned, oddly, into a pillar of salt. And Lot? He runs off to a cavern, where he drunkenly copulates with his daughters and gives them children. There is much sinfulness in that story—and it isn't among the Sodomites.

Historically, the voice of the noble outlaw has conveyed from the frontlines urgent messages of impending struggles. Seldom has that voice been more relevant today, when politicians openly propound a "heterosexual ethic," vaunting exclusive "traditional values." Violence against gay people leads all other hate crimes. Gay men and lesbians are encouraged to join the army—and become hypocrites. Our rights are put to a vote. Our art is the real object of the attacks on the National Endowment for the Arts.

It is a time, therefore, when we must ensure that our voices are heard beyond our ghettos. How? Let me state one way that may seem like blasphemy: I suggest that our writers resist the label of "gay writers," that we allow, indeed *invite*, the writer who is gay to write about what heterosexuals call their world but which is ours, too, to locate ourselves fully on the widest landscape of literature, where we belong. While we provide a picture of the world that no one else can convey as we can, we will also teach—even force—the world that shuts us out to see us fully within it, as we, and only we, know that we truly are.

What is this knowledge to which only we have full access?

At times we ourselves forget our heritage of unique courage. We need to be reminded of it—and to let it be recognized widely.

Who else can convey what it is like to live in a world that renders us strangers in a million ways, by excluding us, by pretending we don't exist? Who else can remind the world that through witch-hunts, inquisitions, internment in concentration camps, jailings, bashings—our largely ignored history—we have not only endured, but we have created some of the world's greatest art? Every gay man who was sexually active during the "profligate years" now possesses what might be called a graveyard of memories; someone is remembered and the question quickly arises, "Has he survived?" Whether HIV-positive or not, every gay artist has been jarred into an awareness of cruel, early death, as the number of obituary columns grows daily. Yes, even in this time that requires for many a thousand acts of daily courage, some of our best writers continue to live fully, from day to day, and to produce, just as fully, some of the finest writing anywhere. That literature will come, as well, from lesbians whose support of gay men through our holocaust has been steadfast and noble, a display of the grandest solidarity between us. All these factors will produce and are already producing a body of literature like no other, a literature of urgency, anger, and courage that will instruct all.

Certainly it is only we who will be able finally to illuminate the real metaphor of AIDS, which lies not in an indictment of our sexuality but in the outside indifference to our dying.

Let me state as an aside that I hope that we will never surrender our sensuality, that we continue to celebrate it in our lives and in our art, that we never become puritans. I hope just as strongly that we will never again flirt with sexuality to the point of bludgeoning all sensations, compromising our feelings, the danger of another time, the time before the dawn of AIDS.

It is the writers, the teachers, the scholars, including the noble outlaws and stereotypes among us, who will carry our singular messages, not only to those who already know them but to those who must learn of them. Those messages should be delivered not only in the justifiably angered language of protest, but also in the careful sentences of the artist.

I congratulate the men and women who are dedicated to asserting that not only are we here now in all our splendid variety, but that we, and our art, are here to stay.

Notes

1. David Bergman, ed., *The Violet Quill Reader: The Emergence of Gay Writing after Stonewall* (New York: St. Martin's Press, 1994).

2. André Gide, *Corydon*, trans. Frank Beach (New York: Farrar, Straus and Company, 1950), 110.

Part Two

URBAN FRONTIERS
QUEER SPACE AND PLACE

7

Pouring On the Past
Video Bars and the Emplacement of Gay Male Desire

Richard C. Cante

So we beat on, boats against the current,
borne back ceaselessly into the past.
—F. Scott Fitzgerald, *The Great Gatsby*

Keep revolving.
—advertising slogan of Revolver

A considerably important institution for urban American gay men of a certain sort, the video bar is an establishment that makes its livelihood through the re-presentation of segments of American mass media texts, especially television programs. The clips are selected, edited, and programmed so as to be broken up by rather long interludes of music video, all with the dual intent of enticing a steady flow of customers into the space and keeping those already there happy enough to stay and, of course, continually purchase drinks. Thanks, technologically, to the "video revolution" of the eighties, at least one such bar exists in each of the more populated urban "gay ghettos" across the country, and in a good number of smaller cities as well. Well-frequented examples include the Midnight Sun, off Castro Street in San Francisco; Splash, in New York's Chelsea district; Chicago's Sidetrack Saloon; Boston's Luxor; and the institution on which I will focus, Los Angeles's Revolver, located on the "Boys' Town Strip" of Santa Monica Boulevard, a portion of the city sometimes called "West Hollywood 'Village.'"

Revolver's imposing street-corner entrance even boasts a video monitor strategically mounted out front, facing the sidewalk—giving passersby a glimpse of the electronic attractions inside and, it is hoped, enticing them to spring for the cover charge (five dollars on weekends) and to check the place out for themselves. Yet the relationship of Re-

A publicity card for the Revolver video bar in Los Angeles
puts its moniker into motion. (Reprinted by permission of
West Hollywood Interests Ltd.)

volver to other institutions of this sort is one that goes beyond mere
representatives. I would like to assert that these specific incarnations
of the video bar phenomenon are spaces that are actually continuous
and coterminous—conceptually as well as psychically and discursively. In other words, these spaces form satellite centers of one especially important American educational institution (or archive) for the
urban and, more important, interurban gay men who make up their
clientele.[1]

   None of this, however, is to deny the idiosyncrasies of any one particular institution. As any highway traveler knows, even a franchise
like McDonald's is careful to differentiate its cuisine according to its
perception of regional flavors. My interest here is primarily in the general rather than the particular: first, the manner in which the video
apparatus is put to use in such spaces by real people; and, second,
the relationship of such spaces of reception and praxis to some of the

discursive fields that intersect and overlap at the (imaginary) site of the "gay male subject" at a particular moment in history.

In arguing for what he calls a "socio-spatial dialectic," Edward Soja (among many others) has critiqued the "essentially historical epistemology which pervades the critical consciousness of modern social theory." For Soja, this is an epistemology that "still comprehends the world primarily through dynamics arising from the emplacement of social being and becoming in the interpretive contexts of time."[2] Proposing instead a descriptive *poetics* of the "new" time/space relations that have emerged from postmodern capitalism, Soja argues for a methodology capable of understanding "spatiality with the same acute depth of vision that comes with a focus on *durée*."[3] He argues, that is, for a methodology that, in Michel Foucault's words, avoids the historiographical vulgarity of treating time as "richness, fecundity, life, dialectic" while relegating space to the realm of "the dead, the fixed, the undialectical, and the immobile."[4] To underline his point, Soja cites Manuel Castells's classic 1977 work *The Urban Question:*

Space is a material product, which exists in relation to other elements, among them men [*sic*], who themselves enter into particular social relations which give to space a form, a function, a social signification. Space is not, therefore, a mere occasion for the deployment of social structure, but a concrete expression of each historical ensemble in which a society is specified. It is a question, then, of establishing, in the same way as for any other real object, the *structural and conjunctural laws that govern its existence and transformation,* and the specificity of its articulation with the other elements of a historical reality.[5]

As "spaces of gay male desire," video bars are also, fundamentally, "spaces where history is," not only in that these sites *have histories,* but also in that history is one of the things that is sold therein. What is the particular reality of these spaces to those who spend their time and money there? What exactly is the role of the video apparatus in such spaces? To what uses are mass-cultural images being put in these institutions? Finally, and most important, in what sense are these spaces, as both material and psychic sites of praxis, articulated with and by particular elements of historical "reality" for a certain segment of the population of this country?

Places of Distinction

In a sometimes absurdly volatile business, which must constantly contend with the capriciousness of "trends," the video bar commonly numbers among the most venerable institutions in a particular gay neighborhood. It often bills itself—for instance, in advertisements in popular gay travel directories such as *Bob Damron's Address Book* and *The Spartacus Guide*—as a "neighborhood bar," a term that implies a certain institutional longevity. Moreover, "neighborhood bar" is a descriptive title that carries a full range of class, generational, and even racial connotations, each of which differs slightly according to geographical location. This title works, in fact, to construct its opposite or other: the "dance bar." It follows that if video bars do indeed function as centralized and centralizing archives that do important work in educating gay men in both general reading practices and specific textual histories associated with gay maleness, this network of institutions may be a (more or less) literal incarnation of the proverbial Old School. Put another way, these bars—in local geographical lexica—sometimes come to represent a "taste culture" associated with one particularly salient historical representation or incarnation (perhaps a white bourgeois one) of American male homosexuality.

A twenty-one-year-old man to whom I spoke on the street outside Revolver said it bluntly: "Oh, no, I don't go there. It's just so old and tired." A cohort of his then voiced his own opinion: "Yeah, it's depressing."[6] It does seem to me that there is a world of difference between the crowd at Revolver and those at the other, most popular dance bars in the neighborhood, all located within two blocks—the Rage, Mickey's, and Studio One. One wonders, though, to what these comments might also refer. While on slower nights like Monday, Tuesday, and Wednesday the crowd does appear significantly older at Revolver (a good deal of the men are, I would guess, over forty), the case for the rest of the week is a much more slippery one.

One thirty-two-year-old man, a public relations executive to whom I spoke in the bar, compared it to the surrounding institutions as "more moderate and WASPy, and better looking on the whole." He then summed up the space in Revolver in relation to the other bars as being not only more "comfortable," but "safer." Likewise, a younger male patron, a twenty-five-year-old law student, told me that the clientele is definitely much "better" than at the surrounding dance bars. In fact, he said he hates the moments when the crowd at Revolver does anything that approaches dancing, as had occurred earlier the night we spoke, when the crowd as a whole had become somewhat physically animated in response to Debbie Harry's video "I Want That Man." This patron went on to tell me that the "adolescent fascination" with dance music and dancing is not really expected here because this is "only a bar, and people should come here only to drink. The dancing just doesn't go with the rest of it."

These representations of the character of the bar must be understood in relation to the general character of the dance bars that are constructed as Revolver's others, by the institution itself as well as by its enthusiastic and/or regular patrons. A quick glance at the respective crowds says it all. At Revolver the patrons are predominantly white and "buttoned down." The surrounding bars' crowds are more significantly Hispanic and black, dressed in a "working class clone" style (T-shirt or no shirt; jeans; necklaces, pendants, bandanas, caps, etc.). This style is markedly different from that of the video bar's crowd, which, for the most part, seems literally "decked out" in its own ethic of "professionalism."

Thus, the outsiders' representation of the bar as "old, tired and depressing," when understood in dialogue with the insiders' representation of their environment as "safer," might not have quite as much as it purports to do with the generational constitution of Revolver's crowd, and more to do with its (non)ethnic constitution and class significations. It is interesting too, then, that these racial/class assumptions, partly masquerading as assumptions about age, involve particular and different representations of one's relation to one's body, and to the bodies of others; issues, essentially, of physical motility. These issues are, apparently, an important component of patrons' varying conceptions of what "should" and "shouldn't" be done in the space of a gay bar, conceptions that I address more thoroughly later on.

Furthermore, one wonders whether the description of the bar proffered by the "outsiders" has as much to do with the crowd therein as with some conception of the place created on bases other than interactions with Revolver's actual patrons. Might the media texts (including the video images as well as music) presented by the bar be especially important here, for what they imply about the tastes of Revolver's regular patrons—especially since there is a video monitor out on the sidewalk? Might "old, tired, and depressing" refer as much to the outsiders' relations to the images shown on the sidewalk monitor outside as to the types of people whom they perceive to be enjoying these images inside?

These questions are important because, for many of Revolver's patrons, to be "in" the institution should not be taken to imply that one is all-too-complicit with the tastes it presupposes in the selection of its textual materials. A good number of patrons expressed to me their annoyance at the conceptual similarity of the videotaped excerpts the bar selects and displays, be they more recent media materials or older mass-cultural objects being recycled. One man expressed his disapproval by saying that all the clips seem to be selected and presented with "the same exact type of humor." He then declared, exasperated, "I wish they could get outside of that," though evidently he was not willing "to get outside of" the bar's space himself by choosing a different venue.

When I asked another patron what he thought of the tastes of the people who select the videos, the following conversation ensued:

PATRON: See, it's the kind of thing that, once I see it—old stuff—in here, I kind of think it's coming back in again, so I do kind of feel that it keeps me current, even with the videos and stuff [*here he indicated the 1993 Pet Shop Boys' video, a remake of the Village People's "Go West," which we had just watched together*]. So they are kind of a vanguard, I guess, but they're not *really* very current.
ME: Well, who would be more current?
PATRON [*joking*]: Um, like Ru Paul, people in New York . . . you know. It's kind of the vanguard of the mainstream, but not the vanguard of the vanguard, that's what I mean.

Later, the same patron did admit to me that "once you see something in here, you never see it the same way again." If, then, the institution does not necessarily have the power to decide for its patrons what is "hip" (on matters of "hipness" and queer culture see Michael Bacchus's chapter in this book), it might play a significant role in deciding what is and isn't history—and, specifically, what *our* history is and is not.[7] To be sure, the segments of media texts on display at Revolver create a horizon of American "pastness" that stretches with ease across the entire realm of postwar American media. In general, though, that horizon limits itself to the territory between the Stonewall rebellion in 1969 and whatever is currently promoted as the latest major televisual event. As far as older texts go, the bar is most concerned with those that lend themselves to various periodizing effects—in particular, those of the seventies and the eighties. Yet, due to the attempt to keep "current," one can certainly find oneself taken aback by the breakneck pace by which time here becomes history—as I was when, the day after it aired, the "gay scene" from the final *Cheers* episode was already being displayed as a thing of the past. Likewise, something to which one hardly pays attention when encountering it on television might suddenly be made to seem ultrasignificant by the mere fact that it has been selected and redisplayed by the institution: "Someone, for some reason, thinks that *we* will relate to this!"

Not surprisingly, the type of humor that generally guides the selectivity of the institution's memory (and everything displayed here is, in some sense, humorous) is an unmistakably campy one.[8] The texts that involve male stars or characters are typically concerned either with connotationally or denotationally gay themes, or else with apparently "straight" ones put in explicitly homoerotic or unusual (in terms of "classical" heteromasculinity) situations. Most of the selections, though, pivot around images of females. Not at all unusual in the vein of contemporary camp, the institution fixates on various permutations of some noticeable types: the "powerful" woman (e.g., Samantha Stevens of *Bewitched*); the brash, "fallen" or "working" woman (Elvira, Mistress of the Dark); the bitch and/or hyperelegant woman (Erica Kane from *All My Children*, Joan Collins's character from *Dynasty*); the fat woman (Roseanne); the Jewish woman (the obligatory "Babs"); and the black woman (Oprah).[9]

Interestingly, the bar's "veejays" comment on the texts in ways much more explicit than selection alone, often making "periodization" the heart of their jokes. For instance, one of Revolver's signature techniques of bricolage is the reediting of famous "cat fights" (Alexis and Krystal's from *Dynasty* is but one) so as to repeat *ad absurdum* each of the blows administered, with the addition of outlandishly pumped-up sound effects—thwacks, smacks, and so on. Oprah Winfrey's (in)famous 1993 interview with Michael Jackson has likewise been recut to include a veritable barrage of inserts mocking the sincerity and integrity of both interviewer and interviewee. Another "intellectual montage," which would probably make Sergei Eisenstein roll over in his grave (or maybe not!), continuously dissolves back and forth between Toni Basil's 1980s cheerleading-themed music video "Mickey" and Marcia Brady's traumatic tryout for the pom pom squad more than a decade earlier.

If, as already mentioned, Revolver expects (and banks on) a certain response to their texts, that expectation is both discomforting and enjoyable for the bar's patrons. In this sense, such viewing environments could be seen to re-create, at the level of reception, the same closeness/ distance paradox built into the campy selection criteria in the first place: the pleasure of one's revulsion. Thus, the video bar, as a cultural space, aspires to the blanket commodification of a type of text-spectator relationship that may exist as nothing more than a fantasy, a guise, and/or a self-conscious masquerade of a reading position from which even many of the bar's regular patrons feel quite alienated and distant. Indeed, I have found that in Revolver this text-spectator relation is commonly adopted only self-consciously and with a certain accompanying anxiety.

Still, many of the men to whom I spoke in the bar told me that the stereotypical representation of gay men as hyperconsumers, libidinally close to mass-media textual objects—even if they simultaneously distance themselves from those objects via ironic reception procedures like "camping"—does, in their opinion, hold a degree of truth. What arises here is the question of whether or not this information should be taken as surprising; these are all people who, for whatever reason, had chosen to be present in this space when I encountered them. Furthermore, an interesting and related regional peculiarity of Revolver is that a (not at all) surprising number of individuals who attend the bar are employed by the Los Angeles culture industries.

In summary, the taste culture deployed in and commodified by the bar—only partly through texts that are literally "old"—markets to and advertises a version of gay male identity that is obviously endangered by these complex articulations of generational, class, ethnic, and racial realities that remain foreign to it. This version of gay male identity is constructed, ultimately, by the taste of the institution itself and embodied by its selection of texts. This particular brand of "gay maleness" is articulated by at least some of the bar's patron as phantasmatic but also as being somehow based in reality, and always available. Simultaneously, it is articulated by at least some of the bar's "outsiders" as being both real and obsolete. These perceptions of this reception environment—this habitus of subcultural taste—exemplify the ambivalence of gay males to their own position vis-à-vis media culture in this country, even (or especially) when media culture is presented with a difference, a difference represented as being "our" difference.

In its periodizing selection of texts, Revolver and institutions like it operate partly on a notion of historical time that, though it is a structural nexus of the habitus, is also radically effaced by Revolver's own methods of combination/display. Moreover, Revolver puts this temporal dialectic to work in evoking the closeness/distance problematic of a reading practice discursively associated with gay maleness, creating spectator positions into which gay male patrons, ideally, find themselves always already interpellated. The "problem" is that this spectatorial position is simultaneously perceived as a dead one by real historical individuals: as dead as the texts continuously resurrected to reanimate it, and as dead as the "gay identity" that these texts together embody—an identity already under assault from many sides.

Representing itself as the major etymological shift in the development of homosexuality since "homosexual" became "gay," "queerness" takes upon itself the task of the annihilation of cultural spaces like this one by proposing itself as an antidote to—even while writing the requiem for—that "old, tired, and depressing" identity that is embodied by the "tastes" of an institution like this one.[10] This is yet another sense in which a bar like Revolver forms a "space of history."

Swallowed up into its own vortex of the past, it is itself in danger of blowing away as a mere remnant, or as debris.

Queerness, in all of its incarnations—as real behavior, as ethic, as academic/institutional construct—is nothing more than a fantasy, or a word, to be more precise. The desire to which it responds is an absolutely real one, though, and it needs to be considered as much as an oppositional discourse that tries to usher something *out* as a revolution that tries to usher something else *in*. The concept "queer" enters the field of critical theory at precisely the point of horrific impasse to theoretical and real (socioacademic) gender relations that has resulted from the solidification of identities based on an *exclusively* same-sex desire. A male version of this identity lies at the base of Revolver's and other video bars' existences, in that this fantasized if unreal identity becomes the implied spectator and ideal consumer, created by the reception-environment-as-moneymaking-institution.

Therefore, as a concept and as a speech act, "queer" has a murderous side that has been largely overlooked. It aspires to killing off, by exclusion, all those "old, tired, depressing" gay male entities (real or ideal, it apparently makes no difference) who *haven't already actually died*. It is an attempt to relegate them, literally, to the realm of the past by recourse to their "obsolete" tastes, predilections, and practices. Eve Kosofsky Sedgwick has recently argued, with characteristic rhetorical skill, that *queer* exists in its most substantial form as a first-person performative, the way "I Dare You" or "I Thee Wed" exist mostly in what they perform as speech acts. She also implies that *queer* is purely additive, existing only *in addition to* other manners of sexual identification, like "gay" and "straight."[11] But Sedgwick's argument, like many of those that accept the same basic tenets, fails to address those situations wherein *queer* is much more than that; situations wherein it becomes a term that makes coming out of the closet as a gay man—or as a lesbian, for that matter—as difficult as, if not more difficult than, it used to be. Discursively, then, the project of queerness and that of the men to whom I spoke outside the bar is one and the same, though each exists for different reasons. For now, whether or not their historical coincidence is providential remains an open question.

Looks, or the Performance of Response

Traditionally, television reception studies have understood the roles that individuals adapt toward the television apparatus in terms of the family, a network of social relations taken to condense larger power structures.[12] Other important work has investigated reception pro-

cesses and the readings they produce in relation to alternatively structured "interpretive communities."[13] But the reception and use of television texts (as well as the video apparatus itself) in public spaces
outside the home is still generally neglected, since the field of "living
room television studies" remains libidinally attached to feminism's
scholarly project of recuperating the "domestic sphere."

If a general assumption of this tradition of work has been that television spectatorship, as opposed to moviegoing, necessarily involves the
realm of sociality in active negotiations for meaning, the case of the
video bar is a particularly interesting one in that this space involves
responding to media texts while being situated in a network of relations involving the constant relay of looks around the room of which
one is, in general, highly conscious. More specifically, the video bar is
an interesting case of a public reception situation because the bar's
lattice of gazes is, if one wants it to be, an explicitly sexualized one.
This is not to say that "cruising" is the only thing or even necessarily
the most important thing going on in these spaces, but it is an extremely important aspect. In fact, the potential for making connections
with other individuals on the basis of various types of desire, only one
of which is sexual, is one of the bar's primary purposes. Hence, the
viewer's response to texts in such a situation can be seen as necessarily
and inherently performative, since one knows that one's responses are
always, to a greater or lesser extent, under surveillance.[14] Thus, perhaps the actual media images presented by such institutions should
not be overvalued in their importance: the text might be logically re-
conceptualized as a pretext here, a pretext to sociality of one sort or
another.[15] This reception environment, then, is perhaps an expression
par excellence of the type of television viewing context in which it is
the general presence of the image apparatus rather than of any particular texts or "meanings" that is most important.

If the primary concern one confronts as a lone body in search of
something in a gay bar is "How do I look?" running a close second is
another question: "*Where* do I look?" The development of the video
bar, as an institution, aspires to offer a solution to one of the key problems of singles bar patronage in general—how to be, or at least appear,
comfortable while consciously having to endure functioning as a lone,
intermittent object of countless evaluative gazes. The video apparatus
serves the important function, in this setup, of absorbing your look by
giving you something to look at so that you, in turn, can *be looked at.*
Thus, these institutions implicitly advertise comfort in being watched,
privilege in watching, and even alibis for not being interested in being

a particular person's sexual object ("I'm just too engrossed in this clip to notice you"). And, the video bar adds another convenience to the complexities of cruising. Should you not be finding what you think you are after, you do not necessarily end up as "bored and annoyed," in one patron's words, as you might be in other bars.

Conversely, though, the media apparatus—as potential solution to the problem of the gaze in these spaces—re-creates exactly those complications which it apparently attempts to remedy. Quite a number of men to whom I spoke expressed the frustration that "everyone just watches the videos, and it makes it hard to talk to anyone." One even dismissed the whole situation as a shabby pretense, deeming it "absolutely ridiculous" that "at the height of laughter, during clips, if you watch the crowd, everyone's eyes are just darting around watching other people. If they want to look, why don't they just look?"

That gay bars should eventually become sites where each patron's gaze is potentially refracted through such a complex, spatialized, institutionally controlled, and—from one standpoint—downright Riefenstahlian ocular "machinery," just so that individuals can make sexual connections with each other, is even more ironic than it might seem initially. When this is examined in the light of gay male history in this country, the reason becomes clear.

The whole post-Stonewall, minoritizing project of the creation of the "gay ghettos" in which these bars are situated was precisely one of creating a "safe" public space for the homosexual male gaze, a space where men can specularize each other as erotic objects without fear of doing this to the wrong person (read: a "straight," "homophobic" man) and thus suffering the consequences (presumably, being beat up). With the development and popularization of gay bars as spaces within these safe spaces, such consequences are, for the most part, reduced to "rejection," since any male who enters does so only on the condition that he potentially become an object of other men's gazes. Hence, the structural position of the video apparatus in these bars functions, ironically, to recontain the very gaze we have worked so hard to set free, a gaze which, apparently, has *its own* inherently terrifying consequences. The nonconsideration of the terror of the male homosexual gaze could be seen to follow logically from the "looksist" legacy of the promiscuity-based gay liberation agenda which, to an extent, is the foundation for all gay bars as we now know them. In this regard, the gaze is a "problem" in these spaces not only in and of itself; it now functions as the unappreciated return of a "classical" gay male liberation theory that had supposedly been, for the most part, *dead and buried.*[16]

Of course, the gaze is not a problem that the institution believes it can solve. It would be naive to assume that the unrefracted gaze is, from the standpoint of the profit-driven institution, now some kind of nuisance. On the contrary, Revolver, as a physical space, seems constructed for the ideal specularization not only of video images, but of actual bodies and inanimate objects as well. From the Picasso cum Giacometti cum Keith Haring art work that graces the walls of the back bar, to the actual writing on other walls, to the kitschy cherubs (reproduced in numerous places as the bar's trademark image) that hang from the ceiling above the crowd, the whole place screams out for attention, if not interpretation. The gilded revolving door from which the bar takes its name is situated in a symmetrical spatial relation, across the large front room, to the prominent and most attended to of the space's seven video screens, which hangs above a corner of the actual bar. Forming opposed absorption points for the gaze of the crowd as a whole, these two sites duke it out for attention; often, not surprisingly, the revolving entrance seems to deliver a somewhat more valued "consumable" to the patrons' hungry eyes—real male bodies.

Moving through this space, one is at once a flaneur in an excessive field of textuality and a text like any other. The male patron is simultaneously the spectator and spectacle, at once the spotlight itself and the proud, horrified, and/or stagefrightful object in its beam. And the mention of such a "spotlight" here warrants the brief consideration of a body of critical work that considers gay maleness as "always already performative" by giving a sociostructural explanation/justification for this notion of a specifically gay male mode of performativity.[17]

The explanation goes that from growing up isolated from each other and not being able to identify each other readily, gay male individuals each become individually aware of the possibility, if not the necessity, of passing for straight, of playing the role of a straight man. What results is an unusual and atypical awareness of the "mainstream as a mainstream,"[18] of social roles as social roles, and of the theatricality and artificiality of that which presumably seems "natural" to straights. This is taken as the basis for a gay sensibility and a gay aesthetics. For instance, the processes of "camping," in the production both of texts and of meanings from texts, would logically follow. As far as this argument goes, the closeness/distance text-spectator relationship continually associated and reassociated with gay males, through institutions like this branch of the critical apparatus ("gay theory") as well as ones like Revolver, is specific to this population and differs fundamentally from the rampant currency of similar spectatorial practices under the regime of the postmodern. For gay men, camp, along with the performativity that produces it, is nothing less than a technique for (social and/or physical) survival.

Such approaches generally suppose that there is a gay "sensibility," and that this sensibility is the foundation of gay male cultural production. This sensibility develops out of a notion of the lived experience of homosexual individuals that has essentializing tendencies (though it is not quite an "essentialist" notion). This is because it elides all sorts of real differences—in particular race, class, and geography—that fracture and expose as illusory any unified notion of "the American gay male" or even "the gay community." For the most part, the patrons of Revolver seem more closely to satisfy the experiential conditions for this "sensibility" than, for instance, the men who frequent the surrounding bars. However, I have found that in Revolver the patrons' perceptions of their own sociocultural positions often preclude the type of performative response already written into many of the texts on display in the bar and even written into the physical space itself (the architecture, the interior layout, the decor, etc.). In other words, the alienation from this institution's tastes—which was articulated as a generational concern for the men outside Revolver—is precisely that which constructs and constricts the horizon of possibilities which guides patrons' performance of textual "response" in such an environment.

Consider the following conversation that I had with a patron in his early twenties. When I asked him whether he thought Revolver could exist as a straight bar, he answered by proposing a surprising relationship between the tastes of individual customers and those of the institution, the latter of which he implicitly linked to "gay sensibility":

PATRON A: I would just have a lack of faith in straights to do it in any interesting way, and yes [*responding to an earlier comment of mine*], I do think straight men would find it emasculating to sit around laughing at television comedy in a bar.
ME: What do you think it'd feel like to be in a straight bar of this sort—for you, being gay? I mean, do you feel really connected to the response of the crowd here, then?
PATRON A: We'll, I think I'd feel . . . here I do feel really connected to the response, but not so much to individuals in the crowd. I think in a straight bar I'd feel more connected with the individuals and less with the general response.

Similarly, two men whom I met at the bar asked me what my research was about. I explained to them the idea of the "performance of response" in these spaces, an idea that most men either welcomed very enthusiastically or mentioned on their own. The following dialogue ensued:

PATRON 1: That makes sense. I agree with that.
PATRON 2: I don't. I think what's going on is just entertainment.
PATRON 1 [*to Patron 2*]: Yeah, but you wouldn't, like, hurl insults back at Joan Crawford in here [*the "no wire hangers" clip from* Mommie Dearest *had just been played*].
PATRON 2 [*seriously*]: Well I wouldn't do that *anyway*.

Each of these two conversations documents an impulse to express alienation from those aspects of reading practice that presumably delimit Revolver as a unified, stable "interpretive environment" in the first place. The first exchange typifies the manner in which, for many in this "community," the bar's network of gazes is differentiated in its experiential reality into dualistic components. In this case, one aspect is a totalized vision of the crowd, the "general response" with which Patron A says he identifies more than with the particular individuals enacting that response. We might note that this notion of a general response implicitly collapses the crowd into the institution itself—that is, into the excerpts Revolver presents for the crowd's response, and into the preferred responses already encoded into these texts through the style of their representation. Put another way, for some patrons "the crowd" in Revolver acts as a sort of superego that is part and parcel of the institution. Simultaneously, though, particular individuals in the crowd are conceptually conditioned to maintain their distinction from this entity. Thus, it is not only gazes that are present in this space; The Gaze is embodied there as well.

The second exchange demonstrates that readings, more so than actual meanings, must be carefully negotiated, through performance, so that the manner in which one presents oneself to these (individual) gazes and to The (fantasized general) Gaze does not veer too close to the reading/selection practice of the "house." Patron 2's denial that he would even have *the impulse* to enter into the type of spectator-text relation that is encouraged by the bar exemplifies this. The performance of response is perceived to proceed under the gaze of a sort of Big Other that is Revolver's phantasmic incarnation of the always preexistent "social totality" that supposedly witnesses and oversees all subjective individuation. This Big Other dictates, for any given individual, what is not to be done as well as what may be done, and it is feared not only for its authority, but for what it actually and ultimately is: a projection of the (gay male) self. Therefore, responding to texts in a manner that reveals one's gaze to be The Gaze performs complicity with the "tastes" of the institution. This complicity, by implication, displays "gay sensibility," a stigma to many of the men with whom I spoke, at least in their cruising scenarios.

Patron 2 is careful to position himself as unmistakably "far away" from a response that would "hurl insults back at Joan Crawford," publicly or privately. It is tempting to understand such codes of acceptable performance as mechanisms for the reexternalization of internalized repression or even homophobia.[19] However, such an understanding implicitly assumes that there exists some authentic "kernel" of response that is being modulated and/or blocked by the patron's recourse to the excuse of the Big Other. Further, it assumes that the release of such repressed acts would be, first, pleasurable to the individual, and, second, beneficial to the community in political terms. Of course, such assumptions are open to debate.

In her very early work on female impersonators, Esther Newton makes a relevant observation. She notes that camp, at least as it is instantiated in the language of drag, is fundamentally incompatible with seduction, and often stands in as a substitute for "real" enactments of gay sexuality.[20] More generally, camp can be read as a representation of the inherent "failure" of all human sexuality. A man as drag queen restages the frustration or impossibility of "straight" homosexual desire (to be desired by a man as a man) by dressing as a woman. Also, he distances himself ironically from *all* forms of representation, including the codes of gender and sexuality, through his campiness. Thus, in acting to cede his "gay" desire he ends up restaging its frustrating blockage. Reading this "acting out" of desire as a failure is compatible with a repressive hypothesis of homosexuality; in this sense, all gay sexuality is *doomed to somehow "fail."* Alternatively, one could view this scenario through the lens of Slavoj Žižek's controversial work. Žižek repeatedly, and almost obsessively, reminds us what desire is—in the strictly psychoanalytic sense. In Lacanian terms, desire is that very thing—embodied in language, or the symbolic order (the Big Other)—that, through fantasy, continually re-creates itself by repeatedly restaging the frustration of that lack of fulfillment for the sake of which we supposedly act.[21] In Žižek's understanding, then, the failure of the drag queen's desire *is* his desire. In this regard, one could explain gay performativity, whether it be drag or its seeming antithesis (the performances of rigid "masculinity" at Revolver, by consciously veering away from campiness) not as inherent, repressive failure, but as *smashing success!*

An argument propped on a repressive hypothesis might lead us to the conclusion that the boundaries placed on performative-reception behavior in spaces like Revolver are not only "antisexual" but "heinous," since they seem to reify dominant behavioral codes based on a rigid distinction between the masculine and the feminine—and on the binary relation between heterosexual and homosexual that functions in tandem with those of gender.[22] The conspicuous *absence of, ejection from,* and possibly even *hatred of* real female bodies in these spaces adds only another tier of importance to this consideration. Leaving aside the somewhat banal position that flatly denies the seriousness of such charges, I am suggesting that recent psychoanalytic elaborations on desire offer a means of problematizing any such condemnation in the first place. Though such a line of argument is problematic and potentially controversial because it universalizes the dilemma in the specific manner that commonly enrages opponents of psychoanalytic critical theory, it still very compellingly drives us to its conclusion: that these "insufficient" means of performance (or "acting out") *are* sexuality in its very essence, and that they *are* sexual desire in its most universal form. For is not sexual desire precisely that thing to which *all particularities* are irrelevant in the wake of its most general and irrational force—aching want?

Discussing the horizon of preferred performative responses that sexuality regulates in a reception environment like a gay male video bar, many men were able specifically to cite texts at which they would be unwilling to laugh in a potential cruising scenario. For example, one Revolver patron here mentioned "that totally faggy queen from *Kids in the Hall* who talks directly to the camera." He proceeded to recount a situation wherein he "basically had to pretend it wasn't even on," even though he found it funny, because he knew he was being watched while it was being shown. I asked him why laughter at such an effeminate representation isn't sufficient to the critical distance from effeminacy that he wished to perform. He replied that laughter would only have signaled a recognition of some part of the character in himself. In other words, he represented himself as having been in danger of being perceived as acting on an "identification."

I would assert that the notion of the other to which such performances of response reply as discourse is constructed partly as the (ideal) *heterosexual male spectator who is always already absent from the space.* This is the aforementioned, imaginary heterospectator who "would find it emasculating to sit around laughing at comedy in a bar." The mechanisms that police performative response by incarnating this other as their watchdog are particularly interesting to me because they aspire to hold in check, and possibly even to invert, all those aesthetic/economic logics of television, and of postmodernism in general, according to which "too much is not enough."[23] In the semipublic use of media texts at Revolver, for some males at least, too much (response) is disastrous in that it risks having one understood and received as exactly that which one is already supposed to *be*, simply by being present in this particular bar as opposed to some other—a gay man whose tastes run toward the grand, excessive, "old," and declassé, though maybe still endearing (but not *sexually*, of course) style.[24] At the same time, "too little" response remains, well, not enough. Here one runs the risk of being a "wallflower," and of not being noticed at all, except perhaps by someone interested in wallflowers.

The following conversation resulted when I asked a patron, a friend who is a twenty-five-year-old graduate student in literature, if he recalled ever having met someone through a particular text or textual response in a video bar:

PATRON: Well, this is kind of stupid, but I remember I met this guy who was a cook—because of an Annie Lennox video.
ME: Which one?
PATRON: *Precious*. It's in black and white. It's kind of a takeoff on *Wings of Desire*.
ME: What happened?
PATRON: Well, I actually kind of get chills when I see that. I really like Annie Lennox. And sometimes, you know, how you'll actually gesture when something like that comes on?
ME: What kind of gesture?
PATRON: Well, like a nod of recognition, or, I don't know, my hand or something, just because you're excited to see something. And we were both obviously excited to see it.

Despite the hyperperformative aspect of spaces like Revolver, this example illustrates a connection forming between individuals on the basis of media texts that involves the specific kinds of responses that seem momentarily to derail self-conscious performativity. This is the interesting, exceptional case in which too little *is* enough. At these moments, some authentic kernel—or "piece of the real," in Žižek's terms—erupts, if only accidentally, onto the surface of the performative mask.[25] Paradoxically, what is here perceived as the "piece of the real," the gesture, is of course visible only as performance. Following Žižek, we can make perfect sense of this paradox: this "piece of the real" is authentic only *because* it is mere signification.[26]

This patron's comments suggest that such an authentic kernel is a treasure for which at least some of Revolver's patron are on the lookout in an otherwise excessively performative field. But if gay maleness is performativity in its most "exquisite" form, as it is in the critical/discursive tradition we have already briefly surveyed, then nonperforma-

tivity is something radically different: realness, maleness, nonhomo-
sexuality—another fantasy continually reincarnated in its impossible
absence from "gay space," and successfully performed, paradoxically,
only in its failed delivery.[27]

Sites, or Mixing Memory with Desire

A gun. A gilded entranceway. A Beatles album that seems today, to the
aficionado, to have marked a definite turning point in the group's style,
the beginning of a whole new period. The referent of this bar's name
is indeed a slippery one. Dangling from the word *revolver* are a number
of connotational strings that, in their dialectical entanglements, do
quite a bit to represent the bar. In that this space is a material product
like any other, its name operates not unlike those of other consum-
ables: *Crest, Cheer, Tropicana.* On the one hand, there is the absolute
linearity and finality of the word's Thanatological connotations—guns,
bullets, endings, death. On the other, though, there are those of Erotic
"circularity"—the penis, the phallus, and all those vortices of desire
that are continually refigured around the sites where both death and
desire are circulated and advertised.

Therefore, it is important that, like many "cruise" bars, Revolver is
set up to facilitate repetitive circular motion (or revolution) as one
scans and is scanned by the crowd. Its trademark motto, "keep revolving," appears in its print advertisements, on its T-shirts, and on the
stack of paper cards, available from the bartenders, that patrons commonly use to exchange phone numbers. This slogan is always super-
imposed over images of the plastic cherubs that hang from the bar's
ceiling, but don't themselves actually revolve. The bar's name and its
motto collude in their invitation to the continual circulation of the signifiers of desire in this space of consumption.

But you only need literally to read the writing on the wall, literally,
to notice that this slogan and the bar's name also allude, as does the
visual image of the angel, to the most obvious threat of a detour out
of "circulation" for a gay man at the time of this writing. The writing
on the wall is an ultra-explicit invitation to the practice of "safe" sex,
which anyone coming out of the bathroom is doomed to encounter.
Significantly, it comes in the form of postmodern icon Sandra Bernhard's altered lyrics to EMF's song of erotic obsession "Unbelievable,"
which are painted on this wall in very large letters. Bernhard sang this
to Tom Jones in a segment of her 1991 Showtime special, helping to
secure the male crooner's return to hipness. The clip has a prominent
place in the bar's canon and is shown there quite often.

This wall hints at yet another path of signification leading away from the word *revolver*. Circularity *here* involves the recirculation, with a difference, of the mass-cultural materials or even "detritus" (like the EMF song and Tom Jones himself) that the bar not only sells but uses to deliver its patrons to its own "advertisers": the liquor bottles that will be in turn recirculated by The System once they have been emptied of *their* souls. In this manner, Revolver, as a name, transposes the continuous circularity of the televisual apparatus—and of postmodern epistemology more generally—onto the space of the bar itself, but only at the cost (or added benefit, depending on how you see it) of evoking that which "the system" itself must construct as other: the deadness of what little it leaves behind and forgets absolutely, and the bullet-train, linear progression of Time and History in which we, as mortal beings, *are still* and *will always be* situated.

Thus, the bar's name and its slogan present us with the fantasy of directly "jacking in," cyberfiction style, to the very apparatus of desire. But, by connotational implication, this fantasy is a strange and highly improbable one—that of continually and ecstatically revolving in the bar's glass entranceway, the revolving door that the bar's name and slogan also evoke. As we all know, to even *consider* this would be "loony." You would find yourself, like a giddy kid at a department store, tossed out by some strong gestapo type before you could even say "Mercy." You might get, at best, nine or ten revolutions; hardly enough to build up any substantial ecstatic momentum. And, worst of all, once you're violently ejected, you just might not even know which side you have landed on—since the outside and the inside, and the street and the cruising place, and the realm of the image and the realm of the Real are all so confusingly similar. In other words, the violent, seemingly inevitable end to your spin into gay male desire, and the necessary brevity of that spin, are the preconditions of its very possibility. Thus, they are advertised quite "honestly" (surprise!) by at least some of the ways in which this bar discursively markets itself as space, since Revolver wears its articulation with the structural and conjunctural realities that govern its existence—in particular, the HIV pandemic—in plain sight, on its proverbial sleeve.

Slavoj Žižek, following on the work on spatiality described in the first section of this chapter, has agreed that the crisis of postmodernism is a fundamentally *spatial* one for the following reason: everything, including History, gets so near that it becomes distant, or so visible and so close that we lose it.[28] Video bars barrage us with "historical periods," and, consequentially, with the breaks, ruptures, and losses that create these. But they periodize so mechanistically, and so officiously, that not only do they smooth over those losses and breaks, they present them for what they are: sites fixated only by fantasy and by historical representation itself, losses only masquerading as other losses. In this sense, as conceptual/technological spaces (based on the video apparatus) and as spaces of fantasy, these bars are constructed at the very site of this crisis. In fact, video bars *are* this crisis, erected smack in between our desire for the past and our absolute terror of its return.

All this has recently found concrete expression at Revolver, where a prominent wall was temporarily transformed into an *objet* in a very interesting manner. Into this wall, five rows of regularly placed (presumably fake) skulls were installed, and covered over so as to appear deeply embedded in the stark white plaster. This made spatially present what is so saliently absent from the bar's media images—namely, the many, many gay American gazes already "glazed over" by painful *physiological* processes. In this wall-as-public-art-object, as well as in the forms of the cherubs that benevolently ogle the crowd from above, these gazeless visages can now assume their rightful place in that network of gazes that is the sexualized space of the bar. Significantly, though, the skulls have been cemented into the white wall with one peculiar effect. They look, to the semidistant observer, like those "theatrical masks"—we all know the ones, Comedy and Tragedy—that would have in themselves been so apt in designating this space for what it is. In this way, the wall dually marks this space as a theatrical one (a site of performative sexuality) and as a space of death.

To explore these implications, we must recall the spatial project of the gay ghetto and the related narrative of the generation/origination of video-bar space in general. The impetus for the construction of such spaces was and continues to be the "safety" of the gaze. The goal has been the colonization of a site where this gaze can become what it is already supposed to be, or where it can break out of its repressive shell to reveal its "authentic kernel"—Eros, the life drive, desire itself. But the inescapable consequence of the existence of such spaces (from bars to bathhouses to cruisy ghetto streets) has not only been the successful commodification of the gaze and of all that the gaze implies.[29] The consequence has also been a facilitation, particularly during the seventies and early eighties, of the rampant spread of HIV among those who have patronized these sites.

In total, this narrative of generation is one whose implications are obviously dangerous—that we got, literally, what we asked for. In fact, it has become a primary site of disavowal (for a cultural catastrophe

that is already all about disavowal) for both the AIDS activist imperative and, predictably, for the "institutions of the gaze" that are implicated by this schema. Beyond all the horrendous suffering and death,
which has been bad enough, and beyond even the swift mechanisms
by which the epidemic basically continues to be ignored by heterosoci-
ality, the real tragedy of HIV, then, is precisely that it *is* a tragedy, a
specifically postmodern version of that Gatsbian historical/narrative
economy whereby The Rise (gay liberation) *is* The Fall (HIV), and from
which there is no way out, even after the fact.

The problem, then, is not that the master narrative that governs the
emplacement of our desire in history is lost to us in its incoherence, its
violence, or in its inaccessibility to us in some canonically high modern
way (note the closing line of Fitzgerald's novel, cited as one of this
chapter's epigraphs, or the opening lines of Eliot's *The Waste Land*, for
that matter). Instead, the problem is that our master narrative is lost
because it *must* be lost. And it must be lost precisely because it makes
the scandalous move of becoming *coherent*, or because it takes on values and valences of meaning that representation is not, by definition,
supposed (in both senses of the word) to possess.

Contrary to popular understandings of AIDS discourse, the problem
is not that Eros is unmasked by this historical scheme for who he "really is," Thanatos. As I have tried to show in the previous section, gay
men are far too "sophisticated" for such a simple deception. We can
discipline our bodies, we can control our images and our voices, we
can perform our desires like no one else; we know that and we are
known for that. We *know what a performance is,* and always have.

The real problem is a much more sticky, as Žižek knows: "Embodiments of pure drive *wear a mask*—why? . . . The real is thus not an
inaccessible kernel hidden beneath layers of symbolizations, it is *on the
surface* . . . the death drive resides in this surface deformation, not in
what is beneath it. The real horror is a stupid laughing mask, not the
distorted, suffering face it conceals."[30] Hence, the rhetorical problem
with the historical scheme on which these spaces are both materially
and psychically built is that Eros *is* Thanatos, mask and all. Hence, the
grand historical irony that curses these spaces and curses all of its
surfaces—from its bodies to its objects to its mediatexts—is *not at all
ironic*, since it says, precisely and totally, that which it means to say. In
effect, this scheme allows history to do the "impossible": it allows history to overcome its alienation from and ignorance of History, to repair
its own split, to get back, so to speak, into its mother's body. And it
allows representation to enter into a conversation with the Real that

we *aren't even prepared to believe* it can have, since the two have always spoken such positively incompatible languages. In Žižek's terms, the more general horror becomes that of suddenly finding out that the Real can, after all, "answer back" to representation.[31]

In this sense, video bars are temples to Truman Capote's "answered prayers," which are much worse in their consequences than unanswered ones. They arise out of a postmodern wish's being granted, out of a crisis of representation performing itself as an epidemic.[32] In the modernist version, Oedipus finds out that his "wish" has been granted and destroys his faculty of sight. Our version ends not in bleeding blindness, but in the splendid, excessive ocularity of these spaces and their "pleasures." Still, these spaces are cursed by their own "guilt." This is obviated by their attempt to keep hidden The Thing that has resulted, since to allow that Thing to invade the depths, or more precisely the *nondepths,* of Revolver's video attractions could only be in poor taste (clips from *Longtime Companion*?). And there is only one place where anything could possibly be hidden in a space as hyperperformative and surface-oriented as a gay male video bar. Luckily, this just happens to be a place where no one in his right mind would ever even think to look: on the surface itself. Thus, The Thing is "hidden" not only in the bar's name and in that which it markets, but in its most basic concept and in the practice that arises from it.

The term *nostalgia* was first formulated in 1688 as a medical diagnosis, by the Swiss doctor Johannes Hofer. A combination of the Greek words for "return" and "sorrow," the term was developed to describe a pathological disturbance resulting from one's separation from one's normal surroundings, that which affects exiles such as soldiers, mercenaries, and "country folk" newly transplanted to the city. This concept has come to underpin contemporary psychoanalytic and popular conceptions of the "desire to return" and its connection to the loss of childhood, the loss of "oral satisfactions," and, by implication, the loss of the mother and her body.[33] When viewed in this light, then, it should not be surprising that HIV has been taxonomically designated as a *retro*virus, since nostalgia is the technology of HIV, and HIV is the technology of nostalgia. The cases for which Hofer's diagnosis was originally formulated even bear a striking resemblance to the popular iconographic countenance of gay male AIDS, which is associated, through pictoral and discursive association, with melancholia, a condition with similar symptoms. Some of these original cases of "nostalgia" were so extreme that the individual would "languish, waste away, and finally perish" in his (the documented cases are male) increasingly acute desire to return to the time and space *before the break.*[34]

A key question arises here: *Why* should a designation such as "retro-virus" hold so many avenues of biological, cultural, social, and histori-cal reality together at such a stable intersection? HIV is an invisible or diseaseless disease, one that reduces the opportunistic infections it allows to attack the body to the mere status of *symptoms*. Thus, it func-tions through the breakdown of various mechanisms of distinction: the self from the other at the immunocellular level, the symptom from the disease at the medicoscientific one, and the image from the "real" in the sociocultural sphere. It is "logical," then, that HIV should be spa-tialized and emplaced, in the form of nostalgia, at the sociocultural site of the video bar, since the epidemic is imbricated, at the deepest roots, with a historically specific incarnation of the machinery of nos-talgia (the postmodern apparatus, as embodied by the "video revolu-tion" that made these bars possible). It is no more coincidence, then, that both "developments" made their way into American public dis-course concomitantly, in the eighties.

Therefore, locating the "historical break" in 1981 that gave rise to the "AIDS era" is a haltingly dubious business. Even the popular press in this country has discovered this. The year 1981 is only a fantasy that functions, if in an only semisatisfactory manner, to fixate for us not only the slippery question of when the break occurred, but also a com-panion enigma: *What exactly was that break?*[35] Placing the origination of the epidemic at 1981 (phase 3), along with the founding of "gay libera-tion" at Stonewall in 1969 (phase 1), produces a three-phased period-izing scheme. This historical structure allows for the efficient post-modern mass-production of a retroactive gay male desire for phase 2, the seventies. This collective desire for the space and time before the break, the desire for the orgy or bacchanalia that the seventies has come to represent in the popular queer imagination, is manufactured (or, to say the least, *made visible*) by the same postmodern "video revo-lution" that makes possible the hyperpresence of the past that charac-terizes gay male video-bar space.

So we have located the *phylogenic break* on which these spaces de-pend and from which their practices of rampant periodization obtain their force in the psyches of Revolver's patrons.[36] Yet if nostalgia's "ob-ject" is ultimately the gaze of the child, or the desire to see as one saw when a child, we must now acknowledge the importance of another break. This is the *ontogenic break*, that equally phantasmic moment at which one assumes a homosexual "identity"—or any sexual identity at all. Psychoanalytically, video-bar space is an enticing consumable in that it "sells itself hard," as a space of fantasy, on the simultaneous reparation of both of these breaks—the ontogenic one and the phylogenic one. In fact, it collapses the two into each other. In other words, these bars aspire to the fantasmatic reconciliation of two separate "befores" and "afters" for their gay male clientele.

The patron actually purchases, with his five-dollar cover charge, his complicity in wanting to be "cured" of his alienation from two separate before-the-breach times and spaces. The first, the phylogenic, are those spaces/times when sex was not only safe, but freewheeling, easy, cheap and, most important, satisfying. Every pre-1981 image shown by the bar bears the invisible trace of this nonexistent period of pure and satisfying promiscuity. The second, the ontogenic, are those spaces and times when images similar to and even the same as those shown in the bar were apprehended innocently, nonperformatively, and in *no way a campy manner*—when they were apprehended by the gaze of a presexual version of the self. This originary ontogenic scenario is typically associated with the parents' living room, which is, conveniently for us, the living room of traditional television reception studies.

But let's speak about all of this more concretely, remembering the case of Revolver. Evoking again those seventeenth-century Swiss country clients of Hofer afflicted by nostalgia when transplanted to the "city," the suburban, private living room of the ontogenic scenario becomes the impersonal, urbane, performative space of Revolver only while insistently remaining located in the spatial center of West Hollywood's "Village." Likewise, Revolver rigidly designates itself as a "neighborhood bar," always extending a "warm welcome" to the citizens of this quaint(!) community. Similarly, the gaze of the parents, which functioned as that of the Big Other in the ontogenic living room scenario, is finally replaced by a sexualized, collective gaze. Yet, if the Big Other takes the form of The Gaze in the bar, it continues to serve exactly the same function as the gaze of the parents, that of the superego always ready to shake a finger at prohibited behavior.

In essence, the sexuality that is now constructed, after the fact, as *the lack* in the ontogenic living-room scenario is finally emplaced in the space between spectator and text, taking the form of the (homo)sexualized gaze that "obstructs" that spectator/text relation and makes it performative—as ostensibly opposed to "authentic." Likewise, the sexuality that is the tragic phylogenic excess of the bar's periodized pre-1981 images ("If only we'd known") is displaced into our knowing space of reception, keeping the horrific, invisible threat attached to those earlier images positively alive, but only in our contemporary space of much more "enlightened" reception.[37] Thus, the video bar, as an economic institution, sells itself on mastery. And the drive toward mastery must always be acted out in repetition.[38] Nostalgia, of course, necessarily involves repetition. Finally, then, it is through nostalgia, repetition, and mastery that the video bar markets reconciliation not only of one's present to one's past, but ultimately of one's past to the Past.

There is another equally important, and seemingly antithetical, dimension to all of this, though. What goes on at Revolver may indeed be enticing in myriad ways. But we should not forget all those thanatological connotations dangling from the word that represents the space, and all the performance anxiety that the space repeatedly produces for many of its patrons. We might recall that, for Žižek, desire—in continually restaging itself through fantasy, and in acting itself out through the Big Other (the symbolic order)—continually restages/repeats that break from which it purports to have arisen. The primary question posed by both the ontogenic and the phylogenic gay male narratives is "How did *that* (the before) turn into *this* (the after)?" If this is not—to be sure—a question the bar can answer, it *is* one it can continually, maybe even sadistically, repeat with slight variations. Put another way, the video bar is *structured around* the continual, horrific return of that which was not even ever apprehended as something that could possibility make a return—Tom Jones, for instance, or a viral infection through sex before one even knew (or before one chose to believe or had been taught to believe) that there existed anything fatal to be infected by.

Finally, then, we can see the dreaded and continuous return of camp reading practices in these spaces for what it is. At Revolver, camp at once forms a vortex out of which patrons must perform themselves and a deep structural basis for the entire experiential reality of the space—or that which commissions this performance to begin with. This is to say that camp is the mechanism that keeps continually present in this space of desire everything that AIDS activism is (and has been from the outset) working so hard to keep spatially separate and conceptually distinct from our desire; the repulsive, the ugly, the dangerous, the anachronistic, and the asexual.

In conclusion, then, what is a video bar? It is a space of history and memory and desire wherein the three are mixed and served up on the rocks, and it is a space wherein the three are *emplaced* only to be continually *displaced* and *replaced* by each other. All this occurs in cycles that endlessly repeat themselves, acting as if the threat of a mortal being finding his death in this machinery of desire does not exist even while that threat is simultaneously displayed on every available surface and in every imaginable depth.

What are these spaces? They are places where even those things that supposedly cannot "see" us return our gaze, like the bar's video images and every inch of its space. They are places that we repeatedly enter in hopes of spending our desire, but from which we always seem to walk back out into the night only having purchased more of it. And since they are "gay" spaces, we might expect that they would *do something* to distinguish a high modernist Munchian scream in the face of linear time (and death) from the frustrating/not frustrating, postmodern, silent shrug that responds to exactly the same desires and horrors. Ultimately, though, they are only sites that are confused, like the rest of us, about their own spatial and temporal relation to both. So they desperately try to keep themselves pacified and occupied with all that they have and all that they are—their own (brilliant) performance of oblivious *revolution.*

Notes

I would like to thank Lynn Spigel and Debra Silverman, without whose encouragement, scholarly influence, practical help and remarkable patience this chapter would not exist in the form in which it now does. Likewise, I thank Angelo Restivo, not only for his thoughtful comments on an early draft, but for his general intellectual companionship, which has profoundly influenced many of the ideas in this chapter—as has that of Michael Bacchus and Amy Villarejo. Joe Boone, Corey Creekmur, Julie D'Acci, Alexander Doty, Ken Feil, and Martin Meeker all read drafts and responded with incredibly useful comments. Finally, I would like to express my sincere appreciation to all those people who shared with me, during my fieldwork, reflections that many might consider to be extremely personal.

1. Interurbanity is important here because (literal and figurative) "mobility" is one of the sites where both class and generational distinctions, which will be introduced in the following section, become involved in this discussion. For a good extended discussion of the involvement of these issues in the historical analysis of spatial forms, see Aaron Betsky, *Queer Space: Architecture and Same-Sex Desire* (New York: William Morrow, 1997).

2. Edward Soja, *Postmodern Geographies: The Reassertion of Space in Critical Theory* (New York: Verso, 1989), 15. Other theorists and historians who have done influential work on space but will not be explicitly discussed here include David Harvey, Henri Lefebvre, and Georg Simmel.

3. Soja, *Geographies,* 11. This is a problem with Soja's work. He does not seem to consider fully the implications of espousing a "concrete" Marxist social analysis based on space that he ultimately props on the dazzling but to a

large extent rhetorical notions of that holiest of postmodern trinities—Jean Baudrillard, Jean-François Lyotard, and Frederic Jameson. The two most obvious and important examples of such work in the current critical context are probably Jean Baudrillard's *Simulations,* trans. Paul Foss, Paul Patton, and Philip Beitchman (New York: Semiotext(e), 1983), and Fredric Jameson's "Postmodernism, or, The Cultural Logic of Late Capitalism," *New Left Review* 146 (1984): 53–92.

4. Soja, *Geographies,* 10.

5. Manuel Castell, *The Urban Question,* cited in Soja, *Geographies,* 83; emphasis in the original.

6. Since the use of "ethnographic" methods in academic cultural studies has become such a charged issue—with that particular charge being closely related to the power dimensions of "speaking for" and "speaking as" in feminist and lesbian/gay/queer studies—I should include a few words about my attitude toward my own use of interviews in this chapter. My intention in this study is to make a *primarily methodological* contribution to a number of disciplinary and cross-disciplinary endeavors (e.g., studies in cultural space, AIDS, gay male subjectivity, television/video reception, psychoanalytic exegesis, postmodern historicity, and, of course, ethnography). The implicit assertion is that all of these can be usefully layered upon one another, as can the various investigatory methods and jargons associated with each. Indeed, it could easily be charged that my use of ethnography here is "unreflective"; in fact, I have not even formally cited my interviews. This should be taken as, rather than an omission, a *mode of reflection* on the place of ethnography in such a methodological concoction. This is to say that it is my assumption that "talking to people" is, always has been, and always will be a natural part of all scholarly conceptualization, or "research," in the humanities. The fact that we have not (yet) successfully conventionalized a mode of acknowledging this in the socioinstitutionally mandated procedures of humanistic writing, beyond that of the formal citation, is an issue that needs to be addressed, along with the issue of why this has happened—not how we can "solve the problem." (And formal citation is a radically inappropriate mode of inscribing such "talk" when it is situated in subcultural, vernacular knowledges that are being exchanged—the very sort that strategically "evaporate" when we try to pin them down from "outside.") In other words, it is still not clear to me, despite the volumes of literature that exist on the issues, exactly what "reflective ethnography" is, and how it proceeds. But even more important, it is not clear to me why "reflective ethnography" is transcontextually any better than "unreflective ethnography" anyway. Anthropological regimes of difference are, after all, different from one another—are they not?

7. For his influential original discussion of this issue, see Michel Foucault's "Interview on Popular Memory," in *Cahiers du Cinéma's Edinburgh Festival Review* (London: BFI, 1977), 110–25.

8. Some of the more useful (to media studies) explorations of camp include: Jack Babuscio, "Camp and Gay Sensibility," in *Gays and Film,* ed. Richard Dyer

(London: BFI, 1977); Andrew Ross, *No Respect: Intellectuals and Popular Culture* (New York: Routledge, 1989), 135–71; and Susan Sontag, *Against Interpretation, and Other Essays* (New York: Dell, 1969), 277–93.

9. On the relations between gay men and lesbians of some of these "types," see Alexander Doty, *Making Things Perfectly Queer: Interpreting Mass Culture* (Minneapolis: University of Minnesota Press, 1993), 81–97, and Eve Kosofsky Sedgwick and Michael Moon's "Divinity: A Dossier, a Performance Piece, a Little Understood Emotion," in Eve Kosofsky Sedgwick, *Tendencies* (Durham, N.C.: Duke University Press, 1993), 215–52.

10. For influential discussions of "queerness," see: Judith Butler, *Bodies That Matter: On the Discursive Limits of Sex* (New York: Routledge, 1993), 223–42; Doty, *Perfectly Queer*, xi–17; Sedgwick, *Tendencies*, 1–23; and Michael Warner, "From Queer to Eternity: An Army of Theorists Cannot Fail," *Village Voice Literary Supplement* 106 (June 1992): 19–20.

11. Sedgwick, *Tendencies*, 7.

12. Emblematic ethnographic work in this regard includes Ann Gray's "Behind Closed Doors," in *Boxed In: Women and Television*, ed. Helen Baehr and Gillian Dyer (New York: Pandora, 1987), 39–54, and David Morley's *Family Television: Cultural Power and Domestic Leisure* (New York: Routledge, 1986). One influential example of such work in a nonethnographic mode is Lynn Spigel's *Make Room for TV: Television and the Family Ideal in Postwar America* (Chicago: University of Chicago Press, 1992), a historical investigation of the ways in which the complex realm of the "domestic" comes to circumscribe America's dominant, institutional notion of television.

13. See in particular Robert Hodge and David Tripp, *Children and Television* (Stanford, Calif.: Stanford University Press, 1986); Henry Jenkins, *Textual Poachers: Television Fans and Participatory Culture* (New York: Routledge, 1992); Constance Penley, "Brownian Motion: Women, Tactics, and Technology," in *Technoculture*, ed. Constance Penley and Andrew Ross (Minneapolis: University of Minnesota, 1991), 135–61; and Ellen Seiter, Hans Borchers, Gabriele Kreutzner, and Eva Maria Warth, "Don't Treat Us like We're So Stupid and Naive: Toward an Ethnography of Soap Opera Viewers," in *Remote Control: Television, Audiences, and Cultural Power*, ed. Ellen Seiter (New York: Routledge, 1989), 223–47.

14. Robert C. Allen, in "From Exhibition to Reception: Reflections on the Audience in Film History," *Screen* 31, no. 4 (winter 1990), reminds us that all reception is performative, and that this should be a consideration in all reception studies (352). The video bar is distinct and interesting in that it is a case in which the performance of sexuality becomes "visibly" involved with the performance of textual reception/response.

15. To transform from its original function, that is, the use of the term *pretext* by Lucie Arbuthnot and Gail Seneca in "Pre-Text and Text in *Gentlemen Prefer Blondes*," *Film Reader* 5 (1982): 14–23, cited in Doty, *Perfectly Queer*, 106. These authors use this term to describe the role to which heterosexual narrative structures may be relegated by nonheterosexual readings.

16. By a "classical gay liberation theory," I mean one grounded in a promis-

cuity-based critique of heterosexual monogamy and generally associated with the seventies in this country. I thank Martin Meeker for his observation that "perhaps in practice and conceptualization 'classical' gay male liberation theory (as I discuss it here) was more about bodies and touch than eyes and vision." While Meeker's point is interesting, important, and well taken, I remain attached to the notion that any collective aspirationality involved with individual somatic sensation inherently involves, both pro- and retroactively, the possibility of moving its seductions "into the light," a metaphor that I will let speak for itself.

17. See in particular Babuscio, "Camp and Gay Sensibility"; Michael Bronski, *Culture Clash: The Making of Gay Sensibility* (Boston: South End Press, 1984); Richard Dyer, *Heavenly Bodies: Film Stars and Society*, (New York: St. Martin's Press, 1986), 141–95; and Larry Gross, "Out of the Mainstream: Sexual Minorities and the Mass Media," in *Remote Control*, ed. Seiter, 130–49.

18. Gross, "Mainstream," 133.

19. For his critique of the "repressive hypothesis," which puts power in a top-down relation of "prohibition" and "regulation" to sexuality, see Michel Foucault, *The History of Sexuality*, vol. 1, *An Introduction*, trans. Robert Hurley (New York: Random House, 1978), 17–49.

20. Esther Newton, *Mother Camp: Female Impersonators in America* (Chicago: University of Chicago Press, 1972).

21. Slavoj Žižek, *Looking Awry: An Introduction to Jacques Lacan through Popular Culture* (Cambridge, Mass.: MIT Press, 1991), 6.

22. Eve Kosofsky Sedgwick, *The Epistemology of the Closet* (Berkeley: University of California Press, 1990), 35.

23. Jon Wagner pointed out the importance of this phrase to me.

24. Such ambivalence about the pleasures of video-bar patronage, and about gay male institutional taste cultures in general, is particularly evident in conversational exchange among certain gay males in Chicago's Lakeview district. Here, Monday is officially called "Show Tunes Night" at Sidetracks. But the patrons regularly refer to this weekly event as "Nellie Night," articulating their own pleasures only sarcastically and self-consciously—"I'm not *really* nellie" (read: an old style, stereotypically effeminate homosexual who preys on cultural detritus), or, alternatively, "If I am, I am not embarrassed (and maybe I'm even proud)." Furthermore, it is common for gay men in Chicago to jokingly refer to Sidetracks as "Widecracks," linguistically associating in one fell swoop the "excessive" modes of textual consumption and reading going on at the video bar with, first, anal passivity and, second, promiscuity.

25. Žižek, *Looking Awry*, 172–73. On the issue of the real in Žižek, see Butler, *Bodies That Matter*, 187–223. For its implications for film theory, see Angelo Restivo's review of Žižek's work, "Lacan According to Žižek," *Quarterly Review of Film and Video* 16, no. 2 (1997): 193–206.

26. Žižek, *Looking Awry*, 43.

27. For a virtual rumination on this issue of "realness" in gay male culture, see Jennie Livingston's 1991 film *Paris Is Burning*, which complicates this fur-

ther by dealing with performativities of differences that are somehow written onto the body (in particular, race and gender) as well as those which, more commonly, are not (like sexuality and class).

28. Slovoj Žižek, "The Pervert Games: David Lynch and Neil Jordan," paper presented at the Parallel Histories: Psychoanalysis and Cinema conference, University of California, Los Angeles, 13 November 1992.

29. Dennis Altman, *The Homosexualization of America* (New York: St. Martin's Press, 1982), 28.

30. Žižek, *Looking Awry*, 172, emphasis in the original.

31. Ibid., 41.

32. For short but stunningly illuminating considerations of HIV as a certifiably postmodern phenomenon, see Jean Baudrillard, "After the Orgy," "Prophylaxis and Virulence," and "Viral Hospitality," in *The Transparency of Evil: Essays on Extreme Phenomena*, trans. James Benedict (New York: Verso, 1993), and Arthur Kroker, "Sacrificial Sex," in *Fluid Exchanges: Artists and Critics in the AIDS Crisis*, ed. James Miller (Toronto: University of Toronto Press, 1992), 321–29.

33. Jean Starobinski, "The Idea of Nostalgia," *Diogenes* 54 (spring 1966): 86–87. For a similar discussion of the pathological origins of the term, see David Lowenthal, *The Past Is a Foreign Country* (New York: Cambridge University Press, 1985), 3–31. For relevant discussions of nostalgia in relation to contemporary American culture, see Lowenthal, "Nostalgia Tells It like It Wasn't," in *The Imagined Past: History and Nostalgia*, ed. Christopher Shaw and Malcolm Chase (New York: Manchester University Press, 1988), 18–32, and Fredric Jameson, "Nostalgia for the Present," *South Atlantic Quarterly* 88 (spring 1989): 517–37. For an interesting discussion of nostalgia's importance to popular and ethnographic memories, see Henry Jenkins and Lynn Spigel, "Same Bat Channel/Different Bat Times: Mass Culture and Popular Memory," in *The Many Lives of a Batman: Critical Approaches to a Superhero and his Media*, ed. Roberta E. Pearson and William Uricchio (New York: Routledge, 1991), 117–49.

34. Lowenthal, *Past*, 10.

35. Arthur and Louise Kroker have recently proposed that the JFK assassination is the moment of postmodernism's emergence. Following them, I submit this event as the beginning of the HIV epidemic as well—we might as well just get these two moments together for simplicity's sake. Doesn't everyone know by now that JFK was the first of the sad, young, beautiful, and promiscuous men to be swallowed up by his own system?

36. For a discussion that distinguishes between, and considers the relations among, phylogenic narratives (the collective or "centuries long process by which identities are constructed") and ontogenic narratives (the individual story of the identity of "such and such a person") in queer politics and subjectivities, see Sedgwick and Moon's "Divinity," in Sedgwick, *Tendencies*, 226–27.

37. "Enlightened," that is, if one believes "safe" sex discourse to be enlightening. For a related and very eloquent personal/theoretical rumination, see Samuel Delany, "Street Talk/Straight Talk," *differences* 3, no. 2 (summer 1991): 21–38.

38. For his classic argument on repetition (in all its notorious conceptual confusion and difficulty), see Sigmund Freud's *Beyond the Pleasure Principle* (1920), in *The Standard Edition of the Complete Psychological Works of Sigmund Freud*, ed. James Strachey (London: Hogarth Press, 1953–1974), 18: 34–35. For a sustained analysis of psychoanalytic repetition and its relation to HIV narrative, see my "Narration by Numbers: AIDS and the Form of Contemporary Difference" (Ph.D. diss., School of Cinema-Television, University of Southern California, 1998).

8

Unmasking the Homophile in 1950s Los Angeles
An Archival Record

Karin Quimby and Walter L. Williams

(A)History

With rainbow flags lining Santa Monica Boulevard, the main thorough-fare of "gay" West Hollywood, known today for its gay bars, book-stores, coffeeshops, novelty boutiques, gyms, churches, and govern-ment, one can easily forget the very recent past of this urban space where, as gay L.A. legend reveals, the early gay protest movement erupted in 1970 outside of a notoriously homophobic restaurant in the heart of what is now West Hollywood. Protesting the wooden sign, Fagots Stay Out, that had hung outside Barney's Beanery since the 1950s, the Gay Liberation Front began what now has stretched into several decades of visible protest for lesbian and gay rights. Morris Kight, a prominent Los Angeles gay activist who was instrumental in organizing the Barney's Beanery protest, owns that sign today as a prize in his private archival collection.

Such visible signs, however, as any historian of gay life knows, are few and far between. The desire to collect such signs of oppression and victory necessarily must be informed by a profound sense of *lack*—of any trace of gay, lesbian, bisexual, transgendered or otherwise queer existence. The effects of the closet in all its manifestations have given shape not only to queer life, but likewise significantly inform any attempt to construct queer history as a field of legitimate study. The very problematics of re-creating a history defined by gaps, elisions, omissions, as well as the relative instability and historically recent use of terms such as *invert, homophile, gay, lesbian, bisexual, transsexual, trans-gendered,* and *queer* make reconstructing the history of nonnormative sexual groups through material signs all the more fraught with ques-tion. Around the nation lesbian and gay archives face, in very material terms, the theoretical question of what defines such identity groups and who decides what should be collected and preserved, and what should be discarded. The omission of queer histories in the official records of the United States, as well as their absence even in unofficial local lore, not only has made the historian's interpretive work more difficult, but has led to necessarily creative strategies that employ myth, gossip, heresy, and fiction in order to reconstruct a past for sexual minorities. In a sense, writing a queer history is still very much a frontier, a terrain yet to be mapped out, defined, theorized.

The purpose of this chapter is to construct one such history using the resources available in Los Angeles—from the personal testimony of individuals such as the early activist Jim Kepner, who founded what is now the International Gay and Lesbian Archives (IGLA), to an examination of the materials of those early L.A. gay organizations and publications whose archival traces are found in bulging file folders and on the bookshelves of the IGLA. There are various documents—a gay magazine, a gay academic journal, a U.S. Supreme Court ruling, and the rise and fall of two early gay groups, the Mattachine Society and ONE Incorporated—that show how, two decades before the 1969 Stonewall rebellion in New York City, Los Angeles gays and lesbians were organizing to resist police oppression and to educate themselves and the general population about homosexuality. Although the original impetus of this chapter was to present a photographic essay of Los Angeles's gay past, as research at the IGLA ensued, as well as interviews with the late Jim Kepner took place, what became clear was the extraordinary power of the early L.A. gay press to shape the debates and political movement as it came into being, debates that continue in some cases almost in the exact same form today. Also, it became clear through the contentious personal letters found in files among drafts of mission statements and early homophile articles, that Los Angeles's gay history is replete with the personal politics and polemics endemic to much minority group organizing. This L.A. history is as much about imperious personalities, the struggle for power and agendas (resulting in such acts as the heist and holding captive of a collection of gay archives for over thirty years) as it is about any historical document produced, or any political battle won. The attention these early activists gave to putting their ideas down on paper, of preserving their words with such care and ferocity, reveals in fact the core political response to living a life of enforced secrecy. Their desire to preserve these traces, coupled with our desire to locate them, reveals a similar impulse: the desire that a visible, "real" legacy might be pasted together to help shore up a sense of permanence and belonging in a general culture that would prefer, still, that we not speak our name.

In Los Angeles two gay groups decided to organize in response to police pressure and government security programs: the Mattachine Society began in 1950 and ONE Incorporated, a group that splintered off from the Mattachine, was founded in 1952. Both groups organized in response to the police repression that homosexuals were encountering in the city, but ONE Incorporated emphasized educating homophiles, as they then referred to themselves, about their lives and loves. This group of volunteers published the first nationally distributed gay magazine called, *ONE Magazine.* In its attempt to illustrate one way of going about the excavation of a hitherto obscured facet of Los Angeles's gay past, this chapter charts the emergence of this latter organization and magazine. What follows, we hope, is a meditation on the unexpected ways in which a queer history may emerge from the sometimes anomalous, sometimes tantalizing, often ambiguous traces that comprise, in the most theoretical sense of the phrase, the gay archive.

Postwar (Night)Life in Los Angeles, or "Pin Up Your Bobbypins before You Go out the Door"

From the early 1900s, when the growth of the movie industry attracted many creative and bohemian people to Hollywood, Los Angeles served as a magnet to attract sexual nonconformists of all types.[1] Why Los Angeles became the birthplace of these vanguard gay organizations in the early 1950s, however, might best be attributed to its role in World War II. The gay and lesbian population swelled in Los Angeles during World War II, as L.A. served as the departure point for numerous young service women and men leaving for the Pacific front. In addition, many young lesbians working in defense industry plants discovered each other in their new wartime jobs or in all-female boarding houses. At the end of the war, however, as Allan Bérubé details in *Coming Out under Fire,* many of these lesbians in the Women's Army Corps, and gay men in all branches of the service, found themselves facing undesirable discharges.[2] Not able to return to their families, or not wanting to go back to a life of enforced heterosexual marriage in their provincial small towns, many of these returning veterans decided to remain in Los Angeles once the war was over.

As a result of this increased population of gay guys and girls (as they then referred to themselves), gay and lesbian bars began to proliferate in L.A.'s wild night life. Historian and longtime Los Angeles resident Jim Kepner recalls some of the bars that opened in Los Angeles in the late 1940s, including one of the more popular bars, the Tropical

Lt. Doris Putman of the Women's Army Corps, Los Angeles, 1942. One of many photographs documenting aspects of pre- and postwar lesbian life from the personal album of Putman, a Los Angeles lesbian, which she later donated to ONE/IGLA. (Used by permission of ONE Institute/International Gay and Lesbian Archives)

Village, or "TV Club" in Santa Monica, on the beach. The Tropical Village was unusual, Kepner remembers, because it commingled all kinds of men and women and the attire worn was quite varied—from bathing suits to tuxedos. Also in Santa Monica was Jack's at the Beach, with its sister establishment, Jack's Drive-In on Wilshire Boulevard. Officially a hamburger joint, its handsome male waiters on roller skates made it a popular hang out among gay men.

The lesbian bars in that era were mostly located in North Hollywood. Kepner describes them as "rough," with a clientele of butch dykes and prostitutes on their nights off. The If Club, the Open Door, and Joani Presents were among these early establishments. The first L.A. lesbian bars that broke out of the butch-femme stereotype included the Lakeview and the Bacchanal 70, the latter of which did not emerge until the early 1970s. The Bacchanal 70, located in the midtown Beverly Boulevard area, featured cool jazz combos and drew high fashion female models—a precursor perhaps to the "lipstick lesbian" image for which Los Angeles is now known.

Because of the proliferation of gay bars and patrons in Los Angeles during and after the war, police harassment of homosexuals also increased, heightening an aura of suspicion and fear of entrapment. Kepner remembers the euphemism, "doing the two-step," that was used to characterize the closeted gay patron's departure from a bar. The "two-step" meant that when he left the bar, it would only take him two steps to reach the sidewalk and affect the pose of simply walking by. This pose was sometimes foiled, Kepner recalls, by one of the drag queens in the bar who would prepare to leave at the same time as the departing patron. Once out on the street the drag queen would, to the hilarity of some and horror of others, throw his arm around the "two-stepper" exclaiming something like, "Oh honey, wasn't that just a wonderful gay bar?" This tension and play between those frequenting gay bars—between those who were out and visible, like the drag queens, and those who remained fearful and in the closet—comprises a relatively unexplored layer of gay history. The emphasis in historical studies on the frequent police raids that forced these very different patrons of the bars into solidarity, sometimes overlooks the extreme differences in gay identity and degrees of "outness" among these same patrons.

Police harassment appears to have been the main motivation for the start of early gay political resistance.[3] Another reason for organizing, however, was the desire to develop a sense of community outside of the bars. The rise of several gay newsletters and periodicals in the 1950s was particularly significant in forming this broader sense of gay community, and of advancing the movement for gay and lesbian rights.

Sporting different looks: two versions of glamour and grit. At top, Joan Waldor Hannon, who played drums in *Some Like It Hot* and was the popular owner of Joani Presents, a landmark Los Angeles lesbian bar that operated from 1961 to 1973, and, at bottom, the 1964 softball team sponsored by the bar, first called the Gangrenes and subsequently the Schleppers (not all woman participating were lesbian). (Used by permission of ONE Institute/International Gay and Lesbian Archives)

The Rise of the Gay Press in Los Angeles

The first step in lesbian and gay community organizing in Los Angeles might be considered to have begun in 1947 with Lisa Ben's printing of the first American lesbian newsletter, *Vice Versa*. (Like most other gay writers and editors of her day, "Lisa Ben" chose to write under a pseudonym, an anagram for *lesbian*, and still desires anonymity today.)

The newsletter was decidedly apolitical, as were many of the small groups that sprang up around the same time whose focus was on creating networks of friends beyond bars and nightclubs. For example, as Kepner remembers, in June of 1951, a small group of interracial male couples in Los Angeles formed an organization called Knights of the Clocks to provide a social outlet for others like themselves.

Most gay men and lesbians were not politically active and simply wanted to live lives without disruption. They could not do this, however, because of the concerted series of attacks begun by conservative politicians and law enforcement agencies. Responding to the new gay social openness, the Los Angeles Police Department began taking a decidedly antigay stance in the 1950s. Lesbians and gays were increasingly arrested upon any excuse in a determined effort to rid the city of "sexual perverts." This police persecution helped mobilize what would become the first homosexual rights group in the country.

The Battle of the Boys: In-fighting and Outcasting in the Early Gay Movement in Los Angeles

In response to the police harassment, a Hollywood actor named Harry Hay proposed the founding of a society devoted to guaranteeing the rights of homosexuals. This group, which Hay and several other leftist activists organized in Los Angeles, became known as the Mattachine Society. The term *mattachine* refers to a tradition involving medieval dancers who wore masks while performing in public plays critical of their world; likewise, the Mattachine Society itself underwent several different public and many private transformations in its tumultuous twenty-year history.[4]

After meeting and organizing for two years the organization decided in 1952 to start a magazine to express "the homosexual viewpoint." A small core of Mattachine members nurtured this magazine into existence, naming it *ONE* in recognition of the fact that homosexual people shared a common bond that made them "one." They rejected the medical term *homosexual,* and favored using *homophile* to ex-

VICE VERSA

Volume I, Number 1

June, 1947

TABLE OF CONTENTS

...lets ...ying the crudest kind of magazines or pictorial
severely censured were they to display this other type of
publication. Why? Because Society decrees it thus.

Hence the appearance of VICE VERSA, a magazine dedicated, in all seriousness, to those of us who will never
quite be able to adapt ourselves to the iron-bound rules
of Convention. The circulation of this publication, under
the circumstances, must be very limited, going only to
those who, it is felt, will genuinely enjoy such a magazine. This little publication, at present free of charge,

Remember, VICE VERSA is your magazine. If you find a
place for such a publication in your scheme of things,
well and good. But only by contributions of material will
we be able to keep our magazine in existence. Whether you
are an experienced writer or the veriest amateur, submit
your material. And if VICE VERSA should be subjected to
the glance of unsympathetic eyes, let us at least show
that our magazine can be just as interesting and enter-
taining on as high a level as the average magazines available to the general public.

JUST BETWEEN US GIRLS

Fortunately, it was possible to gather together enough
material for a second issue of VICE VERSA, which, at least
at the present time, seems to put this magazine on a month-
ly-appearance basis. Whether your editor can continue to
do this alone or not, however, is doubtful. The only outside contribution in this issue was a very fine letter from

WE TOO ARE DRIFTING, by Gale Wilhelm
    Grayson Publishers, 381 - 4th Avenue,
    New York City 16

(Drifting....
but not far
enough!)

WE ARE FIRES UNQUENCHABLE, by Mary Speers
    Murray and Gee, Hollywood, 1942

(Not so hot)

LOVELIEST OF FRIENDS, by G. Sheila Donisthorpe
    Claude Kendall, New York, 1931

(hostile
propaganda)

EXTRAORDINARY WOMEN, by Compton Mackenzie, Vanguard
    Press, New York, 1928

(dull)

TWISTED CLAY, by Frank Walford
    Claude Kendall, New York, 1934

(sordid story
of mental
disintegration)

A lesbian newsletter is born. Masthead and clippings from the 1947 inaugural issues of
Vice Versa, the first known lesbian publication. Note, in the bottom excerpt, the review of
homosexually themed literature. (Used by permission of ONE Institute/International Gay
and Lesbian Archives)

A fifties version of direct-action intervention. This "how to act during a police raid" card was distributed to gay bar patrons by the Mattachine Society in the 1950s and attests to the oppressive reality faced by homosexuals entering public space. (Used by permission of ONE Institute/International Gay and Lesbian Archives)

Demonstration against police brutality, February 1967. At this rally in Silverlake, early gay activist Jim Kepner declared in a speech, "After tonight the nameless love that dare not speak its name will never again be quiet." (Used by permission of ONE Institute/International Gay and Lesbian Archives)

press the notion that it was their same-sex (homo) love (philia) that united them, rather than just sexual behavior.

However, within two years of its foundation, Mattachine fractured over debates about how best to accomplish its goals of improving the lives of homosexuals. Harry Hay held a rigid view of Mattachine's development that he modeled on Communist Party ideology. As the Mattachine grew, new activists were shocked to learn of the Communist Party background of several of the leftist leaders of the organization. In the context of the red-baiting McCarthy era of the early 1950s, less radical activists emerged in Mattachine, like Ken Burns and Hal Call, who believed that the Mattachine would never be able to accomplish its objectives if the organization were publicly associated with communism. They wanted homosexuals to be seen as "all-American" and "just like everyone else," which is how they saw themselves.

This early split in agendas, in fact, initiated what remains a central debate in the gay community today, pitting those who believe that gays are essentially the same as straights, and therefore should be treated equally, against those who claim that sexually minoritized people and cultures are intrinsically different from heterosexual society, yet still are deserving of civil rights. People like Harry Hay and Jim Kepner took this latter position. In an article addressing this debate in the Mattachine Society, Kepner wrote a response in the April 1954 edition of *ONE Magazine*, entitled: "The Importance of Being Different." In this article he poses the questions that continue to split the gay community today: "Are homosexuals in any important way different from other people? If so, ought that difference be cultivated, or hidden under a bushel, or extirpated altogether? . . . While the magazine has been relatively clear in its policy, the Mattachine Society has become almost schizoid on the question of whether we're different, whether to admit it, and what to do about it."[5]

Members like Hal Call, a procapitalist libertarian journalist and businessman, felt that a more effective way to gain equal rights was to publicize homosexuality widely and make it a common topic of conversation in mainstream American society. He wanted to use the progay findings of researchers and intellectuals, like Alfred Kinsey and psychologist Evelyn Hooker, to spearhead a public relations campaign to revise public attitudes toward sexuality in general. In contrast to Harry Hay, who stressed the gender nonconforming personalities of homosexuals as separate types of persons who should organize as a minority, Call emphasized sexual liberation for everyone, with a focus on sexuality freed from sexual repression. This focus, according to one source, eventually turned the Mattachine into an all-male "jack off

"We're not in the business of protecting cocksuckers," declared officials from the Harbor Police Station in 1968, which led to this "polite" demonstration by lesbians and gay men, whose preppy outfits and all-American smiles were part of an organized strategy to win public support—although the floral bouquets add a touch of camp humor to the demonstration. (Used by permission of ONE Institute/International Gay and Lesbian Archives)

club." Call reacted against the secretive, left-wing, marginalized approach of Harry Hay, and stressed that communism was no friend of homosexuals (given Stalin's widespread imprisonment of sexual nonconformists of all kinds). Instead, he wanted to see homosexuals succeed economically, to be sexually open and free, and to build a strong presence within mainstream American capitalist society, an agenda that has, forty years later, come to define a certain urban, gay male population.

Under Call's leadership the Mattachine Society moved its headquarters to San Francisco and evolved an increasingly public, mainstream approach to their advocacy of gay rights. Meanwhile, the more radical activists (including radical leftists like Jim Kepner and radical libertarians like Dorr Legg and Don Slater) shifted their emphasis to ONE Incorporated. They focused on publishing *ONE Magazine* out of a belief that the prime need of homophile people was to build a strong

An early recognition of gay identity as performative underlies this graphic design for the Mattachine Society; the term *mattachine* referred originally to medieval masked drama. (Used by permission of ONE Institute/International Gay and Lesbian Archives)

2430 Ellsworth Street
Berkeley 4, California
February 15, 1953

MATTACHINE FOUNDATION
P. O. Box 2833
Terminal Annex
Los Angeles 54, Cal.

Gentlemen:

Through a friend I have just heard of your organization and the Public
Committee to Out-Law Entrapment. I am deeply interested in your work and
would like to do all I can to help. The two-dollar money order enclosed is
the best I can do now in the way of money, but I assure you more will follow
from time to time as I can afford it. I fully intend to tell as many of my
friends as I can about the foundation and trust that even this bit will help
get the ball rolling up here in the Northern California area.

I am curious to know if you might have brochures which might help us to
organize discussion clubs such as I hear are being sponsered by you in the
Southern California area. Perhaps such a group has already been formed here.
Would it be possible to obtain any information from you on this matter? Traditionally, inverts have not be noteable for any great degree of social cohesion,
and I realize fully how delicate the whole matter might be in regard to the
mails, unsympathetic interests, agents provocateurs, etc. But if you feel free
enough to send me some information in this regard, I would certainly be very
grateful to you.

There is another matter over which I am very concerned. I understand that
Bayard Rustin, college secretary for the Fellowship of Reconciliation, has been
arrested in Los Angeles on a "morals" charge. He was right in the middle of a
California lecture tour and we were expecting him here in Berkeley. I am some-

what active in church work in this area and many of my friends (straight) have been shocked by the news. I have tried to assure them by explanations about the police situation in L.A. that perhaps a man of such caliber had not been as indiscreet as sensationalist newspapers would imply. After all, he is a Negro and a pacifist as well, and I suspect that more departments on the police force down there than its vice squad had been interested in his arrest. The details have reached us up here with a good deal of that Los Angeles smog. Someone said he had been caught in a car with two other men, but no one seems to know what they had been doing. Do they have incontrovertible evidence on him? Has he had a trial? If not, is there any way he can be saved? If so, has he been sent to prison? (Knowing Bayard, prison would be his choice rather than any fine.) In short, could you send me any information you can about this arrest?

Thanking you beforehand, I wish to add my heartiest congratulations to you all for the splendid work to which you are dedicated and my sincerest hopes and prayers for your success.

Sincerely yours,

On mailing list
2-23-53
CMR

A moving testimony to the power of early activist organizing and the spread of word-of-mouth information in creating community, this letter is part of the Mattachine Society file at the ONE/IGLA Archives. (Used by permission of ONE Institute/International Gay and Lesbian Archives)

sense of community within the homosexual population. They wanted to use the magazine to promulgate the communication and exchange of ideas needed to break down the intellectual and emotional isolation that disadvantaged homosexual people. As Jim Kepner writes in *Rough News—Daring Views,* "Most gays [in the 1950s], including some on ONE's staff, felt that our only concern was to get the police off our backs. It took a long struggle to get others to see the need for gay education, for building gay community consciousness and institutions."[6] ONE Incorporated's *ONE Magazine,* which unlike *Vice Versa* developed a national subscription list, not only was one of the most potent public forums for protesting the repression of homosexuals in the United States, but simultaneously helped create the first conceptions of a national gay community. Benedict Anderson has argued in *Imagined Communities* that the invention of the printing press and early print culture was instrumental in forming the conceptualization of nationalism through providing a "common language" publication with the power to bring people together into a discourse community.[7] The early gay and lesbian press served a similar function: while it may not have created a queer nation, it provided individuals, especially those living in rural areas, with their first sense of being connected to a larger community. This increased knowledge of one another, enabled through gay periodicals, did much to spur on the later gay rights movement of the post-Stonewall 1970s.

For over a decade, *ONE Magazine* served as the major publication of the movement, along with two magazines that followed it, the *Mattachine Review* and the *Ladder;* the latter was a publication of the Daughters of Bilitis (DOB), created in San Francisco by lesbian activists Del Martin, Phyllis Lyon, and Helen Sandoz. The mission statements of ONE and the DOB were quite similar, suggesting the tenor of the fledgling homophile movement.

The effectiveness of the early gay press in organizing community is perhaps no better verified than by the homophobic claim made in the 1954 *Miami Daily News* of the rapid "spread" of the gay population from Los Angeles to other urban centers. This headline and article were reprinted in the October 1954 edition of *ONE Magazine.* The *Miami Daily News* article, entitled, "How L.A. Handles Its 150,000 Perverts," warns Miami of an impending takeover by perverts, eerily perceived as a kind of gay virus spreading from Los Angeles. The fear expressed in this article was based on the perception that a developing homosexual community, solidified through "their own magazine," was emanating from Los Angeles and infecting other urban centers:

It happened in Los Angeles and it could happen here. In California the homosexuals have organized to resist interference by police. They have established their own magazine and are constantly crusading for recognition as a "normal" group, a so-called "third sex."

They number 150,000 in Los Angeles, their leaders say. They claim kinship by nature with some of the leading literary and business figures in the nation.[8]

Not only does the author of this article inadvertently recognize the power the "establishment" of a gay press maintained in organizing a community, he refers to what was to become another hotly debated strategy of legitimizing homosexual existence—that of "outing" well-known writers, artists, and political leaders in the 1990s.

Creating Gay History

The strategy of claiming "kinship by nature with some of the leading literary and business figures in the nation" served both a political and historical purpose, and is a methodology still practiced today. The need to build a chronology of a gay past out of historical fragments, innuendo, and blank spaces has been the unique and necessary task of the historian of gay and lesbian culture. This strategy of outing famous figures, of constructing history—or truth—through rumor or gossip, has been the basis not only of much gay history but of daily queer existence as well.

The argument for gay rights through claiming kinship with famous figures of the past was identified in Dr. Evelyn Hooker's groundbreaking article, "A Preliminary Analysis of Group Behavior of Homosexuals" (1956), by a Dr. Burgess, who said, "The group lore identifies, not always too accurately, certain famous men past and present, as homosexuals thus providing a justification of their aberrant way of life."[9] The very act of historicizing or claiming gay existence presents the unique problem of a subject always already obscured through the demands of the closet. In gay historical inquiry, therefore, there can be no myth of an authentic or completely knowable subject that has, in the past, informed much mainstream historical investigation. Gay history begins with the overt recognition of the obscured subject, yet the historical/political strategy of "outing" brazenly subverts that obscurity with a claim of knowledge of the subject. Yet despite valiant attempts by the Mattachine Society and ONE to increase knowledge and acceptance of homosexuals through such strategies, the state continued to harass the new gay organizations at each turn.

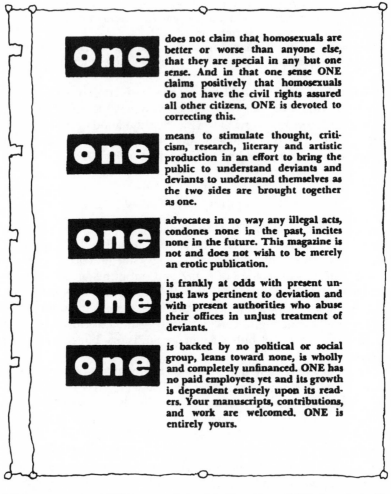

one does not claim that homosexuals are better or worse than anyone else, that they are special in any but one sense. And in that one sense ONE claims positively that homosexuals do not have the civil rights assured all other citizens. ONE is devoted to correcting this.

one means to stimulate thought, criticism, research, literary and artistic production in an effort to bring the public to understand deviants and deviants to understand themselves as the two sides are brought together as one.

one advocates in no way any illegal acts, condones none in the past, incites none in the future. This magazine is not and does not wish to be merely an erotic publication.

one is frankly at odds with present unjust laws pertinent to deviation and with present authorities who abuse their offices in unjust treatment of deviants.

one is backed by no political or social group, leans toward none, is wholly and completely unfinanced. ONE has no paid employees yet and its growth is dependent entirely upon its readers. Your manuscripts, contributions, and work are welcomed. ONE is entirely yours.

Mission statements of ONE Incorporated and the Daughters of Bilitis, from the inside covers of their respective periodicals, *ONE Magazine* (February 1954) and the *Ladder* (October 1957). (Used by permission of ONE Institute/International Gay and Lesbian Archives)

☆ purpose of the

Daughters of BILITIS

A WOMEN'S ORGANIZATION FOR THE PURPOSE OF PROMOTING THE INTEGRATION OF THE HOMOSEXUAL INTO SOCIETY BY:

1 Education of the variant, with particular emphasis on the psychological, physiological and sociological aspects, to enable her to understand herself and make her adjustment to society in all its social, civic and economic implications——this to be accomplished by establishing and maintaining as complete a library as possible of both fiction and non-fiction literature on the sex deviant theme; by sponsoring public discussions on pertinent subjects to be conducted by leading members of the legal, psychiatric, religious and other professions; by advocating a mode of behavior and dress acceptable to society.

2 Education of the public at large through acceptance first of the individual, leading to an eventual breakdown of erroneous taboos and prejudices; through public discussion meetings aforementioned; through dissemination of educational literature on the homosexual theme.

3 Participation in research projects by duly authorized and responsible psychologists, sociologists and other such experts directed towards further knowledge of the homosexual.

4 Investigation of the penal code as it pertains to the homosexual, proposal of changes to provide an equitable handling of cases involving this minority group, and promotion of these changes through due process of law in the state legislatures.

Who's who in gay history? The IGLA's entry in this 1970s Gay Pride parade featured large pictures of known or suspected lesbians and gays as a strategy of historicizing gay existence. (Used by permission of ONE Institute/International Gay and Lesbian Archives)

"Based on No Particular Logic"

The United States Post Office became the next government agency to attempt to halt the emerging homophile voice. Even though *ONE Magazine* was careful not to print sexually graphic language or pictures, the U.S. Postal Service impounded the October 1954 issue of the magazine and labeled it "obscene." Ironically, the same issue that was impounded featured an article by ONE's legal counsel on "The Law of Mailable Material." In this piece the legal counsel reveals the moral and political tenor of the time through its answer to the question, What is printable in *ONE Magazine*?:

First, while I do not want to alarm ONE's readers, I must in frankness say there is one extreme school of legal thought which would say that ONE, merely by its existence, is illegal. That line of reasoning would run as follows: Homosexual acts are made crimes in every State in the Union. ONE is published specifically for homosexuals. Therefore ONE is a magazine for criminals, their edification and guidance. It is, therefore, illegal.

This, however, is too extreme a view for 1954. There is no indication from any quarter that such a view will ever be taken, or could be successfully maintained in a court. It is likelier that a more moderate, sensible position will in fact prevail. This moderate view is in fact the one taken last year by the Solicitor-General.

That view is this: that a discussion of the social, economic, personal and legal problems of homosexuals, for the purposes of better understanding of and by society, is permissible; but appeals to the lusts or salacity or sexual appetites of ONE's readers are not permissible. ONE, in other words, can appeal to the heads, but not to the sexual desires, of its readers.[10]

The legal counsel gives examples of what was and was not permissible to print: "Permissible: 'John was my friend for a year.' Not permissible: 'That night we made mad love.'"[11] The article ends with a comment on lesbians: "Note also that these rules are relaxed somewhat in work dealing with homosexuality among women. Hence, the greater freedom of ONE's February "All-Woman Issue." This is merely a reflection of society's attitudes in general, based on no particular logic."[12] Of course, this writer fails to understand the patriarchal logic (expressed in particular by male sexologists at the time) that has long claimed that women have no sexuality except in response to men, a logic it took the lesbian feminist movement of the 1970s to begin to dislodge.

Despite its careful attention to the government's obscenity rules, the magazine was impounded. The pieces in the October 1954 issue that apparently were salacious enough to warrant the seizure of the magazine were outlined in the court case:

1. The story "Sappho Remembered" appearing on Pages 12 through 15, is obscene because lustfully stimulating to the homosexual reader.
2. The poem "Lord Samuel and Lord Montagu," appearing on Pages 18 and 19, is obscene because of the filthy language used in it.
3. The advertisement for the Swiss publication "The Circle" appearing at the top of page 29, is non-mailable matter because it gives information for the obtaining of obscene matter.[13]

ONE Incorporated brought suit against the United States Post Office, and the case went all the way to the United States Supreme Court. The Supreme Court decision was a summary reversal of the decision made by the Ninth Circuit United States Court of Appeals. The earlier decision of 27 February 1957 had read as follows: "The Court of Appeals, Ross, District Judge, held that [ONE] magazine, purportedly published for the purpose of dealing with homosexuality from scientific, historical and critical point of view, but containing articles which were noth-

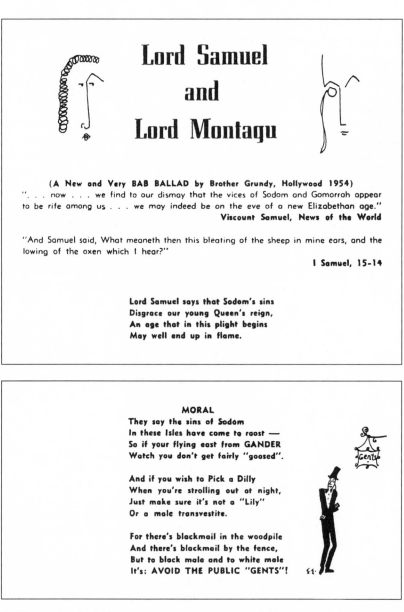

Lord Samuel
and
Lord Montagu

(A New and Very BAB BALLAD by Brother Grundy, Hollywood 1954)
". . . now . . . we find to our dismay that the vices of Sodom and Gomorrah appear to be rife among us . . . we may indeed be on the eve of a new Elizabethan age."

Viscount Samuel, News of the World

"And Samuel said, What meaneth then this bleating of the sheep in mine ears, and the lowing of the oxen which I hear?"

I Samuel, 15-14

Lord Samuel says that Sodom's sins
Disgrace our young Queen's reign,
An age that in this plight begins
May well end up in flame.

MORAL
They say the sins of Sodom
In these Isles have come to roost —
So if your flying east from GANDER
Watch you don't get fairly "goosed".

And if you wish to Pick a Dilly
When you're strolling out at night,
Just make sure it's not a "Lily"
Or a male transvestite.

For there's blackmail in the woodpile
And there's blackmail by the fence,
But to black male and to white male
It's: AVOID THE PUBLIC "GENTS"!

Gay doggerel in the Supreme Court. Excerpted here are the opening and closing stanzas of the poem in the 1954 issue of *ONE Magazine* that was declared obscene and impounded by the U.S. Postal Service. This ruling was eventually overturned by the U.S. Supreme Court, marking the first major victory for the gay press. (Used by permission of ONE Institute/International Gay and Lesbian Archives)

ing more than cheap pornography calculated to promote Lesbianism and other forms of homosexuality, was not mailable."[14]

In the court's decision, lesbianism is singled out as particularly obscene, which is particularly interesting in light of the article written by the magazine's legal counsel claiming that there seemed to be greater leeway allowed in the "All-Woman Issue." The Ninth Circuit Court's summary of the articles under contention instead suggests—once again—that relations between women without men are "nothing more than cheap pornography":

> The article "Sappho Remembered" is the story of a lesbian's influence on a young girl only twenty years of age but "actually nearer sixteen in many essential ways of maturity," in her struggle to choose between a life with the lesbian, or a normal married life with her childhood sweetheart. The lesbian's affair with her room-mate while in college, resulting in the lesbian's expulsion from college, is recounted to bring in the jealousy angle. The climax is reached when the young girl gives up her chance for a normal married life to live with the lesbian. This article is nothing more than cheap pornography calculated to promote lesbianism. It falls far short of dealing with homosexuality from the scientific, historical and critical point of view.
>
> The poem "Lord Samuel and Lord Montagu" is about the alleged homosexual activities of Lord Montagu and other British Peers and contains a warning to all males to avoid the public toilets while the poem pertains to sexual matters of such a vulgar and indecent nature that it tends to arouse a feeling of disgust and revulsion. It is dirty, vulgar and offensive to the moral senses.[15]

The argument in response to the advertisement of the *Circle* reads in part: "Although on its face the information in this article appears harmless, it cannot be said that the purpose is harmless. It is for the information of those who read the magazine and particularly the homosexuals. It conveys information to the homosexual or any other reader as to where to get more of the material contained in 'ONE.'"[16]

The case included a long consideration of the different meanings of the words "obscene, lewd, lascivious, filthy and indecent." The Ninth Circuit Court thereby upheld the original ruling with its Conclusion *777 [3] [4], which reads: "When the approved definitions and tests are applied to certain articles in the 'ONE' magazine, it is apparent that the magazine is obscene and filthy and is therefore non-mailable matter." ONE Incorporated's appeal to the Supreme Court resulted in the issuance of a *per curium* reversal, meaning that the opinion is not one signed by any justice or group of justices but is issued through a more summary process. The Supreme Court ruling of January 1958 in favor of *ONE Magazine* reads simply: "The petition for writ of the certiorari is granted and the judgment of the United States Court of Appeals for the Ninth Circuit is reversed" (no. 290). The Supreme Court's decision was based solely in *Roth v. United States,* 354 U.S. 476, 77 S. Ct. 1304, 1 L. Ed. 2d 1498.

This court decision laid the basis for the legal distribution of all subsequent lesbian and gay newspapers and magazines. ONE Incorporated capitalized on that move for legal change, publicizing a "Homophile Bill of Rights" in 1961, that presaged the lists of demands presented at the lesbian and gay Marches on Washington, D.C., in 1979, 1987, and 1993.[17]

Culture Building(s)

In Los Angeles, the small group of committed men and women who published *ONE Magazine* became much more than magazine writers. Led by Dorr Legg, they formed the nucleus of a full-fledged community center. Dorr Legg, who quit his job to devote himself to full-time work at ONE Incorporated later termed himself "the first full time professional queer." ONE's office was open to gay people needing counseling, attorney referrals, information, and it served as well simply as a place to be with like-minded others. The staff organized social events, lectures, political events, and even a gay travel club. In many ways then, ONE Incorporated became a prototype of what would later emerge as gay and lesbian community centers across the nation. It recognized the needs of the gay and lesbian subcultures for social activities extending beyond the bars and protected from a homophobic state; it addressed the issues and needs that have subsequently become some of the main social and cultural services to our community, ranging from the lesbian and gay press to RSVP Travel and Olivia Tours.

Certainly a momentous decision on the part of ONE Incorporated pioneers like Dorr Legg, Don Slater, Tony Reyes, Jim Kepner, Ann Carll Reid, and Stella Rush was the decision to begin holding classes in what they called "homophile studies." They believed that the lack of solid information on homosexuality was a major gap in the effort to improve the situation of the homophile community. Not only did they teach classes on numerous subjects, from history and anthropology to critiques of Freudian psychoanalysis, but they also began publishing, in 1956, the first scholarly publication on homosexuality in America, the *ONE Institute Quarterly: Homophile Studies.*

Unfortunately, ONE lost momentum in the 1960s, first in a reaction by lesbian leaders of the Daughters of Bilitis, like Del Martin, who felt that the 1961 Homophile Bill of Rights proposal was too radical. Instead, she signed a later Brief of Injustice prepared by several San Francisco homophile groups. There were also personality conflicts. Some lesbians got along well with ONE's leader Dorr Legg, but other women (and men) found him imperious and domineering. The 1961 withdrawal of women, and major male writers like Jim Kepner, weakened the organization. In 1965, another split occurred between Dorr Legg and *ONE Magazine* editor Don Slater. Not only did Slater leave, but one night his faction secretly brought in a truck and loaded up ONE's library, archives, and files to take them with him to a new location. For several months rival copies of *ONE Magazine* appeared. Legg and Slater sued and countersued each other in court, the case dragged on for a long time, draining the organization of energy and funds. Finally, the judge ruled that the two factions should split the library and archives in half. This weakened the use of their most valuable assets, as each faction jealously guarded its holdings. As a result, the gay and lesbian community was denied a strong library and resource center at a crucial time in the movement's history.

In accordance with the verdict, Dorr Legg's faction retained use of the name ONE and continued the monthly lecture series as well as other educational activities, but by 1965 the organization had lost its primary role at the cutting edge of the homophile movement. Don Slater's faction renamed itself the Homosexual Information Center, and began a new publication, *Tangents.* Jim Kepner continued to collect archival material (which he had begun doing in 1942) and founded what was then named the National Gay Archives Natalie Barney/Edward Carpenter Library.

After the 1965 debacle, Slater ran the Homosexual Information Center until his death in 1996. Kepner's archives developed into what has become today the International Gay and Lesbian Archives, considered now to be the largest and oldest archives of lesbian, gay, bisexual, and transgendered (LGBT) materials in the world, containing over two million items. Both groups continued to add more books, periodicals, manuscripts, and artifacts to their separate collections, but the original division of resources continued to weaken each's impact. Recognizing this deficiency, in 1994 ONE Institute and the International Gay and Lesbian Archives formally merged to create an organization that carries on the educational mission of the former and the collecting and preserving mission of the latter, thus gathering under the aegis of a new unified institution the historical items of a queer past. After Don Slater's death, the Homosexual Information Center's library also merged with ONE Institute/IGLA, thus finally bringing all three collections together again. The University of Southern California has offered a building to house this unique and priceless collection, ensuring

Claiming public space. Early activist Jim Kepner with ONE Incorporated organizer Dorr Legg outside the institution's new L.A. storefront office. (Used by permission of ONE Institute/International Gay and Lesbian Archives)

Jim Kepner celebrates opening day at the new National Gay Archives Natalie Barney/ Edward Carpenter Library in early 1979. The Archives was opened to house the collection Kepner began in 1942. (Used by permission of ONE Institute/International Gay and Lesbian Archives)

its preservation for the future. Events of the 1990s have thus brought full circle the pioneering work of the 1950s, adding to Los Angeles's potential to once again become an important site for gay and lesbian thought and research.

The Real, the Tangible, the International Gay and Lesbian Archives: Theory into Practice

What does the collecting of LGBT materials mean to queer communities and identities? The daily operations of ONE Institute/International Gay and Lesbian Archives (as it is now known) speaks to the unique issues of gay historicizing, of the drive toward increased visibility that defines in large part LGBT historical and political agendas. In a culture defined by invisibility, the very act of collecting LGBT materials is political in that it allows an actual visual and material representation of the self. Cultural theorist Susan Stewart suggests that "The ultimate term in the series that marks the collection is the 'self,' the articulation of the collector's own identity."[18] This desire to articulate the self was precisely what the founder of the International Gay and Lesbian Archives, Jim Kepner, was following when, in 1942, he went looking for some visible trace of his gay self and history and found none in the San Francisco Public Library or other repositories of American cultural life. His decision at that time to begin to collect and keep every book and artifact he could find that related to gay and lesbian life was an impulse that reflected an entire subcultural need to have the self represented. The ongoing and primary gay agenda of working toward "visibility" is informed by the same motivations.

The drive toward the collection and display of LGBT artifacts brings to bear on (mostly hidden) gay history a certain material question of authenticity. Archival collections speak to a mainstream notion of what it means to have a history. For a culture often defined through artifice and apparitions, costume and camp, performativity and impersonation, the notion of authentic artifacts, of material objects—housed in an institution—"legitimates" gay culture on another level. Recognizing the value of such an enormous archival collection, the affiliation of the ONE Institute/International Gay and Lesbian Archives with a major research institution's library collections suggests a level of institutional support for the documentation of gay life, if not gay existence itself, that crosses a new frontier.

The mission statement for ONE Institute/International Gay and Lesbian Archives reads: "The Archives shall, without bias, identify, collect, organize, preserve and make available documents, artifacts and information relating to the lives and concerns of LGBT people in all times and places." The Archives, however, has been engaged in a prolonged discussion and disagreement on how to interpret the phrase "relating to the lives of LGBT people" for it raises the difficult question of what it is exactly that defines gay, lesbian, bisexual, or transgendered identities. For example, if there is a novel that contains no overt LGBT content that is written by a "suspected" lesbian, should that book be preserved? Or, in another case, because the dance industry has been heavily populated by gay men, should every book, program, flyer, and artifact relating to dance be preserved since it may in time yield clues to gay identity, even, let's say, through its absence of mention of the gay dancer? Some have claimed that Shakespeare was queer; should all his works be on the shelves of the Archives, or only ones that hint at this queerness? What about male-produced lesbian pornography? Does nonlesbian-identified feminist material belong on the shelves?

On one extreme are those who believe there should be no classification scheme that would limit the Archive's collecting practices. Those who hold this position believe that anything or anyone's works suspected to be gay or queer should not be discarded from the collection or from donations received. Although this may appear an unpractical position to some, it in fact represents what has been touted as a basic tenet of queer theory that suggests that the so-called opposition between homosexual and heterosexual definition is such a troubled, indeed an artificial one, that to make a distinction between gay and not gay is theoretically impossible. Eve Kosofsky Sedgwick has argued that "many of the major nodes of thought and knowledge in twentieth-century Western culture as a whole are structured—indeed, fractured—by a chronic, now endemic crisis of homo/heterosexual definition."[19] If one were to put this argument into practice in an archive one would have to, in fact, collect *everything*! As both Michel Foucault and Sedgwick have argued, silences and absences are as telling and defining of (gay) sexuality as are overt representations or knowledge of (homo)sexuality.

Putting theory into practice is often a complicated process that can either change the theory, the practice, or both. In the case of gay archival collecting, the issue may have more to do with the need and desire to remember and be remembered, not only to see and touch lives that too often have been violently marginalized, but to pass on one's life, especially in the absence of progeny. For many, our history of struggle is a history that should not be forgotten even—or especially—as we move into new freedoms. It remains a political act to save the evidence of our existence, both past and present. It was only a little over forty years ago that Jim Kepner began to assemble his own gay archives because he was not able to find a trace of his gayness anywhere in the San Francisco Public Library system; in such cases, the individual gesture, bred from desire, becomes a radical political *act* whose consequences—as the queer 1990s evidence—are at once material (a building, a collection, the sources from which to re-create history) and ontological ("we're here, we're queer, because you, too, can read about it").

This chapter is dedicated to the work and memory of Jim Kepner, 1923–1997.

Notes

The authors would like to thank Debra Silverman for her insightful comments on drafts of this chapter and for her patience in editing.

We use *queer* in this context to refer to the myriad forms of same-sex and other nonnormative kinds of desire that have come to inform certain specific identity groups. At the same time, we acknowledge that many of those from the generation about which this chapter is written find this term offensive. Later in the chapter, we will use the term *gay* when we write about what was in fact a mostly male homosexual movement.

1. The saying, "Pin up your bobbypins before you go out the door," was the common farewell to someone leaving a gay bar in the 1940s and 1950s, meaning, "straighten up."

2. Allan Bérubé, *Coming Out under Fire: The History of Gay Men and Women in World War Two* (New York: Plume Books, 1990).

3. Interview with Jim Kepner, Los Angeles, 7 August 1997.

4. See Stuart Timmons, *The Trouble with Harry Hay: Founder of the Gay Movement* (New York: Alyson, 1990) for a discussion of the Mattachine Society's transformations.

5. Jim Kepner, *Rough News—Daring Views: 1950 Pioneer Gay Journalism* (New York: Haworth Press, 1997), 6.

6. Kepner, *Rough News,* 3.

7. Benedict Anderson, *Imagined Communities: Reflections of the Origin and Spread of Nationalism* (London: Verso, 1991).

8. *ONE Magazine,* October 1954, 17.

9. *ONE Institute Quarterly: Homophile Studies* 29 (winter 1959):29.

10. *ONE Magazine,* October 1954, 6.

11. Ibid.

12. Ibid.

13. Case no. 15139.

14. Ibid.

15. Ibid.

16. Ibid.

17. This Bill of Rights was never completed. For a copy of the questionnaire see W. Dorr Legg, "Homosexuals in American Society: The Society of a Subculture," in *Homophile Studies in Theory and Practice,* ed. W. Dorr Legg et al. (San Francisco: GLB Publishers and ONE Institute Press, 1994), 128–45.

18. Susan Stewart, *On Longing: Narrative of the Miniature, the Gigantic, the Souvenir, the Collection* (Durham, N.C.: Duke University Press, 1993), 162.

19. Eve Kosofsky Sedgwick, *The Epistemology of the Closet* (Berkeley: The University of California Press, 1990), 1.

9

Lesbian Activism in Los Angeles 1970–1979

Yolanda Retter

I know that much of what I call history others will not. But
answering the challenge of exclusion is the work of a lifetime.
—Joan Nestle, *A Restricted Country*

As liminal spaces replete with promise and possibility, frontiers have
often been conceptualized as geopolitical terrains unburdened by a
surfeit of social controls. In these spaces, old rules and strictures find
themselves suspended, while new ones are in flux or in a polymorphic
state. In the classic "whitemale" fantasy, the frontier is a metonym for
yet another parcel of "virgin" territory to be possessed, under the control of a gaze whose actual and theoretical intent is to conquer and
colonize by pushing back whatever resistant other is inconveniently in
the way. I would like to use the metaphor of the contested frontier to
describe a history of struggle that reverses the terms of this patriarchal
fantasy of possession. In the following pages I argue that the continuing struggle to carve out a place for "lesbian-specific" life and women's
culture in the sometimes wild and infamous frontierland of Los Angeles has built its ideals of community within a landscape first liberated and appropriated by lesbian and gay activists in the homophile
and civil rights movements of the 1960s and 1970s.[1]

The "queer frontiers" announced in the title of this book not only
loom as an index of future possibility but are part of a past we need
to reclaim for its own defiant resistance to the mainstream or normative. These outposts of early gay liberation arose as a response to the
circumstances of what John Rechy (in this anthology) has described as
being "born into the opposing camp"; those who inhabit such a space
outside the mainstream are faced with the option of either assimilating
into the dominant culture or creating a territory of their own. The latter
was the collective decision made by lesbian feminists in Los Angeles

throughout the 1970s. For almost ten years, these lesbian feminists energetically engaged in political activism on behalf of various social causes and also developed a complex woman-focused institutional base and culture located within the interstices of the heterosexual, gay male, and dominant white cultures, carving out liminal spaces that were frontiers of same-sex activism and politics in otherwise hostile environments. My goal in the pages that follow is to give discursive shape to this largely unwritten story of lesbian activism in Los Angeles along the political and social frontiers of the 1970s and, by doing so, to make space for further conceptualizations of the "lifetime[s] of exclusions" (to paraphrase Joan Nestle) that in fact contribute to a revisionist definition of queer "history" itself.

Prelude

In the 1970s, members of the diverse lesbian activist communities in Los Angeles energetically engaged in institution-building, political action, and internecine conflict.[2] Unlike other civil rights groups, lesbians—as well as gay men—had no developed institutional foundation from which to draw moral and financial support for their activism; consequently, in the lesbian movement, institution-building developed in tandem with political activism. The public plexus of the Los Angeles movement passed through three phases during this decade: in the initial separatist phase,[3] lesbian-focused groups and all-purpose centers staffed by volunteers were the norm; during the second separatist phase, groups and centers focused on an issue or area of service, a few centers found funding, and lesbian culture blossomed; during the final phase, lesbians and gay men joined forces to combat a homophobic backlash. At that point, portions of the lesbian and gay movement switched from grass-roots organizing to co-gender leverage advocacy.[4]

During the first two of these phases, three dynamics common to groups that lack formal hierarchies and leaders had a significant impact on the character and fate of activist lesbian organizations. First, while the admonition "the personal is political" was meant to guide the individual toward higher political consciousness and individual agency, the egalitarian imperative required one to subsume one's ego within the group "consensus."[5] This paradox created cognitive dissonance in individuals and discord in groups.[6] For example, in late 1970, Del Whan (a veteran of the Southern California Gay Liberation Front and then a member of Lesbian Feminists), concerned about the need for services for lesbians, took the initiative to rent a storefront in Echo Park on her own. When some of her sisters in Lesbian Feminists judged her proactive effort as "elitist" and "an ego trip," Del left the group to continue with the project on her own.

A second source of conflict arose when groups set about the task of building nonpatriarchal organizations, some argued for an egalitarian structure ruled by consensus while others, fearing that consensus would lead to endless processing and chaos, wanted a more traditional structure. At the Los Angeles Women's Center (LAWC), then the hub of feminist activity in the city, there were ongoing debates between radicals and reformists about what kind of structure was desirable. A third problem area was the diverse backgrounds, ideologies, and agendas of community members. At conferences, participants often divided between those who had come to organize at a political event (the "politicos") and those who had come to network and spend time with other women ("cultural feminists").[7]

Over the years, both in Los Angeles and other locations (for example, Chicago), differing agendas sparked interest, ignited debate, and sometimes exploded into intracommunity conflicts—the so-called lesbian civil wars. During the 1970s, Los Angeles lesbians fought one another over sexual styles, sexism, worker-boss disparities at the Gay Community Services Center (GCSC), and the lesbian community's indifference to racism. Internecine conflicts had a marked impact on the city's activist lesbian community for they divided lesbians, damaged organizations, reduced the coherent energy available to work on an issue, and left more than a few with "activist posttraumatic stress syndrome."[8]

In the midst of contentious dynamics, institution-building nonetheless proceeded at a rapid pace.[9] Before Stonewall, the institutional base of lesbian culture in Los Angeles consisted mainly of bars, private homes, strips of beaches, and softball fields. When gay liberation emerged onto the social movement scene, the opportunities for lesbian institution-building multiplied exponentially. While advocating on behalf of lesbian rights, lesbians across the United States also created a lesbian media, woman-focused cultural productions, and women-only spaces in community centers and at conferences and festivals. Institution-building was also a form of "boundary construction,"[10] which provided an internal environment that both affirmed identity and fueled political activism.

First Phase: Gay and Lesbian Liberation, 1970–1972

Within weeks of the Stonewall riots,[11] the New York Gay Liberation Front (GLF) was organized,[12] and within six months the Southern California GLF was founded as the first "in your face" gay/lesbian political action group in Los Angeles.[13] However, by the summer of 1970, co-gender groups had divided over the issue of sexism. Daughters of Bilitis (DOB) leader and homophile veteran Del Martin wrote a scathing letter to gay men arguing that their culture was as oppressive to lesbians as heterosexual culture was to homosexuals. Following the example of women who had left the sexist New Left movement to form the feminist movement, lesbians began leaving gay liberation and homophile groups to form their own movement. Los Angeles lesbian activists from this decade came from a variety of backgrounds. Some were "red diaper babies," a number had participated in the social movements of the 1960s and 1970s before "finding a home" in the lesbian movement, some were lifelong lesbians who had been involved in homophile groups for years, and others were women whose lesbianism had been catalyzed by their involvement in the feminist movement.[14]

The varied backgrounds of these activists informed their projects and ideologies. In 1970, Del Whan, who had a social services inclination, launched the first known lesbian social services center in the United States.[15] Named the Gay Women's Service Center (GWSC), this organization offered consciousness-raising and rap groups, referrals, classes, dances, potlucks, and temporary housing. Its demise in 1972 was attributed to factors that would soon become a familiar refrain: "as with many organizations, there were not enough women to share the responsibility of the work involved in providing these services."[16] This dependence of the lesbian movement on volunteers was due to a lack of reliable sources of funding. In due time, after the novelty of building a movement wore off and after activists burned out or changed their priorities, volunteerism declined, and concurrently so did lesbian-specific institution-building around the United States.

While the GWSC was attempting to provide social services to lesbians, a 1950s group founded in the shadow of the McCarthy era was attempting to retool its identity to fit an "out" and confrontational 1970s movement. One can follow the Daughters of Bilitis's attempts to adapt to a new political climate by noting the changes in this chapter's newsletter. The first issues of the *Lesbian Tide* state that the DOB is "a nonpolitical, non profit organization" whose goal is to "actualiz[e] . . . personal pride in the lesbian" through education.[17] The January 1972 issue announced that it was now independent of DOB and a "working collective"; two months later, the *Lesbian Tide* declared itself to be an "independent, lesbian/feminist magazine."[18]

A third activist Los Angeles group was born out of a confluence of lesbianism and feminism. This group, named the Lesbian Feminists (LF),[19] was formed by lesbians new to the lesbian liberation movement (feminist lesbians) and feminists who had just come out (lesbian feminists).[20] Most were between their early twenties and mid-thirties, and they came from varying class backgrounds.[21] Unlike the DOB and GLF lesbians, LF lesbians were heavily influenced by feminist analyses of sexism as the root oppression and calls for equal rights for women, and some of its members also identified themselves as progressive leftists or socialists.[22] Lesbian Feminists' ideology promoted consciousness-raising (CR) for personal change and political activism for collective change.[23]

Unlike the Gay Women's Service Center, which tried to provide social services for all lesbians, Lesbian Feminists focused on providing political support to all progressive causes in the tradition of what sociologist Herbert Blumer called a "general social movement," or a movement of "broad range."[24] Members helped organize gay-straight dialogues hosted a popular Saturday night coffeehouse as an alternative to the bars, helped picket the Sybil Brand (County Jail) "Daddy Tank,"[25] and participated in antiwar activities.[26] Some of their projects were also political responses to personal issues. When one of the group's members was kidnapped and raped while hitchhiking, Lesbian Feminists organized a Sisters-Give-Rides-to-Sisters campaign.

While the general political goal of the Lesbian Feminists included changing the larger society, a more immediate goal was that of transforming the reluctance of heterosexual feminists and closeted lesbians to acknowledge their lavender kin. Lesbian Feminists led a campaign to support the L.A. National Organization for Women (NOW) lesbians working on a prolesbian resolution. The resolution outlined the numerous problems associated with being a lesbian and criticized NOW's reluctance to support women who had supported their heterosexual sisters on issues such as abortion. The passage of the resolution at NOW's national conference, held in Los Angeles in September 1971, was considered a first and important victory for lesbian rights because it came out of the most influential and visible feminist organization in the United States.

The Lesbian Movement Diversifies

By the summer of 1971, these three groups (LF, GWSC, and DOB) offered a variety of services and activist opportunities for L.A. lesbians. At that point, Lesbian Feminist member Sharon Zecha suggested that since each represented a different ideology, an umbrella organization

might serve to maximize available energy and minimize potential conflicts. Her suggestion led to the creation of the Intergroup Council. In
July of 1971, the Council produced the "Lesbian issue" of *Everywoman*,
a feminist Los Angeles newspaper. This was a significant breakthrough, since the periodical was publicly circulated and was not a
lesbian publication. The issue contained articles by lesbians on diverse
subjects including socialism, older lesbians, and the recent Gay Wom-
en's West Coast Conference. The Council had been instrumental in organizing the conference, another landmark in coalition building in the
area.[27] The number and the geographic diversity of the approximately
350 participants surprised everyone involved. One attendee reported
that "women pulled in from Wisconsin, Minnesota, Michigan, Seattle,
Salt Lake City, Portland, even Boston."[28] At the same time, the conference's varied intragroup dynamics reflected the ambivalence participants felt about coalescing. In one workshop, the lesbian mothers
group agreed to form a union to lobby for friendlier child custody
laws, while in another, arguments broke out between the "old gay" and
"new gay" women over the issue of gender roles and sexual identity.

While lesbian groups worked together through the Council, some
lesbians were also active in a new organization that appeared to many
to be resistant and/or oblivious to lesbian needs. The organization,
the Gay Community Services Center, which was founded in 1971, was
based on a mixture of Gay Liberation Front, counterculture, and leftist
ideology.[29] Early female participants in the Center included former
GLF member June Herrle and GWCS veterans Mina (Robinson) Meyer
and Sharon Raphael. Although uncomfortable as feminists in a male-
dominated environment, Meyer and Raphael joined "hoping to help
strengthen and enlarge the women's program," and the former was
elected to the Board of Directors, while the latter became director of
research and facilitated rap groups.[30]

Due to the volume of service users, the requirements of funding
agencies, and the developmental process of most organizations, the
GCSC soon abandoned its egalitarian workplace ideals. According to
some, it also continued to ignore the needs of lesbians. In 1973, Meyer
and Raphael left the Center. The former explained that "the Center is
more in keeping with models in the gay [male] movement. . . . I feel it
[the Center] is a positive endeavor, but there is a gap in consciousness
between the place and feminist oriented lesbians in the women's and
or lesbian movements."[31] Meyer also noted that at one point she and
several men attempted to abolish the Center's "boss/worker dichotomy" but failed.[32] This first public break between lesbians and the Center was a portent of troubles to come.

When the L.A. Women's Center closed due to a lack of energy and structure and Lesbian Feminists disbanded, lesbian activist energy drifted to the GCSC and to the feminist alternative that had opened in 1972, the Westside Women's Center (WWC).[33] This center was a typical first-phase center. A former staff member remembers twelve-hour days during which WWC staff struggled in true feminist tradition to provide everything to everyone with next to no funding. Services included a self-help clinic, rap groups, and "gay-straight" dialogues. The WWC also collaborated with women from GCSC and former LF members in organizing the First National Lesbian Kiss-In at the Los Angeles County Museum of Art, as an affirmation of lesbian visibility and the right of lesbians to be affectionate in public.[34]

Westside women also organized the Los Angeles Radical Feminist Therapy Collective (LARFTC) and the Fat Underground (FU); these groups influenced the way that lesbians and feminists looked at therapy and fat oppression. The LARFTC critiqued psychotherapy as a "method of social control" and worked to "help women take back their power."[35] For several years, the collective offered contact raps, problem-solving groups, community mediations, and training. It eventually disbanded due to ideological disagreements between members and amid community criticisms about the collective's alleged abuses. As one former member explained, "instead of being [a] revolutionary group, [LARFTC] became a group that had a lot of power in the community. . . ."[36] This position was antithetical to its original philosophy of spreading rather than holding power.

The Fat Underground, formed by Judy Freespirit and others in 1973 during the same time period as the LARFTC, provided a cognitive space where women could politicize their oppression around issues of "looksism" and "sizeism," and raise awareness about how they, like most people, had internalized the "slim and young" standards disseminated by the media. According to a former member of the group, "I had spent a lifetime being oppressed as a fat woman. . . . I learned to see that this was part of women's oppression. . . . we were very militant. . . . we did all kinds of demonstrations, educating within the lesbian community, interrupted medical conferences. . . . we were a force to be reckoned with. . . . we didn't allow diet soda at the [Westside] Women's Center [*laughter*]. . . . it was a wonderful time."[37] During the 1970s, the women at the WWC, and in the LARFTC and the FU, raised the awareness level of many members of the lesbian and heterosexual feminist community. Some, however, felt that the groups did not welcome views that diverged from their own and that on various occasions, they had misused their power. The conflicts that the managing collective of the WWC in particular dealt with during the 1970s illustrate how issues of authority and power differentials posed problems in most lesbian feminist groups.

Civil Wars I

When activist lesbians recall this decade, they express a mixture of nostalgia and pain, since many were involved in and/or affected by the lesbian civil wars.[38] Following on the heels of lesbian feminist attacks on male sexism and straight feminist homophobia, Los Angeles lesbians began to battle over the behavior of members within their own diverse communities. Conflicts over sexual styles included, for example, lesbian feminist opposition to monogamy and the tradition of butch/femme role-playing. The antimonogamy perspective was based on a feminist criticism of oppressive structures built into the institutions of marriage and the nuclear family. Lesbian feminists who had been married were more likely to espouse an antimonogamy philosophy than feminist lesbians who had longer histories of identifying themselves as lesbians and who, having had fewer socially approved opportunities for relationships, were less averse to the idea of partnering.

During the time that monogamy was under attack, the most common form of lesbian partnering prior to the 1970s, butch/femme, was also under fire for being a misguided imitation of the male/female roles institutionalized in heterosexuality. This attack has been analyzed as an attempt on the part of anti–butch/femme advocates to separate lesbian feminist philosophy from lesbian sexuality in order to gain acceptance from the heterosexual feminist community. Ironically, however, while lesbian feminists criticized those who subscribed to the butch/femme ethic, "dyke" attire was de rigueur in the lesbian feminist community: blue jeans, workshirt, short haircut, and "sensible" shoes or boots. (A good example of this attire can be seen on the cover of the *Lesbian Tide*'s May 1972 issue.) Later in the 1980s, the war over sexual styles would resurface and the arguments would include issues of sadomasochism, pornography, and the relation of both to violence against women.

Second Phase: The Waxing and Waning of Activism, 1973–1976

In December 1972, Del Whan reported that a friend had complained that "All of the old groups are dying! Nobody is coming to meetings any more." An article in the *Lesbian Tide* blamed a lack of structure and organization for the demise of many centers and groups while Bonnie Zimmerman, a former member of a Chicago newspaper collective, thought of the short life span of most lesbian groups as a "natural" process.[39] Although the first wave of centers and groups did fold, the second wave brought with it centers and groups that were focused on one or a few, rather than all, issues. Also during this time, lesbian gatherings grew larger and more public as lesbians grew more confident about being out.

During this phase, the institutional base of the Los Angeles lesbian community grew larger due to both the increasing numbers of women coming into the movement and to divisions that sometimes led to the demise of projects, but at other times led to new projects and groups. Across the nation, lesbian literature, music, and businesses proliferated, and there was a growing interest in lesbian history both in the community and in the academy, where some departments grew more willing to offer classes in lesbian and gay studies. Other positive developments included the election of the first "out" lesbian to political office (Elaine Noble, to the Massachusetts State Legislature in 1974) and the passing of progay ordinances in such cities as Berkeley. There were legal gains in the areas of child custody, with one landmark case being successfully argued by a Los Angeles lesbian who was still in law school.[40] Even the media began to modify its negative portrayals of lesbians and gays.

One indication of the growth of the movement was the size and site of the 1973 West Coast Lesbian Conference. Over fifteen hundred women from twenty-six states and four countries outside the U.S. came to the University of California, Los Angeles (UCLA) to attend a catalytic event that was exhilarating for some and an experience of division and frustration for others.[41] On the evening of a Friday the 13th in April, with a full house in Moore Hall, the first of several highly charged arguments erupted. At issue was the presence of a male-to-female preoperative transsexual who was scheduled to sing. In the end, the singer was allowed to perform, but as a consequence "several hundred women walked out."[42] According to Sharon Raphael, another division occurred between "those who had come to the conference to celebrate lesbian culture and those who came to organize at a political event."[43] For Sharon, however, the competing agendas were not a problem, instead, they were a sign of diversity and choice: "It was wonderful because you could experience both . . . you could be anything you wanted to be . . . you had the sense that this was a mini Lesbian Nation and you were living it out on the campus of UCLA for that weekend. . . ."[44]

This "mini" Lesbian Nation also experienced traumas over the presence of socialists and the underaddressed issue of racism. During this time period socialists were suspected of trying to infiltrate and take over women's groups (In this regard, see chapter 8 of this volume on splits within the Mattachine Society.) When socialist literature found its way into conference packets, some participants, including Robin Morgan, accused the organizers of being socialist dupes. However, on the issue of racism, Morgan, who delivered the keynote speech, was vague. Although L.A. lesbians of color were not yet militant about racism within local lesbian feminist groups, women of color from other areas were. A statement from the conference's black caucus asserted that "Racism is here. We don't like it and we don't want to see it anymore, particularly from our lesbian sisters." Reference was also made to white DOB activist Del Martin, who in her travels across the country had not seen one lesbian organization that she felt had successfully dealt with the issue of racism. Judging from articles and letters in subsequent issues of the *Lesbian Tide*, a number of white women were offended or perplexed by the intense debate that had taken place over this issue.[45]

Some of the differences that emerged from this memorable 1973 gathering were to arise and divide lesbians at every subsequent general lesbian conference, leading some to suggest that cultural conferences were more productive than political ones—a suggestion unacceptable to politicos who continued to advocate for mass mobilization as the "politically correct" method of social change.[46] The reality was that most lesbians in the Los Angeles community spent less time following a radical lesbian path than they did working for personal and collective change. Mirroring some of the problems of large gatherings (and vice versa), efforts to create lesbian specific spaces were often curtailed by a lack of funds and a surfeit of internecine conflict. During this time period, there were two notable exceptions to this pattern. The first, the Alcoholism Center for Women, has, due to its fundable mission (substance abuse prevention, recovery, and education) had uncharacteristic longevity. Funding for the program was first obtained in 1973, as a one-million-dollar grant (for a period of three years) from the National Institute for Alcoholism and Alcohol Abuse for services to women at the Gay Community Services Center. This grant marked a "first" for the Center, and for lesbian recovery services everywhere.

The other exception was the L.A. Woman's Building (WB), cofounded in 1973 by three feminists, including lesbian Arlene Raven, an art historian interested in developing what she called a "lesbian sensibility in art."[47] The WB was an attempt to reincarnate the spirit of the 1893 Columbian Exposition Women's Building in Chicago, where a closeted lesbian presence was represented by Mary Cassatt, whose work had been displayed there. At the new WB, lesbians were always a visible and key part of management and programming. In the 1970s, lesbians at the WB generated projects such as the performance art piece *An Oral History of Lesbianism* and hosted "LA LA LA," a grand cultural event created through the collaborative efforts of an uncharacteristically large number of white lesbian groups. While many enjoyed the event, some—including one *Tide* reporter—criticized the event as apolitical, noting that the event planners had neglected to include those who had contributed to the advancement of the political goals and social condition of lesbians; these critics felt that culture devoid of politics was just entertainment.

While perhaps not "correct" in a "politico" sense, this emergence of lesbian culture and art formed a positive reaction to the dearth of images, music and words in prior representations. In the 1970s, "women's music," and "women's art" came into their own and music festivals and art projects became community staples around the country.[48] The use of "women" as a euphemism for "lesbian" was common during this decade; its use was strategic, for example, as a method of attracting a wider audience to a concert or selling more musical recordings. While objectionable to some, the ploy seemed to work, and had its positive points. Lesbian culture—or "women's culture"—served a consciousness-raising purpose that went beyond the lesbian community.[49]

While lesbian music grew profitable, other lesbian businesses had a difficult time balancing profits and politics. Community studies show that institution-building on the part of target groups always includes dreams of financial independence from the mainstream oppressor, and although lesbians have always owned businesses, it was not until the 1970s that some consciously attempted to combine their livelihood with their political beliefs. The first businesses to do so across the nation were women's bookstores, and Sisterhood Bookstore, which opened in L.A. in 1972, became a prototype of this new approach. Two of the original owners had been deeply involved with the Westside Women's Center and brought their politics into their business venture. Like other women's bookstores across the country, Sisterhood became a community institution. It sold books "by and for women," served as a "safe" woman's space, offered a community bulletin board, and provided a venue for readings. For the first fifteen years of its existence, Sisterhood benefited from its location in Westwood, near both the UCLA campus and a major freeway. Ironically, when mainstream book retailers across the country began to stock and underprice materials that women's bookstores had been the first to carry, many of the latter were forced to close. They fell victims to their successful mission of promoting women's, lesbian, and feminist literature.

In contrast to Sisterhood, most lesbian businesses that catered to the lesbian community faced insurmountable difficulties. Some of these difficulties lay in the politics of the community. For example, at the Women's Saloon, a restaurant and bar, ambience, service, and fare had to be carefully balanced in order to meet the standards of the politically correct (should Sweet 'n Low be banned?), as well as of those women who desired a pleasant dining atmosphere.[50] Another source of difficulty lay in economics. Many activists, among them Shirl Buss, pointed out that while most feminist businesses dealt in luxury or novelty items, the items and resources needed for daily existence were still marketed and controlled by men.[51] In other words, community women with limited incomes were more concerned about paying the utility bills than about buying a woman's liberation pendant. In addition, the policy of "pay more if you can, less if you can't" was too often taken literally (and sometimes abused), thereby forcing lesbians offering services and products to work outside the community in order to make ends meet.[52]

While lesbian businesses struggled with the paradoxes of ideology, lesbian groups that represented an increasingly wide spectrum of political positions emerged. For example, in 1975, a group of white grass-roots lesbians and heterosexual feminists founded Califia, a group that became known for its weeklong camp outs and its intense workshops on classism and racism. During the classism workshops, women from privileged backgrounds were asked to "pass"—that is, to listen and not speak—a policy that caused great unease for the privileged but was cathartic for working-class women. The racism workshops were even more problematic. As Marilyn Murphy recalled (in an understatement), "the race presentation has a stormy history."[53] During that workshop, women of color and white women intensely struggled, sometimes together and often against each other, across the divide of race and ethnicity.

While grass-roots Califia wrestled with controversial issues within the community, the newly formed Southern California Women for Understanding (SCWU) had a different focus.[54] Founded in 1976, the organization was seen by some as too white and politically conservative (a kind of au courant DOB catering to middle-class and upwardly mobile women). Others, however, saw it as providing a comfortable environment in which lesbians from white-collar professions could "come out" and socialize with kindred spirits. Members who had power, money, or access to both, began to advocate for lesbian and gay rights at levels significantly different from those of their grass-roots sisters. In the late 1970s, SCWU used this leverage to help defeat an anti-lesbian/gay amendment.

Civil Wars II

Shortly after the Gay and Lesbian Community Services Center received its grant for the Alcoholism Program for Women (as it was then called), long-standing resentments rose to the surface. Local legend attributes what took place to factors ranging from alleged mismanagement of funds, to infiltration of the Center by an FBI provocateur, to women being tired of sexism within the organization and wanting to run their own program. In the midst of these conflicts, in 1974 the Program received permission to incorporate as an independent non-profit agency at which time it was renamed the Alcoholism Center for Women (ACW). The Center, however, still faced charges of elitism and sexism that were not resolved and, when its governing board fired a number of workers for reportedly sending inflammatory information packets to funding agencies, a strike was called. Pickets took up posts outside the Center in 1975 and the strike continued until 1978. Lesbians who stayed with the Center were ostracized by the community and even those who tried to remain neutral were penalized.[55] Jinx Beers recalls that when the group Lesbian Activists declined to take sides and voted to be neutral on this subject, "we were thrown out of the Westside Women's Center."[56] Shortly thereafter, as part of the political fallout, the Lesbian Activists' ads for meetings were declined by both *Sister Newspaper* and the *Lesbian Tide*. Jinx and friends responded by founding the *Lesbian News*, which is now the oldest lesbian publication in Los Angeles, and one of the oldest in the country.

While lesbians fought each other over the policies and politics of a co-gender agency, they also continued battling over sexual styles. Beginning in the second phase of the seventies and continuing into the nineties a persistent source of contention was sadomasochism. In late 1976, the *Tide* published a transcript of a workshop entitled "Towards a Feminist Expression of Sado-Masochism," which opened community debate on the issue. Strict feminists were not amused, and at those conferences where S/M groups were allowed to present their points of view, their workshops were crowded with women ready to argue with them. Pro-S/M groups like Samois asserted that S/M was a form of sexual dissent, while groups like Women against Violence against Women felt that S/M promoted antiwoman violence and pornography. The former group was made up of "prosex" or sexual liberationists, while the latter generally consisted of lesbian feminists concerned about violence against and by women.

Third Phase: Girls and Boys Together, 1977–1979

The final phase of the decade was characterized by increased lesbian visibility and the increased influence of co-gender groups, and it began in 1977 with the government-funded International Women's Year Conference held in Houston, Texas. At the conference, lesbian delegates (many from Los Angeles) and their allies worked overtime to gather support for a prolesbian resolution, which passed by a wide majority. Although the larger society would not be influenced by this decision, it was nonetheless a groundbreaking event since lesbians had persuaded a large group of feminist women to pass a supportive resolution at a government-sponsored, high-profile gathering. After the conference, jubilant lesbians returned to L.A. to work on the next item on the agenda, the defeat of the Briggs Amendment, also known as Proposition 6 (a ban on gay schoolteachers).[57]

Since the proposition would have adversely affected both lesbians and gays in California, the two groups set aside their differences and went to work to defeat the proposal. As part of the resistance, SCWU organized several upscale social events where mainstream power brokers from the political arena, the media, and Hollywood mixed with "out" and closeted gays and lesbians dressed in formal attire. Gone were the blue jeans preferred by grass-roots gay liberation activists. The power brokers were duly impressed and offered unprecedented support and money. Support also came from the general public, for in November of 1978 the proposition, which at first seemed likely to pass, was defeated 58 percent to 42 percent.

After the Briggs Amendment was voted down, portions of the co-gender coalition responsible for defeating it continued working for lesbian and gay rights within co-gender political groups such as the Municipal Elections Committee Los Angeles (MECLA) and the Stonewall Democratic Club. The new breed of activists represented by MECLA (the first gay political action committee) lobbied for lesbian and gay rights on local and national government levels. Mass demonstrations were replaced by leverage advocacy, which included entreaties and deals over lunch, telephone calls, small group meetings, personal and professional connections, and the creation and collection of political debts. Less than a year later, in 1979, the L.A. City Council passed an ordinance protecting lesbians and gays from specific discrimination.

Civil Wars III

Although there have always been lesbians of color working within white groups, it was not until the mid-1970s that they formed their own "out" groups, and several years passed before they became a significant presence in the white-dominated lesbian activist community.[58] In 1978, the lesbian of color agenda in L.A. received unexpected support at the National Lesbian Feminist Organization (NLFO) founding convention, held in Santa Monica. Shortly after the conference opened, a white delegate asked about participation by women of color. Few lesbians of color had come as delegates, and most were there as observers and staff. In an unprecedented move, the lesbians of color present were recruited as voting delegates. After much debate, delegates passed a resolution stating that in the new organization "a minimum of 50% of all women involved in the level of planning and decision-making (must) be women of color of various class backgrounds." Both the resolution and the percentages were groundbreaking, and as two white delegates noted, "For the first time in our experience, white lesbians were forced to deal with an issue of parity for women of color in a concrete way."[59]

Shortly after the NLFO conference, the group Lesbians of Color (LOC) was organized in Los Angeles. According to one flyer, the group's mission was to "facilitate [the] personal, social, cultural and political growth of its members." While LOC worked on behalf of many women's issues, some declined to use the term *feminist* because they felt the term had connotations of "white and middle class."[60] Although many women of color felt that the effort to raise white consciousness around racism was useless, LOC sponsored a number of antiracism workshops and worked in collaboration with several white women's antiracism groups.[61]

Along with other lesbian and gay people of color groups, LOC was present at the grand finale of this eventful decade—the first lesbian and gay March on Washington, D.C., in 1979.[62] Planning for the march started amid disagreement among activists about the proposed event's political timeliness and doubts about the ability of organizers to generate a large turnout. Without the initial support of influential segments of the gay and lesbian community, the march was organized at the grass-roots level. At a planning meeting in Houston it was agreed that "third world" women, followed by white lesbians, would lead the march. Prior to the march, lesbians and gays of color attended the First World Gay and Lesbian Conference, held near Howard University. The march was held on 14 October 1979, and both United Press International and the Associated Press reported between fifty and seventy-five thousand participants. At the rally, lesbian activist Arlie Scott reminded the audience that lesbians and gays had always worked on behalf of other causes and movements and that it was now their turn to take center stage. She also underscored the new direction of the lesbian and gay movement: "we are moving from gay pride to gay politics."[63]

Conclusion

The first decade of the post-Stonewall movement offered many opportunities for the development of political and personal identity. It served as a social movement laboratory that offered apprenticeships in politicization through participation in rap groups, marches, conferences, cultural productions, educational panels, publishing, and lobbying. It also encouraged the development of a lesbian culture that included women-only spaces, businesses, gatherings, and artistic endeavors. Although Los Angeles can be credited with a number of firsts, gains on many fronts were not specific to that city, but paralleled those in other U.S. urban areas where energetic lesbian activists were also at work.[64]

In Los Angeles, along with progress and moments of "communitas," lesbian activists also had much to criticize and regret.[65] They had spent a lot of time and energy "trashing" each other. Issues important to lesbians of color were generally ignored until late in the decade. Most of the groups and centers established in the 1970s failed to outlive the decade, most had been badly funded and were dependent on volunteers who inevitably burned out, many were resistant to reasonable structure, and some imploded from cliquishness. Part of the failure could be attributed to the "natural" life process of groups and movements and to the inclination of many activists to spread themselves too thin. As Jeanne Cordova pointed out in 1973, "We've been everywhere fighting under everyone else's banner for five or six years now, for centuries."[66] Larger factors also conspired against grass-roots efforts as the social movement impulse of the sixties and seventies began to wane. Yet for many lesbians, after years of monolithic repression, the combination of being out, politically proactive, and part of a nascent lesbian culture generated a heady feeling and a surfeit of energy. Civil wars notwithstanding, the decade of the 1970s was a time when changing the world seemed possible,[67] and so for many lesbian feminist veterans, Robin Tyler's assessment that those days were "the golden age of lesbianism" rings true.[68]

Ironically, twenty-five years later, the largely separatist women's agenda described above has been supplanted by a co-gender movement encamped along the "new" frontiers of "PomoHomo" culture. Faced with this shift and consequent displacement from the center of lesbian politics, lesbian feminism and lesbian separatism have gone into what Verta Taylor calls an "abeyance" mode,[69] and adherents now find themselves holding the line against further erosion of the ideologically and temporally situated outposts they created in the 1970s. Ironically, in the 1990s, lesbian feminists of all ages find themselves having to defend their "opposing camp" not only from the mainstream but also from those lesbians and other "sexual outlaws" who have taken center stage within the "queer" neighborhood or community. Los Angeles lesbian activist pioneers who braved the frontiers of same-sex politics in the 1970s remain steadfast in their resistance to the "dominant symbolic,"[70] and in their commitment to what once seemed the outposts of a new dispensation (the dream of a "Lesbian Nation"), but now all too often seem to be isolated islands amid the (co-gender) urban sprawl of contemporary queer-identified life and culture.

Notes

1. *Lesbian-specific* is a term used by lesbian activist Robin Tyler to identify XX chromosome lesbians who in the 1990s are still committed to a lesbian feminist agenda.

2. I follow Allan Johnson's definition of community as "people who share something in common . . . without necessarily living in a particular place. It can be a feeling of connection to others, of belonging, of identification. . . ." A community is often diverse and divided, thus one definition cannot encompass all individuals. See Allan Johnson, "Community," *Blackwell Dictionary of Sociology* (Cambridge, Mass.: Blackwell, 1995), 42.

A fourth dynamic (after institution-building, political action, and internecine conflict) usually considered private territory, had at times public, collective consequences. The term *Lesbian Loveland* was suggested to me in the early seventies by Toni X, a member of Lesbian Feminists. What she was somewhat humorously referring to was the intricate network of personal relationships in a small politicized community. Under this rubric I also include the political impact of some of these relationships, noting that historically, personal desires and relationships (e.g., that of Henry VIII and Ann Boleyn) have had political consequences. On a more local scale, the behavior of lesbian activists was at times directed and/or affected by their friendships and intimate relationships. This in turn had an impact on the political direction of a project or issue. For example, the first meeting held between The White House and lesbian gay activists (1977) was partly the result of intimate lesbian connections put into the service of the lesbian and gay rights agenda.

3. Separatism, always a charged subject, did not wreak havoc in Los Angeles as it did in cities like Chicago. The concept of separatism was a logical progression for some and a revelation to others. Gahan Kelley defined separatism as "building an alternative culture/society based on values we've just begun to explore (i.e., woman-identification)"; Gahan Kelley, "Separatism: Building Alternatives," *Lesbian Tide*, May 1976, 29. Jeanne Cordova explained the varieties of separatism circa 1973 as a "political direction that calls for the economic, psychological, cultural, (and) emotional separation from men and all they have created"; Jeanne Cordova, "Radical Feminism? Dyke Separatism?" *Lesbian Tide*, May 1973, 19. See also Michal Brody, *Are We There Yet?: A Continuing History of Lavender Woman, a Chicago Lesbian Newspaper, 1971–1976* (Iowa City: Aunt Lute, 1985), 82; Sara Hoagland and Julia Penelope, eds., *For Lesbians Only: A Separatist Anthology* (London: Onlywomen Press, 1988); and Dana Shugar, *Separatism and Women's Community* (Lincoln: University of Nebraska Press, 1995).

4. Leverage advocacy uses techniques of behind-the-scenes persuasion, uses social and political connections, creates and collects on political debts, uses subtle threats of civil disturbances and when necessary actually uses grass-roots mass mobilization and civil disobedience. As in other social movements, the success of leverage advocacy is partly based on historical foundations created in this case by repression era activists (homophiles) and social movement era radicals (the Gay Liberation Front, Lesbian Feminists).

5. The phrase "the personal is political" is attributed to Carol Hamisch; Maggie Humm, *The Dictionary of Feminist Theory* (Columbus: Ohio State University Press, 1990), 162.

6. For a psychological analysis of lesbian feminism and issues of power see Sherry McCoy and Maureen Hicks, "A Psychological Perspective on Power in the Contemporary Lesbian-Feminist Community," *Frontiers* 4, no. 3 (1979): 207–11. Hicks was a member of the L.A. lesbian feminist community during the 1970s.

7. According to Alice Echols, "politicos" attributed women's oppression to capitalism and their primary loyalty was to the Left. The "radical feminists" argued that "gender rather than class was the primary contradiction." They rejected both the politico assertion that a "socialist revolution would bring about women's liberation and the liberal feminist solution of integrating women into the public sphere." This group "succeeded in pushing liberal feminists to the left and politicos toward feminism." In the early 1970s, radical feminism was eclipsed by "cultural feminism," which turned its focus "from opposing male supremacy to creating a female counterculture." Although envisioned as a culture of active resistance, the stance became "an end in itself . . . the focus became one of personal rather than social transformation"; Alice Echols, *Daring to Be Bad: Radical Feminism in America, 1967–1975* (Minneapolis: University of Minnesota Press, 1989), 5.

8. Activist posttraumatic stress syndrome, or "activist battle fatigue," is an unexplored phenomenon.

9. According to Manuel Castells, "In 1969 there were 50 gay organizations; in 1973 there were over 880"; Manuel Castells, *The City and the Grassroots: A Crosscultural Theory of Urban Social Movements* (Berkeley: University of California Press, 1983), 142.

10. Boundaries are "social territories" or the "social, psychological and physical structures that establish differences between a challenging group and dominant groups"; Verta Taylor and Nancy Whittier, "Collective Identity in Social Movement Communities," in *Frontiers in Social Movement Theory*, ed. Aldon Morris and Carol McClurg (New Haven, Conn.: Yale University Press, 1992), 111.

11. The foundation for the lesbian and gay liberation movement was laid by resisters like Henry Gerber in the twenties, Lisa Ben in the forties, and homophile groups like Mattachine, ONE, and the Daughters of Bilitis (DOB) in the fifties. In the mid-sixties, inspired by the militance of other civil rights groups, organizations like Homophile Action League (HAL) in Philadelphia and the Society for Individual Rights (SIR) in San Francisco were formed "as a protest against the sluggishness of the (homophile) movement"; Don Teal, *The Gay Militants* (New York: Stein and Day, 1971), 39. These new groups signaled the emergence of a different ideological and strategic approach to the struggle for homosexual rights.

The riot/revolt at the Stonewall Inn on Christopher Street in New York's Greenwich Village in June of 1969 has been recounted by a number of sources. See, in particular, Martin Duberman, *Stonewall* (New York: New American Library, 1994). Morty Manford, then a student at Columbia, recalled, "The place attracted a very eclectic crowd. Patrons included every type of person: some transvestites, a lot of students, young people, older people, businessmen"; Eric Marcus, *Making History: The Struggle for Gay and Lesbian Equal Rights, 1945–1990* (New York: Harper Collins, 1992), 39. Queens, butches, and politicized students were the homosexuals with the most experience with and inclination toward physical confrontations and thus were most likely to have resisted. One report in the *Advocate* (penned by first-name-only authors Lige and Jack) noted that it was young people who rioted; Lige and Jack, "NY Gays: Will the Spark Die?" *Advocate*, September 1969, 3.

Although drag queens are credited with starting the riot, there is evidence that a lesbian also contributed a well placed spark. Jim Fouratt, who later helped found GLF and ACT UP, reported that "a bulldyke . . . was inside giving the cops a lot of lip about their rights and how the cops should get out . . . they handcuffed and arrested her." She objected, she was hit and was put in a police car from which she promptly extricated herself. She released herself from her handcuffs and started rocking the police car (Duberman, *Stonewall*, 196). This account is discredited by some (Craig Rodwell, in Duberman, *Stonewall*, 197), but dyke or no dyke, at one point the audience exploded. The bar was set on fire while the police were inside. After the fire was put out and reinforcements arrived, thirteen people were booked.

12. In the days following the riots, homophile groups "at odds with each other over strategy" handed out leaflets, trying to take advantage of the incident as an organizing opportunity; Lige and Jack, "NY Gays," 3. Soon after, the Gay Liberation Front (GLF) was formed as a radical homosexual advocacy group. Across the United States, groups with the same name (GLF) sprang up, and following the spirit prevalent in counterculture circles, there was no central, hierarchical entity coordinating the groups. Martha Shelley recalls that although GLF was filled with hope and revolutionary fervor, it didn't last: "We got involved in these endless theoretical debates about what we should do and what our relationships were to other organizations. I think we just talked ourselves to death; GLF disintegrated into so many splinter groups that it just disappeared"; Marcus, *Making History,* 185.

13. When the first anniversary of Stonewall arrived, celebrations and marches were held in several cities. In New York, an estimated ten thousand people showed up, while in Los Angeles, an estimated twelve hundred marched along Hollywood Boulevard as thousands watched; Teal, *Gay Militants,* 331, 333. Karla Jay, then living in Los Angeles, recalled that "I seem[ed] to be one of only nine or ten women . . . who had the courage to march . . . of course it still wasn't quite safe to come out, and the parade was also an act of defiance against our oppressors. . . ."; Karla Jay, "The Decline and Fall of an Idealist, or Why I Ain't Marching Anymore," *Lesbian Tide,* August 1973, 10. Del Whan recalls that she helped to carry the GLF banner, and "there were smiles, happy, loving smiles everywhere. Karla marching behind us was the cheering section. . . . I have never felt happier or prouder in my life . . ."; Del Whan, "Come Out!" *Everywoman Newspaper,* July 1971, n. p. These reactions were typical of those who had spent years hiding from their oppressors and who were now publicly acknowledging their newfound pride even in the face of possible repercussions.

14. "Catalyzed lesbians" are women who have come out later in life and have a heterosexual history prior to coming out. Yolanda Retter, "Identity Development of Lifelong vs. Catalyzed Latina Lesbians" (master's thesis, University of California, Los Angeles, 1987), 45.

15. According to Sharon Raphael, the new social services center "had 'Gay Women's Service Center' printed on the door and the window"; Sharon Raphael, "'Coming Out': The Emergence of the Movement Lesbian" (Ph.D. diss., Case Western University, 1974), 54. Mina (Robinson) Meyer recalls that the center was listed in the phone book, and that one day she got a call from an anonymous woman at the phone company who said, "They tried to drop it [the listing] out of the directory and I'm making sure that it stays in"; Mina (Robinson) Meyer, interview with the author, Long Beach, California, 1995.

16. Mina (Robinson) Meyer and Sharon Raphael, "Women's Service Center Closes," *Lesbian Tide,* November 1972, 16.

17. The statement has no author and is on the inside cover of the September 1972 issue of the *Lesbian Tide.*

18. The *Lesbian Tide* (1971–1980) was the first U.S. lesbian newspaper to have the "L" word on its masthead. Under publisher Jeanne Cordova, it provided

news, information, and analysis to a local and national audience. It now serves
as an invaluable source of information on the early days of the second generation of lesbian activism.

19. J. Freeman has written that lesbian feminism "provided a strategy for
action, [one] that fused purposive and solidary incentives. One did not have
to wait for the revolution; one could revolutionize one's own life now. It was
an overt act of commitment which provided a political strategy which was
consonant with women's traditional style but avoided the onus of traditional
institutions"; Jo Freeman, *The Politics of Women's Liberation* (New York: David
McKay, 1975), 141.

20. "Lesbian feminists" were women who were feminists and later added
the lesbian component; "feminist lesbians" were lesbians who added the feminist component. Although the meaning of the order of the words was not debated in the group Lesbian Feminists, feminist lesbians were more often lifelong lesbians while lesbian feminists included more catalyzed lesbians among
their ranks.

21. Assertions that early lesbian activist groups were primarily from the
middle class does not apply to these Los Angeles groups. Lesbian Feminists'
membership, for example, was comprised of women from a mix of socioeconomic backgrounds. Although classism was an issue for Lesbian Feminists
from working class, socialist, and New Left backgrounds, racism was not.
There were only a handful of women of color in LF, and fewer still in the DOB
and the GWSC. Those of us who belonged to "ethnic minorities" and worked
in predominantly white groups were aware of individually experienced racism
but were not yet politicized around racism in the lesbian community in the
same way we were around sexism and lesbophobia in other communities.

22. The "socialist question" had many facets. Jeanne Cordova's lover, Sally
Anderson, had been deeply involved in the Socialist Worker's Party (SWP),
and this impacted the *Tide*'s coverage of the subject. Some of the lesbian feminists who had helped plan the conference, like Rita Goldberger, identified as
socialists. Attempts by SWP members to infiltrate the L.A. Women's Center
still rankled some lesbians, and the L.A. Women's Union, which was perceived
to be under SWP influence, did not last long. Lesbians like myself believed
that the fundamental problem was not class but gender. I used to tease my
socialist friends, "After you take it from the Rockefellers, you're going have to
take it from the 'fellers.'"

23. In CR groups, women talked about issues relevant to their lives. CR
was intended, according to one account, to "make us aware of the societal
pressures that oppress women. Some women use the awareness gained from
CR solely in their personal lives, without becoming active in the women's
movement.... It is hoped, however, that CR will help to radicalize us as
women, to participate in whatever action is necessary to change our society";
New York Radical Feminists, "Introduction to Consciousness-Raising," in *New
Woman's Survival Catalogue*, ed. Kirsten Grimstad and Susan Rennie (New York:
Conrad, McCann and Geoghegan, 1973), 206.

24. Herbert Blumer, "Social Movements," in *The Sociology of Dissent,* ed. Serge Denisoff (New York: Harcourt Brace Jovanovich, 1974), 6.

25. The "Daddy Tank" was where the overt and suspected lesbians were held and according to some reports, badly treated, "We Mean Business: Predicting the End of a So-Called Model Prison," *Lesbian Tide,* July 1972, 1.

26. Joan Robins recalls that two Lesbian Feminists members "went up to Canada for a women's antiwar conference representing us as lesbians. They met North Vietnamese women and tried to explain lesbianism to them." Joan Robins, interview with the author, Albuquerque, N.M., 1993.

27. The DOB had, much earlier, sponsored the first national lesbian conference. It was held in San Francisco in May 1960.

28. Joan [Robins], "Gay Women's West Coast Conference," *Everywoman Newspaper,* July 1971, n.p.

29. The GCSC became the prototype for other gay centers and is now the largest of its kind, with a nineteen-million-dollar budget. The center's first location was on Wilshire Boulevard near Union Street, and in 1975 it moved to Highland Avenue. In 1992, under the leadership of its first female CEO (Torie Osborn), it moved to a building that once housed the local IRS office. The "L" word was added in 1980; the phrase "Community Services" was taken out in 1996, and it is now called the L.A. Gay and Lesbian Center (LAGLC).

30. Meyer and Raphael persistently fought for a lesbian agenda at the center. Meyer recalls that she "started the first women's clinic. I said they couldn't open their VD clinic unless we could open the women's clinic at the same time ... [this "first"] has gotten totally lost in history.... When Laurie Jean (the present CEO of the GCSC) opened the new [Audre Lorde] clinic [at the Center] she billed it as the first clinic.... Ours was the first for lesbians at the center.... Jane Patterson [M.D.] got volunteered, we had all lesbian nurses and technicians.... We also have to give credit to the women at the Feminist Women's Health Clinic ... [who] trained the staff and helped us get started even though it wasn't their clinic"; Meyer, cited in Raphael, "'Coming Out,'" 71. One lesbian-focused project that the Center did support was the Sisters Liberation House, a living and meeting space. See Lee Hanson Sisson, "Women Come Home!" *Lesbian Tide,* April 1972, 19.

31. Jeanne Cordova, "G.C.S.C. Resignation," interview with Mina (Robinson) Meyer and Sharon Raphael, *Lesbian Tide,* July 1973, 22.

32. Ibid., 23.

33. The WWC had several locations and names. As Womonspace, it lasted until the late seventies. See "Go West Young Woman," *Lesbian Tide,* May 1972, 22; and the cover of *Sister Newspaper,* June 1977.

34. The kissing began at "high noon," with approximately seventy-five people gathered, including supportive feminist heterosexuals, onlookers of various persuasions, and several television crews.

35. Kirsten Grimstad and Susan Rennie, "Los Angeles Radical Feminist Therapy Collective," in *New Women's Survival Sourcebook,* ed. Kirsten Grimstad and Susan Rennie (New York: Knopf, 1975), 60.

36. Gudrun Fonfa, interview with the author, Los Angeles, 1997.

37. Ibid.

38. For example, Gahan Kelley recalls that "during the GCSC strike, that was awful. It divided the community. To this day there are people who will not be in the same room with each other because of the strike"; Kelley, interview with Del Whan, no location given, 1976.

39. Bonnie Zimmerman's take on the situation was that "almost every community project has a lifetime. It's born, it comes to maturity, it dies. I can only think of a couple of projects that ran on more than four or five years"; Zimmerman, cited in Brody, *Are We There Yet?*, 82.

40. Linda Chaffin of Torrance, Calif., lost custody of her children to her parents in December of 1973. In 1975, she was represented by Cheryl Bratman, who won a decision in Chaffin's favor. This was a first. See Jeanne Cordova, "How to Win a Lesbian Custody Case," *Lesbian Tide*, July 1975, 20.

41. Jeanne Cordova, Barbara McClean, and Rita Goldberger, along with the UCLA Women's Resource Center, the UCLA Gay Sisterhood, and others organized the 1973 West Coast Lesbian Conference, held at UCLA. Sheila Kuehl, then a UCLA dean and now a California state assemblywoman, was instrumental in obtaining the site.

42. The battle over the issue of transsexuals abated until 1977, when it was revealed that Olivia Records' recording engineer Sandy Stone was a male-to-female transsexual. The Olivia women (some of whom had been radical separatists not too many years before) quickly moved to mitigate the damage of perceived political inconsistencies, and Olivia weathered the storm.

43. Raphael, "'Coming Out,'" 76.

44. Raphael, in Meyer and Raphael interview, 1995. Regarding the notion of a "Lesbian Nation," Jill Johnston's book inspired the metaphor, dream, or fantasy of a space populated solely by lesbians, one in which we all lived in harmony and the abundance of lesbian culture; see Jill Johnston, *Lesbian Nation: The Feminist Solution* (New York: Simon and Schuster, 1974).

45. Barbara McClean's diary noted that "race and class has really been a big issue at the conference. There are women who are saying that these issues should have top priority in our movement. Cindy Gipple [from Social Radical Women] says that ethnic women should be the vanguard of our movement." "Black Caucus Position," *Lesbian Tide*, May 1973, 19.

46. The terms *politically correct* (PC) and *politically incorrect* (PI) were used in the lesbian activist community years before they surfaced in the mainstream lexicon. In 1977, an article in the *Tide* discussed the terms' meanings, noting that "the list of what is pc is lengthy, complex and changes almost whimsically as the season's fashions." The author warned that "If you aren't pc in the feminist community, you run the risk of getting trashed"; Cheri Lesh, "The New Conformism?" *Lesbian Tide*, January 1977, 14.

47. Before she cofounded the WB, Arlene Raven had confounded Womanspace, a feminist art center and gallery. In 1973, Womanspace (not to be confused with Womonspace, an incarnation of the Westside Women's Center) celebrated "Lesbian Week" with films, a slide show, workshops, music, dance,

and poetry readings. The WB closed in 1991 due to "the recession, a decline in membership, crises in feminism and funding for the arts and the outdatedness of the concept [of having everything in one place]"; Carla McBeath and Lori Medigovich, "L.A. Woman's Building to Close," *Lesbian News*, July 1991, 41.

48. Lesbian culture was blooming. Maxine Feldman's "Angry Atthis [At This]," a 45-rpm record, was sold through the *Tide*. Maxine, who lived in L.A. at the time, also appeared as the opening act for comedians Robin Tyler and Patty Harrison. Local musical talent included Vicki Randle, Sylvia Kohan, Diane Lindsay, Six Women (a multicultural band), The New Miss Alice Stone Ladies' Society Orchestra, and lesbian members of the L.A. Women's Community Chorus under the direction of Sue Fink. Film and theater found a receptive (if not lucrative) audience in the L.A. lesbian activist community. Jan Oxenberg produced one of the first lesbian documentary films, *Home Movie*, and Liz Stevens, a former member of Lesbian Feminists, cofounded Iris Films, which produced and distributed films like *In the Best Interests of the Children*. The performance group Bread and Roses provided song, satire, and skits designed to raise political consciousness. Evan Paxton and friends produced two memorable lesbian talent shows at the Venice Pavilion, and lesbian radio programs included June Herrle's, on KMET, and "Lesbian Sisters" on KPFK.

49. Along with political and cultural community, many lesbians also sought spiritual community; some found it in co-gender organizations like the Metropolitan Community Church, Beth Chaim Chadasim, and Dignity. Feminists lesbians who mistrusted male deities and male leaders looked further and found women's spirituality, which drew from pagan traditions and goddess worship. Z. Budapest, a refugee from the Hungarian Revolution, and friends founded the Susan B. Anthony Coven, which according to one member "was designed to give women spiritual power . . . its name was meant to link it to the feminist movement"; Robins, interview, 1993.

50. The Saloon was owned in part by former Lesbian Feminist member Collen Mckay. One visitor described it as "a place a woman can go after marching and speeching [*sic*] . . . and not feel depleted and overwhelmed by the abundant incongruities of the patriarchy"; Ann Doczi, "'whelmed' by the Women's Saloon," *Lesbian Tide*, September 1975, 20. Unable to deal with ongoing organizational and financial problems, the Saloon closed in 1977.

51. Buss later became one of the owners of Building Women, a licensed contracting company that in order to make ends meet worked both within and outside the lesbian community.

52. By 1977, there were enough lesbian and women's businesses to make the first issue of the lesbian-produced *L.A. Women's Yellow Pages* viable.

53. Marilyn Murphy, "Califia: An Experiment in Feminist Education," in *Learning Our Way: Essays in Feminist Education*, ed. Charlotte Bunch and Sandra Pollack (Trumansburg, N.Y.: Crossing Press, 1983), 148.

54. SCWU was founded by lesbians who had separated from a co-gender organization, the Whitman-Radclyffe Foundation.

55. Casualties included Lillene Fifield, who, like the Lesbian Activists, also

had previous ties with women at the Westside Women's Center who were firmly in favor of the strike. Lillene recalls that "for one solid year anytime I showed up anywhere I was turned away. . . . I was totally ostracized . . . ; Lillene Fifield, interview with the author, Los Angeles, 1994.

56. Jinx Beers, quoted in Ellen Swann, "The Mother of Invention," *Lesbian News*, August 1990, 47.

57. In 1977, singer and orange juice promoter Anita Bryant decided to "save the children" from imagined lesbian and gay predators and her campaign to overturn Dade County, Florida's gay rights ordinance was successful. In California, John Briggs, a state assemblyman with gubernatorial aspirations, managed to place Proposition 6 before the state's voters.

58. The group Latin American Lesbians met in 1974 in Highland Park. Debreta's, organized by Deborah Johnson and Bobreta Franklin in 1977, offered a social network for women of color.

59. Mina Meyer and Sharon Raphael, "National Lesbian Feminist Organization," *Sister Newspaper*, April–May 1978, 1.

60. Lydia Otero, interview with the author, Los Angeles, 1995.

61. The group Lesbians of Color worked most closely with Califia and White Women against Racism, and was active until the mid-1980s. LOC also organized the first National Lesbians of Color Conference in 1983.

62. The Lesbians of Color banner from the 1979 March on Washington can be seen on the official 1997 March poster.

63. Participants remember the event as an exhilarating and emotional historical moment, "a coming of age" for the lesbian and gay movement. Arlie Scott, "Listen America! Gay Push into the 80s," speech delivered at the first National March on Washington [D.C.] for Lesbian and Gay Rights, 14 October 1979; reprinted in the *Lesbian Tide*, November 1979, 18.

64. Throughout this and subsequent decades, lesbians not only organized on behalf of lesbian issues, they also worked with nonlesbians on behalf of many other issues. Lesbians were (are) the backbone of many projects, yet their efforts are often downplayed or omitted from the record. Prior to 1970, Lisa Ben—the name is an alias, an anagram for "lesbian"—published the first known lesbian publication in the U.S. (*Vice Versa*) in 1947 and 1948. Los Angeles lesbian "firsts" between 1970 and 1979 include: The first "out" lesbian publication, the *Lesbian Tide*, (1971–1980); and one of the longest surviving lesbian newspapers (*Lesbian News*, 1975–). Los Angeles was home to the first known "gay" women's services center (GWSC), as well as to one of the oldest women's bookstores in the nation, Sisterhood, which was cofounded by lesbians. Los Angeles lesbians created the first (and by now one of the longest-lasting) alcohol education and prevention programs for lesbians (ACW); they helped persuade NOW to pass a prolesbian resolution (1971); were instrumental in getting the International Women's Year prolesbian motion passed (1977); and helped defeat the first large antigay proposition, the Briggs Amendment (1978). They organized one of the first "out" lesbians of color groups (1974), and the first conference to form a national lesbian feminist organization (1978). Former LF member Joan Robins helped found the Los Angeles Commission

on Assaults against Women (LACAAW), which organized L.A.'s first funded community rape hotline. Women against Violence against Women (WAVAW) was founded by lesbians Suzann Gage, Lynn Heidelberg, and others to protest media portrayals of violence against women. When domestic violence became a public issue, lesbians like Kerry Lobel worked with heterosexual women to obtain public funding for a network of battered women's shelters; later, Kerry was also at the forefront of the movement against lesbian battering. Finally, toward the end of the decade, it was lesbians, at the Women's Building and the Gay Community Services Center, who were key activists in the movement to expose the silence and secrets around sexual abuse.

65. Communitas, explains Joan Cassell, "can be experienced at rallies and 'actions,' when a woman is marching with other women, surrounded by indifferent or hostile spectators; it may appear late at night when a small group of exhausted feminists is racing against a deadline to complete a project. This feeling of intense intimacy and trust, this 'communion of mutually supportive women,' can be an intoxicating experience"; Joan Cassell, *A Group Called Women: Sisterhood and Symbolism in the Feminist Movement* (New York: David McKay, 1977), 153. Some examples of moments of communitas were portions of the West Coast Lesbian Conference (1973), the "Margie, Chris, Vickie" concert in Los Angeles (1974), the first March on Washington (1979), the National Lesbians of Color Conference (1983) and the second L.A. Dyke March (1995).

66. Jeanne Cordova, "Abortion Rally Speech," *Lesbian Tide*, June 1973, 27.

67. New York City activist Martha Shelley recalls that "those of us in GLF [the Gay Liberation Front] felt that the struggles of all people should be united. . . . We had the feeling that the revolution was just around the corner and that we were part of the vanguard. . . . We were young and idealistic and wonderful and brave and naive"; Marcus, *Making History*, 183.

68. Robin Tyler, interview with the author, Northridge, California, 1995.

69. An abeyance structure, explains Verta Taylor, is a "holding process by which movements sustain themselves in non-receptive political environments and which provide continuity from one stage of mobilization to another"; Verta Taylor, "Social Movement Continuity: The Women's Movement in Abeyance," *American Sociological Review* 54 (October 1989): 761. Under adverse conditions, a movement (or what is left of it) may adopt an abeyance stance that sustains a core of activists, ideas, institutions, and resources through a hostile or nonreceptive period.

70. Rey Chow defines the "dominant symbolic" as a "corpus of attitudes, expressions, discourses and the value espoused in them"; Rey Chow, *Writing Diaspora: Tactics of Intervention in Contemporary Cultural Studies* (Bloomington: Indiana University Press, 1993), 100.

10

Presenting a Queer (Bath)House

Ira Tattelman

How to describe a "future" for a social space and architectural site that no longer has a "present"? This is the paradoxical, paradigmatically queer project that this chapter undertakes both to evoke and describe, by imaginatively entering into the lingering memory traces, the once flourishing social activities, and the physical layout of what was once the Saint Marks Baths in New York City and re-creating from its phantasmic outlines and actual blueprints a utopian vision for the future, one that grants a vibrant afterlife, to this venerable landmark of gay life.

As is now common knowledge, bathhouses in the U.S. have functioned as spaces for men to engage in same-sex activity for nearly a century. By the 1970s, gay bathhouses flourished, no longer simply underground or clandestine institutions, attracting a wide variety of men across an equally wide spectrum of race and class and offering multiple venues not only for physical but for social engagement. In the mid-1980s, however, gay bathhouses disappeared from numerous cities, under the cloud of fostering unsafe sexual behaviors conducive to the spread of HIV. While many gays—activists, intellectuals, everyday people—continue to consider the bathhouse disreputable or passé, relics of an already "antiquated" gay history, I use this chapter as a springboard for imagining, in both architectural and social terms, a future for the bathhouse. No longer exclusive to men, no longer cut off from the street, the bathhouse that I describe in the following pages is an amalgam, its relationships constructed out of the realms of the social, the sexual, the geographic, the historical, and the imaginary simultaneously. Because I conceive of this site as an *existing possibility*—not simply impossible fantasy—my strategy will be to talk about it in the present tense, even though the project has no literal "present" except that which inhabits your imagination as you read what follows. An unpredictable, activist, passionate construction filled with acts of self-revelation, the celebration of bodily pleasures, and the interplay of

222

design invention and political necessity, this site is conceived as a space where art, commerce, and work can be brought together, while offering a place in which new relations between one body and another can evolve. By renaming this revitalized structure a "(bath)house," I mean to evoke the connotations of "house" as a space for habitation and use, while "(bath)" signifies that even if, in this new bathhouse, the water facilities have been turned off, the remnants of that original function are nonetheless active in its design and implementation. This (bath)-house thus alters and builds upon an older structure through strategic innovations, rather than creating an entirely new one: in the process the site it occupies takes on a new urban identity, economically, politically, and physically speaking, by working through memory and discovery, by intensifying and linking together what is already present. Sex here is positive and resists mainstream structures of power.

As already noted, this project uses as its springboard the former gay bathhouse located on Saint Marks Place in New York City. This choice allows me to acknowledge its seventy years of operation and ten years of legal struggle, to focus on the particularities of the site, and to communicate my research through active participation. In the process I hope to open a dialogue, metaphorically speaking, between its past customers and its future users. If one considers this existing building structure as a conceptual frame and the new uses I propose for it as an intervention, then this project may be said to reinscribe the bathhouse—both the Saint Marks, and the concept of the bathhouse in general—with untold, fully queer, possibilities. The organization of any building affects social interaction, as Joel Sanders notes in his introduction to *Stud: Architectures of Masculinity,* by "regulating, constraining, and (on occasion) liberating the human subject," for architecture has the ability to create "the space—the stage—where human subjectivity is enacted and performed."[1] While present-day economic, legal, and ideological realities circumscribe social and architectural space within certain parameters, the conceptualization of new spatial strategies to match new or evolving social conditions holds open the possibility of revising those parameters. We are already seeing such an evolution happen in the social sphere as conceptions of queer identity, desire, and community are supplanting older norms of gayness and straightness. What we need to do now—and this is a task that this project attempts—is to create and design "queer spaces" that recognize and validate our unique subjectivities and experiences.

"Queer space" involves the construction of a parallel world, one filled with possibility and pleasure, while functioning simultaneously as an intervention in the world of the dominant culture, replacing its fixed principles and binary modes of thinking with the mutability of our everyday queer actions. By heightening the intensified, disruptive qualities of queer imaginations and sexually coded bodies, queer space provides an alternative means of worldly inhabitation, makes visible the already-in-place hierarchies, and embraces the reciprocity of space and sexual identity. In its space of opportunity, we are free to construct ourselves in flexible, unspecified, and unpredictable ways.

Given my focus on the (bath)house as the locus of such queer space, an explanation is in order here: its queer space is not (necessarily) the same as a sex club, nor is a sex club necessarily constitutive of queer space. Let me state outright that sexual activity is not the primary focus of my project, although I believe sexual activity can occur within and find a receptive space in its design. Indeed, rather than reinscribing this site as an exclusively male gay space, I openly invite women into its habitation. This gesture toward a queer sexuality, where queer-identified or same-sex partners can share information about their lives, experiment among themselves, and venture into relationships with others is not meant to threaten the Saint Marks's traditional patrons. Rather, it is meant to recognize the fact that while men and women may identify as gay/lesbian/queer, we can no longer assume that de-sire for one's own sex is exclusive, or that "crossing the line" and hav-ing sex with the "opposite" sex threatens one's self-identification. To bring women into a space associated with a specifically gay male past is to confront both men's and women's sexual assumptions and to cre-ate the imaginative space for additional choices and desires. If we are serious in exploring the queer frontiers of our future, then women as well as men need to create the terms and spaces in which our lives will be lived and defined.

The pages that follow, then, will take you into the Saint Marks Baths, examine its history, describe its heyday in the late 1970s and early 1980s, document its demise in the late 1980s, and propose a future for a place that has no present. By reoccupying the bathhouse, I intend to record and interact with its forgotten rooms and the primacy of its sensual effects. By exposing the displacements that have occurred within its walls and gay culture alike, by rediscovering the spatial func-tioning of the baths, I will explore ways of bringing a provisional un-derstanding to the myriad feelings, desires, and fears that surround the institution of the bathhouse, while carving out an experimental, queer space occupied by new forms of experience, production, and understanding.

A Site Accumulates over Time

The Saint Marks Baths, first a Turkish and then a gay bathhouse located on the Lower East Side, was constructed in 1913 as a commercial baths. Bathhouses such as this have always offered same-sex enjoyment.[2] Whether watching or participating in these activities, the men patronizing such establishments have traditionally found ample opportunities to engage in various levels of intimate contact. The height of the popularity of gay male bathhouses occurred between the Stonewall riots of 1969 and the onslaught of media surrounding AIDS, beginning with the death of Rock Hudson in 1985. Bringing together a wide mix of strangers, such locales offered anonymity and seclusion from the outside world. Men went to the baths to find others "like me," to find men who like what "I like." In these spaces, men were initiated into a group, assigned an identity, albeit one constructed in an exclusive place, a world apart. One such place, Saint Marks, remained unchanged for seventy years, until it was closed by court order on 6 December 1985, by the New York City Health Department.

Bruce Mailman, the owner and operator of the building since 1979, tried to fight the closing. When the courts failed to allow Saint Marks to reopen, Mailman began a campaign to try to sell the bathhouse in the early 1990s. In light of the commercial boom that has taken place in the East Village and on Saint Marks Place, the building was eventually sold and now houses a video and CD store, a café, and a music studio, with all traces of its former use erased. Like the Gap store and multiplex movie theaters in the area, "safe" and "acceptable" commercial venues have taken over the neighborhood, continuing the trend toward the homogenization of space in urban and suburban sites across the country.

When Mailman took over the Saint Marks Baths in the late 1970s, however, sexual activity and nonconformity were the main events; as a site within the often heterosexist spaces of urban centers, the contained and secretive world of the bathhouse offered comfort and security for gay and bisexual men. Although the required entry fee made the baths inaccessible to some, the consolidation of men within its walls created a commonality of experience that unified everyone in attendance.

The intensity of sexual play within the baths of this period continues to yield a varied literature ranging from memoir to fiction, film to theater, pornography to academic treatise. While the following anonymous testimonies, taken from the *Straight to Hell* (*S.T.H.*) anthologies, are not specific to the Saint Marks, they nonetheless indicate the range

THE LARGEST BATH HOUSE IN THE COUNTRY
6 SAINT MARKS PLACE (8TH ST. AND 3RD AVE.) NEW YORK. 212-473-7929.

This postcard, which was distributed at the Saint Marks Baths, promoted a sense of adventure and wild masculinity. (Reprinted by permission of John Sugg)

of bacchanalian behaviors and the diversity of orgiastic experience exhibited by the thousands of men who attended the baths. For example, one contributor to *S.T.H.* fondly recalls a "first visit to a bath . . . when I was 21. I remember the strange good feeling that went with allowing myself to be passed around every which way and groped, sucked and licked."[3] Another visitor, to the Beacon Baths in New York City, writes that he "experienced the biggest orgasm of my life there. . . . Six or eight men were contributing to my pleasure. . . . While it was happening I was scarcely aware of who these men were or what they looked like or what they were doing. When it was over I sat up on the bed. I thanked the men. We chatted idly."[4] As for raw human sexuality, a traveler to the Washington, D.C., Club Baths in 1978 jokes that "in th[o]se wicked times, it [was] possibly more shaming to reveal bashfulness than to submit to unspeakable outrages."[5]

While most patrons used the bathhouse as a place to get off, its space also served other social, even mating, functions. As Kenneth Read has noted, "while voyeurism or active participation in sex may be the main attraction for most, the settings also provide a meeting place—a place to talk and even, perhaps, to begin a relationship that moves out of the baths, transformed into the personal bond of 'lovers.'"[6] Some found delight in watching beautiful bodies being worshipped. Some used the heat of the sauna or the vapor of the steam room to relax their bodies and heighten their senses. A guide to "more free" and "less guilty" gay sex published in 1978 concurs that "There is a good deal of unobtrusive social interaction taking place in a baths as well as outright sexual activity. . . . Gay men who have been conditioned to be reticent about revealing their sexuality in the hostile society outside must learn to relax and express sexual interest in the baths."[7] Nor did the sexual "expressions" have to lead to one and only one end; indeed, it was not uncommon for men to leave without coming, not because they were unsatisfied, but because the multiplicity of partners and the polymorphous fluidity of exchanges became a worthy object of desire itself: "When I say 'played with,' I don't mean 'had sex to orgasm,'" one regular explained. "I mean played—fondled, talked, perhaps had foreplay. Orgasm is never my goal, though occasionally it will happen."[8]

For such men, then, the baths of the 1970s and early 1980s served multiple functions. Confined in a space of desire where almost any wish could be fulfilled and where the hostility of the outside world was momentarily suspended, men used the baths to make connections, to liberate their fantasies, to experience refuge and self-affirmation. When they walked out, they left a supportive environment and returned to a world of isolation and homophobia.[9]

The spatial layout of the Saint Marks Baths attests to this stark division between "inside" and "out," between an external world of straight surveillance and an interior one of hedonistic freedom. The street entry led up a flight of stairs to the first floor, which housed the admissions/registration window, offices, locker room, restaurant (where cold sandwiches, salads and nonalcoholic beverages were sold), and an orgy room. Another flight of stairs led down to the basement, where the steam room, swimming pool, and showers were located; a sauna and whirlpool were added in the early 1980s. The three upper floors contained as many small, partitioned rooms as possible—approximately 150 single cubicles and 6 double or specialty rooms. On the roof, there was a sun deck for nude sunbathing by day and sex under the stars by night.

By all accounts, the baths were surprisingly clean, congenial, and, better still, always open; beyond its unobtrusive doorway and discrete sign, potential satisfaction awaited the interested or horny passerby at any hour of the day. At peak times, the baths accommodated hundreds of men.

A person's entrance into the Saint Marks inaugurated a series of transactions and interactions involving issues of gender, power, vision, transference, exposure, surveillance, and desire. While the men who came to the baths constructed its activities, the physical structure of the building in turn helped shape those activities. Walls, doorways, and windows determined the flow of bodies, the distribution of activities, and the exercise of visual authority.

The architecture in a space like the Saint Marks also influenced the dispersion and experience of sensual pleasure in other, less tangible, ways. Because buildings are put together with materials, connections, and technologies—components that not only serve the architecture but the lives of its inhabitants as well—one could craft an experience through the sheer tactility of the physical environment, which could include brick, tile, glass block, corrugated sheet metal, chain link, fabric, carpet, and wood. The delight of being in the baths thus resulted from more stimuli than just the flesh of other bodies. Towels, condoms, lubricants, mouthwashes, and blow-dryers offered the body additional sensations.

Buildings also impart signals through the quality and performance of their "stages," and the Saint Marks was no exception, providing a variety of areas for different kinds of involvements, and accommodating a range of moods, objectives, and preferences. The interaction between the imagined and material realities transformed even the most unlikely couplings into viable conduits of passion. Whereas some baths included libraries, gyms, and even dance floors or theaters, at the Saint Marks the café was one of the few spaces where men could talk and laugh without disturbing the general sexual ambience. A second lounge, also on the first or entry floor, featured carpeted platforms for stretching out or resting as a site of pure relaxation; the "wet area" in the basement was also extremely popular. The sauna at the Saint Marks was fairly standard in terms of design; the steam room was more highly styled, featuring multi-level benches, decorative tile, and a window in the door with a view of the traffic flow in the hall beyond. The round hot tub was also tiled; from its central location next to the pool, the entire wet area formed a stage from which one could observe and be observed. Everyone at some point seemed to end up in the showers, an easy site for casing out that person that one had just missed out on, or a hitherto unnoticed object of desire and pursuit.

Upstairs were the individual cubicles, in which anything might occur. The partitions were designed to create the maximum number of "private" rooms in the least amount of space. Also known as dressing, changing, resting, or sleeping rooms, the cubicles measured approximately four feet by six-and-a-half feet, and contained little more than a platform, mattress, small night table with ashtray, and a light on a dimmer switch. In architectural terms, one unexpectedly interesting feature of these "rooms" were their thin walls, which also did not stretch to the ceiling. Contrary to expectation, this absence of complete separation actually contributed to one's sense of security in the baths. Because every moan, slap, compliment, and shriek could be heard in both the hallways and neighboring rooms, disruptions to the baths' code of mutual consent were almost unknown; someone was always within hearing distance and physical reach.

The hallways measured approximately four feet wide, with just enough room for two men to pass each other. On each floor these halls ran continuously into each other with no dead ends. By creating a mazelike layout, complex enough so that newcomers were slightly confused, the baths invited an unending flow of foot-traffic. The men wandering these halls cruised not only each other, but the bodies on display within the cubicles where, with their doors left ajar, other men often stretched out in various provocative poses.

Baths like the Saint Marks may be best known for their orgy rooms and mazes. While private rooms could only accommodate a few individuals, the orgy room at the Saint Marks was designed for large groups and aimed to encourage unrestrained indulgence. Located

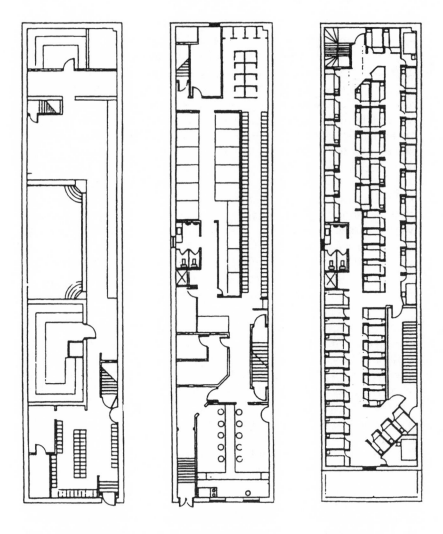

BASEMENT   FIRST FLOOR   SECOND FLOOR

These plans show the layout of the Saint Marks Baths as the establishment existed in
the early 1980s.

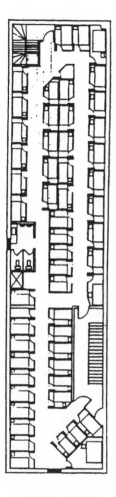

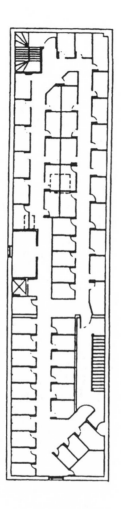

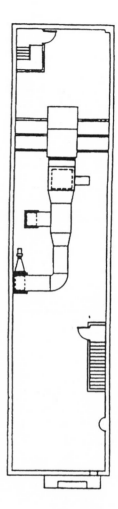

THIRD FLOOR   FOURTH FLOOR   ROOF

at the back of the first floor, the large unlit space was divided with mattresses. If in the hallways communication relied on the eyes, in the darkness of the orgy room one's hands guided one through the space.[10]

The strategy of the bathhouse was to break down as many of the class barriers that separate people as possible, creating a democracy of male bodies. The removal of clothing and the low, tinted-to-a-healthy-pink lighting played a role in this equalizing desire, reducing virtually everyone to one common denominator—a towel draped around a naked male body. Distributed at entry, the towel permitted a variety of styles; the fold of the towel and the placement of the knot were among the codes that signified various sexual interests. Towels folded in half could be drawn tightly around the ass or give a peak at the genitals. Towels hung loosely could suggest any number of surprises underneath, or they might hide some extra fat. Securing the towel so that it parted in back indicated a "bottom," while a front flap often signaled a top. Such codes, of course, were moot in the collective spaces where people removed their towels.

Advance planning, however, was required to satisfy some of the more specific sexual fetishes of some patrons. If accessories such as food and oils, alcohol and drugs (nominally prohibited), leather and rubber, jockstraps and G-strings, dildos and vibrators, or toys and gloves were needed, one had to remember to bring them. One bathhouse visitor revealed a sight of fetishistic display that he had "never, never forgotten" in *S.T.H.*: "[I] passed a room with a door open and there sat this dude, sitting on the edge of his bed drinking beer. He was wearing construction boots, white (very dirty) socks, a worn-out jock strap, and an open shirt with no sleeves. He smiled. He took a sip of beer and let it run from his open mouth onto his jock strap."[11] Clearly this "dude's" effect depended on the props—boots, beer, jock—that, along with the framing offered by the open door, constituted this staged pose. Another patron recalled that in his "favorite bath house in Los Angeles" he liked to "run around naked, just wearing my slave collar and chain. I wandered around looking for someone to mistreat me when I spied some dusty boots at the entrance to one cell. Naturally I crawled in and found a sexy, young, mean-looking stud dozing in Levi's [sic] and leather jacket."[12] One man's props, well placed, communicated clearly to this patron where to find an answer to his desires in this theater of fantasy and display. As such tableaux evince, the language of the baths often had little to do with spoken words. And if some men found the conspicuous silence difficult, they learned other ways to communicate in order to initiate encounters. New arrivals learned the rules that were informally enforced by the regulars and the employees.[13] As a result, explicit exchange of intentions could occur without spoken communication.

In order to facilitate these nonverbal levels of intercourse, the architecture of bathhouses utilized a variety of viewing mechanisms: strategically placed windows, doors, balconies, and artwork all helped to keep up the visual excitement. Everyone was on public display, whether walking around the hallways, relaxing in the wet area, or indulging in an orgy. Frames were designed to outline the body and sexual encounter. The artwork often consisted of erotic images or mottos, contributing subliminally to the sexual atmosphere. Some baths offered paintings that showed scenes "crowded with men, every type you've ever seen at a baths, and more: from a cowboy in boots, hat & towel, to a rotund, cheery troll who is fishing (with rod and reel!) in the pool for a handsome young twinkie."[14] Others used sculpture such as a "large blue neon bird suspended from the high ceiling. The wings are animated, so it appears to be flying. On the wall near it is a large panel, with jaunty lettering which invites all who enter to 'FREE YOUR MIND.'"[15] One famous image, from a series entitled *The Orgy Mural from the Bulldog Baths*, featured a muscular man ejaculating into the mouth of another while being fucked by a man in a jockstrap who is being fucked by a man with his jeans around his ankles. The other panels featured similar exploits, with multiple partners and dripping come.[16]

Men who went to the baths usually wanted sex with few complications, and the bathhouse encouraged physical contact along with ample opportunities for voyeurism and exhibitionism. Every patron was a potential partner. Men willingly transformed themselves into sexual objects. While anxiety and rejection could deflate a person's ego, few men—whatever one's age or appearance—left without getting sex. Sexual energy and technique were the commodities that were traded. One had the opportunity to try, learn about, and reject radically different ways of enjoying the multiple possibilities of the body.

The narrative of the space of baths like the Saint Marks was produced by gay desire and the inventiveness of that desire was visible for all to see. Men moved through the space with intention, navigating the traffic as if they owned the place. Polite assertiveness was rewarded. Curiosity functioned as a means of introduction. The ease of coupling as well as of refusal were intrinsic both to the system's appeal and structure.

What You Get When the Bathhouse Is Seen

Historically, the exteriors of gay bathhouses tend to be as anonymous as possible, often appearing boarded up to ensure some sense of privacy and protection to their patrons. Even when located, like the Saint Marks, in well-traversed areas such as the East Village, doors and windows are often painted black. By looking forbidding or deserted, most bathhouses operate without incident, remaining invisible to those who do not care to know about them. Police departments are usually "well aware of [the baths'] sexuality but [do] not bother them." One reason is their location in "enclosed and off-the-street places where an unsuspecting public is not likely to be exposed to moral outrage."[17] When they do become visible, their existence often becomes the trigger point for conflicting social agendas and the focus for intense civic debate.

Throughout this century, bathhouses have felt the full force of political and social judgments. From the early-twentieth-century progressive movement to establish municipal sewerage and water systems (which took people out of the public baths, thereby establishing the remaining bathhouses as private enterprises for communal respite) to the closing of selected gay bathhouses in the mid-1980s (which put people searching for sex back into the potentially dangerous zones of parks, public bathrooms, and alleys), the baths reveal the complex interactions of competing ideologies. The most dramatic example of social ideologies making the gay baths newly "visible" to public scrutiny and regulation is, of course, the controversy surrounding the bathhouse and AIDS in the past decade.

Confused by conflicting reports and under pressure to do something, government officials and many gay leaders targeted bathhouses for attack as a way of responding to growing concern over the spread of AIDS. This resulted in the vacating of many establishments by their regular patrons, and in the closing of others. In response, the owners of the spaces argued that the interference was misplaced, claiming that the bathhouse could serve as a positive site for AIDS intervention, education, and condom distribution, helping to point out high-risk practices and change behavior: "We feel that closure of bathhouses and private clubs is not the real issue," read a 1984 flyer, ". . . rather, the issue is the education of gay men as to what specific sexual practices involve the exchange of bodily fluids and thus are 'high-risk' for the transmission of AIDS, and to learn and practice low-risk 'safe-sex' techniques wherever and whenever they have sex."[18] Those wanting to close the baths argued that as long as sex at the baths went unmonitored, the transmission of HIV would continue unabated, citing the multiplicity of anonymous partners, the impossibility of knowing who is infected and uninfected, the perniciousness of drug use in causing men to let down their guard, and the confusion of exactly which behaviors were more or less safe. Part of the controversy was also, however, the fault of the owners of the baths. While some put up the initial safe-sex posters and distributed condoms, others seemed to care more about the incredible profits they were pocketing rather than the health and safety of their patrons.[19] As a result, states such as Connecticut, Georgia, Iowa, Kentucky, Maryland, New Jersey, New Mexico, North Carolina, Oklahoma, and Wisconsin no longer have operating bathhouses. New York and California, which collectively boasted a total of seventy-one bathhouses in 1982, had only twenty-two in 1995.[20] Sexual abundance, it seemed, was no longer utopian.

To replace the baths as sites of sexual play, sex clubs have been built over the past few years. In contrast to the baths, these clubs, popular in about a dozen cities, no longer have wet areas or private cubicles. They do, however, maintain the layout and erotics of the maze. Men, now clothed rather than toweled, plant themselves in strategic locations waiting for a partner; others maneuver through the surroundings as if on a hunt wanting to capture their prize. These spaces advertise themselves as men's clubs or naturist compounds with hot weekend action and take all sorts of forms: some are more like gyms with "hands off" cruising than participatory playrooms, others are more like social clubs with lots of small meeting areas, many are unpredictable, dependent on the crowd that gathers inside on a given night.

While I am interested in these new clubs, I cannot help noticing the many ways in which they are similar to the bathhouse even as they adamantly describe themselves as anything but one. The clubs create an atmosphere of sexual competition, developing hierarchies based on cock size and the condition of one's body. Just as the baths could seem to some like "nothing more than a large, subdivided closet where gay men who are already hiding their sexual orientation from the outside world continue to hide themselves in the dark and anonymity,"[21] sex clubs generally maintain dimly lit, enclosed environments and operate as self-contained retreats. Some argue that private rooms make a bathhouse and that such privacy encourages unsafe sex behavior. Lacking these opaque walls, patrons and monitors in the sex clubs can observe and at least hypothetically intervene in such unsafe behavior. The sex club thus attempts to couple a sense of sexual freedom and fluidity with the reality of responsibility.

If communal spaces mark where we are and how to behave, the baths of the 1970s and early 1980s gave gay men a place to congregate with others who shared their desires and rituals. At the same time, they also reproduced some of society's destructive hierarchies regarding race, age, class, gender and ethnicity. Thus, as one participant reminisced in the novel *Tim and Pete*, "it was hard to think of [the baths] as an innocent pleasure palace. Not that I ever did, really. I always had very mixed feelings about it. A lot of cruelty here. Rejection. Everybody looking for the perfect body, the biggest cock. A lot of psychic damage. . . . It wasn't sex as catharsis or redemption, but sex as a drug. A crazed, compulsive abuse of what sex can provide. Cynical and loveless. Sex as ego gratification, as ephemeral validation. Sex as a product, something you need to feel better about yourself for a while. A new shirt, a new car, a new fuck. Capitalism. I didn't like the music either."[22] Marked by the debates of the 1980s, the gay bathhouse has entered public discourse. Recent battles over their reopening or the creation of new ones have been waged in both the gay and mainstream presses. Some critics and activists find little to value in them, while others celebrate their creation of sites for unlimited, anonymous, non-normative sexual gratification. In either case, the bathhouse remains a threat.

Addressing History and Meaning

Having surveyed some of the intellectual, political, social and sexual concerns surrounding the baths, I want to engage this material through my proposal for a queer (bath)house. How to imagine a future use for the former Saint Marks Baths that relates the physical experiences that once took place within its walls to a larger queer community? What traces, what signs, remain that suggest clues for future use? Prior to the building's transformation into a retail establishment in the 1990s, the room dividers had left their trace on the paneled surfaces of the bathhouse wall and along the carpeted floors, though the interior partitions had been removed. The café sign was untouched, boasting sandwiches with 1985 prices. Under a bathroom sink remained a box of Spic and Span and three cans of Barbasol. These were telltale remains of the world of the baths that the following pages identify, celebrate, and undermine in an act of imaginative modification and intervention designed to keep the building "alive." By suggesting new ways to reenvision and reanimate this landmark site, I hope to make more self-conscious the ways in which individuals approach, resist, or idealize their lives. That life, as I envision it, is a queer one.

I begin with the premise that queers (gays, lesbians, bisexuals, transgenders, transsexuals, transvestites, cross dressers, drag queens, alternative straights, and anyone in between) desire to reveal what the norms of mainstream culture try to conceal. They challenge social practice, struggle over control of space, and question accepted orders. As a subculture, queers try to be self-sustaining and self-defined. They develop strategies for making their presence known through clothes, language, style and manner. The results often valorize experimentation, variety, unpredictability, adventurousness, and spontaneity. Identity is not singular, but fluctuates depending on circumstance and desire.

Queer, then, is neither finite nor fixed. Queer can be odd or strange, eccentric or different. To be queer is to manifest the multiple identities that lie within subjectivity without choosing one over the other. To be queer is to decorate one's body and perform one's attitudes. In a society that tells us we do not exactly belong, queers discover their difference and begin to play with their gender and sexual roles as well as their individual and social beings. They explore interactions while planning for new ones.

Similarly, the aesthetics of the queer (bath)house of the future I'm proposing here embodies the potential for both connection and disjunction with the physical realm. Temporality and the dissolution of substance are virtues within this site. Its architecture need not be fixed but can be composed of light, motion, and sound as well as physical matter. This vision of architectural possibility finds its power in memory, illusion, and imagination as well as real-time experience. In designing this queer space, I have used the deliberate layering of multiple functions and multiple techniques of construction to produce unforeseen textures and experiences. Its spaces are described without factual record or fixed image; they are permeable, flexible, places to intermingle or contradict. They are places for resistance, for a (re)location of focus. In providing a visual record for this proposed renovation of the Saint Marks, I sometimes overlap one photograph/program on top of another. The two images/uses remain independent, yet their overlap produces a third image/use. This process heightens issues of scale, sensuality and the viewing frame, all gesturing toward a realization of queer space.

In taking on the contested site of the bathhouse, I also envision a space where the quest to be queer can be experienced as a creative process. By studying bathhouse strategies and spatial construction, and learning from their prior usages, this project attempts to uncover new potentials in this now "inaccessible" site. The general mingling of bodies, diffused eroticism, and leftover environments provide my context. Through programmatic collage and sited interventions, this proposal for a future Saint Marks theorizes a place that breaks down compartmentalization, brings sensuality into everyday life, and transforms an insular space into something more public.

The program I propose for this building does not experience the past as a set of memories or fixed rituals. Instead, it revitalizes the spatial relations and social functioning of the bathhouse without repeating its activities. This is one of the main reasons my project includes women. By being inclusive, I embrace the contradictions within our communities and ourselves. When Rita Mae Brown, disguised as a man, went to a bathhouse in 1975, she revealed that "whatever slender bond these men felt for me as a male would have been shattered if I revealed myself as woman. . . . Their sexuality depended on my absence."[23] Perhaps it is time to take pride in the sexuality of all genders. As a place of relief, touch, refuge and contact, the queer (bath)-house that I am imagining will be open to myriad visitors, spurring each to explore their own behaviors and desires through an experience of shared space.

By taking over the potent site of the bathhouse, this project gives queers a public forum from which to break the silence imposed on their lives. This new Saint Marks is a place where one can revise and rewrite rules, reassert the need for artistic and sexual freedom, and develop a language that articulates queer experiences. My proposal imagines a space in which queers can organize socially and politically—a place to be loud, visible, and sexual in a culture that would rather queers not exist.

Occupation

Foremost, I have imagined the queer (bath)house as a multivalent artistic, social, and commercial space, one that is not an idealized, an isolated, or a homogeneous retreat from the outer, "public" world. Within its walls, people can wander without their movements being restricted by singular paths or solid rooms. Here they inhabit a place of casual reception, void of the mechanisms of surveillance and uniformed guards, where patrons en route to one space may be surprised to find themselves passing through another. The success of the project is dependent upon the participation of all those who enter.

In order to describe its architectural and design features, I have included drawings and images to accompany my narrative. As I map out each floor, these plans and cross-sections can be used as a guide illuminating the relationships between one space or floor and another.

I reinhabit the existing infrastructure of the first floor and basement, reconceive the second floor, and allow the third and fourth floors, which have been stripped of their rooms, to be rebuilt by the people who venture up there. I adapt the baths to include commercial spaces such as a market, a café, and a meeting room; there are art and body spaces for piercing, tattoos, and haircuts, and work spaces for artists, healers, and body workers. Today, art is rarely a painting in a frame. Artists often work with communities and environments, handing out leaflets, interpreting technology, playing characters, or conceptualizing events and installations. Conceptualized as a project that has been funded by an arts foundation that wants to deliver a space in which artists can "create," this place is available to those who do not want to participate in programmed activity, to those who want to choose their own paths and direction, rather than follow a map and look at static objects on the walls.

These multiple uses, retail services, and means of pedestrian access create public and semipublic spaces while leaving open the potential for more private groupings to occur. The option of erotic freedom and sexual release exists even if it is not specified. The bath(house) can suggest social intercourse and pure action. The spaces are both ground and stage; one has full knowledge of what one is doing but need not feel any anxiety to prevent one from doing it. The concentration of social behavior and movement provides the inspiration for new definitions. If patrons can "conceive social relations in a different way," then they may be able to take "pleasure in an immediate relation where the sancrosant difference between public and private, between the individual and the social, will be out of place."[24]

Rearranging the Hierarchy of Bathhouse Spaces: The First Floor Entry

The existing building façade acts as a mask; in my design, a glass curtain wall is placed just behind the brick wall to highlight the separation of the interior from its public face. By framing the human form in movement and in its surroundings, I hope to make visible the subjects' positions as well as to call into question and subvert the expectations that those positions arouse.

Whereas the architectural remnants of most defunct baths in New York City have been cleared out and cleaned up, here the façade is left as it was, with graffiti covering the painted stucco. Inside, however, the building has changed: the heavy, closed doors are no longer restrictive; the baths are now open to both men and women.

As one enters, the old cashier's desk becomes the new structure's orientation lobby. There is no entrance fee. Instead, the former private

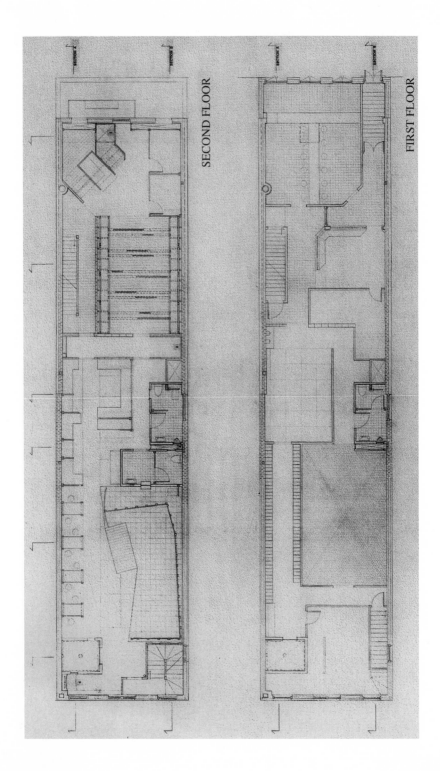

SECOND FLOOR

FIRST FLOOR

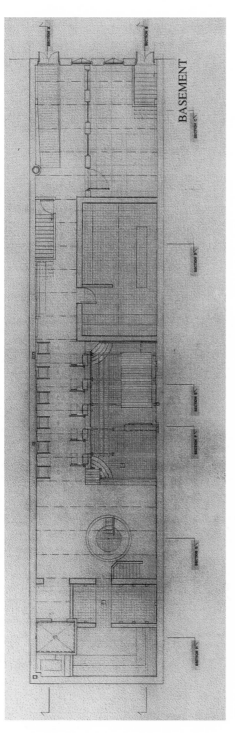

BASEMENT

These updated plans show the basement, first, and second floors of the queer (bath)house.

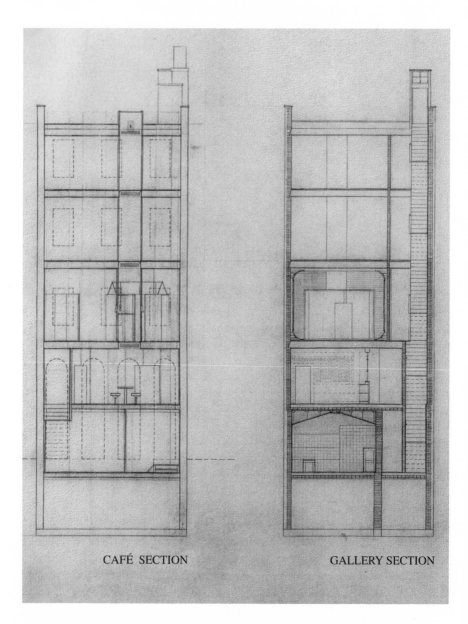

CAFÉ SECTION   GALLERY SECTION

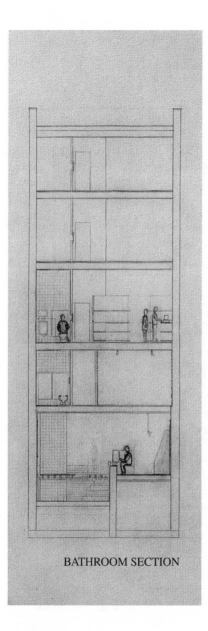

BATHROOM SECTION

These three short sections reveal the relationship of uses as they are stacked one floor to the next.

The façade shows the existing worn, graffiti-covered surface with the glass wall behind it.

office is transformed into a place to get acquainted, read community bulletin board listings of upcoming events, or find interesting personal ads, whether for a new couch or a S/M bottom. Visitors cannot "experience" the bathhouse as it was: the former thresholds have been erased, the old gates are opened. The activities within, however, remain the building's invitation.

Eroticizing Encounters through Intimacy and Surprise: The Basement

One takes possession of a space through action, and it is movement that gives any building its life. Here people move freely and at their own pace, unexpectedly bumping into friends, engaging in physical contact or experiencing the spectacle provided by others' activities. People come here consciously, making a choice to explore the impact that art is making on their environment, sexuality, and lives. This queer (bath)house, hence, should not be thought of as an after-hours sex club.

In the basement, the steam room, formerly blurred by water vapor, becomes a contact room available for wrestling and massage. There are mattresses in the room's center surrounded by tile benches. The mechanical system is no longer the heat producer; people will still sweat, but not passively. Impromptu wrestling matches and sexual encounters are encouraged in this space.

The sauna and showers, traditionally "hot" spots in gay baths, remain open but now as the site of needle exchange, condom handouts, drug distribution "banks," and homeopathy. I am conscious that HIV was (and might still be) transmitted within these spaces. Therefore, I want outside organizations to use this renovated bathhouse as a site of caring and education. The responsibility for safe sex lies within us; safety and protection are an individual choice. An environment can only suggest the parameters of behavior and encourage self-affirming, safe habits.

At the pool, facing a line of mirrors, I place open, coin-operated booths. This is an area of narcissism and objectification. By taking a position in a booth, the thrill of looking and being looked at is itself placed on view. One can pleasure oneself by admiring the reflective surfaces or by indulging the body with sun lamps or vibrating chairs. One can admire others though videos or computers. Such electronic communication technologies also allow access to a realm of virtual possibilities that exist outside the literally visual, since whole communities are now formed within wires rather than on the streets; gender roles and identities are extremely fluid on the Internet, whose maze-

While the pool is no longer for swimming, the use of mirrors, computer screens, and a vertical tiled "water wall" keep the area active.

like pathways and links mimic both the form and pleasures of the former bathhouse's architecture.

Establishing Relations between People: The Second Floor

Upstairs, on the second floor, the bathhouse has been remade by readjusting viewing positions, juxtaposing different kinds of activities, and establishing the proximity of bodies. A "body center" is meant to serve as a reminder of the rooms formerly located here, since these present spaces are rentable on a daily basis and also serve to bring people to a more positive awareness of their bodies. Many experience body shame because they derive pleasure in ways that the dominant culture considers unacceptable, illegal, or sinful. The body center features practitioners who facilitate comfort by intensifying and heightening the client's responsiveness to physical, visual, and aural stimulation. These practitioners could include acupuncturists, chiropractors, tattoo artists, sex workers, or massage therapists. While these rooms are closed to view, any sounds from within the room can be heard elsewhere in the building through open duct work. The exposed infrastructure is an integral part of the daily operations of this project.

A set of paired stores placed in conjunction with a pair of bathrooms create a service core at the center of the second floor. The store space is tight and deliberately constricted like the old bathhouse corridor or sidewalks outside. One store will sell basic needs such as bread, milk, coffee, and toilet paper. The other will sell whatever is being sold on the street. Many have written about the problematic relation between commerce and the gay and lesbian communities.[25] I highlight this dilemma by placing a one-way mirror in the bathroom that looks directly onto the cash register of the store. Acts of consumption are being watched; shoppers participate in more than one event without know-

The ducts are framed like windows and the infrastructure of the building is open to view. The ducts also allow sound to travel from one floor to another.

The store and bathroom are combined through proximity and transparent glass; one function projects itself onto the other.

ing it. If the shoppers at some other time use the bathroom, they will realize that their exchanges may have been observed. While control of vision through one's position may equal power, a central location makes one vulnerable by becoming subject to the gaze from the sides. Through spectatorship, one identifies and desires what one sees, as one in turn is being seen by others.

The bathrooms, one of the few public places where we expose our genitals, are a prime site rather than nonsite within this project. In the bathroom, one performs bodily functions that are considered private, unacknowledged, yet witnessed by those in the next stall. I have allowed one bathroom to keep its locked door and "one person at a time" expectations. But to invert this premise, I have placed a doorless second bathroom across a thin sliver of space beyond the first. Each bathroom has a window facing into this thin shaft. The public performance of bodily functions reminds us of the "libidinal charge when first placed under surveillance by a keen parental eye in order to call forth the subject as he who internalizes cultural power by learning to display an efficient control (one that parents will blithely call 'his') both over his turbulent body and, that mission accomplished, *through* it."[26] The positions of users, from toilet to toilet to urinal, and the placement of the windows call the privacy one assumes in a bathroom into question. It also compresses the spatial distance between subject and object, while heightening the tension of exposure and recognition. Physical contact is momentarily unattainable. One must remember the other through the window and identify her later. At times, furthermore, one's sight through the shaft between the bathrooms will be blurred by water. I have cut a hole in the roof and opened the floors all the way down to the pool, allowing rain water to flow from the roof to the pool. By placing this cut between the bathrooms and creating this tiled "water wall," I question issues of source and waste in our water systems.

While the art and body spaces occur throughout the building, there are areas that are designated as "galleries." The gallery on the second floor is both passageway and labyrinth; the partitions run on tracks and are spaced to recall the dimensions of former room walls and doors. Viewers control the route of progression by manipulating movable partitions. As individuals take on the gallery, they create their own path. Through the act of making these decisions, they affirm their autonomy in "creating," and placing themselves in, this building. Being able to determine their own movements becomes an act of self-definition.

The outer gallery walls are framed in wood and protectively wrapped in latex. In this time of virus and disease, we are all too familiar with the reality of condoms and dental dams. These new walls both comfort and challenge the user by giving these materials alternate uses. While they clothe the old walls, they are also translucent enough to suggest what lies behind them. Surfaces generally create the illusion of continuity even as they hide the equipment, wires, and security devices that run just behind them. In contrast, my design uses materials to intensify boundaries, confuse surfaces, reveal their making, and discover depth. If gender transgression, through clothing or language, is a sign of queer identity, material transgression may be a sign of queer architecture.

The "performance space" opens onto a grouping of tables for eating, reading, or socializing. Its stage can be used for both planned and unplanned events. The passing of a hat can help support these events. The floor consists of a platform raised one step off the old bathhouse floor. There are walls on two sides that bend into a lattice covering to hold lights and microphones. The walls do not reach to the floor. By seeing the new walls in relation to the old walls, by seeing the new platform in relation to the old floor, by seeing the formality of the stage in relation to its back alley (large enough for one person to pass at a time), one always sees the current activities and constructions in rela-

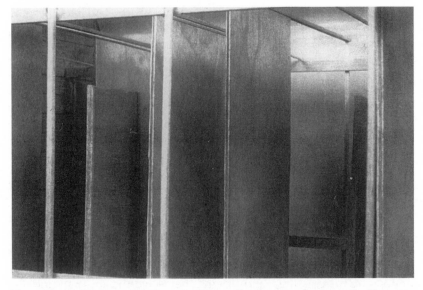

The gallery dividers are on tracks so that they can be moved and arranged by their user.

The long history of the building is revealed in the layering of surfaces found along the walls of the (bath)house.

This computerized image presents a stage set with forced perspective, using the repetition of open doorways and truncated stairs as a play area.

tion to the remnants of the original bathhouse. The interventions can be understood as artificial constructions, ready to be reconfigured or removed when something else comes along.

Some of the design elements will not be immediately apparent to everyone, although they may become more evident through repeated use. Some will function like a code to those who have experienced the building before. I have also included three rooms that serve as "thresholds" to tell the story of the bathhouse to patrons who have never been in one before. These rooms highlight materiality, manipulate sounds, and isolate body positions. By accepting a position in the spectacle, the visitor experiences the apparatus of display.

The first is a solid room, covered with tile and visible to the street. The hard surfaces reflect sound and are cold to the touch. The room may suggest schoolhouse communal showers, the site for many gay youth of same-sex attraction and the fear of discovery.

The second threshold leads into a room with a cushioned platform. The room can be closed off with a roll-down gate creating a cell. Music intermittently piped into the room can turn it into a disco cage. When inhabited by two people talking, it can become a living diorama. The

The three thresholds invite the user to make a choice and enter into the more private realm of a "room."

The confluence of materials such as tile, aluminum, corrugated walls, and framed glass create a contrast to the streetscape below the window.

platform seats are heated to body temperature and conform to the body's contours. An imprint thus remains even when no one is present.

The third threshold is a constructed alcove; one kneels because of the lowered ceiling and passes under a spotlight. This initiation process allows the visitor a privileged view. Cut into the floor is a window that looks down onto the counter of the café below. The meaning of this experience may not be obvious. The counter, shaped like a *T*, divides the service help from the customer. In the "old days," it also divided the clothed patrons waiting to rent a room from the toweled patrons already inside. While the café, a relic of the original design, continues to operate, it no longer divides those on the outside from those on the inside. The café serves the same kind on both sides.

Revealing the Body

Like many bathhouses that are no longer in operation, the old orgy room is now available "for rent." In my design it serves as a meeting room—a collective space for trustee gatherings, water sports demonstrations, safe sex parties, and the like. I can imagine someone having a birthday party in which Twister games rather than mattresses cover the floor, or a networking event, in which business cards are passed from hand to hand.

Since queer space can be described as momentary and unstable, I have left the third and fourth floors, composed of long and narrow rooms, as unspecified; they are open to invention, and the users of the building determine their use. Clotheslines hang through the open space tracing the former rooms and corridors. Sex is most likely to happen on these upper floors, open to those who want to participate, curtained off to those who have no interest. The space is climate-controlled and self-patrolled. People may bring in their own materials, creating their own space; leather pants, rubber sheets, or moiré fabric hanging from the lines could close off a space for private fantasy. Here users become directors of their presentation through self-theatricalization, constructing their identities by showing themselves as they wish to be seen. The queer (bath)house celebrates their choices, appearance, and actions.

Conclusion

As a historical and social phenomenon of the twentieth century, the baths attest to our conflicting and changing views about our lives and our sexuality. In the past, gay baths gave people a private place to congregate with others who shared their desires. At the same time,

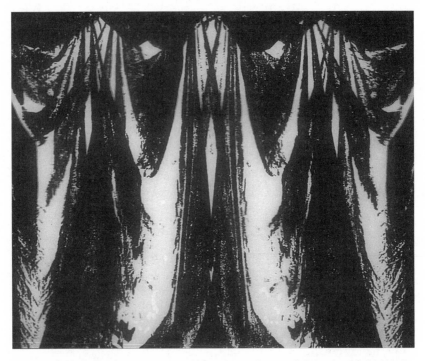

The hanging of fabric on a wire begins to suggest the possibilities for inhabiting the space of the upper two floors.

these out-of-the-way sites allowed for surveillance and containment. Turning surveillance into visibility has been a primary goal of queer activists who choose to challenge and change social relations rather than conform to them. New spaces need to be created to meet their needs.

Hence my blueprint for the queer (bath)house, which offers a network of procedures and practices that transgress the closet and inscribe the improvisation rather than the fixity of bodies. Whereas in most community spaces, for example, we find bodies either standing or sitting, here one also finds bodies kneeling, lying down, leaning, and crouching. As a space for performance, this project attempts to create environments that give people the opportunity to assume positions they would not normally allow themselves to experience, encouraging its clientele to begin to participate in events that highlight their differences from the norm.

In these sites of intimacy and touch, gathering and congregation, mobility and opportunity, patrons are encouraged to disregard the

The queer (bath)house creates a stage on which bodies can be positioned in multiple ways.

social values, beliefs, myths, and injunctions that constrain behavior through actions that are transient, disruptive, and transformative. While the queer (bath)house I have outlined here has been built on the erotic foundations of the baths, its space is more mobile, its definition contingent on its patrons and the assertiveness of their practices. As a site of seduction, subversion, pleasure, and pause, it is a place to live out the multiplicity of queerness itself.

It is obvious to me that every articulation excludes something else. Through a process of regulation and exclusion, commercial spaces sustain a given economic and ideological environment. But these ventures can also articulate the conflicts and maneuver within the structures in which they are situated. Negotiating the spaces between access and contemplation, contingence and security, description and distortion, can make hierarchies more visible and lead to the readjustment or reorganization of orders.

By inhabiting a decimated site of gay male desire such as New York City's Saint Marks Baths, the project researches and reinvents the bathhouse in order to experiment with form and content in ways that are both naive and knowing. By overlaying a distinct organization onto an existing one, an environment is produced that is multiple. Thus, constructions that I propose are concrete, fragmented, and temporary at the same time. They are meant to evolve into a future direction for use; their irregularity creates a condition of possibility, available to new procedures and interpretations. In the process, normative relations come under question.

I believe in queer presence as a requirement for progress. In order to disturb the accepted positions of power, to shift the paradigms of a fearful society, the (bath)house contains a transformative program. By establishing spaces where people congregate in overlapping nexuses of pleasure, the queer (bath)house uses simple devices and construction materials to bring people into contact with one another, to let people share knowledge and reinvent their lives. One can do as well as watch, listen as well as speak, inhabit as well as visit, move as well as rest, modify as well as influence. When queers live out a fantasy in this (bath)house, they also alter reality for others.

Notes

1. Joel Sanders, introduction to *Stud: Architecture of Masculinity*, ed. Joel Sanders (New York: Princeton Architectural Press, 1996), 13.

2. Additional material on the history of bathhouses can be found in my article "The Meaning at the Wall—Tracing the Gay Bathhouse," in *Queers in Space: Communities, Public Places, Sites of Resistance*, ed. Gordon Brent Ingram, Anne-Marie Bouthillette, and Yolanda Retter (Seattle: Bay Press, 1997), 391–406.

3. "Ballsy," in *Flesh: True Homosexual Experiences from S.T.H.*, vol. 2, ed. Boyd McDonald (San Francisco: Gay Sunshine Press, 1982), 112.

4. "New Hope for the Heteros," in *Smut: an S.T.H. Chap-book*, vol. 5, ed. Boyd McDonald (New York: Gay Presses of New York, 1984), 215.

5. "Ass-Licking Today," in *Cum: True Homosexual Experiences from S.T.H. Writers*, vol. 4, ed. Boyd McDonald (San Francisco: Gay Sunshine Press, 1983), 183.

6. Kenneth E. Read, *Other Voices* (Novato, Calif.: Chandler and Sharp, 1980), 33.

7. John Alan Lee, *Getting Sex: A New Approach: More Fun, Less Guilt* (Don Mills, Ont.: Musson Book Co., 1978), 24.

8. Scott O'Hara, "Midtowne Spa/Denver," *Steam: A Quarterly Journal for Men* 1, no. 2 (summer 1993): 129.

9. While I focus on a bathhouse that is no longer functioning (hence, I have put my description of the baths in the past tense), I acknowledge that a great number of gay bathhouses are still open and quite popular throughout the country.

10. The *S.T.H.* anthologies again document the rough and raunchy thrills provided by the orgy room. One account details a patron who followed some-

one he recognized into the dark room. He watched as the man "started to grope a fellow next to him and they walked to a corner and lay down—hunk on his back and the other fellow straddling his face. I decided to renew old acquaintances and went over and kissed his pectorals—real beauties, just a little coarse blond hair sprinkled over the mounds and around his nipples. Thence down his belly to his cock" ("The Sweetest I Ever Tasted," in *Flesh*, ed. McDonald, 136). Another found himself lying on his back when "a dude came in and sat on the bed next to me and leaned over and swooped my soft cock into his mouth and began massaging it with his lips and tongue, while his fingers were working on my balls and asshole. . . . As I lay moaning a tall shape emerged and settled on the bed on the other side of me and began playing with his dick. With the other dude still slurping between my legs, I turned and began working on the cowboy's meat on the bed next to mine" ("Sweet Ass at the Baths," in *Flesh*, ed. McDonald, 145).

11. "The Smell Drove Me Wild," in *Flesh*, ed. McDonald, 86.

12. "Tasty Lump," in *Meat: True Homosexual Experiences from* S.T.H., vol. 1, ed. Boyd McDonald (San Francisco: Gay Sunshine Press, 1981), 84.

13. Further discussion on systems of communication in the bathhouse can be found in my article "Speaking to the Gay Bathhouse: Communicating in Sexually Charged Spaces," in *Public Sex, Gay Space*, ed. William L. Leap (New York: Columbia University Press, 1998), 173–96.

14. Kyle Madison, "The Best Little Bathhouse in Texas," *Steam: A Quarterly Journal for Men* 1, no. 3 (autumn 1993): 187.

15. Ibid., 188.

16. Painted by M. Brooks Jones, the mural, which was on permanent display at San Francisco's Building Baths from 1979–1991, is now part of the collection of the Gay & Lesbian Historical Society (GLHS) of northern California. In 1996, it was on view at the sex club Eros in San Francisco, and it can now be seen at the GLHS archives in San Francisco.

17. Read, *Other Voices*, 36.

18. Bobbie Campbell, People with AIDS flyer, cited in Susan Stryker and Jim Van Buskirk, *Gay by the Bay: A History of Queer Culture in the San Francisco Bay Area* (San Francisco: Chronicle Books, 1996), 91.

19. A scene from *Tim and Pete: A Novel* describes the sentiment:

"You know who owned this place [bathhouse], don't you?"

"Yeah. *Mister* West Hollywood. Talk about scumbags. He kept this place open for *years* after people knew what was going on."

"I know. I think it sent out the wrong message at a very crucial time."

"It was unconscionable," Pete said. "The greedy pig."

"Denial, too. I'll bet. The end of a way of life." (James Robert Baker, *Tim and Pete: A Novel* [New York: Simon and Schuster, 1993], 148)

20. New York and California listings, *Gay Yellow Pages* (New York: Renaissance House, 1982) and *Sexplorers—The Guide* (San Francisco: PDA Press, 1995).

21. Lee, *Getting Sex*, 28.

22. Baker, *Tim and Pete: A Novel*, 149–50.

23. Rita Mae Brown, "Queen for a Day: A Stranger in Paradise," in *Lavender Culture*, ed. Karla Jay and Allen Young (New York: New York University Press, 1994), 75.

24. Guy Hocquenghem, *Homosexual Desire* (Durham, N.C.: Duke University Press, 1993), 111.

25. See, for example, Jon Binnie, "Trading Places: Consumption, Sexuality and the Production of Queer Space," in *Mapping Desire*, ed. David Bell and Gill Valentine (New York: Routledge, 1995), 182–99; Manuel Castells, *The City and the Grassroots* (Berkeley: University of California Press, 1983); John D'Emilio, "Capitalism and Gay Identity" in *The Lesbian and Gay Studies Reader*, ed. Henry Abelove, Michéle Aina Barale, and David M. Halperin (New York: Routledge, 1993), 467–76; Daniel Harris, *The Rise and Fall of Gay Culture* (New York: Hyperion, 1997).

26. Lee Edelman, "Men's Room," in *Stud*, ed. Sanders, 159–60; emphasis in the original.

Part Three

CROSSING FRONTIERS
ACTIVISM AND ACADEMIA

11

Resistance, Representation, and the Subject of Violence
Reading *Hothead Paisan*

Liana Scalettar

My original goal in conceiving this project was to investigate the uses of violence in lesbian cultural production, examples of which seemed to be multiplying everywhere: the Five Lesbian Brothers' recent play *The Secretaries*, the Lesbian Avengers' use of a bomb as logo in their flyers and activist texts, and, as Lynda Hart notes at length, Split Britches' *Lesbians Who Kill*. But again and again I found myself returning to the one example that had at first seemed the least likely candidate for inclusion, as well as the most suspect because of my own rather complex relation to it: Diane DiMassa's cartoon zine *Hothead Paisan: Homicidal Lesbian Terrorist*, a quarterly comic book that has also been turned into two anthologies by Cleis Press.[1] Since that repeated return has proved compelling, this chapter will attempt both to trace the workings of violence in the latter, and to speculate on the terms of my relation to that violence. For, as I hope to show, the textual violence of the zine and the reader's approach to it are intimately connected, and it is ultimately the terms of that connection that this essay interrogates. In short, I would like to argue that *Hothead* has much to say about the connections that exist among the media, violence against women, violence against lesbians and gay men, and potential for resistance in a wholly mass-mediated society.[2] More specifically, I would like to suggest that while the extratextual terms of *Hothead*'s production and reception support a reading that places its violence within a realm of "harmless" fantasy and subsequent cathartic value, another kind of reading is possible. In this other reading, the possibility of political resistance, rather than the "talking cure" of therapy, is at issue. On the one hand, then, *Hothead Paisan* is a cultural product whose popular form and format seems wholly commodified, whose principal selling point seems to be a release from anger and a subsequent accep-

Things get hot in *Hothead Paisan*. (*Hothead Paisan: Homocidal Lesbian Terrorist* [Pittsburgh: Cleis Press, 1993], 34; reprinted by permission of Diane DiMassa)

tance of current political systems and discourses. On the other hand, it is a text whose content provides abundant material for fantasies— potential acts—of political resistance. The reader may rightly ask, then, what kind of text is *Hothead*?

I would like to stress at the outset that the question is not whether our heroine *is* or *is not* subversive—whether her antics do or do not allow us to think in terms of political resistance. Such an either/or stance is antithetical to the major impetus of this chapter, namely, the urgent need that I see within queer studies for vigilant readings, for critiques that can salvage what is useful while leaving behind what is harmful. *Hothead* both partakes of the terms of mass culture and rejects them, so that it is intellectually impossible to classify the work as either "alternative" or "mainstream," pacificatory or resistant. Like so much of our cultural production—and like so much of our lives—DiMassa's zine inhabits an uneasy zone of acceptance and rejection, of capitalist desire (I am tempted to say now more than ever), and revolutionary longing. Such a textual-critical space demands a supple critical practice that can both recognize its own complicities and confirm its own dissents; only with such a practice in hand, can we even begin the work of deciding what a subversive queer culture might look like?

Much recent cultural theory has questioned, if not altogether effaced, distinctions between discursive and material violence. Thus, for example, Lynda Hart's consistent use of the phrase "discursive/material violence," in which the two once-separate terms are brought together into one. Similarly, Nancy Armstrong and Leonard Tennenhouse, introducing their anthology *The Violence of Representation*, suggest that the violence of representation, understood as the excluding force that inheres in any act of writing or naming, cannot be explained away as merely textual.[3] In her chapter in that book, Lucia Folena cites what she calls the "Reaganian discourse" about Nicaragua as a stellar example of an "interpretation of violence [that works] to displace and conceal the violence of [its] interpretation."[4] And Teresa de Lauretis, while arguing that the representation of violence is always gendered in some way, notes that dominant and feminist *representations* of domestic violence are inseparable from *reactions* to that violence.[5] The implications, at least in my reading, are clear: a struggle over maintaining or ending violence means a struggle over how that instance of violence is represented. Again, the discursive and the material appear inextricably intertwined.

Because I call this project "political," my preferred reading is a reading of and for political resistance; therefore, situating the lesbian subject in relation to the question of violence seems particularly relevant. As Hart points out, lesbians have been objects of violence in mainstream representations since the turn of the century; and, according to the results of four surveys tallied by Gary David Comstock in his *Violence against Lesbians and Gay Men*, over 50 percent of lesbians have suffered homophobic physical violence.[6] Comstock's work suffers from an unquestioned faith in statistics—he does not, for example, hesitate to equate the fact that fewer lesbians reported incidences of violence with the "fact" of fewer incidences of violence against lesbians. This fact aside, Comstock's numbers suggest that most lesbians and gay men live in a state of terror, of fear of homophobic physical violence. Likewise, Hart persuasively suggests that early-twentieth-century criminology and sexology produced parallel, if not identical, images of the lesbian as abnormally violent; in mainstream cultural representations ever since, she continues, lesbians have been simultaneously the subject and the object of aggression.[7] Taken together, the findings of Comstock and Hart convey an overwhelming impression of oppression in which lesbians figure as the objects of violence. For even in their status as subjects, the lesbians discussed by Hart are subjected to the violence of being always named the aggressor, of always being labeled as the danger lurking behind the deviance of the "normal" woman who uses violence. That is, they are subjects mainly by virtue of being subject to, and hence the object of, dominant culture's proscriptive discourses.

While acknowledging the very real violences faced by lesbians in streets and homes, I want to stress that the possibility of such material violence against us is bound up with representations that in themselves enact and sanction violence. Even Comstock hints interestingly at this phenomenon when he notes that language is used more often in attacks upon lesbians than in those on gay men, and, furthermore, language that is misogynist ("anti-feminist or anti-woman," in his words[8]) occurs second in frequency to antilesbian verbal violence. Thus it seems that even at its most material moment, its supposedly greatest distance from representation, violence against lesbians "speaks" with great clarity, and in so speaking, represents as it enacts. In speaking, as it were, for itself, this violence obliterates the discursive/material divide that some critics have upheld as crucial for theorizing political resistance. This violence is one of erasure and exclusion as well as the mimetic violence—the literal broadcasting of misogynist and homophobic violence—of what is now often called "violence in the media." As a form of popular media, Hothead Paisan is of course implicated in the latter. But if Hothead abounds with a violence enacted in and through the mass media, it also resounds with the violence of the character Hothead herself, a violence through which, I propose, a nonobjectified lesbian subject can begin to be conceived.

I return here to the extratextual dimensions of Hothead, and to the reading that runs counter to the one to which I have very briefly alluded above. The production and reception of Hothead as a popular phenomenon, and the subsequent reading of the textual violence in it as therapeutic, is, I want to argue, very much connected to the logic of late-twentieth-century consumer culture. According to this reading, Hothead's violence is bought by and sold to women in need of release and cure, women who gain from the zine or book what they might otherwise gain from a therapist—namely, the ability to accept.

Originally produced as a quarterly zine, sold in lesbian and gay and women's bookstores for three dollars an issue, Hothead Paisan's first nine issues were anthologized by Cleis Press in the fall of 1993. While still available in its zine form, Hothead is now also sold for $14.95 as a coffee-table book and has been spotted in otherwise staid bookstores with discreet "lesbian and gay" sections. In addition, each issue of a subscription to the zine arrives with a catalog hawking T-shirts, mugs, buttons, stamps, and other *Hothead* paraphernalia. *Hothead Paisan* in any form undeniably works powerfully as incitation, as witnessed by the packed publication party celebrating the book at the Clit Club in New York City, as well as by the Canadian government's banning of *Hothead* under its recently enacted antipornography law. But this cult status is not due to the "alternative" or "underground" nature of the zine *as zine*. Indeed, the mention of DiMassa in an article on women cartoonists, which appeared as the lead story in the Arts and Leisure section of the *New York Times,* suggests that the underground itself, whatever its former locations as the conscience or goad of the mainstream, is now firmly ensconced within the above-ground glare of the dominant.[9]

If *Hothead* is produced as a commodity, its reception strongly suggests that what is being bought is identification, and via this identification, therapeutic release from anger. Thus several people or magazines whose comments appear on the book jacket compare reading *Hothead* to therapy, or raise questions of sanity, insanity, and cure. Rachel Pepper is quoted as writing that Hothead (the character) and the book are "a lot cheaper than therapy," while according to Jacqueline Woodson, the character Hothead "answers the question *'Is it them or is it me?'*" DiMassa, in her introduction, calls *Hothead* "personal medicine" and explicitly links the writing and reading of the latter to psychoanalysis: "By getting these images out into the light, where they can be examined, I can then move on."[10] And in one of DiMassa's frequent appearances, as herself, in the text of *Hothead,* she argues with a lesbian feminist reader appalled by the strip's violence. In response to Fran Bran's protestations, the DiMassa character labels the text as fantasy and says that "a lot of women need to vent their rage and this works for them."[11] Through the point of view of numerous frames as well, the reader is positioned to see what Hothead sees on television, or even positioned as Hothead as she sits a mere arm's length away from her many screens. This intradiagetic rhetoric of venting, of violence as cathartic, carries over into the extratextual, as evidenced by the allusions to therapy and other comments. So, for example, Brat Attack's reviewer is quoted on the book jacket as saying: "most of us are never going to take the extremist route to female liberation, but we can dream." At another point in her introduction, DiMassa writes, "Hothead will continue to act out fantasies that we would never really carry out ourselves."[12] It is as if constant reassurance that this violence is only "make-believe" is needed, as if even the erstwhile fierce Di-

Fran Bran protests . . . and the author talks back. (*Hothead Paisan: Homocidal Lesbian Terrorist* [Pittsburgh: Cleis Press, 1993], 84–85; reprinted by permission of Diane DiMassa)

Massa and Brat Attack must disavow the violence of the text, in order to place it firmly within the realm of the phantasmatic, the therapeutic, and, ultimately, the pacifying. Readers, they and others suggest, buy issues of *Hothead Paisan* and T-shirts adorned with Hothead Paisan's image in order to identify with a fantasy: this fantasy, apparently universally held, is one of violent revenge against men (and, as important, against some women) for everything from rape to racism to lesbian invisibility. Once it has been successfully identified, the fantasy, in this interpretation, allows the reader to leave the motivating anger behind—at least until the next issue. And, again, in this logic of a need repeatedly invoked and satisfied through consumption—in the production of *Hothead* as an exemplary case of interminable analysis, repackaged and resold every few months—the logic of (some forms of) therapy and of consumer culture come together in the unlikely figure of the homicidal lesbian terrorist.

As mentioned earlier, I position the above reading as extratextual while simultaneously affirming my alternate interpretation (soon to come) as textual, as supported by the implacable details of the text itself. But it occurs to me as I write that the narrative of therapy, of phantasmatic expression of violence leading to calm, of Hothead's place (diegetic, if you will) within consumer culture, also appears in the text. The perspectival positioning of the reader, briefly discussed above, composes one such moment. Additionally, DiMassa creates several characters whose primary attribute is precisely the calmness that Hothead lacks. Through these characters—including Roz, who is blind but able to "see" what Hothead cannot, and Chicken, a cat gifted with human thought and a penchant for yoga and healing rituals—the reader is presented with a running commentary, within the text, on Hothead's character. At various moments, these characters recommend that Hothead should either be committed or should start therapy, or they suggest that her behavior is psychotic. In formal terms as well, the gaps in time and space rendered through the frequent discontinuity between one frame and the next represent Hothead as out of her mind. But her "episodes," while never ending, are always followed by a lucid, calm phase (often connected to or substituted for by a plot twist), during which it appears that the so-called madness is gone. Text, then, mirrors context: the process of watching Hothead vent her anger and madness, becoming calm and enraged in an endless cycle, matches the process of the reader's venting, the endless cycle of potentially maddening rage and promised purchase of recovery to which the discourse surrounding *Hothead* points.

Ironically—or perhaps not—text mirrors context again in the cartoon's representation of the mass media. For Hothead lives and has grown up, as suggested in the additional introductory pages of the book format, in a world in which the power of television, film, and advertising is ubiquitous and unequivocal. Posters of music and MTV stars, from Joan Jett to a felinized Queen Latifah (Queen Latigre), dot her walls; the Madonna of the song "Justify My Love" haunts her dreams. Television is quite literally everywhere, figured as either disproportionately huge and able to fill an entire wall of her apartment, or as proliferating into ten simultaneously showing screens. And what's "on" the screen is always some combination of the following: viciously gendered and raced advertising, horrifyingly biased news that presents itself as self-evident, and film previews with nonsubliminal advertising messages ever present (for Jujubes, Junior Mints, and my personal favorite, "buttery buttery popcorn"). These images exhort both Hothead and the reader, as viewer, to watch and buy, to watch and be calm. The textual Hothead, of course, refuses: her rampages often directly follow time spent watching television or a movie. But in a telling textual moment—comprising another point at which text and context come together rather eerily—consumerist and spectacular logic is made quite clear, as the following paragraph shows.

The DiMassa character, in this same incident, goads her peeved interlocutor, Fran, into remembering an incident of sexual abuse by "Uncle George." In the next frame, Fran violently knocks over the furniture around her, à la Hothead, and in the next is figured in miniature, sitting curled up in the outstretched palm of the cartoonist.[13] Finally, at the end of the sequence, the concluding frame shows Fran offering a check to the now-out-of-the-frame DiMassa. Made out to Giant Ass Publishing, Hothead's actual publisher, the larger-than-life check is meant to cover subscription costs for the now convinced character. A direct link is thus posited between reading Hothead and recovering from past abuse: presumably Fran will now enter the extratextual cycle of incited rage and subsequent calm stemming from the quarterly arrival of the zine. The text does make available a critique of the selling of sexism and heterosexism, of gendered commodities and of the commodification of gender. But the context surrounding Hothead, as well as some intertextual moments that blur the text/context divide, seem all too willing to exhort us to buy, in all senses of the word, what's being sold.

As mentioned above, Hothead's world is one in which an escape from mass media—to a space outside its reach, a space of effective resistance—is impossible. Television becomes anthropomorphized and malignant in the first section of the book version of the comics, in which a woman and a man steeped in the workings of patriarchy emerge from the screen into the three-dimensionality of Hothead's living room. Their explicit mission is to try to scare the young Hothead straight. The woman, desperately clinging to Hothead's ankles, later dangles a pair of high heels from her outstretched hand, while the man, pointing maliciously, asserts the power of the mass media and its inescapable ideological weight in no uncertain terms: "You'll come around! You've got a lifetime of TV, billboard, and magazine poisoning ahead of you! You'll be innocently 'relaxing' in front of the TV, and the next thing you know, you'll be wearing an apron!"[14] In these pages, as well as throughout the whole of issue number 1, Hothead's very self seems to have been shaped, indeed constituted, in all its complexities, by television.

It is in reaction to this scarily alive television that Hothead's alter ego first appears, urging her to be constantly on guard against the on-slaught of media images. And it is against the television that she com-mits her first act of violence, going at it with an ax until it is revealed to be a never ending series of screens. In the beginning of issue number 1, moreover, an omniscient narrative voice wonders about a lesbian (soon after to be named as Hothead) who believes everything she sees on television. Later, a newscaster self-named as "white man" reports the non-news of sexism and heterosexism as ineluctable facts, ending with peals of gleeful laughter at the impossibility of change. And, fi-nally, in issue number 16, we see that material and representational violence are intertwined in film as well as in television. Surrounded by other moviegoers, Hothead is repeatedly confronted by men whose will seems all powerful. One seated in front of her insists on his right to too much space, refusing to remove his hat and ignoring her at-tempts to get his attention; another insists on his right fully to control the volume and tone of his surroundings by yelling at Hothead and Daphne for talking before the movie starts. A third insists that his harmful movements are beyond his control, and that he simply cannot stop kicking the back of Hothead's chair.[15] Concurrently, the previews on screen are blatant advertisements for sexism and imperialism; as Hothead and Daphne leave the theater after Hothead explodes, a filmic man strikes a filmic woman in an echo—or a culmination—of the violence just displayed in the theater and in the previews. But if the media cannot be escaped, if its multiple formats pervade every-thing with an insidious ability to shape human subjects, it also pro-vides the place from which resistance may be conceived. And, shaped as I am in turn by other texts, other mediated moments, I want to turn here to three theoretical considerations of violence and/or resistance in a mass-mediated society that seem to provide an "in" to my reading of *Hothead*'s violence as political resistance.

The first consideration is that articulated by Walter Benjamin in his essay, "Critique of Violence."[16] In Benjamin's formulation of violence as a force monopolized by the law, so that any use of violence by those not representative of the law becomes suspect, I find an apt suggestion of the phenomenon at work in my source text. In Benjamin's discussion, the law suspects extralegal violence not only because that violence may have extralegal ends, but also because that violence threatens law in general. He writes that "one might perhaps consider the surprising possibility that the law's interest in a monopoly of violence vis-à-vis individuals is not explained by the intention of preserving legal ends but, rather, by that of preserving the law itself; that violence, when not in the hands of the law, threatens it not by the ends that it may pursue but by its mere existence outside the law."[17] I take this argument to rest on the subsequent assertion that violence "is the origin of the law," and that all violence is thus "implicated . . . in the problematic nature of law itself."[18] Law is threatened by extralegal violence, I think, not only because of its intimate relation to violence but because this intimacy is a covert one. In the modern state, that is, the law presumably works to hide its origins in violence and to promote itself as allied with order and peacefulness.

Violence in the hands of unauthorized individuals would then threaten to make the state show its "true self," threaten to expose, through incurring its force, the legal violence that has been in place all along. An exposure of heretofore hidden violences whose façade is one of normality and peace—is this not the point of many kinds of political critique, and by extension, sometimes offered as a justification for politically motivated violence?[19] It seems that Hothead's extralegal violence is shown time and again to be a response to the multiple violences perpetrated against her and others; although these mediated violences are not centralized in the state as Benjamin would have conceived of it, they are most certainly sanctioned by dominant modes of representation and in that sense legal or licit. In responding to this legality, Hothead resists the normalizing power of the mass media and exposes their peaceful self-presentations as a fraud. And I would argue further that it is this exposure to which people react the most strongly in condemning *Hothead*. Even the textual and extratextual disavowals of Hothead's violence focus on "her" or on "us," the presumably feminist, presumably progressive, readers who "would never." I would suggest that this focus on her/our violence or potential violence and particularly on its phantasmic quality works to distance the reader from the exposure effected again and again in *Hothead Paisan*. DiMassa's, and some readers', focus on the personal fantasy, that is, works to deny the all too explicit quality of the violences perpetrated against Hothead and, by extension, against her loyal legions of fans (myself included). Again, the point here is not to insist that the text definitively allows or disallows certain meanings. What comes to the forefront when readers focus on the narrative of therapy and fantasy may recede into the background when those same readers focus on little girls with guns.

Although the above passage may have entertained a rhetorical distinction between Hothead's violence as fantasmatic and mass-mediated violences as real, I hope it is clear that I do not consider such distinctions to be ultimately tenable. The realness of any representation, along with the representational quality of any reality, is one of the primary points of *Hothead*'s narrativizing of violence and resistance. The text's complete saturation with mass media, and its representation of subjectivities as constituted by them, points to the utterly naturalized place of the media in contemporary culture. And I turn here to my second theoretical consideration. An essay by Henri Lefebvre, which outlines his idea of the "everyday" as an interpretive category, helps to underscore this naturalization.[20] In Lefebvre's terminology, which distinguishes between the categories *daily life, everydayness,* and *the everyday,* the latter term is daily life brought within the epoch of modernity: it is "the object of a programming, whose unfolding is imposed by the market, by the system of equivalences, by marketing and advertisements."[21] Moreover, in its contemporary manifestations (and leaving aside my qualms about Lefebvre's periodizations), the everyday "is entirely mediated and mass-mediated" and is a "modality of administering society."[22] Within this system of mass mediation, the idea of repetition becomes important to the everyday, as the latter repeats itself constantly. Hothead's textual life, with its endless rounds of mass-mediated rage, mass-mediated pleasure, and mass-mediated leisure (she watches television often, since she has nothing else to do) seems imminently readable in terms of the everyday. Not only do her mass-mediated habits repeat; the images that mediate the habits are themselves endlessly, mind-numbingly, the same.

However, like her habits and the images that produce them, her resistances are *also* figured as mass-mediated events. For example, one of many newscasts is interrupted on the air by an unknown Hothead ally who, thanks to a power saw, provides Hothead and the reader with a graphic view of the broadcaster's irredeemably masculinist brain. It is shown to be, quite literally, centered around a small, phallus-like organ. The ally, having already interrupted the circulation of the images of the everyday, next interrupts their form by co-opting the news broadcast format to give an informational report on men's brains in general.[23] Hothead then hurries to arm herself, but what follows is not a "literal" rampage. Instead, she takes part in her own intervention into the everyday of the mass media, rendering herself the star and subject of an advertisement for her "services." Thus the voiceover proceeds in classic commercial fashion, invoking a need and subsequently offering to satisfy it. It reads, in part, "Is your career suffering due to unworthy penises?? Are you tired of fearing for your life because penises are stalking the planet? Then I am the girl 4U. Never again walk away quietly because there's 'nothing you can do.' This convenient homicidal dyke will come right to your door! Special services for rape and incest survivors."[24] A need and its satisfaction are invoked, and a target audience is appealed to—pure consumer capitalism. We as readers and as mass-mediated subjects have certainly experienced this formula before. We immediately understand the terms of the appeal. But this use of a televisual form is subverted by *Hothead*'s exposure of what is never explicitly revealed in televisual content, namely rampant sexism, systemic violence against women, and the possibility of resisting these wrongs.

At another point, a flashback to or dream of the scene of Hothead's birth opens with a frame depicting a marquee above an open door, followed by an introductory title placed on a strip of film. Later, after the newborn Hothead decapitates her doctor, the flashback is brought to a close with two frames that again render both Hothead and her life as filmic images. In the first, a film projector exudes smoke as the film itself appears hopelessly tangled. In the second, under the title "malfunction in the projection room," another filmstrip fills the frame: this time it repeats the image of the decapitated doctor, but with a central hole in the celluloid through which pokes what turns out to be Roz's cane. When she comes to (with Roz's help), Hothead finds herself on a street that recalls Times Square, resplendent with billboards, advertisements on buses, and neon-lit theaters.[25] Surrounded and shaped as she is by media, Hothead's actions are also mass-mediated, despite her hatred for the premises of the former.

Read in terms of Benjamin and Lefebvre, *Hothead*'s violence might be interpreted as political violence, as mass-mediated resistance to the everyday of mass-mediated culture. But her violence is a specifically inflected one, carried out in particular against misogyny and heterosexism (and also, though less prominently, against racism). A feminist discussion of violence, resistance, and representation therefore forms my third and last consideration. In "Fighting Bodies, Fighting Words: A Theory and Politics of Rape Prevention,"[26] Sharon Marcus takes issue with the claims of some feminists that poststructuralist theory, with its emphasis on language and on the relativism of truth, can have nothing to say about the material reality of rape. Marcus argues instead that feminist antiviolence politics have in fact always stressed the *importance* of language in the politics of rape, and that it has done so by focusing attention on the opposing representations of truth proffered by the perpetrator and the survivor, and on the consistent privileging of the perpetrator's version. In addition, she argues that what she calls a "gendered grammar of violence" places women as the objects of violence and subjects of fear in any violent or potentially violent encounter. Ironically, this grammar is also operative, in Marcus's view, in much feminist antiviolence work that does not consider rape prevention, as well as in more mainstream representations of self-defense.[27] In her words, such representations enact "a gendered polarization of the grammar of violence in which the male body can wield weapons, can make itself into a weapon, and benefits from an enforced ignorance concerning its own vulnerability; the female body is predicated by this grammar as universally vulnerable, lacking force, and incompetent to supplement its deficiencies with tools which could vanquish the penis's power by dissimulating it."[28] *Hothead Paisan*'s representation of gender and violence, I would argue, forcefully interrupts this grammar: men are consistently vulnerable, if still also the instigators of violence. In addition, Hothead, with her extensive knowledge and expertise about a range of weapons, and her willingness to use them, accedes unquestionably to the position of "subject" in this grammar. Most important, she shares her knowledge and equipment with others, as when she inspires vacationing queers to run gawking straight people out of Provincetown, or nonchalantly gives her weapons to a small girl.[29] These acts of violence and education are what make her the nonobjectified subject to which I referred in my introduction. They are also what makes my relation to *Hothead* so complex, for I would suggest, in line with Marcus, that the thought of women as resistant subjects of violence remains unthinkable, even for women. For lesbians who are doubly—triply, if subject to racialized violence—objectified through misogynist and homophobic violence, it may be even more difficult to conceive this accession to the position of subject. In its representation of such an accession, however, *Hothead Paisan* provides a version of feminist political resistance to our mass-mediated world of the "everyday."

How Hothead was born—a mass media malfunction? (*Hothead Pai-san: Homocidal Lesbian Terrorist* [Pittsburgh: Cleis Press, 1993], 34–35; reprinted by permission of Diane DiMassa)

Much later—after *Ellen*, after the Defense of Marriage Act, after more and more smallish media outlets have been purchased by fewer and fewer gargantuan conglomerates—I am asked, by the editors of this book, to conclude my chapter. A rereading does highlight its un-finished state—the ending more a hope or a tentative suggestion than a convinced statement. But I hope that this provisional, questioning end does not equal, for the reader, millennial gloom.

Always and still, there is reading. There is the making and remaking of meaning, the shards of pleasure wrestled from mass culture by queer hands or eyes. As media become more homogenized, as the mo-noculture devours more and more subversion and sells it back to us,

the agile, tactical work of reading—work nurtured by what has always been queer people's need for counter knowledge—becomes more crucial than ever. The same, but different—a dogged shadow clinging to capitalism's rampaging sameness and difference, trying to turn it into something that can be survived.

Notes

1. See Lynda Hart, *Fatal Women* (Princeton: Princeton University Press, 1994). It should be explained here, for those who may not know, that the term *zine* (pronounced *zeen*) refers to any of a number of (often self-published) cultural or countercultural texts that may take the form of newspapers, magazines, comic books, chapbooks, or online publications. The term itself is shortened from the term *fanzine*, which in turn was a shortened 1980s coinage for *fan magazine*.

2. A note on terminology: I believe that elaborating the terms through

which certain uses of defining terms (*lesbian, gay, queer*) are made is crucial to any political/intellectual project. But—as they say—such an elaboration here seems to me beyond the scope of this paper. For the sake of simplicity, I considered and used texts whose titles or named creators contain the word *lesbian.* As will be made clear, however, Hothead's identity is far from a transparent given within the text.

3. See Nancy Armstrong and Leonard Tennenhouse, "Introduction: Representing Violence, or 'How the West Was Won,'" in *The Violence of Representation,* ed. Nancy Armstrong and Leonard Tennenhouse (New York: Routledge, 1989), 9.

4. See Lucia Folena, "Figures of Violence: Philologists, Witches and Stalinistas," in *Violence,* ed. Armstrong and Tennenhouse, 220.

5. See Teresa de Lauretis, *Technologies of Gender: Essays on Theory, Film, and Fiction* (Bloomington: Indiana University Press, 1987), 32–34.

6. See Gary David Comstock, *Violence against Lesbians and Gay Men* (New York: Columbia University Press, 1991), 36.

7. Hart's phrase, "the site of aggression," nicely points to this simultaneity. See Hart, *Fatal Women,* 11.

8. Comstock, *Violence,* 67–68.

9. Roberta Smith, "A Parallel Art World, Vast and Unruly: Beyond Superheroes, Women Are Transforming the Underground Comic Universe," *New York Times,* 20 November 1994, B1.

10. Diane DiMassa, *Hothead Paisan: Homicidal Lesbian Terrorist* (Pittsburgh: Cleis Press, 1993), 9.

11. Ibid., 84.

12. Ibid., 9.

13. Ibid., 85.

14. Ibid., 16.

15. Diane DiMassa, *Hothead Paisan: Homicidal Lesbian Terrorist* 16 (1994): 1, 3, 5.

16. Walter Benjamin, "Critique of Violence," in *Reflections,* trans. Edmund Jephcott (New York: Schocken, 1978), 277–300.

17. Ibid., 280–81.

18. Ibid., 286–87.

19. I am not, needless to say, trying to justify political violence here. But neither am I offering a blanket condemnation of it, and I must confess that this note has the tiresome feel of a mandatory disclaimer. If you take the question of political violence as an open question, and concurrently note that I am trying to argue for a reading of *Hothead's* violence as political resistance, the point will be clear.

20. Henri Lefebvre, "Toward a Leftist Cultural Politics: Remarks Occasioned by the Centenary of Marx's Death," trans. David Reifman, in *Marxism and the Interpretation of Culture,* ed. Cary Nelson and Lawrence Grossberg (Urbana: University of Illinois Press, 1988), 75–88.

21. Ibid., 87, note 1.

22. Ibid., 21–22. These concepts are, of course, not new to cultural studies. Nevertheless, I found the terminology and elaboration offered by Lefebvre to be quite helpful.

23. DiMassa, *Hothead* 1993, 80.

24. Ibid., 82.

25. Ibid., 34–37.

26. Sharon Marcus, "Fighting Bodies, Fighting Words: A Theory and Politics of Rape Prevention," in *Feminists Theorize the Political*, ed. Judith Butler and Joan W. Scott (New York: Routledge, 1992), 385–403.

27. Ibid., 387, 393–95.

28. Ibid., 395.

29. DiMassa, *Hothead* 1993, 55–60; DiMassa, *Hothead* 16 (1994): 9.

12

Eating Eve's Plums
On Citation and Hero-Worship

Michael Bacchus

I

SOREL: Do you think it's wise? You retired so very finally last
year. What excuse will you give for returning so soon?
JUDITH: My public, dear—letters from my public!
SIMON: Have you had any?
JUDITH: One or two. That's what decided me, really—I ought
to have had hundreds.
—Noël Coward, *Hay Fever*

I once wrote a fan letter to Eve Sedgwick. This is another one.

I write this remembering a day when Eve came to speak at the University of Southern California in 1993, when I was still taking classes, and I was planning on meeting her through my adviser, Jim Kincaid (she thanks him in the acknowledgments to her *Tendencies*). After the lecture there was a reception in the English department conference room, replete with cheap wine and bad food, and I was so close I could nearly touch her, but I couldn't, simply *couldn't,* speak. So I left. And I could have been transported back to that episode in my childhood . . . let me explain.

I was in Manhattan with my family, and we were dining out after a night at the theater, having just missed an evening of the wildly successful run of Noël Coward's *Private Lives* with Elizabeth Taylor and Richard Burton, suffering instead through a dreadful revival of *42nd Street*. Anyway, we had just arrived at Sardi's, and were waiting for our table, when there was a commotion on the stairs, someone bumped into me, and I turned around just in time to see Richard Burton say "Excuse me" as he was ushered to his table accompanied by Elizabeth Taylor. Imagine! And I couldn't say a word. I'm certain I stood there and stared with my mouth open, eleven years old and star struck. Of course, with Eve I was twenty-five, but the feeling of being star struck was almost exactly the same after all those years, albeit in such an incredibly different milieu. It seems clear that the rarefied atmosphere of academia has set up its own star system, one that functions in much the same way as Hollywood's. The audience is significantly smaller, as small, perhaps, as Noël Coward's character Judith Bliss's and the stars are not nearly as charismatic (except for you, Eve), but there are still significant similarities. In the pages that follow I will suggest that an investigation of academia in these terms can accomplish goals analogous to those of star theory—namely, an appreciation of the academic star as a media text with real social significance outside of her work

It is no secret that many of our most commodifiable academic stars work in the "frontier" discipline of queer studies. David Shumway blames this fact on the emphasis being placed on "the personal" in academic writing, whose cause he traces to the disfigurations of queer theory: "Personal matters, once regarded as extraneous to disciplinary discourse, have become central to it. Queer theory has made the sexual life of the theorist one of its principal occupations."[1] Recently, many have hailed academic queer studies, predicting its ascendance. Eve Kosofsky Sedgwick heralds its arrival in *Tendencies* (published in 1993), stating, "I suppose this must be called the moment of Queer."[2] Lauren Berlant and Michael Warner, in the May 1995 *PMLA,* note that "Queer theory has already incited a vast labor of metacommentary, a virtual industry: special issues, sections of journals, omnibus reviews, anthologies, and dictionary entries. . . . Queer is hot."[3] And Jon Harned, in *Profession 1996,* remarks, "Queer studies now stands at the threshold of institutionalization as an academic discipline."[4] Academics become stars in the traditional way—through exposure. The stars of queer studies have been helped along by a perception of the vogue of their discipline. But the process through which the star is created—the consistent reference to her work—exists in tension with the identification of an academic frontier. The vicissitudes of star and fan culture rehabilitate the oppositional quite quickly, and the institutionalization of a discipline based so securely in oppositional politics may well evacuate the frontier it seeks to buttress.

But you must not read this as a manifesto against star and fan culture. It is, rather, the opposite. Those who know me will not be startled to hear me come out publicly as the consummate fan. Indeed, I have cultivated a reputation for fandom, so important, I think, for someone who fancies himself a cultural studies scholar: I would much rather be visibly entrenched in the discourse than attempt to present the completely untenable position of one outside of it. I am not, however, indiscriminate about my fandom—quite the contrary. I choose very carefully the phenomena toward which I choose to be abject. But, having chosen, I am able to throw myself into the delirium of adoration with unprecedented abandon. Clearly, my fandom is strategic, particularly strategic for one in my position—an underemployed Ph.D. who numbers queer studies among his areas of expertise. My icons tend to exhibit a particular kind of currency, a position in the cultural or political vanguard. Queer studies, itself, has depended on a stance of aggressive vogue in a profession that is obsessively concerned with tradition, canonization, and "authority," and carefully chosen fandom is one technique of keeping up the appearances of currency and oppositional exuberance that many young gay academic types have found necessary for survival both in departments that continue to live up to their hidebound reputations and in a climate where disconcertingly large numbers of graduate students of all types will be found effectively unemployable. For many in academia, I imagine, the postures of fandom attempt to signal a difference from the properly distant and analytical academic stance. As such, the star-struck academic is an incomparable camp artifact, one who, according to Andrew Ross's definition, "expresses his impotence as the dominated fraction of a ruling bloc at the same time as he distances himself from the conventional morality and taste of the ascendant . . . class."[5]

There may be more to the connection of academe to notions of camp. According to Claudia Roth Pierpont, in the *New Yorker,*

If Susan Sontag's famed definition of camp as "failed seriousness" continues to serve, then American academic writing has taken over from old movies and old drag queens as our culture's leading camp phenomenon. Many American academics who currently write about our culture seem to have known nothing except unending childhood, and so have only this culture to measure this culture by—and they tend to do so with a seriousness in inverse proportion to that of their subject. The new field of "star studies" depends on the examination of "star texts" with the aid of "fan discourse." Tools of critical analysis are brought to bear on episodes of "Mr. Ed."[6]

Add to this analysis Andrew Ross's thoughts on the origins of camp, in which "[t]he camp effect . . . is created . . . when the products . . . of a much earlier mode of production, which has lost its power to dominate cultural meanings, become available, in the present, for redefinition according to contemporary codes of taste."[7] Ross's observation underlines the fact that the camp effect discussed by Pierpont may well be dependent on the fact that today's academics ("the products . . . of a much earlier mode of production") are being redefined by a culture that is in the process of dismantling a higher education system that it finds increasingly perverse and unproductive. For the implication in Pierpont, as in many recent attacks on the academy, is that the academy has bent its attention toward something that it is impossible to be serious about (read: popular culture). It is, therefore, impossible to "produce" any truly "serious work" that interrogates such subjects, and academia is, or should be, apparently, in the business of seriousness. Rather than lament this indication that the academy is still under attack from the mainstream intelligentsia—if only in this instance for titles as innocuous as "star studies" (a far cry, one must admit, from one of the media's favorite titles to ridicule, "Jane Austen and the Masturbating Girl")—perhaps we should just take Pierpont's word for it. The academy *is* camp—ridiculous, comic, and aproductive. And this simple, threatening, celebratory observation might open up whole new vistas for ways of being in and thinking about the academy, demanding that we bring the same kind of scrutiny to bear on our profession as we do to *Mr. Ed.*

If I have been gently implying by means of an insistent subtext that academic star making is a largely queer pastime, it is not simply on the basis of our generally recognized appreciation or arbitration of the camp canon. David Buxton, discussing the star system, notes as one of its "essential preconditions" that "the star be known without reciprocation by a mass of individuals, whose only common point lies in being represented by the same star."[8] While correctly recognizing the star system as an agent that enables connection between individuals, this particular statement ignores the possibility that representation by the same star might be the cause of cohesion on bases other than that of representation, or that the negotiations necessary in choosing to become a fan certainly take into account aspects of identity and affect that could form the foundation of a group identity; which is to say my idolization of Eve became a simple shorthand I could use within the academy to replace the drawn out, often embarrassing process of coming out over and over again to people who probably knew already, as well as a basis for the identification of a like-minded community. If cults form around figures like Judith Butler and Eve Sedgwick, it is, perhaps, partly because their images afford an opportunity for recognition and cohesion among a population that still must believe itself to be oppositional and suspect, no matter how queer-friendly the academy seems to have become, because opposition and suspicion are constructs around which so much of our politics and perceptions are formed.

I was at a conference in Austin, Texas, in March 1994, at which Sarah Schulman was the keynote speaker, and on the last day of the conference I found a note with these words scribbled on it: "People are constantly quoting Butler and Sedgwick saying these really mundane things that many people have said before." When I showed it to a few conference-goers, really just for the humor in it, they told me that they knew Schulman had written it because they recognized her writing, and because she had been repeating that same sentiment over and over for the three days of the conference. Now, it really didn't matter to me who had written it except insofar as I had been thinking about writing this chapter (clearly, I have been thinking about it for a long time) and I "needed" someone to whom to ascribe the authorship of the quote, and Schulman's quasi-recognizable name added a certain cachet. But that is getting ahead of myself. For the moment, just remember that I found it and used it. My apologies to Sarah Schulman, wherever she is, if, indeed, she said no such thing and never even thought it. Schulman's observation, though not, perhaps, particularly astute, is partially true. Butler and Sedgwick were nearly omnipresent during that weekend in Austin, and that is a phenomenon worth investigating. It is clear that, at the Fourth Annual National Gay, Lesbian, and Bisexual Graduate Student Conference, people were wrapping themselves in the mantles of their idols.

On a surface level, it is quite easy to say that both Hollywood's and America's systems of higher education treat their employees in analogous ways. I could begin to make parallels between, for instance, producers and presidents (or chancellors); directors and deans; professors and actors; grad students and production assistants; but that, though amusing, would hardly merit publication. Yet think, for a moment, of the way that academic stars are constructed. Think that their images are equally as false as any media star's (indeed, Judith Butler may be the Madonna of the Ph.D. set). The building blocks of academic stardom, however, are not films, records, television shows. They are not only books, articles, and papers. Perhaps the most fundamental element of intellectual stardom is the citation. It is that little entity that has the most potential for creating various images. The quotation, ripped from its context, can create an impression directly opposed to one the author expects to disseminate, not for the mundane reasons that politicians hate to be quoted out of context, but, rather, because the new environment into which the citation is placed insists that new connections be made between the citer and the citee and the others who become involved in the text. Every time a text is cited it means something different, and this different meaning is reincorporated into the image of the academic star, so she becomes, like the movie star, a complex of many different roles.

The phenomenon under discussion here may well be slightly more complex than is suggested by that easy equivalency, however, for the mechanism is not merely the coagulation of the star's image from the presentation of the star's full, cohesive vehicle or *oeuvre*, but also the use that is made of parts of the vehicle. It is not so much akin to the way that Judy Garland, for instance, became the sum of her parts—in films from *Everybody Sing* to *A Child Is Waiting*—as it is to the way the synergistic calcification of *interpretations* of Judy (both her own and those of others) became "Judy Garland." Indeed, critical discourse seems already to have accepted this relationship between academic citation and "drag." We have come to notice the donning of gingham and pigtails, innocence and a dog as a "citation" of Judy as Dorothy. Likewise, a messy, cropped, gravelly voiced drinker "cites" Judy in the 1960s. If these citations create a star complex, it is certainly arguable that academic citation functions in a similar way.

Moreover, just as the movie star possesses the power of her name and, often, a certain typecasting, to lend continuity to the image, to ground her, that is, for her audience so that she remains recognizable (in pop music, this continuity is offered by the name and, more importantly, by the voice, which tends to remain constant and recognizable no matter what physical changes are endured by the singer), the Professor has her authorial signature (and, often, her area of expertise, the typecasting of academia). This mechanism also works in reverse, so that the citation is no longer made up only of borrowed words or ideas and bibliographic information, but of a borrowed image, as well. In other words, people quote from stars not only because of what they say, but also because of who (we think) they are. Indeed, it seems possible that our citational frenzy might stem from a desire to utilize *image* rather than text. After all, if "people are constantly quoting Butler and Sedgwick saying these really mundane things that many people have said before," then there must be a reason for it. And that reason is, of course, that Butler and Sedgwick are glamorous and hip right now.

It would be disingenuous to deny that glamour and hipness signify status in academia just as they do in the more public worlds of politics and entertainment, though a myopic insistence that our profession operates as a meritocracy may have clouded the realization. Both glamour and hipness depend on nothing if not image. Thus, if they adhere to Butler and Sedgwick, it is not because of the intelligence or insight of the two women, nor because of their power, though these all play a part. Perhaps the ground zero of their images, the most basic reason that Butler and Sedgwick have come to be seen as they are, resides in the fact that they work largely in the area of queer studies. I am not positing that the two simply cashed in on the chic of an established discipline, since, certainly, both helped to create that chic. But it seems likely that a reputation of hipness might accrue more quickly on someone who works in an area that is perceived as current and fashionable. For instance, I have it on quite good authority that Nancy K. Miller is an extremely stylish woman, but she does not now function as an idol in the way that Eve does. Moreover, if Madonna's fame is a result primarily of the controversies she has inspired, so might Eve's be founded on her status as a pioneer in a field that much of the mainstream finds controversial and a little bit wacky.

It is fitting, too, that it should be these two women who are constructed as stars, since they are two of the most "tabloidable" academics America has to offer. This is just to say that their personal lives have become as important as—and sometimes more important than—their professional lives. In Eve's case, this blurring of the personal and the professional is effected in her own essays. Her technique goes beyond the academic commonplace of positioning one in relation to the subject of discussion, and into the realm that D. A. Miller frets about in "Secret Subjects, Open Secrets."[9] She must be well acquainted with the charges he mentions, though whether she is mortified by telling tales in school is another question altogether. Essays like "Divinity" (written with Michael Moon), "A Poem Is Being Written," and, most poignantly, "White Glasses" do not simply locate Eve as author in relation to, say, Divine, or spanking, or Michael Lynch, but they utilize autobiography as a technology of analysis. But the real power—the power we would probably rather not acknowledge—is in the titillating factoids they proffer, ripe for gossip-mongering. Certainly, what's *really* important is her intellectual work. But it would be both foolish and disingenuous to deny the power of gossip, of "real life" dirt, in star-making. Hollywood has consistently constructed stars with both their professional and personal lives in its eyes. And, significantly, lesbian and gay communities have relied heavily on published gossip, and unpublishable dish, to create their own connections to more conventionally constructed star images. As for Judith, she has been the subject of a fanzine (one whose existence, I understand, she is none too pleased about). However, Butler's position is qualitatively different than Eve's because, if one were wont to talk in such a way, one could say that where Eve asked for it and even provided some juicy info (perhaps she has mastered the "leak"), Judith has done no such thing, or at least in no such public way. But Judith has also become academia's sweetheart, a dyke Mary Pickford for the intelligentsia. She is, to put it bluntly, a sex symbol. And that confers a certain kind of attention and responsibility. So we have a fanzine, as well as some knowledge that she continues to disavow, that she used to write antipornography tracts under the name Judy Butler. This sort of information adds another dimension to traditionally flat academic prose and personality.

Returning to Schulman's rant, it occurs to me that there is something odd and vaguely haughty about the tone of this found object, as well as something that points to a slight misunderstanding of the politics of academic citation. What is being objected to, it appears, is not so much that these two names have been invoked so often, but, rather, that these are the wrong names to be invoked. The first function of academic citation is, of course, one of simple attribution. It is a way to avoid passing off a quote or an idea as your own, and therein to avoid the attendant trouble that arises in academic circles when that happens (and you get caught). However, the aesthetics of citation, to which Schulman seems to be appealing, demand something more. If someone is going to be cited, it is not enough to resort to the most recent or easiest source. Someone else, someone *before*, needs to get the credit. And, in certain ways, this is the academic's work—the tracing back of ideas to a properly venerated source. We are all, I assume, familiar with the process by which we purchase a book primarily for its notes and bibliography, so we can perform the genealogical labor, the Alex Haley–esque task of uncovering the roots of an argument. This process of textual excavation is really the search for an origin, for the author who can be considered the owner of an idea. And once this is found, it can be built upon to erect a proper argument, one which has a more compelling claim to originality than the one that takes the easy way out and resorts to the less work-intensive citation. This privileging of the intellectual origin points to the malingering Romanticism that still exists at the heart of traditional academic criticism. And, just as the Romantic Ideal of the Author (you know the one—Wordsworth and all that) obscured the intertextuality of any (specifically artistic) production through its insistence on the solipsism of the creative process, so this practice serves to efface complex structures of intertextual indebtedness even within intertextual argument. This genealogical project implies some direct communication between a previous commentator (who functions as owner/originator) and a current one, the "channeling," if you will, of an expert through a medium. What this structure ignores or effaces, of course, is the work of critics produced between the originary text and the current one, texts that have had as much influence in creating the meaning of the former as the original text did itself. Moreover, this privileging of origins can be seen to mirror the artificial separation of "primary" from "secondary" texts, in which the "primary" is the object-in-itself, the artifact that is directly commented on, and the "secondary" the work that does the commenting.

The fact that we are required to cite *ideas* taken from other texts is interesting given that copyright laws—laws that govern the ownership and distribution of intellectual property—have never been able to legislate the ownership of ideas. According to Eaton S. Drone, in his 1879 treatise on intellectual property, "that there can be no property in thoughts, conceptions, ideas, sentiments, &c., apart from their association is clear; for they are then incapable of being identified or owned exclusively. But their arrangement and combination in a definite form constitute an intellectual production, a literary composition, which has a distinction of being capable of identification and separate ownership, and possessing the essential attributes of property. The property is not in the simple thoughts, ideas, &c., but in what is produced by their association."[10] It is, clearly, the exact expression of the ideas that can be identified by law, and, hence, can be owned. The structure of citation, however, allows ideas themselves to be retroactively constructed as property, since once an idea is expressed, the idea, according to academic standards, must be cited no matter whether the specific arrangement of words (or "expression") of the original is being reused or not. The important distinction does not seem to be between metaphysical categories of idea and expression, but in sheer physicality, that is, the intangibility of one versus the tangibility of the other (specifically in publication). In this practical distinction lies the possibility of proof. And so, though there may be a fantasy of exhuming the original intellect, all that can possibly be found is the physical remains of one who may or may not be an origin. In a way, then, it does not matter whether Sarah Schulman actually said what I say she said. I've got my found object, and it is *attributable*. And therein lies its power.

In tandem with providing a comforting illusion of origins, citation is a way to lend credence, to give authority to a text. Of course, it is equally dishonest (in academic circles) to say that someone said something that they never really said, as such a situation circumvents intellectual property statutes and wanders into the realm of libel. Among the situations I have listed for my composition students who ask when to use a quotation is that instance, perhaps rare, when a published source has expressed something in a particularly skillful way. But the attribution of a quotation or idea to an author or authority has power beyond the idea being expressed or the way the words are linked together. It corrals an author-complex for use in a paper, offering not only intertextual, but also extratextual aid, which is to say that, just as any specific citation adds its layer to the overall image of the star, the image of the star *up to the point of a specific citation* becomes intertwined with the text in which it appears. Once again, however, the focus is on the author, both of the cited bit (the author whose name is being invoked as proof) and of the stuff surrounding it (the author who knows enough to cite the citee). Situations like this are particularly absurd in certain poststructuralist writings, particularly those that seek to problematize authorship and question its efficacy. Indeed, it is difficult (though getting easier) to begin such a project without relying on the work of Michel Foucault and Roland Barthes, even though such reliance ironically creates texts that question the place of the author (particularly in the role of foundation/origin) at the same time that they insist on fixing particular authors as foundation by citing (the) two venerated sources, (the) two Masters of LitCrit. This contradiction is so obvious that it's a bit embarrassing to point out. However, it seems that critical theory, the discipline from which much of this questioning comes, continues to insist on authorship. Take, for example, the famed public debate between Nancy K. Miller and Peggy Kamuf, which took place first at Cornell and then in the pages of *Diacritics*, and continues taking place in other name-making venues via the technology of anthologization. I first read the exchange (with addenda titled "Parisian Letters") in a volume called *Conflicts in Feminism*, edited by Marianne Hirsch and Evelyn Fox Keller—that is to say, a volume that invokes two "authors" on its cover, and is sold primarily by means of the recognizable nature of these two names, as well as those of its contributors, two of whom are conducting a debate on authorship that consistently cites not only Foucault and Barthes but also Kamuf and Miller. The effect of this layering of author upon author upon author, while perhaps implying some sort of collective authorship, also insists on a certain acceptance of an author's right to claim ownership over her work, and reiterates that insistence again and again through the necessity of invoking the name of the author as a means of identifying text. Moreover, this exchange certainly served to create, or at least solidify, the names (or should I say "signatures") of these two academics. All of this suggests that the technology of authorship is perhaps inescapable, no matter what theoretical stance is being promulgated.

This tension is not played out only in literary theory; it is part of the foundation of our notions of ownership, particularly the ownership of intellectual property. Certainly, the form of citation privileges authorship. No matter what citational fad is followed, what comes first and what stands out as subsequently recognizable is the name of the author, which, like the name of the Father, serves to organize the symbolic structures of which it is a part. Without this structure, the rehearsal of words or ideas from a published work in another work would certainly constitute unfair use, which is an infringement of copyright. Plagiarism, though usually talked about as an academic integrity violation is, in instances where text is borrowed from published work without a reference and/or permission, a statutory violation. It is important to realize, however, that permission or litigation derives not from the author, but, rather, from whoever is the copyright holder—in most cases, the publisher, who pays the author royalties out of the money the publisher makes from owning the text. The copyright, then, is not a means of protecting the author's rights, but, rather, the owner's (publisher's) right to restrict the circulation of a text and protect his investment. Insofar as copyrights exist for limited amounts of time, they do not appeal to an author's natural right to her own intellectual property. Indeed, the statutory limitation is an attempt to balance the two conflicting purposes of copyright: "On the one hand," Herman Jaszi tells us, "copyright aims to promote public disclosure and dissemination of works of 'authorship' [here we see statutory limitation functioning as an antitrust technique—an attempt to limit the monopoly a copyright holder has over a copyrighted work]; on the other hand, it seeks to confer on the creators the power to restrict or deny distribution of their works."[11] Such opposing claims force a recognition of the alienation of the author from the work—indeed, it is only because of this possible alienation that intellectual property can be called property at all. Ronald Bettig discusses this paradox in terms of capitalism:

The hierarchical class structure of capitalism means that the actual creators of a good produce more than they get in return, while the class on top gets more than it actually creates. Such class relationships and control of the labor process and surplus are "usually expressed legally in a set of *property rights*" (Bowles & Edwards, 1985, pp. 66–67). . . . copyright law governs the relationship between labor and capital in the mass media and information sectors of the economy: It determines who owns the "results" of intellectual creativity. Despite the fact that most artistic and literary creativity is collective in nature, ownership of the "results" of this labor still rests with capital.[12]

So, though protection is not usually accorded to the author, copyright law relies on the myth of the creative subject, and thus creates one out of the available material.

This discussion of the contradiction not only within copyright law, but also between poststructuralist thought and citational technique may be a necessary background for understanding the function of citation, but it still leaves unaddressed some of the most compelling reasons for citation in contemporary academia. Indeed, whereas previous critical trends tended to valorize texts with few references to other critics, the current climate demands citation. We are rabid citers, and the motivation of this frenzy cannot be explained solely in terms of plagiarism or copyright infringement, or with traditional Marxist analysis. This phenomenon does, however, seem to have some affinities with the mechanics of late consumer capitalism, in which the advertisement is the most useful product of all.

The other day, walking down the hall of the English department, a fellow student mentioned to me that she had just cited me in a paper. My gratification was less a function of whatever respect was bespoken by the gesture, and more of the free and easy access that such a citation might give other scholars to my work. The reference is an advertisement—and it didn't cost me anything. The meaning of this advertisement differs depending on the position of the product (and in this case, the product is not necessarily the written text, but, rather, the text's author). It can lend currency—for the graduate student, in the job hunt; for the assistant professor, in the quest for tenure; and for the tenured professor, partly in filthy lucre but mostly in reputation. The citation can thus also function as a sound bite or a slogan, as a way not only of creating interest in, but also of representing, the product. This product can be defined variously as a single written text, a series of written texts, or as the creator of such written texts—the persona of the writer. What this should make clear is that, in being cited, an academic is participating in the project not only of selling intellectual property, nor only of creating image, but also of selling image. We are all in the business of marketing.

With this cult of personality, we are not citing the same way at all. The persistence with which the name of the author presents itself is, however, necessary to this new fashion. To extend the metaphor of film, if "the real creative subject within copyright law governing film is capital [as authorship is assigned to the producer, and ultimately to the filmed-entertainment corporation which she represents],"[13] then it becomes even more clear that our "authors" can be seen as stand-ins. Perhaps we can talk about Sedgwick's "Tales of the Avunculate" the same way we speak of Elizabeth Taylor's character Martha in Edward Albee's *Who's Afraid of Virginia Woolf*, that is, knowing that authorship is conferred elsewhere—for instance, on Duke University Press. But this does not discount the importance of the author as stand-in, for it is still she who functions, in culture, as the creative subject. Still, even this construction requires some retrofitting. The point, you see, is not that this confusion emphasizes the arbitrary nature of authorship—not that, since authorship can be ascribed to almost anyone or anything, it does cease, or should cease, to *mean*. We live in an era where authorship matters. Shumway affirms that "The invention of stars' public images needs to be understood as a collaborative project, but the success of that invention clearly depends on audience response."[14] According to Steve Jones, "It is audiences who care passionately about authors, who seek confirmation that individuals are expressing their own thoughts and feelings through their chosen medium. It is necessary to have an author to lend credibility and authenticity to a work, and that is why image creation and maintenance are of paramount importance in the entertainment industries."[15] If you can accept the postulate that we critics are in an entertainment industry (we are, at least, entertainment for our students, for other academics, and, more and more frequently, for the public, at large), then you can see that, though the author may be dead, the birth of the reader has required her resurrection. Or perhaps it is a reincarnation, because she is an author with a difference. It is useless to argue that the author's history and biography should have little bearing on her work, for the academic star system makes that impossible. But the history, biography, and gossip about the academic stretches the boundaries of authorship, so that the author is not a person, but an image, just as the film star is. Certainly she becomes larger than life. And so it is not her history and biography that matter, but, rather, the history and biography that have been created for her in culture. This has particular significance for the idols of queer culture. Presented with a sanitized image of a star, in a world where passing is a viable (necessary?) option, queer culture is often responsible for creating its own connection to the star, creating its own image through sources disavowed by those who proclaim to be in control of the packaging. We can read against texts to create new, queer readings, or excavate hidden queer histories. Modes of knowledge like gossip allow for new, less-sanctioned histories and narratives to be written, which are then incorporated into the construct called "the author." The self-consciously hidden becomes visible again. The author has not, then, been jettisoned, but inflated to an unrecognizably queer size. And with this advancement into the realm of entertainment media, comes the very real influence of the extremely important mechanics of hipness.

If image is seen as coterminous with subjectivity, then the image must be policed with an equal amount of rigor. In academia we have emphasized the rhetoric of consistency to do this policing. Given what have been identified as the building blocks of academic subjectivity (read: image), it would seem that the academic must find herself in a difficult position, a position in which her work must always be accessible to the structure that has given it currency, or else risk the damning charge of inconsistency. What better way to explain the horror with which academics greeted the possibility of Paul de Man's fascism? De

Man was a known quantity, he could have no secrets and still be de Man. If, however, secrecy is the "mode whose ultimate meaning lies in the subject's formal insistence that he is radically inaccessible to the culture that would otherwise entirely determine him,"[16] then the bourgeois ideal of individuality (as well as the heteronormativity that is taken for granted as part of this bourgeois self) seems endangered in this profession.

The insistence on consistency means, conveniently, that when we need a quotation to illustrate a certain point or stance, we invariably know to whom to turn. An adjunct of this is that, when one needs a quotation to illustrate a certain stance or point, one will invariably use the same source, indeed, often that same quotation. Dorothy Parker is reported to have said that she must "even by accident, have said other things worth repeating, if the lazy sons-of-bitches bothered to find out."[17] So, I imagine, must Butler and Sedgwick feel, when they realize that people are constantly quoting them saying things that have become really mundane. And it is here that Schulman's observation displays its own astuteness. It could be that she is simply extraordinarily sensitive to the tides of academic hipness. Mundanity in academia is strictly outré; we trade in progress. The production and acceptance of each new dissertation, article, or book depends on a perception of its novelty. The academic product is supposed to break new ground, while at the same time being recognizable as a product of its author, that is, consistent with her image. As both the academic and her work are constructed, largely, by citation and gossip, this has repercussions not only for the functioning of the academic, herself, but also for the reception of her work, for, if her marketing requires the citation, it must also guard against the kind of overexposure enjoyed by Butler and Sedgwick in Austin. Such overexposure mitigates the operative designations of originality and freshness and can result in the star, herself, becoming perceived as mundane. If the overexposure of Madonna threatened to end the career of a woman with stacks more money and power than any professor I know, then what might it do to an academic star?

II

All I ever hear about is Marcia! Marcia, Marcia, Marcia!
—Eve Plum as Jan Brady, *The Brady Bunch*

I intend my use of an intentionally "unhip" word to designate hipness—that is, "hip"—to illustrate the speed with which concepts, people, things which depend on the mechanics of hipness are produced, become obsolete, and are discarded (and then resurrected). Along with speed, hipness depends on perspective. I want to think about Schulman's quote alongside Jan Brady's and suggest that one motivation for the charge of mundanity might simply be an irritated response to repetition, rather like Jan's famous whine. Has the work of Butler and Sedgwick become mundane through its seemingly endless repetition? Or are these two women, working in arguably one of the "hippest" of academic subjects—queer studies—(still) hip? Certainly the most identifiable aspect of hipness is the swiftness with which it both attaches to and abandons a phenomenon. The fickleness of hipness is not an index of necessity or significance; rather, hipness is simply the leading edge of a fad that may never become a trend. Realizing the applicability of hipness in academia must, necessarily, problematize the perception of "authority" in the same field. There seems to be a contradiction, that is, between hipness and authority, which is just to say that the velocity that characterizes the hip mitigates any designation of authority. Once a trend has become established enough to have any claim to authority, it is necessarily no longer hip. At the present moment in academia, queer studies may still have the trappings of fashionability, just as perhaps a decade ago, feminism did. But, quite honestly, we are beginning the new millennium, and we are witnessing the obsolescence of a discipline which was once unquestionably hip, just as the late eighties and early nineties witnessed the decline of academic feminism. We are all, I'm sure, familiar with the situation in which the current trend must become established (read: co-opted) in order to be taken seriously.

Right now, you might choose to look back a few pages, to the place where I made an observation that seemed so plain as to be indubitable—namely, that Butler and Sedgwick are hip. I wonder what negotiations with the truth must be completed for such a statement to seem self-evident, what blinders must be worn for it to be believed. Tenured professors and occupiers of endowed chairs may be radicals, but they are not hipsters. Certainly if I am calling Sedgwick and Butler hip, then I am not really talking about hipness, but about the academic establishment. The risk taking (as you might call it) of Sedgwick can end up with her being vilified in the popular press as some sort of crank (someone whose crazy ideas have little claim to authority), while cementing her position within academia, thereby granting her more authority. What is particularly beautiful, though, is the fact that we (academics) really believe that figures like these *are* hip, which is to say that our notions of opposition, authority, and fashion have become insanely muddled. The joke is, most certainly, on us. We continue to lionize our stars as public figures, and endlessly quote them, conceding their authority in a sphere where that designation is excessively fraught. Perhaps this is the root of the problem I have run into in classes, where students and professors speaking out of the tradition of, for instance, established feminism, rail against Sedgwick or Butler for their perceived lacks; where a queer authority is granted and, concurrently, challenged, much as it is in Hollywood. Could Eve Sedgwick and Judith Butler be the Bette Davis and Joan Crawford of the fin de siècle?

I quoted Ross earlier on "the camp effect," but his comments on changes "in the mode of cultural production" and the redefinition of their resulting products "according to contemporary standards of taste" have relevance here, as well. Few would deny that there has been a significant change in the mode of production of academics, when about half of the people who receive Ph.D.s from English departments in a given year cannot find jobs in English departments; when the Modern Language Association defaces reams of paper discussing the horrendous state of the job market, and the solution to the problem is to slash the number of students admitted to doctoral programs in English. The decline of the Hollywood studio system (which guaranteed employment to large numbers of actors) has allowed us (according to Ross's formulation) or forced us to appreciate its stars in different ways, most of which rely on hostility, nostalgia, parody, or some combination of the three. The decline of academic departments across the humanities may force us to do the same.

Admitting the impact of hipness on academics is simply one way to recognize the omnipresence of fashion in our culture. Theorists and critics no longer attempt to find answers to the questions we pose, for the "truth" of these "answers" depends on what happens to be in fashion at the time. It all comes down to what we are wearing, you see. And as definitives are not really possible, the concept of planned obsolescence seems destined to find its place in academia. Such a concept not only recognizes the limited pertinence of the written word, but also, it seems, quite clearly realizes that texts live on only in citation. Indeed, the lingering purpose of the to-be-obsolete text is its usefulness excerpted in the texts of others, but even this is a short-lived service. Exploitation of the freedoms that planned obsolescence might give the academic text could result in its self-conscious denial of the text's own integrity and the importance of itself as a whole, much like the way sampling denies the integrity of a piece of music. But the importance of the text as a function of citation is, in addition, impacted by its metamorphosis into cliché. When I began graduate school, it seems that all I ever heard about was Bakhtin (Bakhtin, Bakhtin, Bakhtin!), so that concepts like dialogism and the carnivalesque, though not rendered meaningless, certainly did become annoyingly omnipresent and ceased to seem interesting. They had become clichés. The descent of a text into the realm of cliché leaves some of its residue on the author of the text, bruising, as it were, not only her work but also, often, her persona as behind the times, tired, mainstreamed into oblivion, like the stars of old Hollywood, or the new Madonna. Moreover, the use of cliché can also mark its user as pedestrian, less than current, and, certainly, mundane. The simple citation of obsolete business, then, allows the accrual of obsolescence in the citer, as well as increasing the perception of the business as obsolete in itself. Of course, there are further steps in this process, steps in which the originary author completely disappears, leaving a citation effect, perhaps, without a citation. Once a phrase or concept becomes thoroughly immured in a culture or subculture, it becomes public domain. The utilization (for it is not technically citation anymore, or at least does not employ the cosmetics of citation, such as quotation marks and parenthetical notes) of such a text, then, clearly implies a history, and imposes such history on the text in which the cliché is used, but that history is vague and undefined. If the text used is truly so hackneyed as to become cliché, then its authorship is problematized either through contempt (what a surprise, what a cliché) or through real confusion (as a result of its unlimited repetition, both with and without attribution—its repeated reauthorship). Notable here is the way that authorship detaches from one persona and attaches to another, for the cliché (as well as the plagiarized text) can easily become attributed to any writer who uses it.

One possible upshot is that the utterance becomes, for many intents and purposes, authorless. As "everyday language" (and please note that the "everyday" changes, not only from one day to the next, but also from one context to the next), its attributability ceases to be a focus. Authorless and overexposed, the only way to infuse new interest is to invest the cliché with new meaning. Far, then, from residing in a state of meaninglessness, the cliché can become full of new and diverse meanings. Michel de Certeau theorizes this mechanism of meaning making in relation to the proper names of city streets which the pedestrian passes every day:

Disposed in constellations that hierarchize and semantically order the surface of the city, operating chronological arrangements and historical justifications, these words (*Borrégo, Botzaris, Bougainville* . . .) slowly lose, like worn coins, the value engraved on them, but their ability to signify outlives its first definition. *Saints-Pāres, Corentin Celton, Red Square* . . . these names make themselves available to the diverse meanings given them by passers-by; they detach themselves from the places they were supposed to define and serve as imaginary meeting-points on itineraries which, as metaphors, they determine for reasons that are foreign to their original value but may be recognized or not by passers-by.[18]

The names have been evacuated of their original meaning and filled with new ones. This, too, is the way we make Davis, Crawford, and Garland mean differently.

Cliché, then, mimics the mechanism of allusion, the literary convention that is recognized as confusing ideas of ownership. The allusive text utilizes the ideas, and often the words, of another—*without* credit. Indeed, in the citation of a highly allusive text ("Sweet Thames, run softly till I end my song, / Sweet Thames, run softly, for I speak not loud or long"[19]), it is, once again, only the most recent author, often a citer, who is credited. Indeed, the above discussion of cliché obtains, almost word for word, here, perhaps because cliché is a vague sort of allusiveness, not so direct and distinct as the sort utilized in traditional allusion, where the structure of indebtedness is traceable: whereas an allusion has an author, the cliché is effectively authorless, if only because of its constant reauthoring. Traceability, however, implies the single most important distinction between the two (that is, cliché and a "traditional" allusion). For there is, certainly, a trace of something in the allusion, but, as any undergraduate English major will tell you, it is not always obvious. It is, I would go so far as to say, necessarily hidden. Allusion hides its indebtedness in a way that cliché, because of its omnipresence, cannot. The appreciation of allusion depends on a reader's specialized knowledge—a familiarity with, say, T. S. Eliot and Edmund Spenser, or with *The Brady Bunch*. As such, it, too, utilizes the mechanics of hipness, and the predilection of the hip to distinguish a cognoscenti from an ignorati. The allusive must be elusive, or it would no longer function as a vehicle for authorizing a text by assembling a history for it, and imbuing that history with an importance by its very use, while at the same time allowing that importance to accrue in the text that utilizes the allusion. The authorization or importance is further created by an elitism that allows a certain audience access to a "more complete" meaning. This addressed audience is produced in the recognition of the allusion. Allusion, then, which complicates authorship, focuses attention on the reader and, in so doing, re-creates an authorial hand in the formation of the audience, a hand that smacks of intentionality. Once again, the Death of the Author has required the birth of the reader.

Sarah Schulman's offhanded remark seems a comment on hipness. Hipness and irritation. For, among other things, it implies the redundancy of the academic who says things (and gets quoted as saying things) that, quite simply, everyone already knows. If this is an indictment of an academy, it is not one that condemns it for being out of touch or off the wall, but for being, really, behind the times. The concerns of academic hipness are patently unhip in any real world sense. And this seems a function of the quest for authority, in many senses. Popular culture does not have the same sort of investment in authorship. While undeniably important, it also does not need to be quite so exact a science. And so Edward Albee, Elizabeth Taylor, and Mike Nichols can each, in turn, author Martha. The academic's pursuit of authorship is what makes a career, for it is a step in establishing authority—an authority that, because of the practical necessities of study, submission, and publication, requires a time lag ensuring staleness.

So what about the pioneering spirit of books like this one? And why have we chosen to utilize a metaphor that cites America's Manifest Destiny, the push of the frontier westward until it reached the ocean, and its continued reach across the ocean, to the South Pacific, the Caribbean, the Panama Canal, suggesting that that destiny, apparently, is continuing to manifest itself? Our destiny is not manifest: there is no queer frontier. That is an anachronism and a cliché, not only because the frontier has moved away from queer studies, but more fundamentally because the discourse of frontiers and pioneering is no longer particularly useful in academia. Planned obsolescence must radically change the relationship of the author to history as well as the relationship of the author to the (production of) text. This chapter is probably already obsolete. Moreover, perhaps a different relationship obtains between camp and the academy, a relationship that Alan Sokal and Andrew Ross and the other editors of *Social Text* might do well to appreciate.

So, this may not be a fan letter to Eve, but a eulogy, and, as such, I must report that I do not find Eve's plums rotten, but perhaps just a bit bruised.

Notes

1. David R. Shumway, "The Star System in Literary Studies," *PMLA* 112 (1997): 96.

2. Eve Kosofsky Sedgwick, *Tendencies* (Durham, N.C.: Duke University Press, 1993), xii.

3. Lauren Berlant and Michael Warner, "What Does Queer Theory Teach Us about X?" *PMLA* 110 (1995): 343.

4. John Harned, "Queer Studies and the Job Market: Three Perspectives,"

in *Profession 1996*, ed. John Harned (New York: Modern Language Association of America, 1996), 82–90.

5. Andrew Ross, *No Respect: Intellectuals and Popular Culture* (New York: Routledge, 1989), 146–47.

6. Claudia Roth Pierpont, "The Strong Woman: What Was Mae West Really Fighting For?" *New Yorker,* 11 November 1996, 118.

7. Andrew Ross, *No Respect,* 139.

8. David Buxton, "Rock Music, the Star System, and the Rise of Consumerism," in *On Record: Rock, Pop, and the Written Word,* ed. Simon Frith and Andrew Goodwin (New York: Pantheon, 1990), 430.

9. ". . . we are all well acquainted with those mortifying charges (sentimentality, self-indulgence, narcissism) which our culture is prepared to bring against anyone who dwells in subjectivity longer than is necessary to his proper functioning as the agent of socially useful work. (It is bad enough to tell tales out of school, but to tell them in school—or what comes to the same, in a text wholly destined for the academy—would be intolerable)." D. A. Miller, *The Novel and the Police* (Berkeley: University of California Press, 1988), 193.

10. Eaton S. Drone, cited in Herman Jaszi, "Toward a Theory of Copyright: The Metamorphoses of 'Authorship,'" *Duke Law Journal* (April 1991): 465.

11. Ibid., 463.

12. Ronald Bettig, "Critical Perspectives on the History and Philosophy of Copyright," *Critical Studies in Mass Communication* 9, no. 2 (June 1992): 150; emphasis in the original.

13. Ibid., 152.

14. Shumway, "Star System," 86.

15. Steve Jones, "Critical Legal Studies and Pop Music Studies," *Stanford Humanities Review* 3, no. 2 (August 1993): 151.

16. Miller, *The Novel,* 195.

17. Dorothy Parker, cited in Marion Meade, *Dorothy Parker, What Fresh Hell Is This?* (New York: Penguin, 1987), 373.

18. Michel de Certeau, *The Practice of Everyday Life,* trans. Steven Rendall (Berkeley: University of California Press, 1988), 104.

19. Eliot or Spenser? Note that the passage is not in quotes in the text of *The Waste Land*. There is, however, a footnote, one which, in the context of Eliot's ironic notes, could (should?) be seen as a comment on the very idea of allusion and authorship. Why should this one not be seen as jokey and misleading, as are the rest?

13

The Queer History and Politics of Lesbian and Gay Studies

George Chauncey

Author's note: The following was written for presentation at a banquet honoring longtime Los Angeles activists Jim Kepner, Morris Kight, Jeanne Cordova, Ivy Bottini and others at the culmination of the "Queer Frontiers" conference in March 1995. For the purposes of its reprinting here, I have opted to maintain the "present tense" of the talk's presentational style, although I have silently updated some of the information within to accord with more recent events and developments of the past five years.

I want to begin by thanking and commending the organizers of this conference both for taking on the unbelievably massive task of organizing this event, which they've done incredibly well—and it is an effort for which they can never and will never be thanked enough—and for their wisdom—indeed, their inspiration—in organizing this powerfully moving event: bringing together three generations of activists and scholars across the gulf of half a century, to thank and honor these pioneers who can never be thanked enough.

It is deeply moving for me to speak tonight, in this hall full of the men and women who pioneered the lesbian and gay movement almost half a century ago—and full of men and women who represent some of the bright hope for the next generation of the movement. Even though I've been to a lot of these conferences by now, it's still astonishing to me—as someone who came out four years after Stonewall—that such a conference could happen, and I think it must seem even more incredible to our honorees.

It must also be hard for most people in this audience to imagine the degree of courage required of the men and women who founded the movement forty-five years ago. I had to spend a long time in the archives—reading court records and FBI records, police files and censorship files—and talking with more than seventy-five older gay men, including a few of the men being honored here tonight—before I began to really comprehend what their world was like.

They began organizing at a time when the police regularly raided the places where gay people gathered, including bars, restaurants, and even private parties. In New York City, literally hundreds of bars were raided between the mid-1930s and the mid-1960s, simply because they let women dance together or wear pants, or let men call each other Mary or talk about the opera or try to pick someone up.

From the mid-1920s, when cruising was specified in the state criminal code as a kind of disorderly conduct, to the mid-1960s, when the pre-Stonewall Mattachine Society of New York waged a successful campaign to stop most egregious uses of police entrapment, more than fifty thousand men were arrested in New York City alone on homosexual charges. In the most brutal years—in the late 1940s and early 1950s during the great antigay reaction following World War II, when these men and women seated before us tonight were forming the Mattachine Society in Los Angeles—more than three thousand men were arrested every year in New York City alone. The significance of this came home to me when I realized that half of the seventy-five men I interviewed for my books were arrested at least once in their lives on a homosexual charge—and that all of them had many friends who had been arrested. Other men I interviewed had been contacted by the post office and warned about receiving gay publications in the mail. They lived in a world in which the police sometimes shut down whole newsstands on busy city corners because they dared to carry early gay magazines like *ONE* or the *Ladder*. Faculty were regularly fired from their university jobs when they were exposed as gay by being caught in a tearoom, or for receiving gay publications—pornographic or academic—at home. Although this level of repression is almost unthinkable today, it shaped everyone from that generation, and, to varying degrees, continues to shape even most of us who came of age after Stonewall.

This is the world the movement developed in, and these were the issues people fought, which gives you some sense of the courage it took for men and women to announce themselves as gay, to take on the police, to take on the government and the media and the church—all targets of the early movement and the Stonewall-inspired movement, a generation or more before ACT UP and queer nationalism came to the fore.

I want to begin with that dual image—of fearful repression and fearless courage—because it seems to me crucial that those of us who are younger realize that we are the beneficiaries of two generations of organized struggle on behalf of the gay and lesbian cause and that we would not be here today if countless people had not taken risks in their families, in their jobs, in their neighborhoods, and in the academy.

Tonight I want to chronicle very briefly how we got from there to here—not in the world at large, but in the academy itself, in part because it is easy to lose sight of even our most recent history, and in part because I think it's important to celebrate our victories, including the stunning growth in the field of lesbian and gay studies in the last decade. But I want to devote most of my remarks to the tremendous challenges we face now that the academy and our place in it have become central battlegrounds in the culture wars presently dividing this country. There are all too many opponents of the changes in the academy who want to return us to the climate of the 1950s, and they leave me deeply concerned about the future of people just beginning academic careers and about the future of our collective project.

Many of us have begun to excavate the intimate connection between this history of the gay academic project and the first and second waves of the gay movement occurring in turn-of-the-century Germany and in Cold War Los Angeles. The Institute for Homophile Studies, established in Los Angeles in the mid-1950s, set the pattern for much of the scholarship of the next twenty years: it was undertaken by nonacademic intellectuals who were deeply tied to the organized gay movement and who sought to create a store of knowledge and particularly a usable past for that movement.

As recently as the late 1970s, much of the (relatively small amount of) gay studies work being published was still produced by nonacademics. The first major collection of historical documents related to gay American history was published in 1977 by Jonathan Ned Katz, a movement activist and playwright who didn't even have a bachelor's degree. A number of community-based local lesbian and gay history projects and archives were started in the late 1970s, although only a handful of them, such as those in San Francisco, New York, and Buffalo, as well as the much older archives in Los Angeles, are still active today. For a period in the late 1970s and early 1980s, historical studies were at the cutting edge of work in gay studies, as they were in women's studies, and several community-based historians toured the country giving slide-illustrated lectures about their research on, for instance, the lesbian pulp novels of the 1950s, or the lesbian and gay writers and entertainers of the Harlem Renaissance. In the decade before Allan Bérubé published *Coming Out under Fire*, his groundbreaking study of gay men and women in World War II, he presented slide shows about his work in more than a hundred living rooms and auditoriums. As gay men and lesbians struggled to create a public presence for themselves in the 1970s, many sought to reclaim their historical presence as well—sought to affirm themselves in the present by affirming that they had a past, and to construct a collective identity in the present by imagining they shared a collective history.

It was only in the wake of the growth of the militant gay liberation movement in the early 1970s that lesbian and gay *academics* began meeting to develop a more gay-affirmative intellectual project, although it was one which, in retrospect, appears often to have treated the category of the "homosexual" as uncritically as the more hostile project of antigay academics had. Yet most gay academics remained too afraid of the all too real professional consequences of conducting such studies to follow the lead of community-based scholars. Although in 1973 a group of New York–based academics started the Gay Academic Union, which organized a series of conferences and publications before collapsing, most scholars who published in the field in the mid-1970s already had tenure. When Yale University's John Boswell published his monumental study, *Christianity, Social Tolerance, and Homosexuality,* in 1980, he became one of the first untenured scholars to risk publishing a book on a gay topic. In those years, not very long ago, graduate students were regularly forbidden to write on such topics, or at least strongly advised not to do so. In the early 1980s I wrestled with the decision to write a gay history dissertation for nearly two years: my closest advisors at Yale, feminists and gay scholars, who were strong supporters of gay research and who had my best interests at heart, advised me not to do so because they feared it would be professional suicide. There were only a handful of us writing gay or lesbian history dissertations in the whole country through most of the 1980s.

The police weren't arresting gay academics anymore, in other words, but the climate of fear was so pervasive and powerful as recently as the early 1980s that the "Queer Frontiers" conference and other large meetings of graduate students in the field would have been unthinkable. It's important to remember this history of a lack of (our) academic freedom every time someone accuses advocates of multiculturalism or "political correctness" of stifling academic freedom.

Nonetheless, a growing number of academics did take risks, such as publishing in gay studies before they got tenure, or even before they got a job. And they began to create organizations and programs that would support that work. Gay caucuses were established in most of the major professional associations like the Modern Language Association of America and the American Historical Association, which orga-

nized panels at some of the major conferences and published newsletters containing reviews, notes on publishing, and news of academic
successes and horror stories. A steady stream of publications began to
appear—first primarily in history and anthropology, and then, increasingly in the 1980s, in literary studies, film studies, and critical theory—
mirroring the shift from the social to the textual, from the archival to
the theoretical, that was taking place in gender studies and race studies
as well.

Then, almost overnight, everything changed. As almost everyone
who's been working in the field for more than a decade would agree,
the late 1980s and early 1990s witnessed a sudden, unprecedented,
and extraordinary growth in the field. Several university presses and
commercial publishers began lesbian and gay studies series, including
Columbia, Oxford, Chicago, and New York University Presses, as well,
of course, as Routledge, and many more university presses joined in
the intense competition for good gay-studies manuscripts. Every forward thinking academic journal in the nation, or so it sometimes
seemed, published a special issue on lesbian/gay studies or queer
theory—*South Atlantic Quarterly, differences, Social Text, Signs, Feminist
Studies,* and *Radical History Review,* to name a few, and a new interdisciplinary queer journal, *GLQ,* began publishing in 1993. There was an
explosion in the number of gay studies courses offered in English,
French, history, film, anthropology, and women's studies departments
at colleges around the country. Moreover, almost all of the students
taking these courses in the 1980s were lesbian, gay, and bi-identified,
it is now common for the majority of students taking them not to be
queer-identified in any sense.

Perhaps most remarkably, a legion of graduate students began work
on queer-themed dissertations in the early 1990s. When I attended the
first North American lesbian and gay history conference held in Toronto in 1982, I counted about fifty people, including a dozen present-
ers and a handful of graduate students. When the first annual national
conference in lesbian and gay studies was held at Yale in 1987, there
were about two hundred in attendance. Two years later there were five
to six hundred. The next annual conference, held at Harvard in 1990,
drew some sixteen hundred registrants, and the conference held at
Rutgers in 1991 was the largest ever, drawing more than two thousand
participants and showcasing almost two hundred papers, making it
one of the largest annual academic conferences held in the country.
Although all of those national conferences have featured a heavy representation of work by graduate students, the organization of annual
graduate student conferences like "Queer Frontiers," beginning in

1990, is another sign of the tremendous growth in interest in lesbian, gay, bisexual, and queer studies at universities around the country.

Why the Growth?

How can we account for the growing visibility of lesbian and gay studies in the academy? Two processes seem particularly important.

The social change brought about by the feminist movement and the lesbian and gay movement is the most crucial. The movement both emboldened individual scholars to take on these projects and helped reduce the general prejudice against gay people that previously deterred research by effectively stigmatizing students of homosexuality as well as homosexuals themselves. Moreover, as anyone who has been observing the lesbian and gay scene at American colleges for the last decade can report, every year more freshmen arrive who have *already* come out as gay: young gay people have more role models, more information, and more support than ever before, and this has made it easier for more of them to come out at an earlier age and produced a larger constituency for such courses on college campuses. Among graduate students, the loss of fear is even more striking. If anything, I sometimes worry that the current generation of graduate students underestimates the professional dangers involved in choosing to work in lesbian/gay studies, an issue I'll return to in a moment.

If it was only possible for the field to emerge because of the movement, it has only been possible for the field to gain visibility, influence, and even prestige because so much of its work has been *so good*. Much of the new work in the field addresses issues that are of central concern to multiple avenues of contemporary academic inquiry, and such work has helped shape the direction of that inquiry. Women's studies and gender studies played an essential role in paving the way for gay studies, in part because they insisted that the academy as a whole take seriously questions about gender, sexuality, nonstatal power, subjectivity, identity formation, and disruption. These questions are at the core of many recent projects in critical theory and cultural studies more generally, and as gay studies along with gender studies has begun to pioneer ways of formulating these questions, it has become a more influential force in shaping postmodern thought. Moreover, given that one of the major intellectual projects of the last decade has been to rigorously question and deconstruct the naturalized categories through which we were taught to understand the world and find our place in it—race, gender, nation, sexuality, individualism, and identity—queer theory has also come to play a pivotal role, for "queerness" provides a powerful vantage point from which to interrogate and destabilize normativity. Lesbian/gay/bi studies has also contributed to the breaking down of disciplinary boundaries involved in cultural studies and feminist studies.

The outpouring of new scholarship in the last decade has made this, then, an exciting moment to be involved in lesbian and gay studies. We have begun to reconstruct some of the social and cultural histories that have been systematically erased from the historical record, and to challenge the dominant categories of thought which that erasure made possible. We have built an important theoretical foundation for future work, but we still have almost *everything* to learn about almost *everything*. Unlike graduate students in many fields, students in lesbian and gay studies and queer theory are not going to need to fill in other people's footnotes; there are still vast unexplored terrains to chart: your queer frontiers to explore.

The Right-Wing Reaction

It is important that we recognize and celebrate this success, and that we acknowledge the courage of the many lesbian and gay academics who took the risks that have made these advances possible. At the same time, though, it is important to recognize that the future of lesbian and gay studies is anything but guaranteed. The foothold we have in the academy is a fragile one indeed, and the ground is shifting beneath us, particularly in the wake of the right-wing resurgence in American culture and politics. I want to turn to those threats now, because they concern us all.

In the academy itself, we face a crisis because we have not been able to institutionalize lesbian and gay studies. There are some notable exceptions. A handful of schools have established research institutes. The Center for Lesbian and Gay Studies at the City University of New York Graduate Center is deservedly the most famous of these, because it has organized a series of significant public conferences on gay studies issues. There are also centers already established or under consideration at a handful of other schools, and the University of Southern California's new programs are extraordinarily ambitious and welcome. At the University of Chicago, where I teach, we have established the Lesbian and Gay Studies Project as part of the Center for Gender Studies, which coordinates courses, organizes conferences and ongoing workshops, and provides research grants to graduate students.

A number of other schools have stressed the teaching of gay studies more than research, and in the last decade minors or certificate programs have been established at a number of schools, including City College of San Francisco; the University of California, Berkeley; the University of California, Los Angeles; Cornell University; and the University of Wisconsin–Milwaukee. Establishing these programs and minors has allowed faculty organizers to coordinate the courses already being taught and given them leverage to campaign for more departments to offer courses.

Whether or not establishing gay studies programs is the best strategy for the field is not altogether clear. Like people working in gender studies and various ethnic studies programs before us, we have to weigh the relative merits of building a program, because even though it serves to legitimate and guarantee support to a new line of intellectual inquiry, it also threatens to ghettoize it and relieve other scholars and programs from the burden of transforming their own courses by bringing queer perspectives to bear on them. We also face the problem that any such institutionalization of intellectual inquiry threatens: namely, to reify and naturalize the very categories it was initially designed to critique, and to freeze a rapidly developing field at a particular moment in its evolution. Simply naming such a program lesbian and gay studies, lesbian gay and bisexual studies, l/g/b/transgender studies, queer studies, gender studies, or critical studies of sexuality is to mark yourself—and perhaps institutionally freeze yourself—at a singular moment in the development of a rapidly developing and always transforming field.

My own sense is that there are good reasons to institutionalize support for such inquiry, despite these dangers, and I am glad to see their development here and elsewhere. But the very visibility of the existing programs masks two central problems. First, there still just aren't that many of them, and in this age of retrenchment it may become even more difficult to establish them. More important, though, almost none of these programs have produced new jobs in lesbian and gay studies. They are almost entirely staffed by faculty from other departments— history, English, film, and the like—rather than by people specifically hired in lesbian and gay studies. To use the institutional lingo, there are almost no "lines" in gay studies, only in conventional departments.

This is grim news for people writing gay studies dissertations, because despite the blossoming of gay studies in recent years, most departments are still extremely reluctant to hire people working in this area. Gay studies is still a highly contested field in most departments, dismissed by many and actively attacked by some, and getting departments to hire entry-level Ph.D.s—and then to tenure them—remains one of the fundamental hurdles to the field's development.

I discovered just how much resistance there is to making the investment that such hiring entails during my three years on the job market.
Through the grapevine I heard stories of outbursts in hiring committee meetings about what it would mean to hire someone "like me";
at interviews I got some very peculiar and sometimes very offensive
questions; and in 1991, the search at one school, where I was one of the
four short-list candidates brought to campus, was abruptly terminated
when several faculty members strenuously objected to the overt and
unrestrained gay baiting engaged in by some members of the department during the decision-making process. This, I might add, was at a
well-known liberal arts college in the Northeast, and it is hardly the
only story of its sort I've heard at either the hiring or the tenuring
stage.

Some of this opposition results from personal bigotry on the part of
hiring committee members, or *homophobia* in its classic sense: that is,
the committee members' fear and hatred of homosexuals, which in
many social settings can still be expressed more freely and overtly than
other kinds of bigotry (not to minimize the persistence of other forms
of bigotry in American culture as a whole or academic culture in particular). But more of the opposition to hiring gay studies candidates results from institutionalized *heterosexism,* since the questions that gay
studies might ask of the work of Walt Whitman, Willa Cather, or Hart
Crane, for instance, or about the development of urban culture, or
about the social ties that fostered the Harlem Renaissance, have so long
been so actively repressed. Lesbian/gay inquiry, in other words, has for
so long been so actively excluded from the curriculum and otherwise
marginalized that it now appears "marginal," or "narrow," to use the
most common code word.

As a result, the number of new gay studies Ph.D.s resulting in jobs is
shockingly low. When I was hired by the University of Chicago history
department in 1991, I became only the second Ph.D. with a gay history
dissertation *ever* to be hired by an American history department (John
D'Emilio was the first, and he'd been hired by the University of North
Carolina at Greensboro eight years earlier—after his dissertation had
already been published by the University of Chicago Press). More candidates with gay studies Ph.D.s have been hired by English departments—Rutgers, Iowa, Yale, Chicago, Duke, the University of Illinois
at Urbana-Champaign, and several other schools have made such hires
in the last decade—but even in English departments the numbers are
small. Other fields, such as anthropology, are even farther behind. I
suspect that even now no more than two dozen of us who wrote dissertations centrally focused on gay issues have gotten jobs in any field.

Indeed, almost *no* departments *set out* to hire people working in gay studies; at best they will hire people in social history, critical theory, or Victorian studies whose work happens to focus on gay issues. The University of Chicago was certainly not looking for a gay historian when they advertised the job I applied for. While the growing undergraduate interest in gay-related courses and the growing vigor and visibility of the field intellectually mean that there will be some growth in the number of jobs advertised that mention lesbian and gay studies along with other fields, it is highly unlikely that there will be a dramatic increase.

It is crucial, in other words, that if you plan to write a dissertation in gay studies you must do all that you can to relate it to other fields—so that you can persuasively argue that it is a dissertation in urban history or Victorian studies or feminist theory or whatever the appropriate field is. This is not all bad. Our work is almost always better when it is deeply contextualized and engages with a wide range of issues and literatures, and it is harder for others to ghettoize and marginalize it when it addresses multiple sets of concerns. But even those who do not share this intellectual commitment need to broaden their work if they want to have a chance on the job market. Given the dismal state of the job market, anyone who goes into graduate school these days is taking a risk, but students in lesbian and gay studies are taking a bigger risk than most.

Unfortunately, those risks are only growing in the wake of the right wing's campaigns against us. Gay educators and gay-positive education are some of the primary targets of the powerful right-wing movement in this country.

We can see this targeting at every level of political struggle in the United States. Local school-board elections, for instance, have become one of the primary organizing vehicles for the right wing around the country. In town after town, from New York State to Missouri to Washington State, Christian fundamentalists have found that the most effective way to win support in their efforts to take over the education of children is to warn parents of the dangers of gay-positive education—that books like *Heather Has Two Mommies* and *Daddy's Roommate* might turn up in the school library, or that gay teachers might come out in the classroom. Only once they are elected do their actions reveal their full agenda, including restoring prayer and creationism to the curriculum. This sometimes results in their being voted out of office, but their campaigns against gay-positive education provoke remarkably little opposition. Even in New York City, which has one of the most powerful gay communities in the nation, proposals for the Rainbow Curriculum, a multicultural educational program teaching respect for diversity, generated enormous controversy because it was going to teach respect for sexual as well as racial and ethnic diversity, which led the School Board to exclude such issues from its agenda. Likewise, Project Ten in Los Angeles, which seeks to offer counseling and support to gay youth in the schools, has also been denounced across the nation and become a centerpiece of antigay organizing. At the state level there have been regular attacks on gay curriculum in state legislatures. The vote by the faculty senate of the University of Wisconsin–Milwaukee to establish a gay studies certificate program, for instance, was denounced in the state legislature and in a vicious newspaper campaign.

Even more ominously, the anti-gay-rights referendum campaigns launched around the nation in the early 1990s often targeted gay-positive education. Some did so only implicitly, but others—like the initiative defeated in Oregon and one proposed in Washington State— would have explicitly prohibited any state moneys from being spent on gay-positive instruction or counseling. If such initiatives were passed, state schools could not officially recognize gay student groups, could not put gay studies books in the library, could not hire gay studies scholars or even bring gay scholars to campus, and could not offer courses with any serious gay content. Even when these campaigns lose, they are dangerous because they become the occasion for the right wing to flood a state with antigay hate literature, which makes the linkages between antihomosexualism and all the old targets of the Right abundantly clear.

Much of that hate literature picks up on old anti-Semitic stereotypes, depicting lesbians and especially gay men as rich white cosmopolitans who live in big cities and control the media. These campaigns also masterfully manipulate white racism by demanding that gays be given no "special rights" or "minority rights." In the days before it was politically acceptable to attack affirmative action directly, this formulation tapped into the white antipathy to affirmative action and to minority rights of any sort, and I think helped lay the groundwork for the growth of anti-affirmative-action rhetoric that we are hearing now. It also helped the right wing mobilize some support in other minority communities from people deeply concerned about the barrage of attacks on their hard-won and all too fragile gains. This makes it clear, I think, that the coming fight to defend affirmative action on campuses deserves the support of all gay academics, not only because it is right in itself (which of course it is), but because the growing attacks on minority rights today are so closely linked to attacks on gay rights.

We may have turned a corner in the fight against antigay state initiatives, since in the 1994 elections most of them did not even bolster enough support to make it to the ballot, although they continue to pose a danger. Even more dangerous right now is the national mood, with right-wing zealots from the most conservative parts of the country having taken control of Congress. As long as there are Jesse Helmses in Congress we can expect continuing antigay education amendments. Right wingers continue to pour through the files of the NEA, looking for examples of support for gay projects with which to further damage the reputation of the Endowment. And the National Endowment for the Humanities seems to have responded by avoiding funding potentially controversial gay projects. No academic should expect to get federal support for a gay studies project anytime soon. The right wing is already so powerful that it can prevent such support for gay research. The forces of censorship are riding high.

If it is an exciting time to be involved in lesbian and gay studies, then, it is also a sobering time. The two are connected, of course. It is always important to remember that reactionary movements are reacting *to* something, and in this case they are reacting to very real changes that the gay and feminist movements have brought about in the gender and sexual order of this society—and in the new ways of thinking they have made possible. Indeed, it seems to me that as gay academics we are doing a number of things that it is perfectly understandable the right wing wants to suppress. The stakes for them—as for us—are very real. I want to talk about two of them.

Suppressing intellectual freedom is important to the right wing in part because they want to control history, because controlling history is important to anyone who wants to control the present or future. Indeed, our work in gay studies, as well as feminist studies and other kinds of multicultural studies, seems dangerous to many conservatives in part because it challenges one of their most treasured and effective cultural strategies: their claim that their vision of the best social order has the sanction of history, which they usually call tradition. Of course, tradition alone should never be a sufficient rationale for a public policy. The Supreme Court rationalized its decision to uphold state sodomy statutes in the notorious *Bowers v. Hardwick* decision in part by evoking the history of centuries of antigay hostility in the Christian West, as if this could justify such an infringement of rights. And more than a century earlier, the Supreme Court upheld the right of the states to sanction slavery in its notorious Dred Scott decision in part by invoking the history of centuries of slavery in the Christian West.

Tradition shouldn't govern our decisions about the kind of society we want to live in. But it does carry weight in the culture wars, which is why history has been so hotly contested in recent years, from the *Enola Gay* controversy at the Smithsonian, to the controversy over instituting so-called history standards in public education. We face this most often in the right wing's inaccurate—but highly effective—invocation of the supposed domestic bliss of the American nuclear family in the 1950s as the traditional and "natural" model of the family life to which we should aspire. Their very invocation of this tradition is contradictory, of course, since they are insisting on the need for social policies to construct a nuclear family artificially, at the very moment when they claim family to be a natural creation.

But the invocation of tradition becomes even more tenuous when we look at the actual history of the so-called traditional nuclear family of the 1950s in the way that several feminist historians have. It turns out not to have been so natural at all, but the product of intensive social engineering. First there were the *welfare* policies such as the GI Bill and the Veterans' Administration housing policies that made it possible for veterans—who constituted virtually an entire generation of white men—to purchase detached single-family homes in segregated all-white suburbs, often for nothing more than a one dollar downpayment—and which refused to subsidize the purchase of anything else. Then there was the provision of the GI welfare bill that paid for the education of those men, and sent them generous welfare checks every month to pay for their housing and their living expenses while they were in school. Then there were the *affirmative action* programs for men coming out of the war. The GI Bill made it so lucrative for schools to enroll veterans (by giving them direct subsidies for the construction of veteran student housing) that literally hundreds of thousands of women who had enrolled in American colleges in 1945 were forced out of school so that men could take their place. Then there were the affirmative action programs at work, which forced hundreds of thousands of other women out of jobs in heavy industry at the end of the war—many of them black—so that men returning from the war could have those jobs.[1]

In other words, the nuclear family constellation of the 1950s was engineered by a series of welfare programs and affirmative action programs that gave white men access to the best jobs at the ground level of the American economy just as it was launching into its vast postwar expansion and that made it extremely difficult for women to support themselves without a man. That family was located in the suburbs by a series of housing welfare programs that, for all their generosity, refused to support home purchases anywhere else. Of course I don't mean to suggest that none of those people would have gotten married and moved into nice houses with yards without these policies, but I *do* mean to suggest that this sort of social engineering left many of them with few alternatives—and that the extraordinary demonization of homosexuals during the postwar era left many people afraid to pursue those few alternatives.

The idea that this socially engineered 1950s family—this white, suburban family on welfare—represents the traditional, natural family becomes even more tenuous when we realize, as feminist and gay historians have pointed out, that the decade of the 1950s was an utter anomaly in American history—that a higher percentage of the American population married in that decade than in any other decade in American history, including the colonial period, and that throughout much of the nineteenth and early twentieth centuries 30 to 40 percent of all men and women over the age of fifteen were unmarried at any given time.

The appeal to an antihomosexual tradition becomes even more tenuous when historians show, as I did in my book *Gay New York*, that many of those unmarried men, and even many of the married ones, interacted with queer men openly and publicly and with the support and encouragement of their peers, and even had sex with them; that there were saloons—open to the public on the busiest commercial streets of the Italian Lower East Side of Manhattan—where so-called normal Italian immigrant working men went to buy the sexual services of young male prostitutes or to watch the show put on by the fairies who gathered there and entertained the "normal" men with their campy repartee; that the records of the police—not just the wishful memories of older gay men—show that sailors regularly went to Times Square to pick up gay men and that gay men regularly went to sailor bars to pick up straight men; that whatever else it took for a sailor or an Italian immigrant worker or many another man to claim the mantle of normality in the early twentieth century, it was not necessary for them to claim the mantle of heterosexuality; that heterosexuality—no less than homosexuality or bisexuality—is a socially constructed and historically specific identity; and that, in an important sense, *there is no tradition of heterosexuality in this society.*

As even this brief excursion into recent American history suggests, one reason that the right wing is so worried about intellectual freedom and rigorous scholarship on American history and culture is precisely that such scholarship offers a fundamental challenge to their appeals to "tradition" in support of their social policies. When people appeal to tradition they are almost always projecting the present onto the past—not their perception of the reality of the present, but their conception of what an *ideal version* of the present would look like.

When they appeal to tradition, then, such advocates are really making a case for the future, and the possibility that we will be in their future is what really frightens them. We are engaged, as both they and we should realize, in a deep struggle over the future of this society— over social reproduction in the broadest sense—and that is why we, as academics, are not and cannot be just observers and commentators on the sidelines, but are necessarily on one of the forefronts of that struggle. Teachers and scholars, after all, educate their children, and the control of children is one of the central issues in this struggle.

Since the end of World War II antigay forces have regularly demonized homosexuals as child molesters. Waves of panic about the homosexual menace swept through large states and small in the postwar decade, prompting massive police crackdowns on gay bars and cruising areas, and attempts to suppress gay political activity and free speech. Indeed, as I will show in more detail in my next book, it was during this period that the image of the homosexual as a psychopathic child molester was created.

This powerful image has continued to inspire some of the most successful organizing against gay people, from Anita Bryant's successful 1977 campaign to "save our children" from a gay rights law in Dade County, Florida, which launched the current wave of organized antigay reaction; to the most recent efforts by Jesse Helms to censor any gaypositive instructional materials in the nation's primary and secondary schools.

Children are almost always the focus of such hate-mongering campaigns, because children are a powerful force for the forces of hate to mobilize around. Concerns about children tie together people's most broadly conceived concerns about the security and reproduction of the social order and their deepest and most intimate concerns about whether their own children will be safe—and will reproduce their way of life. Hence the tendency of dominant groups so often to stigmatize outsider groups—be they Jews, gypsies, or homosexuals—as child stealers or child molesters, since this scapegoating allows them to express and to mobilize people's deepest fears about social and familial reproduction.

Now at one level the fears of antigay activists are utterly groundless, of course. We aren't going to molest or seduce their children. In that respect those children have got a lot more to fear at home than they do at school. But they are right in another sense. *We do want to change their children.* And by our presence as openly gay educators whose every word and action challenges the demonization of homosexuals and bisexuals, *we will change their children.* As educators, gay and straight, who express our respect for gay people and who show students how homosexuality has been a part of our culture and other cultures, and who give people the skills and the predisposition to develop a critical analysis of their world, *we will change their children.* When we say we want to educate young people, we are saying, like all other educators, that we want to change them.

We are not saying that we want to change them all into homosexuals, though we do want to make it easier for gay kids to figure out their sexuality. But we do want to change all people into people who accept and respect sexual diversity, because that will make our lives and the lives of gay children and those other children's lives better.

Response?

How do we respond to this assault? I'm not going to presume to offer a general plan for the movement, but I do want to suggest some of the things I think we can do as academics.

Part of what we have to do is to fight for our rights as full members of the university community, which means fighting for domestic partnership benefits, support for gay students, and support for gay studies. There are also times when scholars can offer support to activists working outside the academy. But while work on specific public policy questions can be crucial, I also think that a wider range of *intellectual* work is also crucial, and that we have to be prepared for the fact that some of our work will conflict with the short-term political agendas of some activists. Very few activists outside of Queer Nation (or even in it) have much enthusiasm, for instance, for the ways in which many of us subject the idea of a unitary, transcultural, and transhistorical gay identity and subculture to critical examination.

But, at the same time, I also think we need to think more about some of our research priorities. It strikes me as troubling that after a decade of dazzling theoretical ruminations and cultural studies, we have a more complex and nuanced understanding of Madonna's popularity than of Reagan's popularity.

As a result, most of us did not anticipate the conservative resurgence in the 1994 congressional elections, and most of us still don't understand how the right wing continues to triumph so decisively. You would think we would: we had twelve years of Ronald Reagan and George Bush in which to figure it out. But most of us didn't try. Many academics fought them and ridiculed them—an easy and satisfying thing to do—but not enough of us tried to understand them. By contrast, Stuart Hall and the other leading theorists of cultural studies in Britain devoted much of their work in the 1980s to analyzing Thatcherism. They didn't stop Thatcherism, but at least they tried to come to terms with it, and they developed a much fuller analysis than queer cultural theorists in the United States have of the ways in which the right wing has been able to mobilize the politics of race, class, gender, and sexuality into wide popular support for a reactionary political movement.

There are good reasons for us to have focused so much attention on the sphere of popular culture. It is one of the arenas where the gay movement has had most success, and it is the site of tremendously significant and consequential cultural struggle. There have been moments when we put that analysis to good use. The generation going into graduate school in the mid-1980s was the same generation that launched the militant direct action politics of Queer Nation and ACT UP, and many graduate students were—and still are—personally involved in this sort of political work. The analysis of cultural representation and of the power of regimes of knowledge to define and shape the world, which lies at the heart of cultural studies, played a critical role in activists' thinking about the AIDS crisis. Analysis of how the media and the government attempted to construct the crisis and to use it to stigmatize and attack gay men, drug users, inner-city dwellers, Haitians, and other people of color was and continues to be a critical part of AIDS political work, and it has laid the basis for some of the most imaginative efforts by ACT UP and other groups to contest those representations.

The extraordinary vitality of that moment, though, in which cultural studies informed activism and was informed by activism, seems to me to have passed. And in the last several years, the right wing has demonstrated that it, too, is acutely aware of the political significance of the struggle over cultural representation, and that, in fact, it can be much more adept at playing cultural politics than we are, that it has a deeper and more sophisticated grasp of how to manipulate cultural politics than we do. If nothing else, this is one of the grim lessons of Willie Horton and Save Our Children.

This is the crisis we face. And in the context of this crisis, it is crucial for all of us to do more to connect our work to the broadest political and intellectual questions facing our culture today. As I've already said, you need to do this to get jobs. But, even more important, we all need to do this if, collectively, we are going to understand and overcome the challenges before us.

Notes

1. The account of postwar American gender history in the following paragraphs draws on several sources: Susan Hartmann, *The Homefront and Beyond: American Women in the 1940s* (Boston: Twayne, 1982); Stephanie Coontz, *The Way We Never Were: American Families and the Nostalgia Trap* (New York: Basic Books, 1992); Elaine Tyler May, *Homeward Bound: American Families in the Cold War Era* (New York: Basic Books, 1988); and Joanne Meyerowitz, ed., *Not June Cleaver: Women and Gender in Postwar America, 1945–1960* (Philadelphia: Temple University Press, 1994).

14

The Final Frontier
A Roundtable Discussion

Moderated by Tania Modleski

On July 11, 1997, keynote speakers Sue-Ellen Case, John Rechy, and George Chauncey (who joined us via speakerphone) reconvened at the University of Southern California to consider what two years had done to shift and shape "queer frontiers." The roundtable, joined by coeditors Martin Dupuis, Martin Meeker, Karin Quimby, Debra Silverman, and Rosemary Weatherston, produced an open dialogue about the increasing presence of and continued resistance to queer theory and identities in academics, politics and popular culture. Subjects covered in the wide-ranging discussion include the gay and lesbian debate over queer politics, the relationship between second-wave queer theorists and preceding generations of lesbian and gay activists, the isolation of sexual politics from other civil rights movements, the effects of increased queer visibility in mainstream media, and the commodification and popularization of *queer*. This examination of the present queer moment raises keen questions and observations that portend the future of queer frontiers.

TANIA MODLESKI: We are gathered together two years after the landmark "Queer Frontiers" conference with keynote speakers Sue-Ellen Case, George Chauncey, and John Rechy to discuss some of the many changes that have occurred in queer politics and cultures since the original conference took place. Since we are beginning this discussion two years after each of you delivered your keynote address, I'd like to begin by asking whether the views regarding queer theory, commodification, and activism expressed in each of your keynote addresses have changed, and, if so, how?
SUE-ELLEN CASE: Actually, I feel much less challenged by the notion of queer theory than I did two years ago. As a term, *queer* seems to have fallen into more disuse in the circles that I'm in. I spent the fall teaching

at a few universities in Europe, and the students and scholars I met over there didn't have anything to do with "queer theory" as we know it in the United States. They felt it was an American term, and didn't serve their needs at all. So, whereas the term *queer* felt very oppressive to me a couple of years ago, and challenging to a certain kind of political position, it seems less oppressive to me now. I feel that it's gone a little bit out of fashion and it has less power.

MARTIN MEEKER: Could you situate these circles and communities of scholars a little, specifically in terms of their geographical location and fields of expertise—and maybe speak to why you think they aren't particularly influenced by the term *queer*?

CASE: I'm referring to the communities I interacted with while I was at the University of Stockholm, Trinity College in Dublin, and one of the campuses of the University of London. What I found in those communities is the sense that *queer* represents just another facet of American cultural imperialism—we ship out our blue jeans, we ship out our politics—and there is necessarily some resistance to that. Their ideas of homosexual, or gay and/or lesbian—whatever term they happen to use for their own historical and material conditions—didn't seem to be very influenced by what seems the specifically American notion of queer, although there was some queer tradition in England through ACT UP. All in all though, they felt that *queer* was simply a kind of academic term and that it had lost its currency in the activist movements. Earlier, in the 1980s, it was useful to create an umbrella term for AIDS activism. Although I think the term ACT UP served better. As a critical term, however, it had no referent. By the time it had a critical reception, it had lost the activist one. I didn't do a survey or anything, but this was the impression I had.

ROSEMARY WEATHERSTON: Would you say that queer activism still exists in the United States, or have queer practices pretty much become scholarly pursuits cut off from activism?

CASE: Gee, I'm not ready to answer that. Does somebody else want to?

MODLESKI: George, what's your impression? Do you feel queer theory and queer scholarship are currently divorced from queer activism?

GEORGE CHAUNCEY: I think that's hard to say, because what queer theory—or for that matter *queer*—means is so incredibly varied across academic culture and political culture today. You see a lot of people who call themselves queer, in effect developing the same kind of critique of established gay and lesbian institutions that in an earlier generation people who were self-identified as radical lesbians or gay men would have developed. In other contexts, it becomes a sort of pseudonym for *gay* or *lesbian*. In other contexts, I think it really represents a generational shift in consciousness. But, I'd be reluctant to generalize because I think that it is a term of such varied meanings.

MODLESKI: Maybe we could pursue this notion of the generational shift in consciousness because it really gets to the heart of this anthology. One of the major claims made by the editors of this volume is that it highlights and represents "second-wave queer theory"; not even second-wave gay studies, but second-wave queer *theory*. I was wondering what "the second wave" meant for those who came up with this notion, and what it might mean for those people who have problems using the word *queer* at all.

WEATHERSTON: There are actually several ideas behind our use of the phrase "second-wave queers," one being the changing characteristics of people who now self-identify as "queers." A key question being raised and addressed in the anthology is, what happens when new people begin to affiliate with the queer movement, people such as "straight queers," or transgender or transvestite individuals? What are the implications when people of color identify with the term *queer* despite the fact that it has traditionally been seen as a largely white movement? Part of what we are looking at are the implications of this broader association or self-identification. Another idea behind the notion of a second generation of queer scholars and activists is the fact that there now exists a significant number of scholars, activists, artists, et cetera, who have "grown up" with both the terminology and concepts of both lesbian and gay politics and cultures, and with the terminology and concepts of queer.

MEEKER: I think these types of concerns were also reflected in the conference's keynote speeches and subsequent essays, specifically in their attention to what we might call first and second generations of lesbian and gay studies. Each of the keynote addresses are, in fact, analyses of generational differences and their consequences. Collectively, they may be read as a critique of, or even a series of stern warnings directed at, a new generation of people doing lesbian and gay studies or queer studies. In different ways, Case, Rechy, and Chauncey each issue warnings about how we—as mostly young (or young in the field), self-identified queer scholars—are situating ourselves in the academy as a new, if not a second, generation. For instance, Case cautions against a too eager embrace of "queer" identity; Rechy makes a plea, on behalf of an earlier, now stereotyped generation, that the past may hold examples of resistance and style that are still useful today; and Chauncey, while less concerned with social or sexual identities per se, urges this next generation of scholars not to define their professional identities too rigidly as, say, "queer theorists." Maybe the panelists want to reflect upon how your essays are addressing the second generation and if, indeed, warnings are being issued?

MODLESKI: John, I'd be interested in your response to the questions of different "waves" and different self-identifications, because you are not in the academy and you directly address the notion of generations in your essay.

JOHN RECHY: I do believe that a major factor in our lingering oppression has been in the names that we men choose to call ourselves, allow ourselves to be called. *Gay* was offensive to many of us. We even preferred *homosexual. Gay* makes us seem, in the original definition of the word, only flippant. Christopher Isherwood said the collective noun *gays* made us sound like "bliss ninnies." When AIDS emerged, the word was coupled, and we heard the terrible phrase "gay death," powerfully judgmental. Now, the word *queer* emerges. But other than referring to it in quotations, I will never use the term *queer* to identify myself or any other homosexual. It's a word that my generation—and my companion, who's twenty-five years younger than I am, feels the same way—will never hear without evoked connotations—of violence, gay-bashings, arrest, murder. The negative power of that word is such that I believe it will impede us from moving forward. There's already a terrible separation on the homosexual front between young people and older people, and that word will separate us further: "You're gay, I'm queer."

MODLESKI: Could I ask you about that in connection with your keynote essay? Because the essay is a defense of stereotypes, and there are certain stereotypes you want to embrace, that a lot of people, as you point out, would find offensive. At the same time, it appears, there are words that you see, like *queer,* that you don't think are redeemable. How does one draw the line between stereotypes that one does want to claim or reclaim, and those that one needs to keep at a distance?

RECHY: *Queer* was used only among ourselves, when we were in non-hostile territory, the way that black people use *nigger* with each other, the way perhaps that lesbians use *dyke* with each other. More popular than *queer* was the word *queen,* which was quite grand. I don't know why we gay men don't call ourselves "kings."

MODLESKI: Where's that leave us women?

CASE: Men have been calling themselves kings for years.

RECHY: You have *lesbian.* I wish we had something that good. I've suggested *trojan.**

*Readers should know that during this conversation, we were seated fifty yards from a statue of the University of Southern California's "mascot"—a beefy Trojan warrior.

CASE: "Trojan?"

RECHY: Yeah.

CASE: What's her name, Ellen. Miss TV-coming-out person said she hated the word *lesbian* and she would never use it because it sounded like an illness or something.

RECHY: Well, *lesbian* has a historical and a mythological connotation. It's wonderful. I wish we had gotten the term before you did.

MODLESKI: George, what would be your reaction to the idea of different generations? It sounds like we're almost talking about four generations now: the two generations within people who associate themselves with gays and lesbians, then first generation queers, and, if you accept the anthology's premise, second generation queers. Have you seen evidence of these splits in the two years since your keynote address, in which you were, perhaps, offering warnings to other generations?

CHAUNCEY: I think that we are witnessing a generational transformation, which is to say an historical transformation. However, because we tend not to think in historical terms, the way the debate often gets played out is through a series of ahistorical critiques in which people often talk across generational divides and consciousnesses that are difficult to cross. Much of the current queer movement and queer consciousness was made possible by the success and the courageous struggles of the lesbian and gay movement of the previous generation. The movement has succeeded to a much greater degree than any of us imagined possible in terms of increasing lesbian and gay visibility and the integration of lesbians and gay men into the dominant culture, even though the success of this integration is still highly contested throughout the country and the country is deeply polarized over these issues. But a measure of the real degree of success is that the gay political project has been producing a series of critiques of itself. Part of that has been a kind of radical gay—now called "queer"—critique of the cost of those successes of the gay movements. For instance, the fact that wealthy, white men tend to be the most effective political actors in the established political structures, and so have come to dominate many gay organizations and much of the so-called official gay political agenda; or that a high degree of commercialization of gay culture has been made possible by the success of the gay movement in decriminalizing gay businesses and gay meeting places and gay visibility. One consequence of this has been that gay businessmen have increasingly come to establish the terms of the modalities, the locations of lesbian and gay culture, much as Sue-Ellen pointed out in her keynote address. So, there has been tremendous success in many aspects of the gay movement, but it's come at a terrific cost as well. A new generation of queer activists—some of that new generation—are unwilling to accept those costs.

KARIN QUIMBY: At the same time the younger generation is critiquing past costs, would you say they, or we, are also building on past successes? Do you think any new possibilities are being brought to the table?

CHAUNCEY: I see a shift in consciousness made possible by the successes of the gay movement that has to do with new possibilities of sexual consciousness and practices. I see this, for example, in the emergence of bisexuality as a much more common subject position and political position amongst younger people than would have been the case fifteen years ago. I also see this in the growing possibilities for people to explore a variety of sexual subjectivities and positions and to not feel as forced to identify themselves as one way or another, in a way that my generation did because of the kind of stigmatization of homosexuality. And so there's a sense in which the very success of the gay movement in destigmatizing homosexuality has created a new kind of cultural moment. Which in the end is somewhat disconcerting to the people who created that moment because it's not producing necessarily the same stable gay identities and gay culture that they might have hoped for. But I think that it's in part an effect of their success and that it is a new cultural moment.

CASE: I still find it interesting that you see the shift as generational. About a year ago I taught, along with Eve Sedgwick, an intensive course in what was called at that time "Queer Identities." The point is that there wasn't a generational difference between me and Eve Sedgwick—we'd both "come of age" as feminist scholars. In that class, I'd brought up the fact that there is a certain kind of coalitional consciousness that came through women's studies, where you understand you have to do some work around issues of race and class in order to create conditional coalitions. No umbrella term would have been acceptable—not even a permanent coalition; only through antiracist, antihomophobic work together might you find a way to work across differences toward specific shared goals. Eve's response was to categorize old-fashioned coalition as a simply additive process, "because that's sort of one-plus-one," and to assert a greater interest in "affiliation." To which my reply was, "I think what you're talking about is identification." Coalitions, in contrast, are built upon politically constructed identities that are useful as a kind of placeholder in the negotiation of differences.

WEATHERSTON: What do you mean by "identification"?

CASE: One of the things that has surprised me about the queer political movement is that one wants to identify with a certain position. That's very different from coalition politics where I don't try to identify with African American women, for example. But *queer* means that somehow we are able in this room to identify with one another through a kind of sexual slippage. I found that a very interesting sort of politics, that somehow we were all going to be the same, or united by a similarity or a possibility of oscillation of sexual practices, rather than coming together through differences. Yet I think that this slippage reveals an ongoing problem between lesbians and gay men, in that it's not so easy to make that affiliation. One just can't presume identification, and it very often breaks down. It's broken down in Pride parades and lots of other activist places, because there's a certain amount of work that has to be done about our differences that isn't done in that queer camp. I guess I'm saying that the shift that the editorial collective has identified might *also* be generational, but I don't think it's *only* generational; there are radical differences among some of us in that same generation.

CHAUNCEY: I certainly would agree with that. That's partly why I said at the beginning that I'm reluctant to talk about *queer* in monolithic terms, because I think its political balance varies so much from situation to situation. And that part of it, I do think, is a kind of generational shift, and maybe even in the context of what you said, a shift in what kinds of differences are seen as particularly salient.

CASE: I would answer that by stating that I feel politically closer to many young women who are in Lesbian Avengers—who are in their late twenties and are part of what we are referring to as the second wave—than I do to some other people of my so-called generation who differ with me politically. So, again, I'm not sure if the difference is generational.

CHAUNCEY: I would still argue that part of it is generational, but that's by no means the only sort of cultural or political valence of *queer*. And I do agree with you that it can often signify a much broader kind of political difference that is intragenerational.

RECHY: I don't see why there's such a pervasive desire to bring everyone together—anymore than heterosexuals are brought together—other than through our mutual battles and struggles. As far as giving ourselves a collective name, I feel pressured by the academic faction to celebrate so-called "queer theory." This is going to sound terribly arrogant. In 1977, in a book that I wrote called *The Sexual Outlaw*, much of what is now being bandied around as new "queer theory" is set out.[1] I think gay people are too concerned about giving a collective name to what is quite individual. When artists are asked to toe a line of any sort, there's danger. I think this type of "mandating" is occurring from "queer studies" programs.

MODLESKI: How have you felt this pressure to "toe a line," and from where has the pressure emanated?

RECHY: I have felt it in the insistence on the word *queer* instead of *gay*. In the essay by me included in this collection, I did not accept some editorial suggestions that I adjust, even change, certain references from *gay* to *queer*. Holding the artist to any kind of political nomenclature or attitude is really impossible. Yes, I do feel pressured to uphold certain views currently held by academics involved in programs that emphasize the politics of identity. An example: In a few academic circles the question used to be asked whether I could be considered a Chicano writer—my mother was Mexican. The assumption was that I couldn't be a gay writer and a Chicano writer. I've read criticism of my work that really baffles me, criticism from the sole perspective of what is at the time politically acceptable.

MODLESKI: In the specific case of lesbian and gay, or of queer academics, though, I have to wonder if the ability to exert even this relative type of pressure extends beyond the confines of a few, selected academic departments. The editors of this anthology seem to think so. They're arguing that subjects like the social construction of sexuality are beginning to permeate a wide range of disciplines, including those not immediately associated with the study of sexuality, like architecture. They claim that for the up-and-coming generation of scholars, issues of sexuality have always been a part of the intellectual fabric. Yet, when I read George's paper in which he talks about how marginal gay studies has been in the university, and I think about my own experience of how few discussions there are in any courses about issues having to do with sexuality in particular—gender, yes, but not sexuality in particular—I wonder if it is really true that there is a body of scholars who, as the collective puts it, have "grown up" with both gay and lesbian, and queer, discourses of gender and sexuality? If you believe this, why keep the phrase "grown up" in quotations marks? I mean, this is great news if it is true, but this has not been my experience, in the classroom especially.

MEEKER: That assertion arose from the realization that in the 1980s and early 1990s there was a proliferation of gay and lesbian publications— of theory, of cultural studies, of histories—so much that we can't possibly keep up with it all. I think this situation differs greatly from the 1970s, when one could probably read almost everything that was published about sexuality from an academic press. With this proliferation of written materials came college courses on gay and lesbian literature, then history, and now queer theory in its countless manifestations. However, most young scholars very likely came to queer theory on their own by reading everything we could get our hands on. Now that queer theory has moved into the classroom it seems possible to imagine that other scholars will "grow up" with queer theory. Instead of having to seek out queer scholarship and queer mentors, this new generation, we believe, has better access to both. Sitting in a seminar room and working ideas out with other scholars seems a completely new and empowering experience. This, perhaps, is a marker of the generational difference we've been talking about in that the so-called first wave paved the way for younger scholars who will have more of a possibility of taking graduate or undergraduate courses in gay/lesbian studies or queer studies, and of studying with mentors.

MARTIN DUPUIS: In terms of a generational shift, when the "Queer Frontiers" conference was put on in 1995, it was the Fifth Annual National Gay, Lesbian, and Bisexual Graduate Student Conference. When the conference was first held in 1990, there weren't many gay and lesbian graduate student conferences. Today, there are so many of them that you can pick and choose which to attend. So, even in the last two years, it seems there's been an incredible increase in the amount of, and opportunities for, presenting research in gay and lesbian issues. There has also been an incredible change in popular culture. We've seen a shift: now when Ellen comes out on her television show, it's considered a newsworthy event. There are more gay and lesbian elected public officials, more and more gay and lesbian characters being readily accepted by the popular culture.

WEATHERSTON: I would agree with the idea that a new type of "critical" or "near-critical mass" is being reached in both cultural and academic arenas. ACT UP recently celebrated its ten-year anniversary. The Los Angeles gay/lesbian film festival celebrated its fifteenth year of bringing new queer cinema to the screen. I think we keep the idea of our generation having "grown up" in quotation marks to emphasize both the increasing visibility of queer culture, and an uncertainty about what exactly are the implications of that new visibility. I suggest a critical mass, but I still need to ask, critical for whom? The term *queer* is firmly a part of the conversations we have, conversations that have shifted but that were begun years instead of months ago. At the same time, though, does our "comfort" with the term *queer* merely offer a new subject position? Or, does it have an impact on what it means to have had a queer history? These are important but troubling questions.

RECHY: I think a main factor that separates our generations is our respective views of history. We have a very long oral history, but a very short recorded history. Younger people, though still having to deal with discrimination and prejudice, don't even know that, not too long ago, just to enter a gay bar, to dance with a member of the same sex, exposed you to arrest. That younger generation was not on Hollywood Boulevard when police roundups of "queers" occurred, cannot even relate to the fact that for inviting a consensual sex act, usually through entrapment, you could be imprisoned, sentenced to years in prison if the charge claimed an actual sex act—or forced into gruesome forms of "aversion therapy." Victims still exist from that time. Gay men arrested decades ago, men now in their sixties, are still required by lingering laws to register as "sex offenders" every time they move or leave the city. Leap forward, to a central element of historical confusion, the arbitrary demarcation of generations that emerged out of the emphasis on the Stonewall riots—before it, all repressed; after it, all liberated. I think that's nonsense. Much pride and defiance occurred before Stonewall and beyond New York; and much self-hatred, unexplored, has been left unattended. It may sound flippant to say that the emphasis on Stonewall emerged in significant part because it occurred in New York; but it's a fact that to too many people an event has to occur in New York to be considered important or to have a significant cultural impact.

CASE: Especially if it's theater.

RECHY: In California in the fifties we had the Black Cat raid and weeks of defiance, gay men and queens heckling cops. So many other "riots" before Stonewall. The emphasis on that one admittedly important event to the exclusion of all others contributes to the sense of separation between generations. The word *queer* does the same thing.

QUIMBY: John's comment about the persecution, our nonexperience of persecution as a younger generation, does indeed separate us a great deal. Having grown up, come out in 1982, and then come to do graduate work in gay studies in 1992, I have felt almost completely free from persecution as a lesbian. And certainly in the academy, here at USC, I felt utterly supported to do gay and lesbian work. So I think that is a real difference in experience.

MODLESKI: I thought that there was still a lot of persecution going on. One of my graduate students recently took a job in Denver, where he was the victim of a vicious gay-bashing with a brick—all this in a seemingly progressive urban area.

RECHY: There's more persecution than anyone acknowledges.

MODLESKI: So, maybe you can say that in certain enclaves, like gay graduate studies at USC, there is freedom from persecution, but step one foot out of these enclaves and it's a different story.

DEBRA SILVERMAN: Such freedom is often a question of geographical location.

RECHY: Not entirely. In Silverlake, just a few miles north of USC, punks still beat up gay people while shouting, "Queers!" I don't think they mean that in the sense of queer theory.

CASE: Maybe we should suggest that the younger generation have affairs with the older generation and in this way, we could have an intimate exchange.

RECHY: I wouldn't want that.

DUPUIS: Even in the academy, though, as George raises in his essay, there's still a very serious question about the marginalization of gay/lesbian scholarship. Most of us have been on the job market, or will be on the job market soon; I was hired as a professor *despite* my gay scholarship, not for it. Most of my research has been on gay and lesbian politics and gay/lesbian litigation and law strategies, and it really was not something that the department into which I was hired embraced.

CHAUNCEY: The recent incident at Yale is indicative of how academic institutions regard gay and lesbian studies or queer theory.[2] They are willing to entertain supporting it—or rather the idea of supporting it—on a short-term and ad-hoc basis, but are still very reluctant to invest in a long-term support of this sort of inquiry. They were willing to use money to hire people on one-year visiting professorships, but, like Yale, would refuse a gift of two or three million dollars to establish an endowed chair in lesbian and gay studies. That's pretty remarkable when a university is willing to give up two or three million dollars.

CASE: The Yale incident came to mind when Marty [Martin Dupuis] was talking about going on the job market having written a queer theory dissertation. I wonder about that job market.

SILVERMAN: I wonder if we might shift the conversation away from the question of generations and the ever-vexing job market. As I've been listening to the conversation, I've been thinking about the ways in which the term *queer* might be becoming, in some sense, an apolitical term. This thought comes from the discussions that we had earlier about how queer has become an overarching, leveling affiliation where you group a whole bunch of people under an umbrella and bring them together. The problems associated with this type of strategy are addressed in all of the keynote essays. *Queer* might have started as something that was connected to activism, but is it still connected? Marty's comment about Ellen "coming out" on television triggered this train of thought: one could argue that Ellen's coming out is not exactly a political or shocking thing at this historical moment. I'm thinking also about our comfort in talking about queerness and queer theory in the academy, sitting in a university located in Los Angeles. Have certain coincidences or privileges of location, and certain tendencies toward ahistoricism resulted in a comfort level which depoliticizes the whole notion of something called "queer theory?" Even those individuals in the academy who insist on the radicalism and resistance inherent in the concept of queer tend to cite the same canon of queer theorists. In fact there's one person who contributes to the anthology—Michael Bacchus—who writes about how important it is to cite the proper queer theorists, and to cite the proper queer theorist citing the proper queer theorist, and how this sort of creates a comfort canon. I wonder if other people see the term *queer* becoming apolitical?

MODLESKI: I think that's a really interesting question in light of a recent classroom experience of mine. I'm always sure that most of my students are homophobic and if they don't express it, then I push them to. They are reluctant, but I want to drag out their attitudes. In this particular class, one of the students who is very, very thoughtful and introspective said, "Well, there is a sense in which in high school we're talked to about it [homosexuality] and we have a kind of liberal relation to it, and sometimes that prevents us from really going deeper and finding out what's underneath." I think that anecdote supports Debra's sense that there's a comfort level, but also that underneath there is a seething cauldron.

CASE: Well, I live one hour outside Los Angeles in Riverside and it's not comfortable out there, let me tell you. It's terrible.

MODLESKI: Even at the most superficial level.

CASE: At the most superficial level. You wouldn't dare express what we are discussing today—it's like the fifties out there. That's one hour outside of Los Angeles; it's still in California, it's not the Midwest. I think there's an urban-class presumption of comfort that doesn't even go one hour down the freeway.

SILVERMAN: On the most superficial level, I often experience a kind of quizzical dissonance when I'm sitting in a stadium full of baseball fans, for example, and they're all dancing to the Village People's "YMCA." It's interesting to me because gay and lesbian visibility can create a liberal veneer that masks or covers up larger problems.

CHAUNCEY: But most of the fans have no idea what they're doing and they don't care. We shouldn't assume that they do. It's just another example of how those gay codes can still work effectively. I think it's clear that we live in a society increasingly polarized around gay issues, as around many women's issues, issues of race, and so forth. There are places where there have been really dramatic increases in not just tolerance—but acceptance of and support for lesbians and gay men. And other areas of the country where people are horrified to see that happening. There are still people who come into L.A. to beat up queers. But at least in L.A. and New York and Chicago and some other cities such behavior is now recognized as a hate crime and as something that local politicians have to speak out against, just as they would speak out against racist violence or antiwomen violence. Yet, there are other parts of the country where judges are still letting teenage boys go when they murder gay men and lesbians. Basically, those kids are just doing what the judges themselves would have done when they were young.

RECHY: I was the object of a hate crime just a few months ago. Two punks robbed me in the middle of the day while everyone ignored the matter. I was advised by a cop to simply drop the matter. I didn't. If it had not been that I had some money, some clout, the two punks would never have come to trial and been sentenced to jail. If you have laws and they're not carried out, especially by a persistently homophobic police force, which we have, then the laws are ineffective. Most often it's a real struggle to assure that laws involving hate crimes are upheld.

MEEKER: I think our discussions of queer identities versus gay/lesbian identities, academics versus nonacademics, or one generation in opposition to another represent only one dimension of the debates taking place today. For instance, a debate receiving much print as of late seems to be more ideological and less identity oriented than the few we have discussed thus far (though this characterization should also be up to debate). Here I am referring to the often heated conversation that has ensued between queer theorists like Michael Warner and the assorted sex radicals of Sex Panic! in contrast to conservative gay writers such as Gabriel Rotello, Andrew Sullivan, and Bruce Bawer—and to a certain extent Michelangelo Signoreli and Larry Kramer.[3]

MODLESKI: Martin, for those who aren't familiar with these debates, could you briefly describe what's going on?

MEEKER: Like I said, though there are elements of the age-old academia versus nonacademia debate, not to mention the lesbian feminist sex wars of the 1970s and 1980s, the increasingly vocal confrontation I'm speaking about seems more ideological than identity-oriented. At issue are conflicting perspectives on the relation of sexuality to mainstream politics, the sexual behavior of gay men and lesbians, and more specific questions about marriage and the military. On the one hand, Rotello, Sullivan, and Bawer seem to making an ideological stand that is both politically and socially conservative. They look for the advancement of gay civil rights by working within the current system of lobbying and legislation; and it follows that the items which work well with such methods are related to matters of public policy like the integration of gays into the military and the legalization of same-sex marriage. Why people like Rotello extend this to demand that gay men pursue monogamy is perhaps another, more vexing issue. On the other hand, published queer theorists like Warner and grass-roots organizations like New York's Sex Panic! have placed themselves in opposition to the best-selling and apparently quite popular journalists like Rotello and Sullivan, claiming that the heart of queerness, like that of sexuality, lies in its radical nonnormativity, its resistance to mainstreaming of any sort. I think the root of their opposition to the conservative program is less a disagreement with the traditional liberal political strategies than with the conservative social agenda which has, perhaps, enabled stepped-up police harassment of gay bars and public places where anonymous or free-floating sex happens; succinctly, the anger in the debate comes from the impression that the conservative authors and opinion makers have given tacit authorization for a policing of the more illicit sexual proclivities or practices in the gay community—anonymous sex, S/M, and the like—from the outside. Can anyone here speak to this description of increasingly vocal gay conservatives and their apparent power inside as well as outside urban queer worlds?

CHAUNCEY: I think it's a problem that these people are writing more for the public and trying to participate in broader public debates outside of the academy. Of course it's increasingly difficult to do so; the more radical your critique of existing social arrangements is, the harder it is to find a venue in which to express that critique. But I often feel that it's not just that some theorists or writers get more press because their views are more easily assimilated into the dominant, conservative zeitgeist of the times, but because they also try harder to speak to those larger audiences and are more committed to engaging in that kind of public debate. It's not just important, it's *vital* that queer theorists and lesbian and gay intellectuals of all kinds start trying to engage in that public debate more than they have.

CASE: Well, I think part of the lack of widely ranging, mainstream public debates on these issues can be linked to the way that sexual politics has isolated itself from other kinds of politics. If you simply have a one-issue politic and it's organized around sexuality or sexual practices and you lose any critique of other kinds of things, like the military or capitalism, then you have no broader critique on which sexual politics are based and you can go fuck in the bushes, but it doesn't mean that you end up having a very radical agenda other than that. That in itself might be radical, but when sexual critiques are separated from other kinds of critiques, then one opens the door to more conservative agendas. You're easily assimilated into other sorts of dominant values. Sally Munt is doing a book on butch and femme and she asked me to write something for it. I decided to contribute what I call a historical memoir, though that's probably just generational self-indulgence . . .

MODLESKI: [*laughter*] Yes, it is.

CASE: I wanted to write about hippie butches, because what was so interesting about being a hippie butch in the late sixties and early seventies was that we were very much a part of anti-Vietnam demonstrations, and we maintained a daily, confrontational position toward the military. It would never have occurred to us to that it would have been a good thing for us to have a military color guard in one of our political demonstrations. The other thing was that along with a critique of heterosexuality, there was also a critique of masculinity occurring—all these boys were growing their long hair and wearing these flowing clothes. These different critiques were intertwined and informed by one another. This whole idea now that lesbians are masculine or that they're taking testosterone to have hair on their chests would not have occurred to us because of the general sort of political movement in which we found ourselves at that time. In our analysis, masculinity really meant the military; it meant Agent Orange and burning foreign peoples with chemicals. That kind of a general coalition of political ideas has been lost. As you separate a political idea of sexuality from its other manifestations, you can end up having whatever kind of sex you want, in bed with Roy Cohn. And somehow that is considered sexually progressive. That's why I think *Angels in America* is interesting, because it looks at the convergence of so many different types of politics. If gay and lesbian politics had also meant a challenge to corporate structures, I do not think they would have had their recent successes. They would have been far more suspect and therefore restrained.

MODLESKI: [*tongue-in-cheek*] Well, you *do* sound old-fashioned.

RECHY: I think Larry Kramer becomes more strident and louder the more he feels he's not being heard. I think a lot of what he has to say is quite valid, his warnings about the dangers of ignoring what we have just been through, are still going through, with AIDS. That should be listened to. But I don't think he's saying it correctly. Especially not when he declared recently that "nature" will always punish promiscuity. That's reckless of him, to evoke use that killer word *nature* that evokes the ages-long condemnation of homosexuality as being "against nature."

MEEKER: People like Kramer and, to a greater extent, Sullivan and Bawer are being listened to as their books are published in the mainstream press—HarperCollins and Dutton, for example—and are available in the mainstream bookstores.

RECHY: They still are aimed only at gay groups. These books don't make national best-seller lists. There's a whole difference between the gay best-seller list and the national best-seller list. I remember somebody one time whose book was number one on the gay best-seller list calling me up and saying, "Listen, is there anything you could do for our book? It's not selling well." At one time Proust might have appeared on the gay best-seller list.

CHAUNCEY: I think the kind of separation between gay literature and general literature you're referring to can be connected back to the idea of the illusory comfort that is produced by the citing of the "canonical" queer theorists. While we can certainly see the building of a queer canon taking place, we shouldn't mistake that for seeing nonqueer theorists or non-gay-studies people citing those queer theorists. It's not like they've become canonical for all institutes of higher education. They've become canonical for a small subsection of the academy interested in gender issues in general and queer theory in particular. I think we are beginning to see more openness in the academy to some kinds of queer critical work, lesbian/gay history, and so forth—actually, compared to the way it was ten years ago, a rather dramatic increase in that openness and interest. But, it's still pretty marginalized and still pretty ghettoized within the academy. So, even though we feel comfortable citing certain authors, we shouldn't think that anyone else is getting that kind of comfort.

SILVERMAN: True.

CHAUNCEY: So maybe I haven't changed much in the past two years. I'm still pretty gloomy.

MODLESKI: I don't think any of us are any less gloomy than we used to be. Is that fair to say? That we're no more certain about the cultural and political potential of gay studies or "queer frontiers?"

CHAUNCEY: I guess I do feel a little better about the state of queer theory within the academy. Again, I think the culture and the academy is increasingly polarized, but also that while that polarization involves a terrific reaction against the gay movement and gay culture and against queer theory, it also involves a growth in acceptance and influence. While it is still difficult for people who have done work in gay studies or queer theory to get jobs, it is no longer impossible. Although Yale is refusing a million-dollar grant for an endowed chair, they are interested in having one-year positions, which they would not have been interested in ten years ago. The University of Chicago, where I teach, has given a surprising amount of support to the development of lesbian and gay studies. That seems also to be the case at USC. So I think that there are inroads and we shouldn't be overly pessimistic. Rather, we should recognize that we have had some important successes and the trick is to be aware of both sides of that process. We should acknowledge the work that we've done and the things that we've been able to achieve, but we should also be fully aware of the limitations of those achievements, and how hard of a struggle there still is before us.

MODLESKI: For example, it's only been the last few years that institutions have begun adopting domestic partnership policies, and while a lot of them have, those adoptions have not always occurred in ways that represent an unmitigated political "success." In the case of USC, the president and the Board of Trustees had been very resistant to the idea of a domestic partnership policy for gays. The gay and lesbian activists on campus pushed so much that what the administration decided to do is to give domestic partnership status to everybody so that the gay people wouldn't stick out from the crowd, and so they wouldn't actually be acknowledging gay relationships. The policy would just acknowledge everybody who had a relationship with anybody that was significant. That suggests, it seems to me, progress, but imbedded within that progress you also see extreme reluctance and the various compromises going on.

RECHY: You see the progress with domestic partnership rights as an institutional attempt to lessen the drive toward the legalization of marriage?

MODLESKI: Right. Exactly.

RECHY: Yes, they would see it as a lesser evil.

MODLESKI: Domestic partnership policies are only a few years old across the country.

CHAUNCEY: That's right. The University of Chicago and Stanford introduced these policies in December 1992 and that opened the floodgates. A lot of schools had been considering it and once two schools of that reputation adopted the policy, then a lot of other schools felt that it was permissible for them to do so, and they'd been under pressure to do so. There has been a really dramatic growth in the number of domestic partnership policies. But they all date since 1992.

MEEKER: It's been occurring in the private sector as well, you see Fortune 500 companies and companies like Disney granting domestic partnership benefits on an increasing level in the last few years.

CASE: I just don't feel very Pollyanna-like here. If you've been involved in political struggles in the last twenty years—for example, women's right to abortion—you've had to fight it every, every, every, year. And here in California, the loss of affirmative action policies has been just devastating. You think, "My God, we've fought this, we thought we had won something. It was a bitter battle when we won it and now we have to start all over again?" So, I never think you get something and you get to keep it. Or that seeming progress means that there's not still a lot of hatred out there or that things might not return to the place you started from very easily. I mean, if you've been involved in political struggles, you can see their seeming progress fall back, fall back, fall back again and again.

MODLESKI: It's true, but it's important to see that you can make a difference, even if you, unfortunately, don't make it permanently. Otherwise, it's just political despair, which is certainly an option.

CASE: Right.

MODLESKI: We've brought up Disney and we've been bringing up Ellen, so I'd like to turn to a question that is near and dear to my heart, which is the popular culture question: What do we make of the current mainstream popularity of drag queens or the fact that *Vogue* magazine called lesbians "the Hula Hoops of the nineties"? We love that, of course, but is *Ellen* a breakthrough or a diversion? Does visibility or acceptance in popular culture have any relation to visibility in legal or political arenas? Any or all of those questions.

RECHY: I just want to say about Ms. Degeneres that the only surprise was that anybody *didn't* know. With any degree of sophistication, one would know that she is a lesbian. What stuns me is the putative closetry of actors who could really make a difference—like John Travolta, who has been outed in the tabloids, most prominently by a famous male prostitute.

QUIMBY: I don't know how much more radical an actor of Travolta's stature coming out would be than Ellen's. I want to return to Debra's comment in which she suggested that it was not radical or political for Ellen to come out. I think a lot of people certainly read it that way, especially those of us in urban centers. But in fact I think *Ellen* represents a paradox of modern gay culture, or perhaps the generational shift in the gay political agenda toward assimilation politics. That is, Ellen—the character and the woman—can be perceived as both radical and assimilationist. She's radical in the sense that she declared herself a homosexual on national television, yet she is decidedly not radical in her self-description, and the wide appeal she has garnered as "the girl next door" . . .

RECHY: The boy next door.

QUIMBY: . . . In this sense, *Ellen* is a far remove from John's discussion of the "sexual outlaw" stereotype in his keynote address, an image I know many lesbians as well as gay men have embraced. I think something is lost—perhaps an insistence on our emotional, sexual, political difference—when the new lesbian prototype becomes "the girl next door." Still, Ellen's coming out remains a radical political move, and herein lies the the paradox.

SILVERMAN: I didn't mean to imply that Ellen's coming out on television isn't political. What I was trying to get at was the dichotomy between popular culture—at a time when lesbians are so hip, like the Hula Hoop and when it's cool to be queer—and the social reality of being lesbian or queer. What does it mean for Ellen to come out at the same cultural moment in which *Vogue* magazine is saying that it's cool to be a lesbian? Not that her act was not political, but what kind of climate is her coming out participating or complicit in? And can queer or queerness remain a political word or movement within this climate?

RECHY: *Ellen* did enable some people to come out with ease, and that would justify the whole thing.

SILVERMAN: That's why this is such an interesting question, the question about popular culture's relation to law and politics. It's almost as if there is a line that's drawn between popular culture and politics and there's no crossing it. You have *Vogue* and *Ellen* at the exact same time that politics and the law are moving so far to the right. Popular culture is becoming more "liberal" and the law and politics are drifting in the opposite direction. Why this gap, and what does it indicate?

MODLESKI: I'm not sure how much TV is moving to the left, despite an occasional exception. It seems to me it's a mixed bag.

MEEKER: I also think the gendered aspect of sexual politics in popular culture is interesting. Lesbianism is in vogue right now, but gay males who have anonymous sex or multiple partners are still the outlaws, even according to many chroniclers of the queer community.

MODLESKI: You have the vogue of drag queens. But that also lines up under femininity.

RECHY: Chic femininity is in vogue. Drag queens around Santa Monica Boulevard are nightly arrested.

MEEKER: This goes back to the point about Sullivan, Rotello, and Bawer. They're gaining "gay" celeb status in the larger public sphere now, but they're actively denying any sort of wildly overt, public, and extramarital gay sexuality. Perhaps sexual politics and sex itself in that instance does make things more radical, sort of reradicalizing an identity that's entering into the public sphere under the guise of a funny woman, Ellen. So perhaps the only way *Ellen* can have a more authentically radical impact would be if the show's producers would add not just romance but sex to the character's experience; and, by extension, if Bruce Bawer or Andrew Sullivan were actually "outed" as people who enjoy sex out of marriage—or even have it at all—we might be closer to a more honest discourse on queer sexuality—an honesty that is more important now than ever as it enters the public sphere and the mass media. Sue-Ellen, you look mystified . . . ?

CASE: I don't know what "raw" sexuality is.

RECHY: Too bad.

CASE: Lesbians have had serial monogamy as a practice for many years. So within monogamy I think there's some sexuality. I don't know if you mean that sexuality is not "raw" when it's in monogamous practices. I feel like you're talking about monogamy here, somehow, and that "raw" sexuality is outside monogamy. So I just find that very confusing, because much of the practice of lesbian sexuality has been more in monogamy.

MODLESKI: Historically speaking.

MEEKER: I'm afraid you are conflating lesbian serial monogamy with the idealized "till death do us part" image of heterosexual monogamy. In reality, lesbian serial monogamy seems closer to the nonmonogamy of some gay men than it is to the supposed lifetime monogamy of married heterosexuals.

CASE: No, it's not lifetime, but it's a monogamous kind of thing. Lesbians don't have a typical profile of a lot of sex, here and there in the bushes and various things.

RECHY: Too bad.

CASE: I do think it is too bad. We've all missed that and wished we could have done it in movie theaters. *Especially* the movie theaters. I've always envied you with that one. But on the other hand, it doesn't mean it's not "raw" sexuality just because it's with a partner. Those terms are weird to me.

MEEKER: What if Ellen perhaps had a sexual partner, a series of monogamous sexual partners? Would that somehow push her character across this divide between the merely liberal and the radical representation that some of us wish her to be?

MODLESKI: Sure, that'd be good.

MEEKER: Would that radicalize her character?

CHAUNCEY: How would it radicalize her character?

MEEKER: We were talking about the comfort zone, a sort of identity or a presence of identities detached from what may be less palatable to the average American. We can think about Ellen on the cover of a magazine, right? She's attractive, she's from Hollywood, she's a television star. But, actually bringing the specter of real sex, I'm not saying "raw" sex, but even real sex with a monogamous partner may be another step.

MODLESKI: I think it would be a huge step forward. Huge. You know, she wanted to end the program right after coming out. She didn't want to stay there, and I think it's because the next step is, well, okay if she's gay, then it's not just a matter of saying it but of doing something. I think it'll be really interesting to see what happens next.[4]

WEATHERSTON: I hope I'm wrong, but I really wonder if the networks are going to take that next step any time soon. *A* lesbian is one thing; *two* lesbians having sex seems to be quite another. In a way, I'm still surprised they actually went through with *Ellen* at all. Can you imagine this taking place two years ago? Even though it almost seems ordinary now?

CASE: Well, in some cases the networks can afford to be more liberal, because capitalism is in such a good place right now; it's having a world victory. Yesterday, Poland was made part of NATO and "came home to itself," in English, with red, white, and blue balloons, which cracked me up. We're at such a celebratory moment for American cultural imperialism and economic global capitalism that sexual politics are simply not as threatening. Business is there, the energy is there, and sexual politics are not tied into global, socioeconomic politics. They're certainly not offering any critique of it. If sexual activists were Trotskyites, if all homosexuals were Trotskyites, then sexual politics might have a really different valence at this particular moment.

CHAUNCEY: Well, yes and no. I don't think you mean to reduce all serious politics to class politics. I certainly agree with you that capitalism is resurgent, indeed triumphant, around the world today and that this is going to have awesome implications for all of us in the years to come. But at the same time, sexual politics are still significant politics within the United States. It took a lot of micro struggles in the television industry and in Hollywood for Ellen finally to be able to come out on national TV. And it has, after all, led the Southern Baptists and other groups to urge a boycott of Disney. They take this as a very serious threat. And while I don't think we should overestimate the significance of having a star like Ellen come out, I also don't think we should underestimate it either. The right wing is correct in some ways to be afraid of the implications of this. Because it does mean that there'll be kids all over the country who on *Ellen* and on other TV shows, will be seeing gay people who are accepted as such, shows that are taking more or less a progay line. And that's one fact of the increasing tolerance and even acceptance of gay people around the country. It's not the only thing, but it is one significant arena of struggle, which is why the right wing is so terrified and why the right wing has focused so much of its energies on trying to censor the media.

MEEKER: Back to the question of global capitalism and sexual politics.

Can or should *Ellen* be exported? If we're talking about the validity of sexual politics, or the genuine oppositional qualities of the representation of sexuality in the public sphere, it's interesting to explore the question of whether or not the sexual commodification proliferating in the United States can be exported. Is that something which can contribute to this global capitalism? Can sexual commodification be a part of global commodification as well?

CHAUNCEY: Sexual commodification has for a long time been a part of global capitalism, of course. Everything from American tourists all over the world seeking sexual services from women and boys, to Japanese businessmen in Korea, southeast Asia, and so forth. In that sense, sexual commodification has been a crucial part of capitalist expansion for a long time. But I do think what you're asking raises a crucial issue, or touches on a crucial process that we can see underway now in the sense that lesbian and gay identities and cultures are rather distinctly products of the modern West. Homosexuality and heterosexuality alike are being increasingly exported along with many other western commodities and subject positions. And so, across the world you see a growing tension between local sexual cultures that are not organized in terms of a hetero-/homosexual binarism having to engage with increasingly powerful and globalizing institutions and ideologies of heterosexuality and homosexuality. The globalization of AIDS and the development of an international AIDS industry is probably one of the most important specific technologies involved in the effort to institute heterosexuality and homosexuality around the world.

SILVERMAN: Which suggests a rather troubling dimension to the metaphors of "queer frontiers" we've adopted here.

MODLESKI: Perhaps that uncertain note would be a good one on which to end. Are there final thoughts? Would anyone like to say something about future frontiers?

RECHY: The *Advocate* did a "roundup" article for their thirtieth anniversary, in which they asked thirty people to write on certain subjects about what they foresee for the future. I was asked to do the one on male sexuality.

CASE: What do you foresee?

RECHY: More of the same. A confusion about promiscuity. There's a vast difference between sexual abundance, which I've always championed, and the throttling of all feelings other than sexual sensations. The latter moves into such extremity that nothing is enough, sex is no longer sex, becomes the mimed, ritualized violence of S/M, which is nothing more than punishment for homosexual desire. I think as soon as the message is perceived that AIDS may be coming to an end, there will be a desire on the part of the young generation to "catch up," even outdo the excesses we were flirting with, signs of horrible psychic danger, the extremities of S/M, humiliation, whipping, fisting, acts that finally had nothing to do with sex and everything to do with self-oppression.

CASE: I can't see anything that is called pleasure as self-oppression. For myself, I have this old thing, I have never thought that lesbian politics were simply about sex. Maybe that's because I come out of lesbian feminism. Even in the bad old days when we were oppressed and everything, I always managed to have sex. Quite a lot of it. And quite a number of partners, in spite of many different kinds of historical conditions. But when I finally became political, it was actually through lesbian feminism—where I thought I was in coalition with other kinds of causes—that my sexual practice, which was called an identity, came up against other kinds of practices and other people's oppression. This is where we looked for collective liberation. That's where I'm really still marked, as a lesbian feminist. Sex to me is one thing and the term "identity politics" means to me doing something in the broad spectrum of political action. I never thought I was doing anything political when I was having sex. I really wouldn't want to think so, actually. It might get in the way.

RECHY: The only time it's political is when you get arrested for it. As I'm sure you know, arrests didn't—and still don't—necessarily have to occur in the bushes, on streets. There is still entrapment, not rare. So acts do become political. I long for a time—I don't see it now—when among gay men sex will be an enrichment but not an obsession, not all that matters.

MODLESKI: Sue-Ellen, any final predictions? Will sex become an enrichment and not a means of obsession or oppression?

CASE: Well, one hopeful one, and I do see signs of some growth, is that sexual politics will conjoin with transnational ones. We will become more aware of the "American" valence on our critique, and we will work to put together something with people working in other countries that will help us understand sexual politics within global strategies.

Notes

1. John Rechy, *The Sexual Outlaw* (New York: Grove Press, 1977).

2. Larry Kramer offered to donate three million dollars to Yale University to endow a chair in lesbian and gay studies and the university refused the money, deciding that the gift constituted advocacy and they would rather continue their policy of hiring scholars to teach on a one-year contract. (Yale also stated their reason as, simply, gay and lesbian studies was too trendy and they

didn't want to be obligated to hire in a field they imagine will not exist years from now!)

3. Contemporary gay conservativism perhaps began with Bruce Bawer's *A Place at the Table* (New York: Poseidon Press, 1993) and *Beyond Queer: Challenging Gay Left Orthodoxy* (New York: Free Press, 1996) but is amplified by Andrew Sullivan's *Virtually Normal* (New York: Alfred A. Knopf, 1995), Gabriel Rotello's *Sexual Ecology* (New York: Dutton, 1997), Michelangelo Signorile *Life Outside* (New York: HarperCollins, 1997), and Larry Kramer's particularly strident article, "Sex and Sensibility" (*Advocate*, 27 May 1997, 59, 64–65, 67–70). The opposition, though a bit muted and absent from the lists mass-market publishers, is beginning to be heard; see Michael Warner, "Media Gays: A New Stone-Wall" *Nation*, 14 July 1997, 15–19, and Douglas Sadownick, "From Gay Rights to Gay Right" *LA Weekly*, 11–17 July 1997, 16. For a more thorough summary of this debate than was included here, see Caleb Crain, "Pleasure Principles: Queer Theorists and Gay Journalists Wrestle over the Politics of Sex" *Lingua Franca* (October 1997): 26–37.

4. The sitcom *Ellen* did indeed go off the air at the end of the 1997–98 season.

AFTERWARDS/AFTERWORDS

15

Back to the Future

Richard Meyer

We believe that if queer people do not preserve our own
history, most of it will simply disappear.
—Willie Walker, archivist, Gay and Lesbian Historical Society
   of Northern California

A column of string connects six black, cardboard arrows. Each arrow
is inscribed with two words—one on either side of its face—printed
in white block letters. When hung from the ceiling, the object functions
as a mobile, its arrows rotating, at different speeds and in alternate
directions, around the central core of string. As each arrow turns, it
reveals first one side (or word) and then the other and so changes the
larger configuration of words and directional markings. Like a roulette
wheel, it is impossible to determine in advance how the mobile will
read when it stops rotating. The twelve words printed on the mobile
are as follows: HETEROSEXUALS, SATYRS, HOMOSEXUALS, HERMAPHRO-
DITES, BISEXUALS, APHRODISIACS, TRANSSEXUALS, INFORMATION, UP-
TIGHTS, VIRGINS, CURIOUS, UNDECIDED. Although each arrow bears two
different terms, none of these "pairs" constitute familiar opposites
(e.g., HETEROSEXUALS shares its arrow not with HOMOSEXUALS but with
SATYRS). The mobile enacts a kind of exchangeability (rather than a
clinical demarcation) of its various sexual terms. Homo-, hetero-, bi-,
and transsexuality (not to mention undecided and curious) are situated as potentially complimentary, not mutually exclusive, categories.

In its undoing of sexual binaries and its insistence on shifting identifications, this mobile echoes a great a deal of recent queer theory. Yet
it dates not from the 1990s but from the mid-1960s, at which time it
was used by activists and educators to trouble, however playfully, the
distinction between normal and deviant sexual identities. In 1998, the
Sex Terms Mobile, created by an anonymous collective, was included in
a remarkable exhibition entitled "Queer and Kinky Danger," which
was mounted at the Gay and Lesbian Historical Society of Northern

Sex Terms Mobile, mid-1960s. (Photograph by Richard Meyer; used by permission of the Gay and Lesbian Historical Society of Northern California)

California in San Francisco. The show's curator, Willie Walker, offered the following description of the object in the exhibition brochure:

Originally owned by Phyllis Lyon & Del Martin [longtime lesbian activists based in San Francisco], this mobile came out of the budding effort to increase people's knowledge of sexuality, and develop sex education classes for youth. . . . The mobile itself reflects the idea that sexuality is variegated and complex, challenging the monolithic model then in place that heterosexuality was the normal and ideal form of sex and the resultant labeling of all other sexual interest as perverse and degenerate. This was, in effect, an early expression of queerness.[1]

The mobile does indeed express "queerness" as that word has come to be used today—namely, as a radical critique of normativity fueled by alternative forms of sexual identity and pleasure. It is worth noting, however, that QUEERS is not among the twelve terms that the mobile variously presents. In the mid-1960s, *queer* would likely have signaled a violent denigration of homosexuality rather than a radical critique of heterosexuality. As John Rechy argues in this volume, for many gay people the term *queer* can never be uncoupled from its prior use by gay bashers and homophobes. "That word," Rechy writes, "will always belong to the violent enemy."

While I respect Rechy's position, I think it might be useful to broaden the question of queer beyond issues of word choice. *Queer* is not merely an old term set to new tasks, not simply a 1990s recoding of a pre-Stonewall epithet. Current constructions of *queer* are part of a larger history of gay and lesbian resistance to assimilation and to fixed binaries of gender and eroticism. While the use of *queer* as a form of defiant self-identification may be a relatively recent phenomenon, the symbolic work performed by such identifications constitute a crucial part of our history.

In my own work as an art historian, I have become interested in pre-Stonewall images that manifest what we would now call a queer sensibility without making reference to the term *queer*. Many of the objects included in "Queer and Kinky Danger" demonstrate, on visual and historical terms, the kind of work I have in mind. Consider, for example, a souvenir dishtowel from a 1966 carnival held by the California Motor Club, an early gay biker organization. Against a backdrop of balloons and striped tents, the towel offers the image of Mr. Carnival, a young leather stud in biker jacket, boots, and tight jeans. This dishtowel, an object tied to domestic labor, to housework, here becomes a carnivalesque display of leather manliness, one which suggests that the towel may find uses outside the kitchen—perhaps as a "come

The Mr. Carnival 1966 souvenir towel, California Motorcycle Club. (Photograph by Richard Meyer; used by permission of the Gay and Lesbian Historical Society of Northern California)

rag" (for post-sex clean up) or as a means to spit-polish one's Harley-Davidson. In its crossing of homoeroticism and domesticity, of biker boots and kitchen dishes, the Mr. Carnival towel topples the traditional divide between men's and women's work, between machismo and housewifery.

An object from "Queer and Kinky Danger" that more explicitly (but no less wittily) contests conventional codes of gender is the cover of a 1959 publication titled *Adonis in High Heels*. The cover presents a figure "split" between masculine and feminine appearance—half sportjacket, tie, and hat; half garters, bustier, and panties. The figure is encircled by various props and accessories: a pair of thigh-high boots, a blond wig, black spike heels, a red corset, and what appears to be a set of strap-on mannequin arms. Although the title *Adonis in High Heels* would seem to suggest a "straightforward" case of a man in drag, the cover image complicates this assumption. Notice that the female half of the body is depicted in underwear while the male half is fully dressed. At first glance, the female side thus seems closer to the "truth" or material ground of this body. Yet, both the male and female halves of the figure's face seem equally "made up" with cosmetics, and the circle of nearby props seem to constitute a womanly "drag" that has yet to be donned. The cover image simultaneously suggests, then, both

Queer performativity before queer theory. Cover of *Adonis in High Heels,* 1959. (Photograph by Richard Meyer; used by permission of the Gay and Lesbian Historical Society of Northern California)

a male and female cross-dresser, both an "Adonis in high heels" and an "Amazon" in suit and tie. Within the terms of this representation, there would seem to be no authentic ground beneath the costuming and performance of gender. It is the surface, as Judith Butler might say, that counts, and here that surface is dizzyingly reversible.

Historical artifacts such as *Adonis in High Heels,* the Mr. Carnival towel, and the *Sex Terms Mobile* can only perform their queer work if they continue to be seen by contemporary audiences. For this reason, exhibitions such as "Queer and Kinky Danger" are of crucial importance to our community. Through the presentation of some two hundred works of art and material culture dating from 1930 to the present, "Queer and Kinky Danger" maps an alternative history of leather, kink, and S/M subcultures in and around San Francisco. The exhibition includes paintings, prints, photographs, and sculptures originally displayed in local bars, clubs, bathhouses, and alternative galleries, as well as more popular materials (posters, matchbooks, buttons, ephemera) that publicized gay and lesbian parades, organizations, events, or places of business. More than any art exhibition I have seen, "Queer and Kinky Danger" demonstrates that gay and lesbian visual culture extends far beyond the production of strictly sexual images.

One quite moving aspect of this show was the care with which it presented such items as the enamel pins and metal buttons that marked membership in gay motorcycle clubs of the 1960s, or the plaster replica of Michelangelo's David in boots and biker's cap that once graced Fe-Be's, an early San Francisco leather bar. The show lavished curatorial attention on objects that would never be granted display within traditional art galleries or historical societies; hence, it not only documented but also performed a kind of queer cultural history.

Earlier in this volume, Karin Quimby and Walter Williams offer the following observation about the importance gay and lesbian activists of the 1950s placed on documenting their work: "Their desire to preserve these traces, coupled with our desire to locate them, reveals a similar impulse: the desire that a visible, "real" legacy might be pasted together to shore up a sense of permanence and belonging in a general culture that would prefer, still, that we not speak our name." Quimby and Williams speak of their desire, as queer scholars, to recover historical materials that have been largely ignored, suppressed, or even destroyed by the dominant culture. But they also speak of the desire of earlier subjects—in this case gay and lesbian activists of the 1950s—to document their own experiences and efforts. Throughout their chapter, Quimby and Williams enact a kind of dialogue of desires, an exchange between the present and the past. Among other things, that dialogue tells us that queerness is not an invention of the 1990s. Attempts to complicate (and multiply) the possibilities of gender and sexuality, to highlight the performative aspects of identity, and to oppose the tyranny of the norm are woven into the historical fabric of gay and lesbian life.

In its summoning of a "frontier," the title of this book suggests a space of future exploration. And yet, as the expanding field of gay and lesbian history attests, the queer frontier exists not only in the future but also in the past. At their best, contemporary constructions of queerness enable us to see the past differently, to recover otherwise lost representations, and to renew the creative and collective force of alternative sexualities.

In a 1970 manifesto, the gay liberation activist Charles Thorp defined the term *gay* as both a manifestation of the homosexual past and a radical break with it: "Gay," wrote Thorp, "is our history and the history we are just beginning to become."[2] Judith Butler has made a somewhat parallel claim, suggesting that "if the term queer is to be a site of collective contestation, the point of departure for a set of historical reflections and futural imaginings, it will have to remain that which is, in the present, never fully owned, but always and only redeployed, twisted, queered from prior usage."[3] Even as we name and claim ourselves as queer, we cannot but echo the former uses and legacies of the term, including the homophobic ones. Yet the term *queer* also insists on a difference from its own history, on a gap between where it's been and where it is going. Like the word *queer*, the future of queer cultural production and political activism will both draw on, and radically reinvent, the gay and lesbian past. In this sense, what lies on the queer frontier "is our history and the history we are just beginning to become."

Notes

I would like to thank David Román, Willie Walker, and the Gay and Lesbian Historical Society of Northern California for their help with this essay.

1. Willie Walker (for the Gay and Lesbian Historical Society of Northern California), "Queer and Kinky Danger: Art of San Francisco's Leather/SM/ Kink Worlds," exhibition essay (Gay and Lesbian Historical Society of Northern California: San Francisco, 1998): unpaginated. My epigraph for this chapter is also drawn from Walker's essay.

2. Charles Thorp, "I.D., Leadership and Violence" (1970), in *Out of the Closets: Voices of Gay Liberation*, ed. Karla Jay and Allen Young (New York: Jove Publications, 1972, 1977), 353.

3. Judith Butler, *Bodies That Matter: On the Discursive Limits of Sex* (New York: Routledge, 1993), 228.

16

Visa Denied

David Román

But the question is still the same. Stay or go? Stay or go?
—Chay Yew, *A Beautiful Country*

Frontiers, like borders, are understood and experienced differently depending upon one's relation to them. For many people, frontiers and borders are inextricably linked with migration and exile, with the domestic and the diasporic—that is, with the politics of home. Within the context of the United States, the history of the frontier has been written as a narrative of national expansion and progress, of Manifest Destiny and American imperialism. Within the global context, America has mythologized itself as the very frontier of possibility, a myth, as Una Chaudhuri has explained, that privileges America as "the place of both literal and metaphorical openness, where the history of the future can be worked out."[1] In both these contexts, frontiers reveal much about transnational power relations and local negotiations of geopolitical space.

California in general, and Los Angeles in particular, occupy a specific position in relation to these issues. With Los Angeles now serving as the primary point of entry for new immigrants, and with minority populations increasingly shifting the racial demographics of the state, California has become the location where the apparatus of the nation-state is most immediately evident and most vehemently preserved. California has historically registered as a national bellwether, and as Joseph A. Boone argues in the introduction to this collection, "In the popular imagination, California has long loomed as the endpoint of the continental U.S. and the 'final frontier' of the mythic Old West; and Los Angeles has become the nation's premiere psychic embodiment, unlike any other city in the U.S., of racial diversity and ethnic hybridity, of mass culture and celluloid dreams, of futurism and apocalypse, . . . of unrest and mindlessness, of sexual promiscuity and perversity, of the Pacific Rim's meeting point of Asia and America, and, as recent immigration controversies have highlighted, the meeting point of North and Central America." Given the weight of these projections, we might want to consider whose imagination constitutes the "popular" in such formulations of California as frontier. The network of associations Boone lists composes the primary narratives about the region and sets the foundation for official accounts of it. In order to complicate further this dominant understanding, I would like to address what might be called the "vernacular imagination" of immigrant subjects whose experiences of California or of Los Angeles are often shaped by the very myths of America that exclude them.

My emphasis here on the social experiences of race, ethnicity, migration, and diaspora is not meant to be a corrective to, or a displacement of, the social experience of sexuality foregrounded in this anthology. Nor do I wish to set these experiences against one another. Instead, I want to identify and examine contemporary cultural work that considers the interrelation among them. In part, I am interested in naming and promoting modes of performance that provide counterpublicity to the popular myths of Los Angeles. The archive for this work remains, for the most part, undocumented and unexamined. It exists in oral history, cultural memory, social ritual, communal folklore, and local performance—media that do not rely on print culture for their preservation. Because this archive often exists outside of official culture, it is frequently undervalued or even derided. So too are most efforts to recover it. José Muñoz, writing about the archives of queer culture, explains one of the main reasons for this occurrence: "Because the archives of queerness are makeshift and randomly organized, due to the restraints historically shackled upon minoritarian cultural workers, the Right is able to question the evidentiary authority of queer inquiry."[2] Muñoz goes on to argue against this critique of queer theory, in part, by advocating for the performativity of queer scholarship, or what he calls "queer acts," and by positing "ephemera" ("all those things that remain after a performance, a kind of evidence of what has transpired but certainly not the thing itself") as a kind of critical residue that enables the archives for our scholarship.

Muñoz's efforts to expand the archive and challenge the authority of official evidence opens a critical space for scholars and activists interested in the alternative histories, memories, and performances of minority subjects. While, in this instance, Muñoz is primarily focused on defending queer theory, his basic premise extends to postcolonial and critical race studies as well. When we consider or foreground racial and ethnic minorities, the concern over the undocumented archive and the question of "evidentiary authority" often corresponds to larger cultural anxieties concerning nation and citizenship. For the immigrant, this issue of documentation is central. Documentation determines access to citizenship. Mining the archives that preserve the interrelations between the social experiences of race and sexuality may in fact help us perceive more critically the ways in which such norms of citizenship have been constructed and enforced historically. Through this understanding, we may even find ways to respond to contemporary exclusionary forms of nationalist discourse currently in practice throughout the United States, but especially here in the state of California.

Recent work by a new generation of queer playwrights calls attention to the rich archives of memory that exist in the vernacular imagination of the queer immigrant subject. These new works thus participate in a larger cultural project, already underway, exploring histories and memories that exist as alternatives to those that circulate as the "popular imagination," or more firmly as "official history." Chay Yew's saga of Miss Visa Denied, a Malaysian immigrant and drag queen, in *A Beautiful Country* (1998) stands as a case in point. The play is a collaboration between Chay Yew, a Los Angeles–based playwright who is one of the most significant new voices in American theater, and Cornerstone Theater, a Los Angeles–based company that, according to its mission statement, "builds bridges between and within diverse communities." The play recovers a history of Asian American immigrant experience—150 years of Asian American history—through "dance, drama, and drag," as the program notes put it. A multimedia and multidisciplinary performance, *A Beautiful Country* chronicles multiple stories of pan-Asian immigration and exile to the United States, ranging from Filipino migrant workers in the 1930s to Hmong refugees in the 1970s and 1980s; from the effects of the 1882 Chinese Exclusion Acts to the internment of Japanese Americans during World War II; from the Negro Alley Massacre in Los Angeles in 1885 (where fifteen Chinese men were hanged and four others were shot or stabbed to death during an interracial riot) to recent hate crimes against new Asian immigrants. These stories are performed by a multiracial cast composed of professional actors and community members from the Chinatown neighborhood where the play is presented.[3]

A Beautiful Country is neither a chronological history play nor a docudrama of Asian American history. In this sense, it departs both from the traditional Asian American history play where, as Josephine Lee explains, "the personal stories of individual valor told in these plays threaten to eclipse the larger social situation," and from the conventional dramatic realism of Asian American theater, which "promises a coherent subjectivity, an authentic voice, a truth within the stories."[4] Rather, Yew stages the various contradictions of Asian American experience, the ways in which racial and national identities are forged historically through—in Lisa Lowe's telling phrase—"immigrant acts," a term that at once summons forth the exclusionary practices of U.S. immigration laws and policies and the performances generated by Asian immigrants and Asian Americans who have found themselves often enmeshed within these shifting historical conditions and constraints.[5] At the same time, *A Beautiful Country* mines the official archives of U.S. culture, including the dates of specific immigration laws and the first interventions achieved by Asian Americans, presenting this information on slides projected onto the back wall of the performance space in both English and Chinese. But other archives are also summoned forth, including the oral histories of various community members, which are interspersed throughout the performance, and the diverse cultural arts of the Asian diaspora, which are performed throughout the production. Yew enriches this fabric still further by staging earlier representations of Asian Americans in U.S. popular culture, including a scene from Henry Grimm's 1879 racist play *The Chinese Must Go!*—a theatricalization of the anti-Chinese sentiment resulting from the shifting economic conditions of U.S. labor forces in the 1870s, and a humorous dramatization of a 1941 *Time* magazine feature that attempts to distinguish, for the white majority, the difference between the Chinese and Japanese. It is precisely this tension between official and undocumented archives, between popular and vernacular imaginations, that propels the drama of the play.

Just how these historical concerns transect with queer concerns is evident in Yew's decision to place at the heart of his play the figure of Miss Visa Denied, an immigrant drag queen from Malaysia who is meant to be, according to the program, "a metaphor of duality experienced by most immigrants: a person caught between two continents, two cultures, two languages, and two homes."[6] The play's dramatic structure, indeed, is framed by Visa's efforts to gain entrance into the United States. At first, we see Visa as a silent diva "dressed like Madonna," being interrogated by a U.S. immigration officer. This opening scene captures the official force of nationalist surveillance as Visa, unable or unwilling to speak in return, remains mute:

OFFICER: Passport please
     Passport
     Name?
     Purpose of this trip
     Purpose

Cast members of Chay Yew's *A Beautiful Country* perform "The Dance of the Migrant Workers" scene. (© 1998 by Craig Schwartz Photography; used by permission)

Eric Steinberg, Chris Wells, and Page Leong perform Henry Grimm's *The Chinese Must Go!* in Chay Yew's *A Beautiful Country*. (© 1998 by Craig Schwartz Photography; used by permission)

Nancy Yee performs a scene from Chay Yew's *A Beautiful Country*. (© 1998 by Craig Schwartz Photography; used by permission)

Why are you here?
Business?
Pleasure?
Working?
Vacation?
I see
How long will you be here?
How long?
Days?
Weeks?
Months?
You cannot stay for more than three months[7]

The scene ends with Visa being led away for further questioning. Throughout the play, Visa literally oversees the 150 year history that *A Beautiful Country*'s narrative unfolds. Visa is played by three actors: a male actor who embodies Visa on stage but does not speak, another male actor who speaks Visa's inner thoughts but only from an offstage microphone, and a female actor who is meant to represent Visa's "soul" and performs only through dance. The duality assigned to Visa in the production notes is therefore misleading: while she may serve as "a metaphor for the duality experienced by most immigrants," the fact that Yew chooses three actors to perform the character suggests not simply duality but multiple fragmentation. The play thus powerfully demonstrates how the experience of immigration not only displaces immigrants geographically, but how it also enacts a kind of symbolic violence or fragmentation on the level of the individual subject.[8] Yew dramatizes this sense of fragmentation by distributing Visa's "body," "voice," and "soul" among three different actors.

This fragmentation of subjectivity, embodied in the play by the three actors, is further echoed by the fragmentation of history that makes up the narrative: out of necessity Yew's ambitious staging of "150 years of Asian American history in dance, drama, and drag" in two hours' playing time presents only fragments from this rich history. In *A Beautiful Country*, history and subjectivity are always interrelated, positioned within a dialectical system of mutual exchange. Hence, Visa's own story unfolds simultaneously with the play's larger historical interests. Throughout the play, Yew stages aspects of Visa's subjectivity— her memories of migration, her nostalgia for home, the erotics of her desire. At no point in the play are we asked to imagine Visa as freak or fetish. One effect of this rather unremarkable presentation of Visa's sexuality is that the queer and Asian immigrant character is presented as a subject *in* history rather than *as* history's spectacle. This is important since Visa's own sense of self feels most complete when she herself is performing, rendered in the play by Visa's full drag lip-synching rendition of Madonna's "Vogue." While this performance announces her queerness, it also forms one of her own "immigrant acts," a performance that only makes sense within the context of the other Asian immigrant acts presented throughout *A Beautiful Country*. Visa expresses this link between queerness and diaspora in an eloquent monologue that describes her subjective experience of America:

> there is so much to live
> to love
> about this beautiful country
>
> everytime
> my feet find this stage
> everytime
> the light drenches my skin
> i am strangely home
> my foundation
> my mascara
> rouge
> my new face
> my lipsynch life
> my makeover life in america
>
> this theatre
> this is my home
> my between home
> between the port of penang
> and the port of los angeles
> forever
> living in two worlds
> forever
> belonging to none
>
> i only wish
> i wasn't lonely

The theme of fragmentation is also brought into relief by the cross-racial and cross-gendered performances of the actors and the overt theatricality of the production. Everyone here is performing a role, a point that Yew's direction does not obscure. (In a debt to Bertolt Brecht's epic theater, Yew's actors perform on a raised platform described as the "acting area"; when they are not performing they sit visibly on opposite sides of the platform along with the play's musicians and dancers.) Yew's actors perform across categories of race, gender, and national origin, and the cross-racial performances, in particular, exploit the theatrical medium's reliance on actors and role-playing to comment on the limited roles imagined and allowed for Asians in America.[9] Within this context, Yew makes it evident that Visa's lip-synching performance of Madonna must be placed in relation to the social and historical forces that have shaped her sexual and racial subjectivity. Although Visa, as the program notes explain, "embodies and pursues the American Dream by wearing the mask of a pop icon and lipsynching words that aren't his," her performance asks to be historicized in the context of a long tradition of Asian immigrant efforts to pass through and into the national culture. That these attempts at "passing" are often tragically unsuccessful—as the dramatization unfolding before Visa and the audience shows—underscores the stakes involved in transnational and diasporic crossings. Therefore Visa's performance of Madonna's "Vogue" suggests she imagines this role not only as quintessentially queer but also—and perhaps even more so—quintessentially American.[10] More to the point, Visa performs "Vogue" as a disidentification with Asian normativity.[11]

At the end of the play, Visa returns to the stage in full drag, once again lip-synching and dancing to Madonna's "Vogue." As she works the runway in all her glamour, slides projected on the back wall convey Visa's day-to-day reality and the world through which she must maneuver. As becomes evident, Visa's performance in this scene takes place on two levels: on the literal level, she performs in the very same space as everything previously represented and staged in the play, and her lip-synching forms the final act in the playing time of *A Beautiful Country*; on the metaphoric level, Visa performs on the very same psychic and physical terrain of those who have historically passed before her, for she is the most recent immigrant in a rich history of Asians in America. All of these past performances haunt her as she enacts her own performance in present-day Los Angeles:

SLIDE: 1998
    Los Angeles
    After my late shift at Starbucks at Pershing Square, I walked
        along lonely Los Angeles Street.
    On the wet street pavement, I could see a blue moon
        dancing.
    As if by command, I ventured down the same street where
        the Chinese lived more than a hundred years ago.
    When I reached the heart of the Plaza, I felt a stirring of
        collective fear the Chinese had.
    In front, a city on fire, eyes silent with hate.
    Behind, wagons, frenzied escape, a forced passage home.

> It was more than a hundred years ago.
> But the question is still the same.
> Stay or go?
> Stay or go?
> I'm staying.
> I'm home.

Visa's performance ends when a technical failure stops the music. Alone and in the spotlight of bright fluorescent lights, Visa is, according to Yew's stage directions, "stunned and embarrassed by being onstage and 'voiceless.'" Left alone to improvise, she summons her other selves: the male actor who has served as her voice and the female actor who has represented her soul appear on stage and help remove her drag. If earlier Visa imagined "this theatre" as "my home, my between home, between the port of penang and the port of los angeles," Visa now questions the security of this belief. Yew cleverly detheatricalizes his central character in order to call attention to the drama inherent in Visa's material world, where the theater provides only a temporary respite from the harshness of America. Home is no longer only "this theatre" but also "the same street where the Chinese lived more than a hundred years ago, the heart of the plaza, Los Angeles." The fragmented narrative of Visa's subjective immigrant experience, which the play has interjected throughout its presentation of Asian American history, now overlaps with the play's own need for closure. It is in this moment that the onstage Visa finally speaks:

> VISA: My
> name
> is
> Wong Kong Shin
> I
> come
> from
> Penang
> West Malaysia
>
> No
> I
> come
> from
> Los Angeles
> California
> United States of America

If "queer acts," as José Muñoz argues, "stand as evidence of queer lives, powers, and possibilities," and if "immigrant acts," as Lisa Lowe argues, "[name] . . . the *acts* of labor, resistance, memory, and survival, as well as the politicized cultural work that emerges from dislocation and disidentification," then perhaps "queer immigrant acts" acknowledge the alternative forms of sociality and community that these interrelated and collective efforts make possible. Queer immigrant acts make possible queer and transnational identities, transforming the social and public worlds in which these subjects travel. Although Wong Kong Shin's queer immigrant act denies Visa's centrality to his sense of self, such an act reintegrates the various fragmented parts of his identity—voice, soul, and body—that have been performed separately throughout *A Beautiful Country*.[12] He speaks now for the first time in his own voice. Such an act, at once, Asian American and queer, locates Kong Shin as a subject in history and as a subject in motion. The play ends with an epilogue that revisits the initial scene with the U.S. immigrant officer. This time, after the interrogation, the immigrant officer stamps Visa's papers and allows temporary entrance: "Welcome to America. Next." Unlike most work in Asian American theater, *A Beautiful Country* explores the interrelation between queerness and diaspora.[13] The play presents various historical and imagined dimensions of Asian American social experience, at once expanding the representational field of Asian American theater and demanding the critical interrogation of race, gender, and sexuality.

In a recent critical project that sets out to link Asian American studies with queer theory, David Eng raises a number of interrelated questions that neither Asian American studies nor mainstream queer theory have previously prioritized. He wonders, "How might we theorize queerness and diaspora against a historical legacy that has unrelentingly configured Asian Americans as exterior or eccentric to the U.S. nation-state? How might queerness and diaspora provide a critical methodology for a more adequate understanding of Asian American racial and sexual formation as shaped in the space between the domestic and the diasporic?"[14] These are also the questions that frame Yew's play and distinguish it from earlier Asian American theater, even including his own previous explorations of gay Asian lives.[15] *A Beautiful Country* participates in what Eng recommends at the end of his important essay: "In the late 1990s queerness and diaspora should be used not only to reevaluate the past but to orient the future of Asian American political projects and strategies whose claims on oppositional politics can be acknowledged as such. This is a moment that should be marked by our definitive shifting away from a politics of cultural nationalism to a politics of transnational culturalism."[16]

This shift to transnational culturalism and a reorientation toward

"I come from Los Angeles, California, United States of America." Reggie Lee and Chris Wells perform the epilogue to Chay Yew's *A Beautiful Country*. (© 1998 by Craig Schwartz Photography; used by permission)

the future through an excavation of the archives of the past seems to me to be precisely what Chay Yew's play has accomplished. It's not so much that he has "queered" the various archives of Asian America (although there's some of that, too, as the play's campy restaging of *The Chinese Must Go!* proves). Nor is it simply that he has thematized queer Asian immigration and brought a meditation on that experience into representation (although the story of Miss Visa Denied also certainly does that). *A Beautiful Country* challenges us to consider the relationship between queerness and diaspora as a productive association, a critical alliance that puts pressure on the normative force of popular imaginations and official archives. After shifting the critical framework—from the national to the transnational, from the domestic to the diasporic, from the normative to the queer—the play brings us back once again, to the politics of home. But the question is still the same: Stay or go? Stay or go?

Notes

I would like to thank Richard Meyer and Karen Shimakawa for helping me think through many of the ideas presented here. Their critical insights and intellectual generosity are much appreciated. Thanks also to Joe Boone for his helpful editorial suggestions. Thanks to Cornerstone Theater for providing me Craig Schwartz's wonderful production photos of *A Beautiful Country*. Special thanks to Chay Yew for sharing with me his work and friendship, for providing me with a copy of his play's text, and for his permission to quote the work in this chapter.

1. Una Chaudhuri, *Staging Place: The Geography of Modern Drama* (Ann Arbor: University of Michigan Press, 1995), 213.

2. José Muñoz, "Ephemera as Evidence: Introductory Notes to Queer Acts," *Women and Performance: A Journal of Feminist Theory* 8/2, no. 16 (1996): 7.

3. *A Beautiful Country*, written and directed by Chay Yew, was commissioned by Cornerstone Theater. The play was copresented by two other theaters in Los Angeles: East West Players, where Yew is a resident director, and the Mark Taper Forum, where Yew directs the Asian Theater Workshop. The play ran from 5 June to 21 June 1998. Admission to all performances of the production were "pay-what-you-can." For more on the history and style of Cornerstone Theatre, see Sonja Kuftinec, "A Cornerstone for Rethinking Community Theatre," *Theatre Topics* 6, no. 1 (March 1996): 91–104.

4. Josephine Lee, *Performing Asian America: Race and Ethnicity on the Contemporary Stage* (Philadelphia: Temple University Press, 1997), 158–59. These are two separate thoughts from Lee's book that I have brought together to emphasize my point.

5. Lisa Lowe, *Immigrant Acts: On Asian American Cultural Politics* (Durham, N.C.: Duke University Press, 1996). Lowe writes: "'Immigrant acts' [name] the

agency of Asian immigrants and Asian Americans: the *acts* of labor, resistance, memory, and survival, as well as the politicized cultural work that emerges from dislocation and disidentification. Asian immigrants and Asian Americans have not only been 'subject to' immigration exclusion and restriction but also have been 'subjects of' the immigration process and are agents of political change, cultural expression, and social transformation" (9; emphasis in the original).

6. Peter Tamaribuchi and Amy Vaillancourt, "*A Beautiful Country:* A Brief History of Asians in America," program notes for Cornerstone Theater production, 5–21 June 1998.

7. All quotations from *A Beautiful Country* are from Chay Yew's unpublished 16 June 1998 draft, © 1998 by Chay Yew.

8. For non–English-speaking immigrants, or for those for whom English is not a primary language, this fragmentation is also experienced through language.

9. In this regard, *A Beautiful Country*'s antirealist investments can also be understood as participating in what Karen Shimakawa explains as "renegotiat[ing] the process of abjection for Asian Americans in representation." See her essay, "Swallowing the Tempest: Asian American Women on Stage," *Theatre Journal* 47, no. 3 (October 1995): 367–80 for a full discussion of this methodology.

10. For some audiences, "queer" is imagined as only American. During rehearsals, for example, some Asian community members were upset by the inclusion of drag and homosexuality in a play about Asian American history.

11. This idea of disidentification is theorized by José Muñoz in his book-length study on the topic, *Disidentifications: Queers of Color and the Performance of Politics* (Minneapolis: University of Minnesota Press, 1999).

12. While this "denial" of Visa may appear to some people as a phobic response to drag, such a view misrepresents the impact of Wong Kong Shin's self-declaration and Chay Yew's overall point here. When I posed this issue to the playwright in conversation, Yew claimed that Wong Kong Shin wasn't abandoning drag completely and that he imagined that the character would return to drag in the very near future. While the playwright's projections for his character's future life might relieve some level of anxiety for those concerned, I think the play itself—as it is *already* written and directed—suggests that drag is much more than just a theatrical trompe l'oeil.

13. David Henry Hwang's *M. Butterfly,* perhaps the most celebrated play in Asian American theater, for all its important cultural interventions, cannot be said to fully address this issue. Consider John Clum's comments in this context: "It is ironic that the best-known play about a gay Asian male, David Henry Hwang's *M. Butterfly,* was written by a heterosexual and used a male-male relationship to comment on white men's attitudes to Asians in general and Asian women in particular." See John Clum, *Staging Gay Lives: An Anthology of Contemporary Gay Theater* (Boulder, Colo.: Westview Press, 1996), 345. In fact, *A Beautiful Country* ironically comments on *M. Butterfly*'s spectacularization of the drag queen through its matter-of-fact representation of Visa. For the histor-

ical interventions achieved by Hwang's play, see Dorinne Kondo, *About Face: Performing Race in Fashion and Theater* (New York: Routledge, 1997). Recently, queer Asian American playwrights and performers such as Han Ong, Denise Uyehara, and Hung Nguyen are, along with Chay Yew, more forcefully exploring the interrelation between queerness and diaspora although the critical bibliography on these and other queer Asian American artists is lacking.

14. David Eng, "Out Here and Over There: Queerness and Diaspora in Asian American Studies," *Social Text* 52–53 (1997): 32.

15. Chay Yew's earlier plays include *Porcelain, A Language of Their Own*, and *Half Lives*. These three plays comprise the *Whitelands* trilogy. For an excellent discussion of this trilogy, see Michael Reynolds's review of their production at East West Players in Los Angeles, *Theatre Journal* 49, no. 1 (March 1997): 75–79. *Half Lives*, the third play in the trilogy, has been substantially revised and is now titled *Wonderland*. In 1997, Grove Press published the first two plays of the trilogy as *Two Plays by Chay Yew*. While these three plays each can be said to explore queerness and diaspora simply by their representation of queer Asian gay men, Yew is more interested in tracing the internal dynamics between Asian gay men and their sexual partners, lovers, and families in these three plays, respectively, than in forcefully positioning these characters as subjects in history. This critique is not meant to slight these plays, but to further underline the significance of *A Beautiful Country*.

16. Eng, "Out Here," 43.

Conference Participants
Notes on Contributors and Editors
Index

"Queer Frontiers" Conference Participants 23–26 March 1995

Jon Adams
Elizabeth Adams
Thomas Albrecht
Pat Alford-Keating
Inna Altschul
Jean Amato
James Andre
Lourdes Arguelles
Daniel G. Bacalzo
Michael Bacchus
Shirley M. Banks
Matthew Bell
Harry M. Benshoff
Robin Bernstein
Rosalee Blumer
Jeff Bohn
Mary Pat Brady
Scott Bravmann
Dee Bridgewater
Kaucyila Brooke
Judith Brown
Richard C. Cante
Kenneth D. Capers
Michael Carbuto
Erin G. Carlston
Sue-Ellen Case
George Chauncey
Elise Chenier
Deborah Cohler
Douglas Conrad
Peter Coviello
Liz Hutchinson Crocker
Quang Dang
Danielle DeMuth
Madelyn Detloff
J. Dallas Dishman

Michael Doylen
Martin Dupuis
Shantanu DuttaAhmed
Caroline Eisner
Douglas Eisner
Rob Epstein
Philip Ethington
Michael Fairchild
Manuel Fernandez
Camilla Fojas
Eric Freedman
Jeffrey Friedman
Julia Gardner
Zsa Zsa Gershick
Marita Giovanni
Judith Grant
Mary L. Gray
Ronald Gregg
Sean Griffin
Christian Gundermann
Donald E. Hall
Kelly Hankin
Stan Harris
Laura Alexandra Harris
Stacey Hart
Joseph Hawkins
Clare Hemmings
Jon Hodge
Lauran Hoffman
Sharon Holland
Mark Hollingsworth
Morgan Holmes
Jill Hornick
Heather Huddleston
Glyn Hughes
Monica Hulsbus

Michele Hunter
Gordon Brent Ingram
Robert Irwin
Katrin Jaeger
Muriel Jones
Mary Kearney
Lynn Kenney
Mark Kerr
Marsha Kinder
Marcy Jane Knopf
Romy Kozak
Richard Kramer
Judith Kunkle
Robbin Ladd
Anique Lamerduc
Jeffrey Langham
Ernest W. Lee, II
Lois Leveen
Harlan Levinson
Brian Loftus
Kristian London
Jaye Lopez
Susanne Luhmann
Lyndall MacCowan
Rachel Laura Madsen
Kirk Marcolina
Alexandra Marshall
Jonathan Massey
Veronica Matos
Martha McCaughey
Sean Aaron Metzger
Katherine Millersdaughter
Christie Milliken
Katie Mills
Cherríe Moraga
Cynthia Morill
Matt Mutchler
Jill Nagle
Peter M. Nardi
Anthony M. Navarrete
Amy Nelson
Nancy Novack
Nii Narh Noye
Shauna Maile O'Donnell
Karen D. Oslund

Monica Palacios
Kody Partridge
Eva Pendleton
Nancy Plooster
James Polchin
Giovanna Pompele
Hugh Porter
John Portmann
Karin Quimby
Jeanne Reames-Zimmerman
John Rechy
Alison Redick
Yolanda Retter
Eric Reyes
Molly Rhodes
Sylvia Rhue
Eric Rofes
Joe Rollins
Amy Rosewarne
Jennifer Ruth
Cindy Sarver
Liana Scalettar
Marc Schachter
Eric Schockman
Heather Schuster
Bill Scroggie
Ann Seaton
Robert Sember
Afzal Shah
Stephen Shapiro
Scott A. Sherer
Debra Silverman
Stephen D. Sinclair
Don Solomon
Jill St. Jacques
Chuck Stewart
Ashley Stockstill
Kimberly Stull
Chris Sturr
Robert Sulcer
Kim Surkan
Ira Tattelman
Nancy Taylor
Alex Robertson Textor
Peter Toscani

Jason Tougaw
Elizabeth VanderVen
Adrian Wagner
John Waiblinger

Rosemary Weatherston
Selena Whang
Walter L. Williams
Gust A. Yep

Notes on Contributors and Editors

Michael Bacchus received his Ph.D. in English from the University of Southern California in 1997. He teaches English at Hunter College in New York City and writes about class, sexuality, and disguise in early-twentieth-century British literature.

Joseph A. Boone, a coeditor of *Queer Frontiers,* is professor of English at the University of Southern California, where he teaches courses in the novel as genre, modernism, gay literature and culture, and queer theory. He is the author of *Tradition Counter Tradition: Love and the Form of Criticism* (1987), and *Libidinal Currents: Sexuality and the Shaping of Modernism* (1998); coeditor, with Michael Cadden, of *Engendering Men: The Question of Male Feminist Criticism* (1990); and recipient of a Guggenheim to work on a project on the homoerotics of Orientalism. He was selected cowinner of the 1997 Crompton-Noll Award of the MLA for his essay "Queer Sites in Modernism: Harlem/Greenwich Village/The Left Bank."

Richard C. Cante is assistant professor of film at the University of North Carolina at Chapel Hill. His chapter in this volume is excerpted from his dissertation, "Narration by Numbers: AIDS and the Form of Contemporary Difference," written in Critical Studies in the School of Cinema-Television at the University of Southern California.

Sue-Ellen Case is professor of theater studies and English at the University of California, Davis. Her articles "Towards a Butch-Femme Aesthetic" and "Tracking the Vampire" have been instrumental in shaping and defining the field of lesbian and queer theory. She has published and lectured widely in the field of feminism and theater and has most recently edited *Split Britches: Lesbian Practice/Feminist Performance* (1996); her latest book is *Performing Lesbian in the Space of Technology* (1997). She was selected cowinner of the 1997 Crompton-Noll Award of the MLA.

George Chauncey is associate professor of United States history at the University of Chicago. His book *Gay New York: Gender, Urban Culture, and the Making of the Gay Male World, 1890–1940* won the 1994 *Los Angeles Times* Book Award for History and the 1995 Frederick Jackson Turner and Merle Curtis Prizes from the Organization of American Historians. He is coeditor, with Martin

Duberman and Martha Vicinus, of *Hidden from History: Reclaiming the Gay and Lesbian Past,* and author of numerous articles on lesbian and gay history. He is currently at work on his next book, *The Strange Career of the Closet: Gay Culture, Consciousness, and Politics from the Second World War to the Stonewall Era,* with the support of fellowships from the Guggenheim Foundation and the National Humanities Center.

Peter Coviello has completed his Ph.D. in English at Cornell University and is now assistant professor of English at Bowdoin College. His present research interests are race and masculinity in mid-nineteenth-century American literature.

Martin Dupuis, cochair of the "Queer Frontiers" conference and coeditor of *Queer Frontiers* while completing his Ph.D. at the University of Southern California, is assistant professor of political science at Western Illinois University. His research on same-sex marriage has been published by Oxford University's *International Journal of Law and the Family* (April 1995).

Morgan Holmes has completed her doctoral dissertation, "The Doctor Will Fix Everything: Intersex in Contemporary Culture," at Concordia University, Montreal. The dissertation combines narrative theory, bioethics, and ethnography to examine interconnected issues associated with intersexuality. Holmes hopes to begin postdoctoral work in fall 2000, working on medical narratives of disease.

Martin Meeker, a coeditor of *Queer Frontiers,* is a doctoral candidate in history at the University of Southern California where he is currently writing a history of the gay and lesbian migration to San Francisco from the 1940s to the 1980s. He teaches in the history department at San Francisco State University and has delivered papers on urbanism, migration, and the history of sexuality at the annual meetings of the Organization of American Historians, the American Historical Association-Pacific Coast Branch, and the Association of American Geographers.

Richard Meyer, an assistant professor in art history at the University of Southern California, was a fellow at the Getty Research Institute for the History of Art and Humanities in 1998. His book *Outlaw Representation: Censorship and Homosexuality in American Art* is forthcoming from Oxford University Press. Selected publications include "Rock Hudson's Body" (1991), "Robert Mapplethorpe and the Discipline of Photography" (1993), and "Warhol's Clones" (1994). In 1996 he curated the exhibition *Paul Cadmus: The Sailor Trilogy* for the Whitney Museum of American Art.

Tania Modleski is a Florence Scott Professor of English at the University of Southern California. An internationally recognized scholar of feminist and film criticism, she is the author of *Loving with a Vengeance: Mass-Produced Fantasies for Women* (1982), *The Women Who Knew Too Much: Hitchcock and Feminist Theory* (1988), *Feminism without Women: Culture and Criticism in a "Postfeminist" Age* (1992), and *Old Wives' Tales and Other Women's Stories* (1998). One of her recent essays on lesbian sexuality is "The White Negress and the Heavy Duty Dyke."

Cherríe Moraga is a playwright, poet, and essayist whose plays and publications have received national recognition, including the NEA's Theater Playwrights' Fellowship in 1993. A San Francisco–based writer, Moraga has premiered her work at Theater Artaud, Theater Rhinoceros, the Eureka Theater, and Brava! Theater Center. Her playwriting includes *Shadow of a Man*, *Heroes and Saints*, and *Giving Up the Ghost*. She is coeditor of *This Bridge Called My Back: Writings by Radical Women of Color*, which won the Before Columbus Book Award in 1986, and editor of *Cuentos: Stories by Latinas* and *Third Woman: The Sexuality of Latinas*. She is author of *Loving in the War Years: Lo Que Nunca Pasó por Sus Labios* (1983), *The Last Generation* (1993), and *Waiting in the Wings: Portrait of a Queer Motherhood* (1997).

Karin Quimby, a coeditor of *Queer Frontiers*, has completed a dissertation on the queer girl's narrative in American fiction at the University of Southern California. She is the author of numerous articles on feminist and lesbian theory, women's music festivals and sports events, as well as Asian American literature. A member of the Board of Directors of the ONE Institute, she was cochair of the "Queer Frontiers" conference.

John Rechy is recipient of the PEN Center USA West Lifetime Achievement Award and an author of international prominence, best known for his landmark gay novel, *City of Night* (1961). His other novels include *Numbers* (1967), *This Day's Death* (1970), *The Vampires* (1971), *The Fourth Angel* (1972), *Rushes* (1979), *Bodies and Souls* (1984), *Marilyn's Daughter* (1988), *The Miraculous Day of Amalia Gomez* (1991), *Our Lady of Babylon* (1996), and *Coming of the Night* (1999); his plays include *Momma as She Became—Not as She Was* (1968), and *Tigers Wild* (produced in New York in 1986). He also writes regularly for numerous publications, including the *Los Angeles Times*, the *New York Times Book Review*, the *Nation*, and the *Village Voice*. He resides in Los Angeles and teaches in the School of Professional Writing at the University of Southern California and conducts writing seminars at Occidental College and the University of California, Los Angeles.

Yolanda Retter is an unreconstructed feminist lesbian and history activist who has been part of the Los Angeles movement since 1971. She was born in Connecticut, grew up in El Salvador, and is of Peruvian and German descent. She compiled the Lesbian History Project web site (www.lib.usc.edu/~retter/main.html), manages the Lesbian Legacy collection at the ONE Institute, and is completing her dissertation, "On the Side of the Angels: Lesbian Activism in Los Angeles, 1970–1990," in American studies at the University of New Mexico. She has taught at several universities and coedited *Queers in Space: Communities, Public Spaces, Sites of Resistance*, winner of a 1998 Lambda Award.

David Román is associate professor of English and American studies at the University of Southern California. He is the author of *Acts of Intervention: Performance, Gay Culture, and AIDS* (1998), which received the 1999 Research Award for Outstanding Book from the Association for Theatre in Higher Education, the professional organization of theatre and performance scholars. He is also the coeditor with Holly Hughes of *O Solo Homo: The New Queer Performance* (1998), which received the 1999 Lambda Literary Award in drama. In the year 2000, he begins a four-year term as editor of *Theatre Journal*. He received his Ph.D. in comparative literature from the University of Wisconsin–Madison in 1990.

Cindy Sarver, a coeditor of *Queer Frontiers*, is writing her dissertation, titled "Seeing in the Dark: Race, Representation, and Visuality in Modernist Literature," in English at the University of Southern California on theories of visuality, the body, and otherness in modernism.

Liana Scalettar holds degrees from Columbia and Brown Universities, where her work focused on lesbian and gay studies, modernism, and cultural theory. She lives in New York.

Debra Silverman, a coeditor of *Queer Frontiers*, received her Ph.D. from the University of Southern California. She has published numerous articles on subjects including infanticide and colonial narrative in Sir Walter Scott, the question of female drag, and exoticism in Nella Larsen's *Quicksand,* for which she received the 1994 Darwin T. Turner Prize for best essay published in *African American Review.* Her book-in-progress is entitled *Prophylactic Practices: Contraception and the Construction of Female Desire from Eliza Haywood to George Eliot.* She is currently putting her research talents to work in the film industry.

Jill St. Jacques is a transsexual performance artist and writer living in Los Angeles. She has a B.E.A. in painting from the San Francisco Art Institute, an M.E.A. in performance art from CalARTS and a B.A. in journalism from California State University, Northridge. His published articles have appeared in *Unnatural Disasters: Recent Fiction from the Golden State* (1996); *Fiction International* (1995); and *Avant-Pop: Fiction for a Daydream Nation* (1994). She has also performed throughout California and in Helsinki, Finland.

Ira Tattelman is an independent scholar and architect living in Washington, D.C. He received his master's degree in architecture from Harvard's Graduate School of Design. His published essays include "The Meaning at the Wall:

Tracing the Gay Bathhouse," in *Queers in Space: Landscapes of Marginalized Sexualities and Communities* (1997), and "Speaking to the Gay Bathhouse: Communicating in Sexually Charged Spaces," in *Public Sex, Gay Space* (1997). He has participated in architecture and art exhibits in various cities along the east coast.

Rosemary Weatherston, a coeditor of *Queer Frontiers* and one of the conference organizers, received her Ph.D. in English from the University of Southern California, where she currently is a postdoctoral lecturer in the College of Letters, Arts, and Sciences. She has published essays on the parallels between the historical treatment of native women informants and the contemporary treatment of women of color in academia and on representations of landscape in postcolonial literatures, as well as interviews with Cherríe Moraga, Nao Bustamante, and Coco Fusco. At present she is revising her dissertation, "Turning the Informant: The Making of Difference in Twentieth-Century U.S. Literature and Culture," for publication and is beginning research on her next project, "Local Color/Localized Color: U.S. Regional and Multicultural Literatures at the Turns of the Centuries."

Walter L. Williams is professor of anthropology and gender studies at the University of Southern California. He is author and editor of several books, most notably *The Spirit and the Flesh: Sexual Diversity in American Indian Culture,* which won the American Library Association Gay Book of the Year Award in 1987. He was cofounder of the Committee on Lesbian and Gay History of the American Historical Association, has been a Fulbright Scholar in Indonesia, and is president of the International Gay and Lesbian Archives.

Index

Index